The EU–Japan Partnership in the Shadow of China

T0361946

Both the European Union and Japan have been major beneficiaries and supporters of the liberal international order, first led by the United States since the end of World War II. During this period, they have emerged as global powers, however, the very order that nurtured their rise is now facing twin threats. First, through authoritarian China's promotion of alternative models of global governance, and second from a crisis of liberalism, manifested in the policies of President Donald Trump and Brexit.

This book explores these challenges faced by both the EU and Japan, providing a multidisciplinary approach to studying the relationship between the two. It analyses their cooperation in terms of security, defence and trade and examines how their shared normative values are ultimately implemented. Having recently concluded an Economic Partnership Agreement and with a Strategic Partnership Agreement in the pipeline, this book asks whether they can convert their latent and modest cooperation into an alternative form of leadership and an antidote to the illiberal tide sweeping the developed world?

As the first book to shed light on the new Economic Partnership Agreement between the EU and Japan, this book will be useful to students and scholars of Japanese Studies, as well as European Union politics and international political economy more generally.

Axel Berkofsky is Senior Lecturer at the University of Pavia, Italy, Senior Associate Research Fellow at the Milan-based Istituto per gli Studi di Politica Internazionale (ISPI) and Research Affiliate at the European Centre for Japanese Studies at the Stockholm School of Economics, Sweden.

Christopher W. Hughes is Professor of International Politics and Japanese Studies at the University of Warwick, UK. He is the author of *Japan's Foreign and Security Policy under the 'Abe Doctrine'* (2015), and co-editor of *The Pacific Review.*

Paul Midford is Professor of Political Science and Director of the NTNU Japan Program at the Norwegian University of Science and Technology in Trondheim, Norway. He is the author of *Rethinking Japanese Public Opinion and Security: From Pacifism to Realism?* (2011).

Marie Söderberg is a Professor and Director of the European Institute of Japanese Studies at the Stockholm School of Economics, Sweden. She is also the chairperson of the European Japan Advanced Research Network executive committee.

European Institute of Japanese Studies, East Asian Economics and Business Series

Edited by Marie Söderberg
Stockholm School of Economics, Sweden

This series presents cutting edge research on recent developments in business and economics in East Asia. National, regional and international perspectives are employed to examine this dynamic and fast-moving area.

For more information about this series, please visit: www.routledge.com/asian studies/series/SE0500

The EU–Japan Partnership in the Shadow of China

The Crisis of Liberalism

**Edited by Axel Berkofsky,
Christopher W. Hughes, Paul Midford
and Marie Söderberg**

LONDON AND NEW YORK

First published 2019 by Routledge

2 Park Square, Milton Park, Abingdon, Oxfordshire OX14 4RN

52 Vanderbilt Avenue, New York, NY 10017

Routledge is an imprint of the Taylor & Francis Group, an informa business

First issued in paperback 2019

British Library Cataloguing-in-Publication Data
A catalogue record for this book is available from the British Library

Library of Congress Cataloging-in-Publication Data
Names: Berkofsky, Axel, editor.
Title: The EU–Japan partnership in the shadow of China: the crisis of liberalism / edited by Axel Berkofsky, Christopher W. Hughes, Paul Midford and Marie Sèoderberg.
Other titles: European Union–Japan partnership in the shadow of China
Description: Abingdon, Oxon; New York, NY: Routledge, 2019. | Series: European Institute of Japanese Studies, East Asian Economics & Business series; 13 | Includes bibliographical references and index.
Identifiers: LCCN 2018010285| ISBN 9780815397984 (hardback) | ISBN 9781351172165 (ebook)
Subjects: LCSH: European Union countries–Foreign relations–Japan. | Japan–Foreign relations–European Union countries. | European Union countries–Foreign economic relations–Japan. | Japan–Foreign economic relations–European Union countries. | China–Foreign relations– 21st century. | China–Strategic aspects.
Classification: LCC D1065.J3 E935 2019 | DDC 355/.0310940952–dc23
LC record available at https://lccn.loc.gov/2018010285

ISBN: 978-0-8153-9798-4 (hbk)
ISBN: 978-0-367-89501-3 (pbk)

Typeset in Times New Roman
by Wearset Ltd, Boldon, Tyne and Wear

Contents

Illustrations

Figures

Tables

Contributors

André Asplund is an Affiliated Research Fellow with the European Institute of Japanese Studies, Stockholm School of Economics. He earned a PhD from Waseda University and has taught on Japanese foreign policy, foreign aid, democracy and human rights in Asia at Yale University.

Paul Bacon is a Professor of International Relations at Waseda University, Japan. His research interests include EU–Japan relations, human rights, and human security. In 2016/17, three of his co-edited Routledge monographs appeared in paperback. Professor Bacon has also published more than thirty book chapters and articles in respected international relations journals.

Axel Berkofsky is Senior Lecturer at the University of Pavia, Italy, Senior Associate Research Fellow at the Milan-based Istituto per gli Studi di Politica Internazionale (ISPI) and Research Affiliate at the European Institute of Japanese Studies at the Stockholm School of Economics, Sweden.

Liang Cai has a PhD in Law from Fudan University. He is a Senior Fellow at the Center for Asia-Pacific Studies, Shanghai Institutes for International Studies (SIIS). His research interests focus on Sino–Japanese relations and the strategic culture of China. His latest book is *Japan's MD Diplomacy Towards China After WWII*.

Markus Heckel works as a Senior Research Assistant in the Department of Management and Microeconomics at the Goethe University Frankfurt. He obtained a PhD in economics at the University of Duisburg-Essen. His research interests focus on the political economy of central banks, institutional economics and labour economics.

Maaike Okano-Heijmans is a Senior Research Fellow at the Netherlands Institute for International Relations 'Clingendael' in The Hague and a visiting lecturer at the University of Leiden. She is also Clingendael's scientific coordinator for the Asia-Pacific Research and Advice Network (APRAN) for the European Commission and the European External Action Service.

Jeffrey W. Hornung is a Political Scientist at the RAND Corporation. Hornung received his PhD in political science from George Washington University and his M.A. from the Johns Hopkins University School of Advanced International Studies. He was also a visiting scholar at the University of Tokyo as a Fulbright Fellow.

Christopher W. Hughes is Professor of International Politics and Japanese Studies, University of Warwick. He is the author of *Japan's Reemergence as 'Normal' Military Power, Japan's Remilitarisation*, and *Japan's Foreign and Security Policy under the 'Abe Doctrine'*, and co-editor of *The Pacific Review*.

Paul Midford is Professor of Political Science and Director of the NTNU Japan Program at the Norwegian University of Science and Technology (NTNU) in Trondheim. He is the author of *Rethinking Japanese Public Opinion and Security: From Pacifism to Realism?* (2011).

Hidetoshi Nakamura is currently Associate Professor of International Relations, Faculty of Political Science and Economics; Head of European Research Unit, Organization for Regional and Inter-regional Studies (ORIS) at Waseda University, Japan. His research interests include EU–Japan relations in a changing liberal world order, security communities, and comparative regional integration studies.

Patricia A. Nelson is Senior Research Fellow, European Institute of Japanese Studies, Stockholm School of Economics and Adjunct Fellow, Center for Strategic and International Studies in Washington DC. Her research focuses on EU–Japan trade, government–business relations, and the structure and organization of business and the business environment.

Marie Söderberg is a Professor and Director of the European Institute of Japanese Studies at the Stockholm School of Economics. She has a PhD from Stockholm University. A central focus of her research is Japanese foreign aid policy. She is the Chairperson of the European Japan Advanced Research Network (EJARN).

Lilei Song has a PhD in Laws from Fudan University. She is an Associate Professor at the School of Political Science and International Relations, Tongji University. She is a member of the council of Shanghai Institute for European Studies. Her research interests are China–EU relations, Chinese public diplomacy, and EU's neighbourhood.

Takashi Terada is a Professor of International Relations at Doshisha University, Kyoto where he teaches IPE and Asian regionalism. He obtained his PhD from Australian National University from which he was also awarded the JG Crawford Award. He used to work for National University of Singapore, Waseda University and Woodaw Wilson Center.

Preface

Increased cooperation between Europe and Japan has been discussed for decades. While there were strong links between Japan and the US as well as between Europe and the US, the Europe–Japan one remained undeveloped until the 1990s. It was to remedy this that the European Institute of Japanese Studies in Stockholm was created in 1992, more than 25 years ago. At that time Japan provided the model for economic growth and there were many studies on Japanese production technology and the concept of just in time. Since then Europe–Japan links have improved, although they remain weak. The rise of China in the twenty-first century proved to be a game changer for European links with Asia. Most Asia research institutes suddenly became effectively China research institutes, and Japan practically disappeared from the scene, except for the fields of culture, food and fashion where it was flourishing.

This was the reason why a group of high-level scholars from all over Europe came together in 2007, now more than ten years ago, and created the European Japan Advanced Research Network (EJARN), from which the core writers of this book are drawn. The network has been holding annual conferences all over Europe, and in Japan. It has also initiated projects producing policy recommendations for government officials. This book project on the EU–Japan partnership started at EJARN's annual 2016 conference, held in June at Warwick University, the same week as the UK Brexit referendum was held. Half a year later Donald Trump, with his "America first" policy, was elected president of the United States.

The environment for EU–Japan relations thus changed again, as it became obvious that there would be no free trade agreement between the US and Europe, nor between US and Japan, as well as another eleven countries around the Pacific. The only large players left that seemed interested in promoting free trade and protecting the liberal world order were Japan and the EU. Negotiations for an Economic Partnership/Free Trade Agreement, which had been going on since 2013, gained new importance and renewed energy, and were finally concluded on 8 December 2017. Negotiations for a Strategic Partnership Agreement covering political and security cooperation between EU and Japan are, at the time of writing (February 2018), almost finished, and this agreement will be implemented in parallel with the Economic Partnership Agreement.

At this historic crossroad the authors of this book analyse Europe–Japan relations from different angels. How are these relations affected by what is happening in the US and China? Is the time finally ripe for further cooperation in the field of economics, politics and security? These are some of the questions we tackle.

On behalf of all the editors and contributors, I would like to thank Toshiba International Foundation (TIFO) for providing generous financial and moral support of this project all the way through. In particular we would like to thank TIFO President Keisuke Omori, Mariko Kuwayama, and Makoto Shirai. We want to thank Warwick University for co-sponsoring the 2016 EJARN conference where first drafts of many of this book's chapters were presented. Finally, we would like to thank Nanhee Lee at the European Institute of Japanese Studies who spent many hours cleaning up our manuscripts.

Marie Söderberg
Series Editor

Note on names and transcriptions

Japanese names are written in the Western order, with first name followed by surname.

The Hepburn system is used in transcription from Japanese, but in names of people, companies or places the long vowel is not marked.

Abbreviations

AAAA	Addis Ababa Action Agenda
ABS	Alternative Bank Schweiz
ACSA	Acquisition and Cross-Servicing Agreement
ADB	Asian Development Bank
ADIZ	Air Defense Identification Zone
AIIB	Asian Infrastructure Investment Bank
ALGS	Autonomic Logistics Global Sustainment
APEC	Asia Pacific Economic Community
ARF	ASEAN Regional Forum
ASDF	Air Self-Defense Force
ASEAN	Association of South East Asian Nations
ATLA	Acquisition, Technology and Logistics Agency
BOE	Bank of England
BOJ	Bank of Japan
BMD	Ballistic Missile Defence
BRI	Belt and Road Initiative
CBDR	Common But Differentiated Responsibilities
CDB	China Development Bank
CFSP	Common Foreign and Security Policies
CPV	Communist Party of Vietnam
CRA	Contingent Reserve Arrangement
CSDP	Common Security and Defence Policy
CZ	Contiguous Zone
DAC	Development Assistance Committee
DAG	Development Assistance Group
DNB	Danmarks Nationalbank
DPC	Defence Production Committee
DPJ	Democratic Party of Japan
EC	European Commission
ECB	European Central Bank
EDA	European Defence Agency
EDTIB	European Defence Technological and Industrial Base
EEAS	European External Action Service

EEC	European Economic Community
EEZ	Exclusive Economic Zone
EFSD	European Fund for Sustainable Development
EIB	European Investment Bank
EIP	European External Investment Plan
EJARN	European Japan Advanced Research Network
EODAS	Electro-optical Distributed Aperture Systems
EPA	Economic Partnership Agreement
EPC	European Political Cooperation
EPSC	European Political Strategy Centre
ESDP	European Security and Defence Policy
ESS	European Security Strategy
ETF	Exchange Traded Funds
EU	European Union
EVFTA EU	Vietnam Free Trade Agreement
FA	Framework Agreement
FACO	Final Assembly and Checkout
FCA	Framework Cooperation Agreement
FONOPs	Freedom of Navigation Operations
FPA	Framework Partnership Agreement
FTA	Free Trade Agreement
FTAAP	Free Trade Area of the Asia-Pacific
FMS	Foreign Military Sales
GATT	General Agreement on Tariffs and Trade
GDP	Gross Domestic Product
GI	Geographic Indication
GoJ	Government of Japan
GSDF	Japan Ground Self-Defense Force
HA/DR	Humanitarian Assistance/Disaster Relief
ICRA	International Conference on Reconstruction Assistance
IDE	Institute of Developing Economics
ILO	International Labour Organization
IMF	International Monetary Fund
ISDS	Investor-State Dispute Settlement
ITA	International Trade Administration
JBIC	Japan Bank of International Cooperation
JCG	Japan Coast Guard
JETRO	Japan External Trade Organization
JICA	Japan International Cooperation Agency
JMOD	Japan Ministry of Defense
JSDF	Japan Self Defense Forces
KAS	Konrad Adenauer Stiftung
KORUS FTA	Korea-United States Free Trade Agreement
LDCs	Least Developed Countries
LDP	Liberal Democratic Party

LMIC	Lower Middle Income Countries
MDGs	Millennium Development Goals
METI	Ministry of Economy and Industry
MHI	Mitsubishi Heavy Industries
MITI	Ministry of International Trade and Industry
MOD	Ministry of Defense
MOF	Ministry of Finance
MOFA	Ministry of Foreign Affairs
MOU	Memorandum of Understanding
MPM	Monetary Policy Meeting
MSDF	Maritime Self-Defense Force
NAFTA	North American Free Trade Agreement
NATO	North Atlantic Treaty Organization
NAVFOR	Naval Force
NBC	Nuclear, Biological and Chemical
NDB	New Development Bank
NGOs	Non-Governmental Organisations
NIR	Negative Interest Rates
NPE	Normative Power Europe
NSC	National Security Council
NSS	National Security Strategy
NTBs	Non-Tariff Barriers
NTMs	Non-Tariff Measures
OBOR	One Belt One Road
ODA	Official Development Assistance
OECD	Organisation for Economic Co-operation and Development
OHCHR	Office of the United Nations High Commissioner for Human Rights
OOF	Other Official Flows
PDA	Private Development Assistance
PCA	Partnership and Cooperation Agreement
PCA	Permanent Court of Arbitration
PF	Private Flows
PKOs	Peacekeeping Operations
PM	Prime Minister
QDR	Quadrennial Defense Review
QQE	Quantitative and Qualitative Monetary Easing
RCEP	Regional Comprehensive Economic Partnership
RECAAP	Regional Cooperation Agreement on Combating Piracy and Armed Robbery
ROE	Rules of Engagement
SCAP	Supreme Commander for the Allied Powers
SDF	Self Defense Forces
SDGs	Sustainable Development Goals
SME	Small and Medium Enterprise

SNB	Swiss National Bank
SOE	State Owned Enterprise
SoS	Security of Supply
SPA	Strategic Partnership Agreement
SR	Swedish Riksbank
SSR	Security System Reform
TOSSD	Total Official Support for Sustainable Development
TTIP	Transatlantic Trade and Investment Partnership
TPP	Trans Pacific Partnership
UNSC	United Nations Security Council
USTR	United States Trade Representative
TZ	Territorial Waters
UK	United Kingdom
UN	United Nations
UNCLOS	United Nations Convention on the Law of the Sea
WMD	Weapons of Mass Destruction
WTO	World Trade Organization

1 Introduction

Now or never?

Marie Söderberg, Axel Berkofsky,
Christopher W. Hughes and Paul Midford

The European Union (EU) and Japan have been two major beneficiaries and sup-porters of the liberal international order led by the United States since World War II. During that period these two powers have emerged as global economic, technological, political and 'normative' powers. Now the very order that nur-tured their rise faces twin threats: from without by the rise of an authoritarian and ostensibly illiberal China promoting (and financing) alternative models of economic and global governance; and from within by a crisis of liberalism, itself manifested in seemingly failing Western leadership and institutions. The EU's position and credibility as a promoter of a liberal world order has been dimin-ished by its travails in responding effectively to repeated financial crises since 2008, and a massive refugee crisis since 2015. The United Kingdom's (UK) vote to leave the EU in June 2016 is a prominent manifestation of the fraying legiti-macy and capacity of the EU. Meanwhile, the election of Donald J. Trump as President of the United States—matching the emergence of populist and xeno-phobic groups and movements in numerous EU member states—points to the emergence of a new wave of illiberalism impacting on the US's established posi-tion since the post-war era as the leader and upholder of the liberal international order.

Set against this background, this edited volume examines the challenges the EU and Japan now face as the two main leading and remaining supporters of the global liberal order in an age of doubt over the durability of US leadership: can they convert their latent and to date modest cooperation in international politics and security into robust action to offer an alternative form of leadership and anti-dote to the illiberal tide sweeping the developed world? Can their political rheto-ric—constantly referring to each other as 'natural allies' in international politics and security—translate into political reality and substance in the years ahead? In other words, can the EU and Japan actually implement together the kind of pol-icies they have listed over recent years in joint statements published after annual EU–Japan Summits?

This volume's central theme is EU–Japan cooperation across the dimensions of trade, finance, development assistance, and traditional and non-traditional security in the context of the challenges of the rise of an illiberal and authorit-arian China and rising illiberalism in the US as well as Europe. It seeks to examine the tasks that Japan and the EU face as two of the leading supporters of the liberal world order led by the US. Can they convert their very modest cooperation into robust action to offer an alternative to the illiberal tide threatening to sweep the world and unsettling the global economy and even peace?

The approach of this volume is a multidisciplinary one, drawing on insights from International Relations, Political Science, Economics, and Business Studies, and achieves coherence by addressing consistently in all chapters the following five main questions. First, how can we assess the significance and impact of EU–Japan cooperation in the areas covered by individual authors? Second, how do China and/or the US individually or through their bilateral relationship affect EU–Japan current or potential cooperation in the areas the volume's authors are addressing? Third, how does EU–Japan cooperation in trade, politics and security impact on cooperation between the EU and China and the EU and the US, Japan and the US, and Japan and China respectively? Fourth, how does EU–Japan cooperation in trade, politics and security affect Sino–US relations? Finally, what is the impact of recent instability in the OECD countries on EU–Japan cooperation? Our edited volume will provide readers with an in-depth analysis of the areas of cooperation that Europe and Japan are currently engaged in, and seek to assess whether the extent of their joint activities is substantive enough to fill the leadership gap the liberal world order faces in the years ahead.

The EU, despite the impending Brexit, is still the main economic and political powerhouse of Europe. However, this does not mean that bilateral relations between some of the major European powers and Japan are unimportant. In this book we will thus provide coverage of EU–Japan cooperation but also Europe–Japan cooperation in a broader sense to encompass also bilateral relations between Japan and some of the principal individual European states.

Judging by the previous and indeed current level of EU–Japanese cooperation, there are understandably doubts about whether political leaders in both Europe and Japan are prepared and equipped with the instruments and resources to enact substantive cooperation. Nevertheless, as this edited volume reveals, the track record of EU–Japan non-military security cooperation in Asia, Central Asia, Africa and elsewhere is not unimpressive, and Tokyo has over recent years increased also military-to-military security cooperation with individual EU member countries, most notably the UK and France. In January 2014, France and Japan held their first ministerial-level foreign affairs/defence ministers (2 plus 2) meeting. During the second 2 plus 2 meeting in 2015, respective foreign and defence ministers discussed the so-called 'Plan of Action for Africa', which included the possibility of joint border security actions in Niger, Mali and Burkina Faso and joint peacekeeping policies and missions in Africa. In July 2014, Paris and Tokyo signed a memorandum of understanding (MOU) to increase defence cooperation, including the joint development of military equipment. This is envisioned to include, among other areas, the joint development of unmanned underwater vehicles.

In April 2012, Tokyo and London signed their first joint weapons development agreement which in July 2013 was followed-up by two additional British–Japanese agreements—the so-called 'Defence Equipment Cooperation Framework' to facilitate joint development of military equipment and the 'Information Security Agreement' facilitating increased cooperation in intelligence. This resulted in British–Japanese joint development efforts in chemical and biological warfare suits and cooperation in missile technology. Furthermore, British and Japanese armed forces have increased the frequency of military exercises, and Tokyo and London in January 2015 held their first 2 plus 2 meeting, involving their respective foreign and defence minister. In May 2014, London and Tokyo initiated negotiations on a bilateral Acquisition and Cross-Servicing Agreement (ACSA), which looks to provide mutual of logistical, material and technical support for both states' armed forces.

EU–Japan cooperation in the shadow of two superpowers

This volume transcends the current literature on EU–Japan relations that in certain cases can be prone to offer little more than self-congratulatory celebrations of the current state of the relationship, especially of elite dialogues and exchanges, which offer very little and often only light empirical verification of the concrete cooperation between the two sides and its broader impact. In other words, large parts of the existing literature on EU–Japan relations limits itself to providing rather superficial, as opposed to in-depth information and analysis, on what the EU and Japan are currently doing as regards concrete cooperation in the field of politics, trade and investment, and security. Moreover, the existing literature on EU–Japan relations tends to overly focus on the bilateral EU–Japan relationship while ignoring the broader international environment within which the relationship is embedded. This bilaterally focused approach and thinking generates an environment that at times unnecessarily creates obstacles to the EU and Japan moving forward and implementing the kind of policies that have featured in the official EU–Japan bilateral agendas over the last fifteen years. Instead, this volume takes a wholly different approach, and applies a critical and empirically based multi-disciplinary methodology to the analysis of bilateral economic, political, and security cooperation between two of the world's largest economic powers.

Although the US and China are always mentioned as number one and two in the rankings of economies, the EU's twenty-eight member states in aggregate make the EU the largest economy in terms of GDP. The EU's trade with the rest of the world accounts for around 16.8 per cent of global exports and imports in 2016. That makes it the world's largest trader (DG Trade Statistical Guide, 2017, p. 25). According to the World Bank, Japan is the world's third largest national economy in terms of GDP in 2016 (World Bank, 2017). The EU and Japan are both mature economies, meaning that they typically record comparatively low economic growth rates and are less affected by fluctuations in commodity and energy prices. Consequently, given the size of the EU and Japanese economies, and their already existing complementarity in trade and investment, it is obvious that the EU–Japan bilateral Free Trade Agreement/Economic Partnership Agreement (FTA/EPA) concluded on 8 December 2017 has the potential to increase significantly bilateral trade and investment flows. A bilateral EU–Japan FTA becomes even more crucial set against the background of the failure of the US-led Transpacific Partnership Agreement (TPP). During his visit to Japan in November 2017, US President Donald Trump, speaking to business leaders in Tokyo, reaffirmed his decision to pull the US out of the trade agreement (Cislo and Takahashi, 2017). Although Japan might continue pushing for implementation with the remaining participants, this is likely to become a considerably weakened agreement. On the European side, the Transatlantic Trade and Investment Partnership (TTIP) is also not moving forward.

In the field of international politics as well, the US and China are usually identified as the two central actors and protagonists, whereas by comparison the EU and Japan receive relatively little attention as contributors to regional and global security. However, if a closer look is taken at the actors contributing to global peace and security through measures such as development aid, technical assistance, and capacity-building in developing and/or post-conflict countries, it turns out that the EU and Japan make very significant contributions. In other words, the EU and Japan are crucial contributors to global peace and stability through instruments and policies which might not always (in fact, almost never) receive front-page coverage but are nonetheless significant, and, indeed, in many cases essential contributions to stability and peace in countries and regions prone to conflict, ethnic tensions, and war. This volume assesses where and to what extent such contributions from the EU and Japan prove to be crucial, whether on an individual or joint basis. To be able to analyse the cooperation some knowledge of the development of EU–Japan relations is essential.

The historical background

Japan, following defeat in 1945, became an occupied country. A programme of 'demilitarization' and 'democratization' was initiated by SCAP (the Supreme Commander for the Allied Powers). Although the occupation was termed 'Allied', European leaders took little interest in Japanese affairs since most of the running of SCAP was in the hands of the American military. At the time European countries also had more pressing issues to contend with, such as economic collapse and identity crises at home. The US came to play an important role in the rebuilding not only of Japan but also of parts of Europe through the Marshall Plan.

The close ties that had developed between the US and Western Europe after the war, and which were reinforced by the Cold War alliances, became tinged with the sense in the US that the European countries with their strong economic growth were not contributing sufficiently to their own defence. The setting up of NATO (the North Atlantic Treaty Organisation) was intended to remedy that and the US was supportive of European integration (Gilson, 2000, pp. 11–15). The

US was even more closely associated with the post-war system in Japan. As Mao Tse-tung and his Communist Party gained power in China, occupation policies changed radically, and in the 'reverse course' there was a move not only to demilitarize and democratize Japan, but also to build up a strong allied country to counter the communist threat (Gilson, 2000, pp. 11–15).

Diplomatic relations were resumed between Japan and various West European states when Japan gained independence in 1952, but US dominance impeded any form of substantive bilateral dialogue. Japan watched the formation of the EEC (European Economic Community) in 1957 with the suspicion that it would lead to a common external tariff, while the Europeans feared a Japanese economic invasion. It was not until the 1960s and the boom in Japanese exports that the European states started signing trade agreements with Japan and bilateral contacts were revitalized. These individual national approaches overlapped with, and occasionally clashed with, the drive for a more assertive role on the part of the EEC, attempting to deal with Japan in a collective European fashion. The Japanese were unsure about the future of the Community, and the Commission of the EEC for its part repeatedly failed to secure a mandate to coordinate trade negotiations for member states (Gilson, 2000, pp. 20–21).

During the 1960s, Japan and the EEC states also interacted in multilateral settings such as the GATT (General Agreement on Tariffs and Trade) and the UN (United Nations). However, it was not until after 1969, when the EPC (European Political Cooperation) was established, that the Commission was authorized to enter into negotiations for a trade agreement between the EEC and Japan. This was further strengthened when the EEC's Common Commercial Policy came into effect in the 1970s. But special rules permitting the retention of certain national measures, some of them directly targeted at Japan, hampered these attempts. The so-called first Nixon 'shock' in 1971, when the US suspended the convertibility of the dollar against gold and decided to place a surcharge on all imports, led to a major increase in Japanese exports to Europe. This increased tensions and the Europeans became more hostile to Japan as the trade deficit grew, even though some 'orderly marketing' measures were agreed to by Keidanren and the Commission (Gilson, 2000, p. 23).

The 1970s was a decade of continued trade disputes between Japan and the EEC, but also produced a new high-level bilateral dialogue. The Japan–EU Joint Communiqué issued after Foreign Minister Ohira's visit to Brussels in May 1973 was not only focused on trade, but also included other areas of cooperation such as East–West issues, as well as cooperation in the financial and energy sectors. The prospects of a real partnership were, however, hampered by trade disputes, as well as by Japan's lack of conviction in the EEC's viability as a single unit. The 1980s went by with the two parties showing only a lukewarm interest in each other. Trade did pose new issues, though, with the Europeans starting to put pressure on Japan to open up its own market, and attention turned to a number of non-tariff barriers (NTBs). High-level bilateral contacts increased, and the idea of a broader cooperative relationship was more frequently raised. This was facilitated by the Single European Act of 1986 giving the EC more of a single external face, and by the fact that Japan had started searching for a new role in the international community. However, only with the fall of the Berlin Wall and the end of the Cold War was this process ready for true take off.

The 1991 Hague Declaration

The collapse of the Soviet Union catalysed change in the Japan–US relationship and EU–US relations. Although the apparent Cold War enemy had been vanquished, the US, burdened with huge military expenditure and the failure of its macroeconomic policy did not appear as a strong victor. The US's dominant role since the end of World War II seemed significantly diminished. In this wider context of international political restructuring, interest grew both in Japan and in the EEC in wider international cooperation, and in creating alternative allies to the US (Abe, 1999, p. 135).

Business relations between Japan and the EEC countries had developed more or less independently of the state of diplomatic ties (Strange, 1996). On the political side, the earlier attitude of mutual indifference was increasingly problematic in the 'New World Order'. In Japan the domestic actor that handled the 1991 Joint Declaration between Japan and the European Community (European Commission, 1991), 'The Hague Declaration', was the Ministry of Foreign Affairs (MOFA). MOFA tried to keep the agreement well fenced off from trade issues, where it would have had to allow to cede influence to the Ministry of International Trade and Industry (MITI) and the Ministry of Finance (MOF). On the European side, the actors were the Commission (which had only limited external policy competence and power) and the governments of the member states. The EC's trade deficit with Japan was growing and there was strong pressure to include economic relations in the declaration. MOFA firmly objected to this proposal, with its intention being to produce a political declaration similar to the Transatlantic Declaration between the EC and the US, and the declaration between the EC and Canada (Abe, 1991, p. 135). The EC states were not united. Some like the UK and the Netherlands sought a political agreement, while others such as France wished to stress economic and trade issues (Abe, 1991, p. 134). In the end the Joint Declaration was mainly a political document with only vague references to trade issues. The declaration led to the initiation of a number of policy dialogues between Japan and the EC.

In the field of security, during the Cold War, discussions between the Japanese government and European leaders generally took place in the context of the European states' NATO membership in which the US presence was significant—to the extent that military issues were considered at all. Generally, security-related issues were understood within the context of economic concerns that were the core of Europe–Japan relations. With the fall of the Berlin Wall in 1989 there was a rethinking of security issues in Europe as former Soviet bloc countries started joining Western European organizations. The Japanese government was also quick to assist countries such as Poland and Hungary to transition to a free-market economy. On the security side there was limited cooperation between Japan and Europe, and the Europeans proposed no consistent security policy. The Hague Declaration, however, pledged cooperation between Japan and Europe in dealing with Central and Eastern Europe as well as the countries in Asia.

Many observers have considered this declaration a watershed in European–Japanese relations (Iwanaga, 2000), and it did indeed lead to political cooperation in various forms, such as the joint proposal for an arms register that was successfully institutionalized by the UN. Overall, however, the political relationship between Japan and the EC (or, after the entry into force of the Maastricht Treaty in 1993, the EU) remained lukewarm. Japan's first priority by far was the US, its second was China, third came the rest of East Asia, and then came Russia. Europe and the rest of Asia competed for fifth place (Lehmann, 1995). Although Japan might have ranked high on the agenda for businessmen in the EC or EU countries, from a political point of view interest was low.

The Action Plan of 2001

Through the Hague Declaration relations between the EU and Japan became institutionalized with regular official political dialogue, at various levels and covering a range of issues. At the same time, both the EU and Japan experienced significant changes at the turn of the twenty-first century. In Europe, with partial economic and monetary union having been achieved, preparations were being made for enlarging the EU's membership. The degree of political integration had increased among the member states and the EU was predicted to form the world's largest market. Security cooperation between Japan and Europe included extensive civilian participation in peace support operations and a focus on issues such as post-conflict reconstruction. This was to be expected, considering Article 9 of the Japanese constitution limits the Japanese Self Defence Forces (SDF) to non-combat missions abroad.

In Asia, which had just managed to overcome severe financial crises, several types of regional dialogues, such as the ARF, APEC and ASEAN + 3, had been established. The power balance in Asia was also changing with the emergence of a stronger and more assertive China that was starting to make its voice heard, at least among its neighbours in Asia. In those years the EU and Japan had both promoted various forms of inter-regional dialogue, as well as cooperation in global venues such as the UN, for, among other things sustainable development and the promotion of peace and stability.

It was in this context, with both parties trying to broaden their influence and partnerships, that the EU and Japan decided to launch an initiative for a so-called Decade of Japan–Europe Cooperation. The New Action Plan adopted in 2001 was to become the main steering document for the relationship during the forthcoming ten-year period. The Action Plan was a long and detailed document covering all areas where the EU and Japan sought future cooperation. Following, the attacks on the World Trade Centre in New York on 11 September 2001, the international environment shifted again and the fight against terrorism became the focus rather than EU–Japan joint civilian-centred approaches to peace and security. Although some joint initiatives were launched, very little of the content of the Action Plan was realized.

The rise of China as a new challenge

For much of the Cold War period China was not a central player in global politics. Largely isolated from the Western world by the US policy of non-recognition (including essentially no economic ties), China did not fundamentally affect the EU or even Japan. A few European countries, including the UK, France, Norway, Sweden, and eventually West Germany, broke with the US policy of non-recognition, although relations remained very limited. Japan felt compelled to abide by the US policy of non-recognition, although it did conduct modest informal trade with communist China. During the Cultural Revolution, China retreated into self-isolation. The main communist threat felt by both Japan and the EU was from the Soviet Union. China's international role, and its impact, became more salient with Nixon's opening of ties in 1971, quickly followed by Sino-Japanese normalization of diplomatic relations, and the beginning of triangular diplomacy between Beijing, Moscow and Washington. Nonetheless, China remained an extremely weak economic power, with nearly 25 per cent of the world's population, but only just over 2 per cent of global GDP (Hyo, 2006). Deng Xiaoping's market reforms and opening to global trade and investment began to transform China from the end of the 1970s, leading to China's rise as first a regional, and then a global economic power over the following thirty years.

Dismissed as late as 1999 as a country that did not fundamentally matter for the West (Segal, 1999), China by the early 2000s truly began to matter for the EU as well as Japan. Following its admission to the WTO in 2001, China became an important issue in EU–Japan, and even trans-Atlantic relations, for the first time by 2004. Identified by the EU as a strategic partner in 2003, proposals within the EU to lift the arms embargo imposed on China in the wake of the Tiananmen Square violent crackdown on student demonstrators, provoked Japanese and US opposition. Although advocates claimed that lifting the embargo would have no practical significance as the EU member state-specific arms export policies would prevent actual EU arms exports to China, strong opposition from Japan and the US prompted the EU to abandon lifting the embargo. This controversy helped launch EU–US and EU–Japan dialogues on East Asian security. By 2010, China overtook Japan to become the world's second largest economy, marking China's arrival as a plausible economic superpower. At the same time, China began to emerge as a regional and then global political power. China's rise posed a distinctive challenge to the liberal international order led by the US and supported by the EU and Japan, due to China's presence as a largely non-liberal power with an authoritarian political system. The so-called 'Beijing Consensus' sees China promoting a model of authoritarian-led economic development challenging Western models of development. China's economic rise arguably helped to undermine the fortunes of working classes in Western countries, while China's political rise itself seemed to challenge the dominance of the Western liberal order and liberalism more generally, as promoted by the US, the EU, and Japan.

The spread of illiberalism as a challenge

China's rise thus appears to be one factor driving the spread of illiberalism globally and even within the Western world. The influence of an increasingly illiberal and revanchist Russia, plus other factors such as technological change that has seemingly decimated blue collar and white collar worker job security; growing domestic economic inequality; massive refugee flows created by the Arab Spring, especially the civil war in Syria; the rise of radical politicized Islam, and perhaps even the balkanizing effects of the spread of social media on news and the loss of objective recognition of facts, have all contributed to the decline of liberalism (Luce, 2017). It is beyond the scope of this volume to analyse these diverse causes. Nonetheless, this spread of illiberalism is a challenge facing the EU and Japan alike.

Even inside the EU and Japan we can see the challenge of growing illiberalism. The economic crises and stagnation gripping the EU have contributed to a rise of illiberalism, undermining liberal democracy in crisis hit states such as Greece. There can also be witnessed the rise of increasingly illiberal regimes, especially in Hungary and Poland, where press freedoms and constitutional checks and balances on the power of ruling parties have been eroded. The challenges faced by the EU have even led to questions about the fundamental viability of the EU as an institution, with the UK's decision to leave being the most challenging example of this. Brexit contributes to challenges to freedom of movement, the free trade in goods and services, and perhaps even the broader EU democratic project, offering a potential revival of nationalism in its place.

In Japan too many observers point to a disjuncture between the self-proclaimed liberalism of Prime Minister Shinzo Abe and evidence of the erosion of media freedoms through the passing of new secrecy laws, ruling party threats directed at journalists, and the promotion of nationalist history education and discourses. Nonetheless, despite these illiberal tendencies in the EU and Japan, these two actors still champion a global liberal order, view it as a necessity, and hold the potential to support its continuation.

In the US as well, still the global liberal hegemon, we see the rise of illiberalism. This already began in the first few years of the twenty-first century, well before the political rise of Donald Trump. The decline in respect for human rights, including a willingness to engage in torture, indefinite detentions of suspects without trial, increasing surveillance of citizens, and a disregard for international institutions and law as embodied in the War on Terrorism and the invasion of Iraq, all reflect a declining willingness and ability on the part of the US to uphold the liberal international order that it created itself. After a limited revival of liberal values during the Barack Obama administration, the election of

Donald J. Trump as US president represented a new backlash against the global liberal order. Protestations of his being a free trader notwithstanding, Trump has signalled his rejection of free trade by rejecting the Trans Pacific Partnership (TPP) treaty and calling for the renegotiation of NAFTA. Trump has also abandoned the Paris Climate Agreement, and questioned US security commitments to Western allies. Trump rejects migration from a range of countries, ethnicities, and cultures, has sought to create a physical border wall between the US and Mexico, and seemingly coerces US and foreign companies against planning investments in America's southern neighbour. The spread of illiberalism globally, most dramatically represented by Trump's election as president of an ostensibly liberal hegemon, poses a grave threat to the global liberal international order, and a great challenge to the EU and Japan, as the remaining hoped-for major supporters of that order. The EU and Japan have reserves of capacity that could make a real difference in turning the tide back towards a liberal international order if they are willing to cooperate in areas as diverse as international finance, leadership in promoting new free trade agreements, post-conflict peace-building, the provision of development aid, and taking some responsibility for deterring and engaging China. The two sides have already declared their willingness to cooperate in all these areas, having concluded negotiations for an EPA free trade agreement, and then having in the pipeline a binding Strategic Partnership Agreement (SPA). The EU and Japan could thereby play a crucial role in stemming the global illiberal tide and leading the world back to a fuller liberal order.

Throughout this book we research various aspects of EU–Japan relations through a multi-disciplinary approach. We divided the book in to three parts, starting first with the political and security cooperation. The second part is concerned with cooperation in the field of economics, and the third contains assessment of EU–Japan relations from the perspectives of the US and China. Finally, the four editors present a conclusion highlighting the key lessons gained from the volume for EU–Japan cooperation and its global impact.

The SPA is the basis upon which EU–Japan political and security cooperation will be built in the future. Axel Berkofsky in his chapter, 'The strategic partnership agreement: new and better or more the same EU–Japan security cooperation?' researches the track record of the EU and Japan in initiating and adopting joint policies on both a regional and global scale and finds that EU–Japan non-military security cooperation (in Asia particular) has yet to reach its full potential. The SPA is aimed at further intensifying and institutionalizing European–Japanese security cooperation on the ground. By the time of writing this volume (December 2017/January 2018) the SPA has yet to be adopted, although an 'agreement in principle' was reached in July 2017, at which time it was announced that there was only 'legal fine tuning' remaining that would be achieved before the end of the year. That deadline has passed, and outside observers and analysts have some doubts about the commitment in both Brussels and Tokyo to utilize the SPA to increase quickly and efficiently on the ground cooperation in international politics and security. This chapter thus seeks to analyse how and to what extent the SPA will facilitate and intensify actual and measurable EU–Japan security cooperation in Asia and beyond.

Japanese Prime Minister Abe has promoted 'Pro-active Pacifism' and 'Values Diplomacy' as hallmarks of his foreign policy. Given the EU's promotion of peace-building, liberal values and the rule of law, the Abe administration's promotion of these two concepts promises the emergence of a new potential for EU–Japan political and security cooperation globally, and in both Europe and East Asia. Paul Midford's chapter, 'Abe's pro-active pacifism, values diplomacy, China, and EU–Japan political and security cooperation', assesses the Abe administration's implementation of 'Pro-active Pacifism' and 'Values Diplomacy' and whether these two concepts really portend greater future cooperation between the EU and Japan, or whether they are rather tactical responses to China's rise that have only limited potential for expanding EU–Japan cooperation.

One of the more important but under-appreciated senses in which the EU *is* relevant to the security shadows cast over Japan by the US and China lies in the realm of ideas. European debates on, and conceptions of, security identity are relevant to, and potentially have an impact on, the way in which Japan conducts itself. Paul Bacon and Hidetoshi Nakamura in their chapter 'Ordinary/civilian, not normative/post-modern: lessons from the EU for Japanese security policy' suggest that Japan needs to learn from European experience and avoid some of the traps into which Europeans have fallen in their self-definitions and actions since the end of the Cold War. The authors posit that the EU's mistakes have led to it being variously characterized as 'hubristic', 'negligent', 'self-righteous' and 'messianistic'. Japan runs the risk of repeating European mistakes, as a result of its persistent and strident references to democracy and human rights in its strategic diplomacy in the Asia-Pacific.

Amongst the array of potential areas for Japan–EU security cooperation the expectation is that the relationship—as with any serious set of security partners—would also extend to include defence technology collaboration, production and exports, and indeed dialogue and cooperation is now moving into this dimension. Japan has concluded bilateral agreements on joint research, development and production of defence equipment with the UK, France, and Germany from 2013 onwards, with other bilateral agreements in the pipeline, and more broadly a range of government and private sector actors maintaining an interest in interacting with and influencing EU defence procurement and arms export policies. Christopher W. Hughes in his chapter, 'Japan and EU defence production cooperation: a strategically important but nascent relationship', analyses how far this emerging defence production relationship can develop, and serve to reinforce and further broaden security ties and internationally significant cooperation.

The EU and Japan share the notion that human rights and democratic principles need to be integral parts in developing successful and sustainable societies. To an extent both actors have used political or economic pressure on un-democratic, human rights-violating regimes—the most striking example being sanctions levied against Myanmar until 2011. However, EU trade policy and the newly concluded FTA with Vietnam, as well as increased Japanese foreign aid to Vietnam, suggest that seemingly normative policy obligations are set aside or circumvented for other more pressing concerns. In 'EU and Japanese aid and trade: legitimising 'Chinese Democracy' in ASEAN', André Asplund analyses how the two self-proclaimed advocates for universal values—the EU and Japan—have come to frame human rights and democracy in their bilateral partnerships with Vietnam. This chapter suggests that increased competition with regional rival and burgeoning super-power, China, over a vibrant Vietnamese economy of more than 90 million (potential) consumers and a rapidly growing middle class, as well as its geo-strategic features, might challenge the otherwise firm normative commitments of the EU and Japan.

In the second part of the book, focusing on cooperation in the field of economics, Maaike Okano-Heijmans and Takashi Terada in their chapter, 'EU–Japan relations in the age of competitive economic governance in Asia', describe how the upsurge in new economic regionalism in Asia and the Pacific constitutes a major toolkit in US and Chinese struggles to form a new regional economic order in Asia. The EU and Japan have taken rather distinct approaches in this field, as illustrated by their responses to the China-led Asian Infrastructure Investment Bank (AIIB) and Belt and Road Initiative (BRI), as well as in trade diplomacy. This chapter discusses the actions and long-term objectives of the EU and Japan and explores to what extent they have set out to coordinate their foreign economic policies. It concludes that momentum appears to be finally building, but much more can be done to coordinate their strategic and geo-economic interests.

In response to the financial crisis, central banks around the globe responded with unconventional monetary policies, including negative interest rates (NIR). Markus Heckel in his chapter, 'Negative interest rate policy by the Bank of Japan from the perspective of monetary policy in Europe', analyses NIR, considering negative side effects of NIR, including declining bank profitability, risks to financial stability, balance sheet policies and global imbalances through currency depreciation. Another focus is on international implications, such as the Brexit referendum and the 2016 US election, which suggest that enhanced coordination and cooperation between central banks is needed to maintain global financial stability and to prevent future crises.

Patricia A. Nelson, in 'Taking the lead in current and future trade relationships', examines the process of the newly concluded EU–Japan economic partnership agreement (EPA). Pressure within Japan to negotiate an agreement increased after Korea concluded its own free trade agreement with the EU. After the catastrophic economic impact of the 3/11 triple disasters, powerful business interests in Japan agreed to open up Japan to the EU. They were even willing to negotiate the removal of non-tariff measures, something the EU had tried to achieve for decades. This chapter analyses how and why the EPA crystallized, and places it in the context of the populist anti-trade stance felt in the UK, namely Brexit, and the US. The vacuum in Asia created by the anti-free trade, anti-globalization Trump administration provided opportunities—and uncertainty—for Japan and the EU with a new trade agreement in an emergent new order.

With the UN adoption of the Sustainable Development Goals (SDG), changes are ongoing in the field of development cooperation. European countries and Japan have followed the OECD's Development Assistance Committee (DAC) standards, although European donors provided more 'soft aid' financed by grants and Japan placed a heavy emphasis on infrastructure. While the Europeans used to dominate agenda-setting, there now seems to be a definite turn towards the Japanese development cooperation model. Marie Söderberg in 'Japan and the EU: SDGs and changing patterns of development cooperation', analyses EU and Japan development policies as well as the cooperation between the two. It also researches Chinese and US influences on global development cooperation.

Part III concentrating on assessments from US and Chinese sides, starts with Jeffrey Hornung's chapter, 'The evolution of America's implicit support of EU–Japan security relations', which clarifies US views of EU–Japan security cooperation. After an examination of US strategic documents and agreements/statements regarding the EU and Japan, the chapter argues there has been an almost three-decade long growth of implicit US support for Brussels and Tokyo taking on greater security roles and many of the specific activities they seek to perform. This is because it is in US interests for 'potential' EU–Japan security cooperation to become 'actual'. While aiding US interests, greater EU–Japan security cooperation can adversely impact upon China as it promises to be a target of joint efforts.

Lilei Song and Liang Cai in their chapter, 'From "wider west" to "strategic alliance": an assessment of China's influence in EU–Japan Relations', seek to answer two questions. First, to what extent do EU–Japan strategic relations have an impact in Asia? Second, what influence does the EU–China strategic partnership have on the current and the future state of EU–Japan relations? This chapter addresses both questions and focuses on the role EU–China relations play in three dimensions of European–Japanese cooperation: security, economy and values. The main argument advanced is that despite the EU and Japan adopting their bilateral EU–Japan SPA, the EU remains cautious about engaging in substantial cooperation with Japan on Asian security that might be perceived as directed against China—such as joint EU–Japanese policies towards territorial conflicts in the East and South China Seas. This is due to Europe's geographical distance to Asia and its close economic and trade relations with China.

Finally, in the concluding chapter the editors argue that the timing is opportune to expand EU–Japan cooperation in regional and global politics and security, albeit perhaps out of dire necessity rather forward-looking optimism. The rise of populism, xenophobia, and ill-fated nationalism in Europe and Japan, Brexit, the election of Trump, and the surge of illiberal policies and regimes, is prompting Brussels and Tokyo to pool resources to counter this tide of illiberalism.

Brussels and Tokyo on 8 December 2017 made an important joint step in that direction by concluding the EU–Japan EPA and being close to adopting the SPA in principle. It might now indeed be possible to see a new dawn for Tokyo and Brussels' joint achievements in international trade, politics and security. However, this volume suggests that EU–Japan cooperation is not yet demonstrating its full capability to lead effectively in these areas and cooperation gaps are likely to remain. There is also a disturbing lack of urgency in Brussels and Tokyo in fully responding to the daunting challenges they face.

References

Abe, A. (1999) *Japan and the European Union: Domestic Politics and Transnational Relations*. London: Athlone.

Cislo, C. and Takahashi, M. (2017) Leaving TPP a Strategic Blunder by Trump, Ex-U.S. Trade Rep Michael Froman Says. *Japan Times*. 9 November. Available from: www. japantimes.co.jp/news/2017/11/09/national/politics-diplomacy/leaving-tpp-strategic-blunder-trump-ex-u-s-trade-rep-michael-froman-says/#.Wgm6uWhSxPY. [Accessed: 13 November 2017].

DG Trade Statistical Guide. (June 2017) Available from: http://trade.ec.europa.eu/doclib/docs/2013/may/tradoc_151348.pdf. [Accessed: 13 November 2017].

European Commission. (1991) Available from: www.deljpn.ec.europa.eu/relation/show page_en_relations.political.hague.php. [Accessed: 29 March 2011].

Gilson, J. (2000) *Japan and the European Union: A Partnership for the Twenty-first Century?* Basingstoke: Macmillan.

Hyo, S. (2006) 'Heiwateki hatten' ni katsuro. *Yomiuri Shimbun*. 23 February, p. 11.

Iwanaga, K. (2000) Europe in Japan's foreign policy. In Edström, E. (ed.) *The Japanese and Europe: Images and Perceptions*. Richmond: Japan Library.

Lehmann, J-P. (1995) Reshaping the US–Japan–EU 'Triangle'. *EIJS Working Paper Series*. Working Paper No. 27 (December).

Luce, E. (2017) *The Retreat of Western Liberalism*. New York: Atlantic Western Press.

Segal, G. (1999) Does China Matter? *Foreign Affairs*. September/October. www.foreign affairs.com/articles/asia/1999-09-01/does-china-matter [Accessed: 23 April 2018].

Strange, S. (1996) *The Retreat of the State: The Diffusion of Power in the World Economy*. Cambridge: Cambridge University Press.

World Bank. (2017) *Gross Domestic Product 2016*. Available from: http://databank.worldbank.org/data/download/GDP.pdf. [Accessed: 13 November 2017].

Part I

Political and security cooperation

2 The strategic partnership agreement

New and better or more of the same EU–Japan security cooperation?

Axel Berkofsky

Introduction

The EU and Japan have – at least on paper – ambitious plans regarding cooperation in international politics and security. The instrument and agreement through which such increased and institutionalized cooperation is envisioned to take place is the so-called Strategic Partnership Agreement (SPA). The SPA will cover EU–Japan cooperation in regional and global politics and security and is planned to give the current EU–Japan ad-hoc security cooperation in various parts of the world an institutional framework. Unfortunately, this chapter is confronted with the difficulty of having to analyse an agreement that has yet to be adopted, and hence it remains difficult to assess whether or whether not the SPA will be a 'breakthrough' agreement paving the way for a significant intensification of EU–Japan security cooperation. The adoption of the SPA, however, is not necessarily a precondition for Brussels and Tokyo to get engaged in on the ground cooperation in regional and global politics and security. As shown in Table 2.1 below, Brussels and Tokyo have over the years signed a number of important agreements and protocols in the areas of non-proliferation, disarmament, human rights, Asian security etc. To be sure, signing agreements and protocols is not the same as adopting joint policies on the ground and the EU–Japan SPA is therefore also aimed at following up on previously signed agreements and protocols with further joint policies. When EU–Japan negotiations were launched in 2013, the EU was able to convince Japan that the Economic Partnership Agreement (EPA) and SPA would not be adopted separately but simultaneously as a 'package'. Convincing Japan required some negotiations and EU insistence, according to what the author was told by EU policymakers involved in the negotiations, as from the onset Japan was more interested in the EPA than a SPA, not least because of the free trade agreement the EU adopted with South Korea in October 2015. Japanese companies (carmakers in particular) were concerned about losing market share to South Korean counterparts. The simultaneous adoption of both agreements, however, did not take place in the end: while the EPA/FTA was adopted on 8 December 2017, the SPA was not and by the time of this writing there is (January 2018) no information publicly available on when the SPA will follow suit.

After the EU and Japan reached an 'agreement in principle' on the SPA in July 2017, both Brussels and Tokyo announced that they intended to adopt the agreement by the end of 2017. The Japanese side assured the author at the time that Brussels merely needed some additional time to complete some final 'legal fine tuning' on the agreements and that this would be completed by the end of 2017. That deadline has now passed and the outside analyst is by now, in view of yet another delay, allowed to have some doubts about the commitment by both Brussels and Tokyo, to use the SPA to quickly and efficiently increase on-the-ground cooperation in international politics and security.

Furthermore, the EU is at risk of jeopardizing its credibility as an account-able and transparent institution, charged with the task of rendering EU policy-making as transparent and accountable as possible. Up until today, the EU has still not made any details of the SPA available, beyond outlining the areas it will cover in a very general manner without providing any details (on EU web-sites). In fact, the information available on European External Action Service (EEAS) websites on the contents of the agreement is very scarce indeed and can hardly be referred to as such. In other words, those looking for information and details on the contents of the SPA should NOT be consulting the EEAS websites as there is indeed next to no information and data available on the actual content of the agreement. While the EU Commission's Directorate-General for Trade (DG Trade) in July 2017 decided to make the EPA draft agreement publicly available, the EEAS did not follow suit. The decision not to make information public gives the impression that EU policymakers think they are operating in an area where transparency and accountability are optional as opposed to compulsory. Or, possibly, the EU Commission, which is in charge of the EU–Japan Economic Partnership Agreement (EPA)/Free Trade Agreement (FTA), took the step to counter accusations of non-transparency while the EEAS chose to ignore such accusations.

Once adopted, the SPA, EU sources tell the author, could be accompanied by the establishment of an EU Commission–EEAS EU–Japan joint committee, i.e. a committee through which the EU Commission informs the EU's EEAS on the state and progress of the more than 40 EU–Japan sectoral dialogues. So far, there are no regular exchanges between the EU Commission and the EEAS on EU–Japan sectoral dialogues, a result undoubtedly of the traditional rivalry and struggle over competencies between the EU Commission and the EEAS. Either way, a joint EU–Japan committee could be an effective instrument for the EU Commission and EEAS to inform each other on respective policies towards Japan. That such a committee has yet to be established reflects a deficit in the EU's ability to formulate and adopt coherent and coordinated policies towards Japan.

Against the background of the global crisis of liberalism, the adoption of the SPA in 2017 would have sent an important message that the EU and Tokyo are serious about joining forces to uphold and defend established standards of inter-national politics and security. While the US under President Donald Trump has sometimes turned to isolationist foreign policies and protectionist trade policies (referred to as 'America First Policies' by Trump), China is, in defiance of liberal norms and – as we have seen when China dismissed the July 2016 verdict of the Permanent Court of Arbitration in The Hague (Permanent Court of Arbitration, 2016), which ruled that China cannot claim historical territorial rights in the South China Sea, also in defiance of international law – promoting its own models of economic and authoritarian political governance on regional and global levels. Against the background of China's global challenge to liberal values, Brussels and Tokyo's failure to meet their deadline to conclude an SPA arguably displays a lack of commitment to defend liberal values and thwarting the challenge posed by China.

Years of negotiations

During the 20th EU–Japan Summit in 2010 Brussels and Tokyo agreed to adopt two legally binding agreements: one to institutionalize and expand bilateral cooperation in international political and security and another to increase bilateral trade and investment ties through a free trade agreement (Tyszkiewicz, 2013). Initially in 2010 the two sides launched the so-called Framework Agreement (FA) (which was later re-named into Strategic Partnership Agreement (SPA) and the EU–Japan Economic Partnership Agreement (EPA)/Free Trade Agreement (FTA). A year later, so-called 'scoping exercises' were launched after the EU–Japan 2011 summit for both agreements, as part of a parallel negotiation process. 'Parallel' in the sense that it was agreed at the time that the two agreements would be adopted together. At that time the European Commission sought the necessary authorization from the Union's member states for negotiating these agreements based on a successful outcome of the 'scoping exercises'. The 'scoping exercises' were launched as part of a preparatory phase, during which both the EU and Japan sides committed themselves to agree on a common platform from which to negotiate both agreements. For the EU, the 'scoping exercises', i.e. regular bilateral working-level encounters, had to result in Japan declaring itself prepared to remove all trade barriers – from procurement and investment barriers to tariffs and most importantly the numerous Japanese non-tariff barriers to trade Brussels (de Prado, 2014). The scoping exercises for the SPA and FTA were successfully concluded in April and May 2012 respectively.

EU–Japan Strategic Partnership Agreement (SPA) negotiations were launched in 2013, and after the 11th round of negotiations in March 2016, the EU and Japan were able to agree on 31 out of 54 articles in the agreement. The outstanding articles – referred to by the EU as 'politically sensitive'[1] – were, as mentioned above, agreed upon in July 2017. The SPA is envisioned to be 'binding' in the sense that it will – at least according to EU sources – feature a well-defined list of issues and areas the EU and Japan will be dealing with in the years ahead. Compared to the previous EU–Japan Action Plan (adopted in 2001 and expired in 2011), the SPA will not be limited by a specific timeframe. The SPA will cover bilateral cooperation in politics and security and it will define

Table 2.1 EU–Japan relations – chronology and key initiatives

• 1959	Accreditation of Japan's first representative to the European Communities (EC)
• 1974	Establishment of the delegation of the European Communities in Japan
• 1987	Japan's Ministry of International Trade and Industry (MITI) and the European Commission establish the EU–Japan Centre for Industrial Cooperation
• 1991	First EU–Japan bilateral summit in The Hague – adoption of 'The Hague Declaration'
• 1994	Establishment of EU Gateway to Japan programme to enhance trade and investment between Europe and Japan
• 2001	Brussels and Tokyo adopt the EU–Japan action plan 'Shaping our common future' (expired in 2011)
• 2002	EU–Japan Mutual Recognition Agreement
• 2003, 2005, 2007	Cooperation on the 'Conference on Facilitating the Entry into Force of the Comprehensive Nuclear-Test-Ban Treaty (CTBT)'
• 2003	EU–Japan Agreement on Cooperation on Anti-competitive Activities
• 2003	Launch of biannual meetings of the 'EU–Japan Troika Working Group on Human Rights'
• 2004	Co-chairing the 'Ministerial Conference on Peace Consolidation and Economic Development of the West Balkans' (Tokyo)
• 2004	Joint adoption of a protocol on disarmament and non-proliferation promoting the acceleration of the implementation of the UN Programme of Action on Small Arms and Light Weapons
• 2005	Launch of EU–Japan Strategic Dialogue on East Asian Security
• 2005	EU–Japan Year of People-to-People Exchanges
• 2006	EU–Japan Agreement for cooperation in the peaceful uses of nuclear energy
• 2008	EU–Japan Agreement on Cooperation and Mutual Administrative Assistance
• 2008	'EU–Japan Meeting on Human Security' in the Western Balkans
• 2009	EU–Japan Agreement on science and technology cooperation
• 2009	EU–Japan Agreement on mutual legal assistance in criminal matters
• 2009 and 2010	EU–Japan joint capacity-building seminars held in Tajikistan
• 2010	Set-up of high-level group to identify options for the comprehensive strengthening EU–Japan trade and political cooperation
• 2011	EU–Japan launch of cooperation for disaster prevention
• 2012	EU–Japan 'Scoping Exercises' for EU–Japan EPA/FTA and SPA concluded
• 2013	Launch of negotiations for a Strategic Partnership Agreement and a Free Trade Agreement
• July 2017	EU–Japan Agreement to adopt both FTA and SPA by the end of 2017

Source: author.

arrangements for regular meetings between political leaders and ministry officials. The SPA is reportedly covering cooperation in over 30 areas. Its conclusion would bring an upgrade in EU–Japan relations, moving from sectoral
agreements to a comprehensive, binding and forward-looking framework.
The SPA would include political dialogue, regional dialogues, promotion of
human rights and fundamental freedoms, and economic, scientific and cultural
cooperation.

What kind of agreement?

EU sources told the author in 2016 and 2017 that it was yet to be decided
whether the SPA would be an EU-only agreement or a mixed agreement. Obviously, the EU Commission is aiming for an EU-only agreement (with the Commission having exclusive competence) while several EU member states wanted
a mixed agreement. A mixed agreement would have to be ratified by all EU
member states, which would likely further slow the eventual adoption of the
SPA. By the time of this writing (February 2018) there is no information publicly available on whether it will be an EU-only or a mixed agreement. Tokyo
always opposed the introduction of the so-called 'Essential Elements Clause'
into the agreement, a clause through which the EU would reserve the right to
link issues such as human rights and non-proliferation of weapons of mass
destruction to trade agreements it adopts with other countries, interrupting those
agreements when violations occur. Even if the clause is reciprocal, i.e. even if
Japan too has the right to interrupt a free trade agreement in response to human
rights violations and the proliferation of weapons of mass destruction by the EU,
Tokyo has nonetheless opposed including this clause. EU sources tell this author
that the EEAS is not 'happy' about having to insert that clause into an agreement
with a democratic country. That clause, EU sources emphasize, has been
'imposed' on Brussels by EU member states, and if it were not for EU member
states' insistence to insert that clause, it would not be in the agreement with
democratic Japan. EU sources tell this author that while individual EU member
states do not have 'essential elements' clauses in their bilateral agreements with
other countries, they expect the EU have such clauses in its agreements.[2] The
treaty-based requirement for the EU to conduct a principled foreign policy is formulated in Article 21 of the Treaty of the Functioning of the European Union
(TFEU). This requires the EU to stipulate in all agreements the commitment for
the respect and protection of human rights and the non-proliferation of weapons
of mass destruction, as well as to find a mechanism to link these political principles to the EU's trading concessions. This concerns not only Japan but also
with other like-minded and strategic partners such as South Korea, Canada, Australia, New Zealand. While this linkage may be a legal requirement for the EU, it
has been contested by some of the EU's partners, including Japan. The legal link
was approved by the Union's Committee of Permanent Representatives
(COREPER) in 2009, through which the EU authorizes itself to suspend a free
trade agreement in case of e.g. human rights violations committed by the other

party of the agreement. To be sure, that is highly unlikely in the case of Japan, but from a Japanese perspective such a clause is without a doubt unwelcome as it – from a Japanese point of view – conveys a message of Brussels 'supervising' the quality of Japanese foreign and domestic policies (Reiterer, 2013, 2015). Japan, however, had to swallow that bitter pill and accept the 'essential elements' clause as a Japanese policymaker involved in negotiations told the author.

The Framework Partnership Agreement (FPA)

In addition to the EPA and SPA, Brussels and Tokyo are currently negotiating the Framework Partnership Agreement (FPA), an agreement aimed at facilitating the deployment of Japanese armed forces within the framework of European Common Security Defence Policy (CSDP) missions (EEAS, 2016a). The FPA would institutionalize already ongoing Japanese contributions to CSDP missions. However, there is no information publicly available on the current state of negotiations other than that they are 'ongoing'. Without the FPA, the EU and Japan are strictly and legally speaking not conducting a joint mission, but are engaged in what Brussels refers to 'parallel coordinated action'. The FPA, as the analyst Andrea Fontini argues, is aimed at creating synergies between the EU's 'comprehensive approach' to security and Japan's 'human security' concept in the Middle East and Asia (Fontini, 2016). However, there are no clear indications as to how and to what extent Brussels' 'comprehensive approach' and Tokyo's 'human security' concept are compatible. Indeed, arguing that they could be compatible and thereby leading to joint EU–Japan policies, applying both approaches of security on the ground (in the Middle East, Africa or Asia) is little more than speculation and guesswork in the absence of empirical evidence. It remains to be seen in both Brussels and Tokyo whether the EU and Japan can coordinate and harmonize the way they operate on the ground. Is Japan prepared to put its armed forces under European command, authorizing its solders to apply EU Rules of Engagement in case they come under attack? Fontini also refers to what he calls 'post-industrial security dossiers' such as counterterrorism, maritime security, resource management (among others water, food and energy), natural disaster prevention and management, cyber-defence, arms control, non-proliferation of weapons of mass destruction and others as areas where the EU and Japan cooperate.

A Trump factor?

Against the background of EU–Japan joint rhetoric, which numerous times in the past suggested that Brussels and Tokyo are 'natural allies' sharing the same values and approaches to international politics and security, EU–Japan preparedness to increase security cooperation should have received a boost with the election of Donald Trump as U.S. President. Perhaps it indeed did in the second half of 2017, when SPA negotiations accelerated, leading to the above-mentioned 'agreement in principle' on the SPA. Abe's EU policy advisors must have advised the Prime Minister not only to invest resources into the alliance with the U.S. under an unpredictable president, but also to make good on the promise to jointly contribute to regional and global stability with fellow 'soft power' EU during turbulent times. To be sure, the Japanese Prime Minister throughout 2017 did not fail to display the sort of strong interest, and even awkward and sometimes obsessive enthusiasm, to stay on Trump's good side; an enthusiasm Abe first displayed when Trump won the U.S. presidential elections. Indeed, after Trump's victory Abe did not lose much time to 'present' himself to the President-elect, travelling to New York in mid-November 2016 for a meeting.[3] Abe, it seemed, was above all interested in making sure that the terms and quality of Tokyo's security alliance with Washington remain unchanged, and that Trump would not after his inauguration act on what he said during the election campaign regarding U.S.–Japan relations.[4] Without offering any details whatsoever, at the time Trump announced that as President he would deal with what he referred to as Japan's 'unfair trade practices'. Furthermore, Trump announced that he would oblige Tokyo to contribute 'more' to Asian security in general, and to the stationing of U.S. military troops on Japanese soil in particular (Ueno and Rich, 2016). None of this as it turned out made it onto the official agenda of the first Abe–Trump summit. In mid-February, Abe and Trump met in the U.S. and Tokyo got what it wanted from Washington: a verbal guarantee that Article 5 of the U.S.–Japan Security Treaty covers also the defence of the Japanese-controlled Senkaku Islands in the East China Sea. This is obviously the kind of guarantee European and EU policymakers cannot give to Japan, and clearly goes beyond the occasional European assurance to continue urging China to solve its territorial disputes in the East and South China Seas peacefully. Against that background and in view of Shinzo Abe's apparently very strong interest to not in any way rock the boat of U.S.–Japan relations it seems rather unlikely that Tokyo will invest significantly more resources into expanding security cooperation with the EU after the adoption of the SPA. In other words, Prime Minister Abe is arguably the 'wrong' Prime Minister to take European–Japanese security cooperation to the 'next level' as EU and Japanese policymakers have often talked about in the past. Abe's his foreign and security policies priorities and his ambitions to expand Japan's role and competencies in the framework of Tokyo's bilateral military alliance with the U.S. point to the conclusion that Abe is much more interested in expanding Japan's territorial defence profile and positioning as opposed to invest more resources into expanding non-military security cooperation with the EU.

Hard security cooperation too?

EU–Japan military-to-military security cooperation dates back to the year 2009, and joint EU–Japan counter-piracy operations in the Gulf of Aden off the coast of Somalia. Japanese Maritime Self-Defense Force (MSDF) destroyers have participated since March 2009, along with two P-3C maritime patrol aircraft added in June 2009. The MSDF unit has been providing information to other countries and has been conducting operations in the field, including with the EU Naval Force (NAVFOR) Somalia-Operation Atalanta, a CSDP military mission operational since the end of 2009. On 18 January 2014 e.g. Japan–EU cooperation led to the capture of pirates when a helicopter from the MSDF destroyer Samidare and a P-3C patrol aircraft detected a suspicious vessel and provided this information to the Combined Task Force 151 headquarters. In response, a helicopter from a French EU NAVFOR naval vessel was dispatched, which led to the capture of five pirates and the release of the vessel's crew. Japan and Europe have been conducting joint counter-piracy exercises since October 2014. In October and November 2014, MDSF destroyer Takanami participated in exercises with Italian, German, and Dutch naval vessels. These consisted of operations such as communications, tactical manoeuvring, helicopter take-off and landing and boarding. Japan's MSDF EU NAVFOR has, since 2010, exchanged information on numerous occasions.[5] However, to refer to EU–Japan information sharing as a 'joint EU–Japan mission' (as the EU and Tokyo have repeatedly done) is probably a bit of a stretch as this data sharing takes place in the framework of a multinational and UN-sanctioned mission combating piracy off the coast of Somalia.[6] That said, however, it should not go unmentioned that Japanese navy vessels escort commercial vessels through the Gulf of Aden in coordination with EU NAVFOR, which is in charge of managing the escorts. Furthermore, the EU and Tokyo are also providing development assistance to Somalia and some neighbouring countries, and are jointly helping to train Somali maritime security officials. Japanese scholar Akiko Fukushima argues that there is further potential for collaboration on capacity building in Somalia (Fukushima, 2015).

EU–Japanese joint interest in informing each other on respective security policies in East Asia dates to 2005. In September of that year, Brussels and Tokyo began discussing Asian security issues on a regular basis by launching the 'EU-Japan Strategic Dialogue on East Asian Security' (Mykal, 2011). The establishment of that dialogue was preceded by the establishment of the 'EU-US Dialogue on East Asian Security' in 2004. However, it is accurate to conclude that the dialogue has not developed into a forum where Brussels and Tokyo discuss and adopt joint EU–Japanese East Asian security policies. In fact, that dialogue – like the Union's dialogue with Japan on Central Asian security – is probably not known to many people outside of Brussels, not least as it is – as EU policymakers have explained to this author – mainly meant to inform each other on respective security policies in the region as opposed to being a platform for adopting joint policies on Asian ground. To be sure, such reasoning comes in 'handy' when EU policymakers are confronted with the task of explaining what concretely has emerged from the dialogue in terms of joint EU–Japan security policies (which is arguably little). In view of the absence of joint EU–Japanese security policies in Asia, stressing the fact that the dialogue exists as a forum to exchange information, as opposed to adopting joint policies, becomes somehow understandable from an EU policymaker's perspective. Given that the EU weapons embargo imposed on China in 1989 has always been the central issue on the dialogue's agenda, it is accurate to conclude that Tokyo's motivation for initiating a dialogue with the EU on East Asian security were identical with Washington's motivations in 2004: institutionalizing political pressure on Brussels not to lift the weapons embargo it imposed on China after Tiananmen square in 1989 (Berkofsky, 2012). Today, that dialogue continues to be focused on informally consulting with each other on respective security policies in East Asia. It has arguably not become – it was never intended, as EU policymakers stress – a dialogue facilitating concrete EU–Japanese joint Asian security policies. To be sure, there is no reason why that dialogue cannot in the future turn into one that also provides a platform for the EU and Japan to adopt and implement joint security policies in East Asia. The adoption of the SPA and the willingness to more closely and more actively coordinate regional and global security policies could provide policymakers in both Brussels and Tokyo with a new impetus to 'upgrade' the dialogue from 'consultative' to 'action-oriented'.

Japanese contributions to Common Security and Defence (CSDP) missions?

In August 2012, the EU deployed a civilian CSDP mission to provide training and advice to Niger's security sector. In December 2014, Tokyo decided to provide grant aid through the UN Development Program to the EU's CSDP mission in Niger. In that context Japan is contributing ¥202 million for wireless communication devices to connect regional government offices with bureaus under their jurisdiction, as well as wireless-equipped vehicles for patrolling in various locations in Niger's seven administrative regions. In April 2014, the EU dispatched a civilian CSDP mission aimed at improving Mali's security capabilities. A year later in March 2015, Japan started contributing to that mission, providing grant aid amounting to ¥492 million for the rehabilitation of Mali's national police school. Japan's cooperation with CSDP missions, Fukushima argues, was facilitated by the expertise Tokyo gained through rebuilding infrastructure in Iraq since the early 2000s (for which Japan used part of its Official Development Assistance (ODA) budget) (Fukushima, 2015).

During the 22nd Japan–EU Summit in Brussels in May 2014, Prime Minister Abe, then President of the European Council Herman Van Rompuy, and President of the European Commission Jose Manuel Barroso, announced the goal of institutionalizing collaboration between the EU's CSDP missions and Japan's assistance and security cooperation initiatives in direct support of ongoing CSDP missions. At that time Brussels and Tokyo also expressed their commitment to ensuring strict export control of arms and dual-use technologies, especially to conflict zones. Finally, Brussels and Tokyo announced plans to further intensify collaboration between Tokyo's humanitarian and technical assistance operations and the EU's CSDP mission in Mali and the Democratic Republic of Congo. They, for example, agreed to strengthen joint capacity building measures of the national military forces of Mali, to jointly support the peacekeeping school of Bamako, jointly assist the improvement of security, antiterrorism laws and enhancement of judicial cooperation in Mali. It was also agreed to jointly assist capacity building measures of police officers and judicial administrators in the Democratic Republic of Congo. Finally, it was agreed to jointly assist the improvement of security, antiterrorism laws and enhancement of judicial cooperation in Niger (European Commission, 2014). Japan applies its so-called 'comprehensive approach' combining development cooperation under its 2015 Development Cooperation Charter[7] with Tokyo's new security legislation adopted in 2013, which has potentially opened additional opportunities for security cooperation with the EU.

During the 2014 EU–Japan Summit, Brussels and Tokyo further announced plans to:

1   promote the anti-Personnel Mine Ban Convention
2   counter illicit trade in small arms and light weapons, especially in Libya and the Sahel region
3   press for the early entry into force and effective implementation of the Arms Trade Treaty.

Bilateral defence ties with France and the UK

In January 2014, France and Japan held their first ministerial-level foreign affairs/defence ministers (2 plus 2) meeting. During the second 2 plus 2 meeting in 2015, respective foreign and defence ministers discussed the so-called 'Plan of Action for Africa', which included the possibility of joint border security actions in Niger, Mali and Burkina Faso, and joint peacekeeping policies and missions in Africa (*Japan Times*, 2015). In July 2014, Paris and Tokyo signed a memorandum of understanding (MOE) to increase defence cooperation, including the joint development of military equipment. This includes joint development of unmanned underwater vehicles.

In April 2012, Tokyo and London signed a first joint weapons development agreement, which in July 2013 was followed-up by two additional British–Japanese agreements – the so-called 'Defence Equipment Cooperation Framework' to facilitate joint development of military equipment and the 'Information Security Agreement', which aims to facilitate increased intelligence cooperation. This resulted, in among others, British–Japanese joint development of chemical and biological warfare suits, and cooperation in missile technology. Furthermore, British and Japanese armed forces began conducting joint military exercises, and Tokyo and London held their first 2 plus 2 plus minister's meeting in January 2015. In May 2014, London and Tokyo initiated negotiations on a bilateral Acquisition and Cross-Servicing Agreement (ACSA), which facilitates the mutual provision of logistical, material, ammunition and technical support for each other's armed forces.

Against the background of the Japanese Prime Minister's strong interest in upgrading Japan's military capabilities, and partnerships (e.g. through the above-mentioned laws authorizing the SDF to exercise the right to collective self-defence), there is obviously the risk that Tokyo under Abe will focus on the development of bilateral hard-security partnerships with European countries such as France and the UK. While that does not necessarily mean that Abe will neglect security cooperation with the whole of the EU, the above-mentioned expansion of bilateral defence ties with Paris and London are an indication of Tokyo's policy priorities. Indeed, Abe might continue to focus on building ties between Japanese and European defence contractors.

The China factor

China's military rise and its increasingly assertive regional security policies in general, and policies related to maritime territorial claims in the East and Southeast Asia in particular, could have been an incentive to intensify EU–Japan security cooperation. However, China's territorial expansion in the South China Sea over the last three to four years has not led to any concrete EU–Japanese policies directed at countering Beijing's unilateral territorial expansionism. Indeed, Brussels will continue to remain very reluctant to get involved in Asian territorial disputes beyond statements urging all involved parties to solve disputes peacefully. Furthermore, it must not be forgotten that the EU's EEAS is not an organization operating independently from EU member states, some of which have strong reservations about getting involved in disputes with China due to their close business and economic ties with China. Furthermore, the EU continues to insist that it is not taking sides in territorial disputes, and it probably does not – unlike the U.S. – have the resources and capabilities in the region (i.e. troops and navy vessels) to deter China from building facilities and military bases on disputed islands in the South China Sea.

The more Beijing seeks to unilaterally change the maritime territorial status quo in Asia in its favour, the more the EU and Japan should realize that consulting with, let alone cooperating, with China on regional security is an illusion that takes place on paper, and paper only. Indeed, China's increasingly aggressive regional policies and policies related to territorial claims in Asia should, from Tokyo's perspective, inject a 'sense of urgency' into European interest in Asian regional security and encourage European policymakers to side with Japan in its efforts to keep China's regional territorial expansionism in the East and South China Seas in check.[8] Doubts about the lack of result-oriented and practical dialogue notwithstanding, the EU and China in 2010 set up an annual bilateral security dialogue, the 'EU-China High-level Strategic Dialogue' (EEAS, 2016b) The last dialogue was held in April 2017 and judging by Federica Mogherini's official remarks on the dialogue, Brussels and Beijing agree on all issues and global crises that were discussed during the three-hour long dialogue (the security situations in Afghanistan and Syria as well as the danger posed by North Korea's nuclear and missile programmes (EEAS, 2017). However, that is probably also the case because potentially controversial issues such as China's (very) assertive policies related to territorial claims in the South China Sea or the problems related to China's less than perfect implementation of UN Security Council mandated sanctions imposed onto North Korea did not make it onto the agenda of the most recent dialogue in April 2017. Since the dialogue's establishment Brussels policymakers among others, hoped that the dialogue would encourage Beijing to become more transparent about its defence expenditures and military equipment procurement and sales policies. However, that is, it turns out, clearly a case of European wishful-thinking, as China will not make any more information on its arms procurement policies available simply because the EU is requesting just that in a bilateral dialogue. When analysts argue that the EU–China strategic dialogue on Asian security is more than anything else an annual window-dressing event as opposed to a dialogue that produces real results, let alone joint policies related to Asian security, EU officials typically point out that the dialogue's objective is not the adoption of joint policies, but rather to provide a platform to informally consult with each other on Asian security issues. While dialogue and consultations are positive as such, the raison d'être of such a dialogue must however be put in doubt if any – even the most 'timid' – European criticism on Chinese foreign and security policy behaviour (such as Chinese assertive policies related to territorial claims in the South China Sea) is either ignored, or worse, called unwanted 'interference' in China's domestic affairs.[9] And that is why Asian territorial conflicts with Chinese involvement did not make it onto the agenda of the above-mentioned EU–China security dialogue in April 2017. Indeed, the reality of Chinese regional security policy conduct has shown that Beijing's preparedness to consult with the EU on security issues which fall under what Beijing refers to as its 'core interests' – the Taiwan and Tibet 'questions' and what Beijing refers to as 'territorial integrity' in Asia's disputed maritime areas – is all but not non-existent. If that is accurate, and if European views and advice on Chinese security policies in Asia are only endorsed during official encounters as opposed to in the 'real' world, then it is fair to question whether the dialogue on Asian security with China is an efficient use of EU resources and political capital.

Regardless of whether or not the above-mentioned bilateral EU–Chinese dialogue on Asian security produces tangible results, this dialogue has, in the past in Japan – the EU's supposed 'natural ally' in Asian politics and security[10] – at times led to the perception that Brussels is not the kind of security policy partner willing to support Tokyo's China security policies aimed at deterring Beijing's territorial ambitions towards Japanese-controlled maritime areas in the East China Sea. In fact, given the currently tense Japanese–Chinese relations, the EU discussing Asian security with Beijing without strongly condemning Chinese violations of Japanese territorial sovereignty in waters around the Senkaku Islands is a de facto confirmation to some Japanese policymakers and scholars that the reality of EU–Japan security cooperation does not live up to the above-mentioned term 'natural ally' in Asian politics and security. In other words, one could conclude that from Tokyo's perspective, the EU, as regards Asian security of direct and vital interest to Japan, is reliable and credible only within limits unless and until Brussels unambiguously sides with Tokyo on its policies related to the defence of Japanese-controlled territory in the East China Sea. To be sure,

Tokyo is probably very aware that – judging by Beijing's insistence on its sacred 'principle of non-interference' on a come-what-may-basis – Brussels openly and on the record criticizing Chinese violations of Japanese-controlled territorial waters around the Senkaku Islands (Beijing refers to them as Diaoyu Islands) in the East China Sea, would probably interrupt (if not indefinitely terminate) the EU–China bilateral dialogue on Asian security. However, this should, from Japan's perspective, not stand in the way of Brussels supporting Tokyo's policies that oppose what Tokyo refers to as unlawful and aggressive Chinese intrusions into Japanese-controlled territorial waters in the East China Sea. However, because the EU – like the US for that matter – officially takes a neutral stance on sovereignty in Asian territorial disputes, Brussels will most probably continue to exercise restraint, and avoid siding with Japan too openly and publicly on the Senkaku/Diaoyu Islands dispute. Then again, the author's numerous off-the-official-record conversations with EU policymakers have confirmed that Chinese policies related to territorial claims in the East and South Chinas are indeed perceived as aggressive and very counterproductive to Asian political and security stability.

To be sure, Tokyo policymakers are aware of the limits of the EU's ability and preparedness to voice unambiguous and outspoken support for Japanese policies related to territorial claims in the East China Sea, and against that background even the EU's 'timid' calls towards Beijing to solve territorial disputes peacefully are probably appreciated all the same in Tokyo. Regarding concrete and sustainable support for Tokyo's policies related to the defence of Japanese territories in the East China Sea, Washington is, and will continue to remain, the most important partner. Washington has, over the last two years more than once confirmed that it is – due to its obligation under Article V of the U.S.–Japan Security Treaty to defend territory under Japan's administration, prepared – to jointly defend the Senkaku Islands with Japan in the case of a Chinese attempt to invade and occupy the islands. Consequently, support from the EU for Asian countries disputing territories with Beijing in the East and South China Seas are helpful and positive as such, but such support does not in any way equal Washington's very concrete support, and the U.S. ability to actually and physically deter Chinese vessels from intruding into maritime areas controlled by other countries, be it in the East or South China Sea. While Tokyo is realistic about Brussels' self-imposed obligation to take – at least for now – a cautious position on Chinese intrusions into Japanese-controlled territorial waters in the East China Sea, joint EU–Chinese statements coming out of the bilateral security dialogue must nonetheless sound 'hollow' to the ears of Japanese policymakers in view of Chinese attempts to challenge Tokyo's control over Japanese-controlled territorial waters in the East China Sea (through illegal intrusions into disputed territorial waters). While the fact that the EU's dialogues on Asian security with Japan and China exist in parallel is not negative per se, it is arguably from an EU policymaker's perspective challenging to explain how a dialogue with a non-democratic country like China, which shares very little, if anything in common with the EU regarding approaches towards regional and global politics and security, can produce similarly constructive results when compared with a dialogue with a democratic country like Japan, which shares similar, indeed often identical approaches, towards Asian security with the EU. In other words, instead of investing more political resources into a security dialogue with its like-minded partner Japan, the EU is investing the same, if not more resources, into a dialogue with a partner, China, that has fundamentally different approaches towards politics and security. As a result, the EU is arguably wasting resources on a dialogue that is not producing tangible joint EU–China policies that reflect European approaches towards regional Asian security.

Jointly checking on Chinese territorial expansionism?

Japan, governed by the pro-defence LDP, and led by Abe, undoubtedly questions the EU a security actor in Asia, able to help defend Japanese security interests in East Asia. While the above-mentioned bilateral defence relations with countries such as UK and France have expanded over the last two years, it is accurate to conclude that the EU as a hard-security policy actor with a role and influence in Asian hard-security issues continues to have secondary importance in Tokyo's security policymaking circles (Pejsova, 2015). That will continue to be the case unless Brussels – against the background of Chinese territorial expansionism in the South China Sea – decided to follow-up its verbal and on-paper opposition to Beijing's building of civilian and military facilities on islands and islets[11] also claimed by other countries, with concrete action, such as maritime patrols missions in the South China, as in 2016 suggested by French Defence Minister Le Drian (see below).

Chinese unilateral territorial expansionism in the East and South China Seas over the last three to four years has led to Tokyo and Brussels voicing joint concerns about China claiming disputed territories in the South China Sea as part of China's sovereign territory. Brussels and Tokyo announced in Hiroshima in April 2016:

> We are concerned about the situation in the East and South China Seas, and emphasize the fundamental importance of peaceful management and settlement of disputes. We express our strong opposition to any intimidating, coercive or provocative unilateral actions that could alter the status quo and increase tensions, and urge all states to refrain from such actions as land reclamations including large scale ones, building of outposts, as well as their use for military purposes and to act in accordance with international law including the principles of freedoms of navigation and overflight.
>
> (EEAS, 2016c)

Even if China is not explicitly mentioned in that statement, it is very clear that it is China's unilateral territorial expansionism that was meant when the statement speaks of 'provocative unilateral actions'. However, such a statement has not been followed-up on by joint EU–Japan policies aimed at deterring

China from unilaterally expanding its territories in the South China Sea. Over the last two years many papers and policy briefs were written, in which it was argued that China's military rise and its very assertive, and indeed aggressive, policies related to territorial claims in the East and South Chinas 'could', or indeed 'should', lead to increased EU–Japan hard security cooperation. That, however, did not happen, even though some EU members recently (e.g. France during the IISS Shangri-La Dialogue in Singapore in 2016) called on fellow European countries to consider coordinated EU patrolling activities in the South China Sea (Roman, 2016). However, suggesting such joint patrol activities is one thing, doing the patrolling quite another, and it remains very unlikely that there will be coordinated European patrolling activities in the South China Sea anytime soon. Then again, should China continue to unilaterally reclaim disputed territories and render the passage of vessels through international waters in the South China Sea difficult in the months and years ahead, it cannot be excluded that Europe, together with the U.S., and Japan, would initiate coordinated patrolling in the South China Sea.

Chinese current policies related to territorial claims in the South China Sea are objectively aggressive, de facto 'inviting' outside actors like Europe and more importantly the U.S. – in view of economic and business interests in the region – to defend themselves against the consequences of Chinese unilateral territorial expansionism. Hiroshima in 2016 was not the first time that Brussels and Tokyo expressed joint opposition to Chinese territorial expansionism.

> We continue to observe the situation in the East and South China Seas and are concerned by any unilateral actions that change the status quo and increase tensions. We support the full and effective implementation of the 2002 Declaration on the Conduct of Parties in the South China Sea and the rapid conclusion of the negotiations to establish an effective Code of Conduct in the South China Sea. We highlight the constructive role of practical confidence-building measures, such as the establishment of direct links of communication in cases of crisis and crisis management mechanisms in this regard.
>
> (European Commission, 2015)

While such a joint statement is positive per se and can be understood as Brussels and Tokyo jointly expressing opposition against Chinese unilateral territorial expansionism, it certainly could have gone beyond 'highlighting the constructive role of confidence-building measures' if the purpose was to send a clear message that Brussels and Tokyo are prepared to be more than just 'concerned' about Chinese aggressive policies related to (largely illegitimate[12]) territorial claims in the South China Sea. Instead, the declaration could/should have called on China directly and unambiguously to stick to what it has promised to do in the past: only talk and negotiate on territorial disputes it has with other Southeast Asian nations as opposed talking while at the same building civilian and military facilities on disputed islands. Instead, Beijing is, through the construction of civilian and military facilities on disputed islands, rapidly and continuously creating facts on the ground, and a timid and very diplomatic EU–Japan joint statement is obviously not changing anything about that. To be sure, a stronger EU–Japan statement in 2016 and a statement, which would have directly called on China to not unilaterally change the territorial status quo in the region would not have changed anything in Beijing's territorial expansionism either, but at least Beijing would have received a clearer message, to which it could have reacted on (as opposed to ignoring the above-mentioned statement). The statement is indeed rather toothless and to the outside analyst (like this author), it looks more like a statement for the sake of making a statement as opposed to a strong statement that is really expected to have an impact on Chinese regional policy behaviour.[13]

Japan's constitutional reinterpretation in 2014, and the adoption of new national-security laws have also been accompanied by debates on whether Tokyo's naval vessels could, or should, against the backdrop of Chinese territorial expansionism in the East and South China Seas, join U.S. Freedom of Navigation Operations (FONOPs) in the South China Sea. While the US currently conducts FONOPs in the South China Sea alone, in June 2015 Japanese Admiral Katsutoshi Kawano, Chief of the Joint Staff of Japan's Self Defence Forces (SDF), declared that the MSDF could consider conducting joint patrols with the U.S. Navy 'depending on the situation' (Gady, 2015).

The U.S. is currently on its own conducting FONOPs in the South China Sea, and while it cannot be completely excluded that navies from other countries can in the future join the U.S. Navy patrols in the South China, it seems unlikely that this will happen any time soon. Already in April of the same year, Washington and Tokyo reportedly discussed the possibilities of conducting joint patrols not only in the South China Sea, but also in the East China Sea (Parameswaran, 2015). To be sure, jointly patrolling the South China Sea with the U.S. Navy could be easier said than done, as Tokyo would have to adopt laws, which authorize its navy to conduct such operations. Indeed, Japan's constitutional re-interpretation of 2014 and the 2015 national security laws do not explicitly authorize Japan's navy to jointly conduct FONOPs with the U.S. and such patrols would indeed be very controversial. In fact, they could be unconstitutional and in violation of war-renouncing Article 9 of the Japanese constitution.

Adopting laws to enable Japan's navy to jointly patrol Asian territorial waters, however, is not the only obstacle Tokyo would have to overcome. The limits of Japanese naval capacities too are an issue in view of the fact the country's naval and coast guard vessels are already engaged in patrolling Japanese territorial waters close (e.g. in the East China Sea around the Japanese-controlled Senkaku Islands) to the Japanese mainland. With regard to the East China Sea, Beijing is clearly very worried about Tokyo authorizing its military to execute the aforementioned right to collective self-defence, as Japan's SDF, together with the country's very well-equipped and state-of-the art coast guard, are authorized to defend US military units when jointly defending Japanese-controlled islands in the East China Sea, against, for example, Chinese attempts to 're-conquer' or occupy the Japanese-controlled, but contested, Senkaku

Islands; Beijing calls these islands Diaoyutai, claiming sovereignty over them.[14] China has, through its intrusions into Japanese-controlled territorial waters around the Senkaku Islands, sought to challenge and disrupt effective Japanese control over the islands and the territorial waters surrounding them. Paul O'Shea argues that this Chinese tactic is part of what he calls the 'sovereignty game' (O'Shea, 2012). To be sure, the author's numerous conversations and interviews with Chinese scholars and policymakers leave little doubt that the islands are part of sovereign Chinese territory as far as Beijing is concerned. Given, however, that the islands and the waters around them are controlled by Tokyo, Beijing, at least for now, will most probably continue to limit itself to challenging Tokyo's control through occasional intrusions.

For Europe there would certainly be repercussions for its ties with China in the case of joint patrolling in the South China Sea, as Beijing is clearly acting in zero-sum terms in this context, and hence EU–Japan military security cooperation would almost inevitably lead to the interruption of the EU–China High-Level Strategic Dialogue. However, in realpolitik terms that should not be of great concern to EU policymakers, for at least two reasons.

First, as mentioned above, the EU–China High-Level Strategic Dialogue has not produced any Chinese willingness to let the EU 'interfere' in China's regional and global security policies. In other words, the part of the bilateral dialogue that deals with security issues is arguably nothing more than 'window-dressing', as opposed to a dialogue that produces actual results, even if Brussels, in official declarations, claims that China is prepared to take European advice regarding Chinese security policies into account. Consequently, Beijing interrupting bilateral consultations on Asian security with Brussels is not something EU policymakers should lose much sleep over, as Beijing never intended to include the EU in its security policymaking in the first place. In fact, over the years the opposite has been the case. Every time the EU and individual EU member states have criticized China's regional foreign and security polices, be it Chinese territorial expansionism in the South China Sea, its policies towards Taiwan, its interference in Hong Kong's domestic affairs, such as the unlawful abduction of Hong Kong citizens to Mainland China, Beijing has reacted by reminding Brussels not to interfere in China's 'internal affairs'. Indeed, many Chinese scholars the author interacted with over recent years have somehow charged themselves with the task of very assertively defending the official Chinese positions on Taiwan, Hong Kong and Chinese policies related to territorial claims in the East and South China Seas. More often not than not this has been an obstacle to constructive academic exchanges (as opposed to Chinese scholars repeating the official government positions) and the author is by far not the only scholar who has experienced such behaviour and interactions when interacting with Chinese scholars. Second, as Brussels has repeatedly stated over many years, it is Tokyo, and not Beijing, which is the EU's 'natural ally' in Asian security. Expanding bilateral cooperation with Tokyo is what really should matter to policymakers in Brussels. The fact that political rhetoric on the EU–Japan 'natural alliance' has yet to catch up with political reality is another matter.

Conclusions

Intensifying EU–Japanese cooperation, the Japanese scholar Michito Tsuruoka argues, requires both Japan and the EU to overcome what he calls the 'expectations deficit' in EU–Japan relations (Tsuruoka, 2013). Today, it is probably fair to conclude that such an 'expectations deficit' (if it ever existed), has been overcome after years of joint experience in non-military security cooperation. 'Overcome' in the sense that both Brussels and Tokyo understand what they can and cannot expect from each other in terms of commitment and resources invested into non-military security cooperation on the ground.

While the official rhetoric seems to suggest the SPA will further intensify bilateral security cooperation, it remains to be seen how and in which areas such cooperation could be intensified in the years ahead. Brussels and Tokyo have yet, after years of mentioning or indeed promising such a legal basis, not adopted the above-mentioned legal framework to enable sustainable Japanese contributions to EU CSDP missions. While the reasons for that are undoubtedly complex from legal and procedural perspectives, the fact that the legal framework has been discussed for years without having been adopted, points to a lack of urgency to institutionalize Japanese contributions to European CSDP missions. Tokyo under Abe, is for the reasons cited above, seemingly more interested in maintaining and indeed intensifying hard security cooperation with Washington under Trump, as opposed to intensifying soft security cooperation with Europe. Indeed, Abe's strong interest to meet Trump before, and then very shortly after, the latter's inauguration must have been perceived as a very clear message that security cooperation with Trump, who on the campaign trail more than once accused Japan of unfair bilateral trade and investment practices and of being a free-rider on U.S. security guarantees in East Asia, is more important than increasing security cooperation with the EU. To be sure, hard security cooperation with Washington and soft security cooperation with Brussels can be complementary, and indeed, they are from a Japanese perspective.[15]

Although it would be desirable for those who call on the EU to take additional responsibility in global politics and security, and more involvement in Asian security in particular, the above-mentioned Chinese territorial expansionism will, in the near future, most probably not lead to more EU involvement in Asian hard security through the above-mentioned maritime patrolling, either alone, or jointly with Japan. However, if Japan decided to start patrolling in the South China Sea, and as mentioned above, there are indications that Japanese defence planners are at least considering the possibility of maritime patrolling in the South China Sea, it is advisable that the EU and individual member states do not a priori exclude the possibility of joining such patrolling activities in view of their economic and political interests in the region. Japan patrolling the South China Sea is, however, as mentioned above, from a constitutional perspective not uncontroversial and could even be a violation of war-renouncing Article 9 of the Japanese constitution. However, in view of equivocating EU reactions to the above-mentioned French proposal for joint European patrolling in the South

China Sea, it remains very unlikely that there will be active consideration of coordinated European patrolling activities in the South China Sea anytime soon. From a strategic point of view, however, EU policymakers were probably ill advised to categorically exclude the possibility of joint European patrolling in the South China Sea. From a legal and operational point of view, there is nothing preventing the EU and European member states from jointly patrolling international waters in the South China. Brussels excluding, at least for now, any consideration of such a possibility does not necessarily add to the credibility of the EU as global foreign and security policy actor.

The arrival of Donald Trump in the White House has not resulted in the Abe administration developing a sense of urgency to rapidly adopt the SPA with the EU as a counterweight to potentially[16] illiberal, aggressive, isolationist or interventionist U.S. policies in Asia.[17] In fact, the opposite, at least it seems for now, has turned out to be the case. As elaborated above, Abe lost no time in presenting himself as reliable and, at least in the eyes of a critical outside observer, as an obedient U.S. ally in East Asia. To be sure, Abe will not stay in power forever, and the kind of security and defence policies he is pursuing could, in the years ahead, be replaced with policies more favourable to the kind of cooperation the SPA with the EU envisions.

Japan's solidarity with the U.S. and the EU in 2014 in imposing economic sanctions in reaction to Russia's illegal annexation of Crimea was an important indication of Tokyo's preparedness to support Western policies aimed at safeguarding international legal norms (Raine and Small, 2015). By imposing sanctions on Russia, Japan has taken a clear position and is without doubt counting on European countries' support for its efforts to deter Chinese territorial ambitions in the East and South China Seas. Indeed, Japan is expecting more European support for Tokyo's defence of its territorial integrity in the East China Sea in the face of Chinese intrusions into Japanese-controlled territorial waters.[18] As mentioned above however, the EU remains reluctant to offer Japan support that goes beyond the kind of verbal support Brussels is providing with Tokyo. It is advisable for the EU and Japan to act to safeguard their individual and joint credibility, and to choose clearly whether or not to strictly limit bilateral cooperation to non-military modalities, which would exclude joint patrolling activities in the South China Sea, or whether to respond to a more unstable security environment by commencing joint military security cooperation in East and Southeast Asia.

Regarding joint capacity-building assistance, some policy experts suggest that the EU, NATO, and Japan could pool resources and consider trilateral security cooperation. However, this has been suggested several times in the past, and expanding bilateral to trilateral cooperation probably does not contribute to making EU–Japan cooperation less complicated and more efficient. 'Pooling resources' is more easily said than done in international relations. All of this points to the conclusion that the SPA, if and when finally adopted, could indeed not turn out to be the 'big bang' of EU–Japan cooperation in regional and global politics and security, but will rather provide existing and future cooperation little more than an institutional framework.

Finally, the fact that the SPA was, unlike the above-mentioned EU–Japan EPA/FTA, not adopted in 2017 allows for the conclusion that neither Brussels nor Tokyo take the agreement and the envisioned benefits for bilateral cooperation in international politics and security seriously enough. Furthermore, it also seems that the EU and Japan did not feel sufficiently obliged to stick to self-imposed deadlines, even after years of negotiations, nor did they care that they left and still leave analysts guessing about the actual contents of the agreement. This is clearly not good enough for two partners who have made repetitive promises about wanting to significantly intensify bilateral on-the-ground cooperation.

Notes

1 Based on the author's conversation with an European External Action Service (EEAS) official in May 2017.
2 Interview with EU official in June 2016.
3 Abe was the first foreign leader to meet Trump after his election victory.
4 The U.S.–Japan security alliance, Trump seemed to indicate during the 2016 campaign, would have to become less asymmetrical in the sense that not only would the U.S. be obliged to defend Japan in the case of an attack, but also vice versa. However, the kind of defence contributions to U.S. national security Tokyo should, in Trump's view provide Washington, would likely go (far) beyond the level Japan currently authorizes itself to provide through constitutional re-interpretation.
5 EU NAVFOR's main tasks are to escort merchant vessels carrying humanitarian aid for the World Food Program, to protect ships in the Gulf of Aden and the Indian Ocean, and to deter and disrupt piracy. EU NAVFOR also monitors fishing activity off the coast of Somalia.
6 Tokyo and Brussels also announced in April 2010 that they would jointly support the establishment of the Djibouti counter-piracy regional training centre, and information-sharing centres in Kenya, Tanzania and Yemen.
7 For details see Marie Söderberg's chapter in this volume.
8 Several interviews with Japanese officials from the Ministries of Foreign Affairs and Defence in 2014 and 2015 confirm this.
9 Numerous conversations with Chinese policymakers and scholars confirm this: they made it very clear that Beijing does not, to say the very least, appreciate European advice on policies related to territorial claims in the South China Sea.
10 'Natural ally' is a term the EU's External Action Service (EEAS) uses when pointing to the (great) potential for EU–Japan cooperation in Asian politics and security. Against this background, however, it can be argued that there remains a gap between this rhetoric and the reality of current security cooperation between Brussels and Tokyo.
11 Some of the geographical features on which the Chinese were building were declared not to be islands by the Permanent Court of Arbitration in July 2016.
12 As the International Court of Arbitration unambiguously ruled in July 2016.
13 When reaching such conclusions regarding Chinese policy behaviour, analysts like this author are often confronted with the counterargument that Beijing reacts very strongly to strong statements regarding its domestic and foreign policies, and therefore such criticism is counterproductive. While that might be true, it must be pointed out that attempts to influence Chinese foreign policy behaviour in general, and in relation to territorial claims in the East and South China Seas in particular, diplomatic

attempts to take all Chinese sensitivities into account have not produced any results either.

14 Article 5 of the US–Japan Security Treaty obliges Washington to defend Japanese-controlled territory.

15 Several Japanese Foreign Ministry policymakers told the author this in 2016.

16 'Potential' as there is a lot of uncertainty and indeed confusion as regards Donald Trump's policies towards Asia in general, and Japan and China in particular. Washington's Asia policies under Trump are potentially prone to contradictions, U-turns and impulsive actions, which makes it very difficult to predict the quality and scope of U.S. involvement in Asian security during his administration.

17 Due to the lack of clarity on the policies and contradictory statements, it could be that all, none, or some combination of these adjectives turn out to be accurate. The fact that Trump earlier announced an intention to revise Washington's 'One-China policy', only to reconfirm soon afterwards his intention to uphold the 'One-China policy', when speaking to Chinese President Xi Jinping, is evidence of the contradictions and lack of clarity in policy.

18 Author's interviews with officials from the Japanese Ministry of Defence in 2015.

References

Berkofsky, A. (2012) EU–Japan Relations from 2001 to Today: Achievements, Failures and Prospects. *Japan Forum* 24(3), pp. 265–288.

de Prado, C. (2014) *Prospects for the EU-Japan Strategic Partnership: A Global Multi-Level and Swop Analysis*. European University Institute Global Governance Programme. Available from: www.eu-japan.eu/sites/default/files/publications/docs/eujp strategicpartnership.pdf [Accessed: 6 February 2018].

European Commission. (2014) *The EU and Japan Acting Together for Global Peace and Prosperity; European Commission 22nd EU-Japan Summit Joint Press Statement*. 7 May. Available from: http://europa.eu/rapid/press-release_STATEMENT-14-151_en. htm [Accessed: 13 December 2015].

European Commission. (2015) *Fact Sheet-23rd Japan-EU Summit, Tokyo, 29 May 2015 Joint Press Statement*. 29 May. Available from: http://europa.eu/rapid/press-release_ MEMO-15-5075_en.htm [Accessed: 22 June 2016].

European External Action Service (EEAS). (2016a) *Shaping of a Common Security and Defence Policy*. 8 July. Available from: https://eeas.europa.eu/headquarters/ headquarters-homepage/5388/shaping-common-security-and-defence-policy_en [Accessed: 9 February 2018].

European External Action Service (EEAS). (2016b) *China and the EU – Political Relations*. 11 May. Available from: https://eeas.europa.eu/headquarters/headquarters-homepage/15394/china-and-eu_en [Accessed: 9 February 2018].

European External Action Service (EEAS). (2016c) *G7 Foreign Ministers' Statement on Maritime Security April 11, 2016 Hiroshima, Japan*. 11 April. Available from: http:// eeas.europa.eu/statements-eeas/2016/160411_05_en.htm [Accessed: 20 February 2017].

European External Action Service (EEAS). (2017) *Remarks by the High Representative Mogherini Following the 7th EU-China Strategic Dialogue*. 19 April. Available from: https://eeas.europa.eu/headquarters/headquarters-homepage/24821/remarks-high-representative-mogherini-following-7th-eu-china-strategic-dialogue_en [Accessed: 9 February 2018].

Fontini, A. (2016) *Advancing the EU-Japan Strategic Partnership in a Transforming Global Environment: Challenges, Opportunities and Prospects*. European Policy

Centre (EPC) Policy Brief. Available from: www.epc.eu/documents/uploads/pub_
6363_eu-japan_strategic_partnership.pdf [Accessed: 4 December 2016].

Fukushima, A. (2015) *Japan-Europe Cooperation for Peace and Stability: Pursuing Synergies on a Comprehensive Approach. Policy Brief Asia Program April 2015*. The German
Marshall Fund of the United States. Available from: www.gmfus.org/publications/
japan-europe-cooperation-peace-and-stability. [Accessed: 4 January 2017].

Gady, F.-S. (2015) Japan's Top Military Officer: Joint US-Japanese Patrols in South
China Sea a Possibility. *The Diplomat*. 26 June. Available from: http://thediplomat.
com/2015/06/japans-top-military-officer-joint-u-s-japanese-patrols-in-south-china-sea-
a-possibility/ [Accessed: 22 October 2016].

Japan Times. (2015) *France, Japan to Discuss Joint Counterterrorism Operations in
Africa*. 11 March.

Mykal, O. (2011) *The EU-Japan Security Dialogue-Invisible but Comprehensive*. Amsterdam: Amsterdam University Press.

O'Shea, P. (2012) Sovereignty and the Senkaku/Diaoyu Dispute. *EIJS Working Paper
Series*. No. 240. European Institute of Japanese Studies, Stockholm School of Economics. Available from: www.academia.edu/3445337/Sovereignty_and_the_Senkaku_
Diaoyu_Territorial_Dispute [Accessed: 8 February 2018].

Parameswaran, P. (2015) US-Japan Joint Patrols in the South China Sea? *The Diplomat*.
1 May. Available from: http://thediplomat.com/2015/05/us-japan-joint-patrols-in-the-
south-china-sea/ [Accessed: 23 September 2016].

Pejsova, E. (2015) *The EU and Japan: Stepping up the Game*. Brief Issue 15/2015. Paris:
European Union Institute for Security Studies (EUISS).

Permanent Court of Arbitration (PCA). (2016) *PCA Press Release: The South China Sea
Arbitration (The Republic of the Philippines v. The People's Republic of China)*. 12
July. Available from: https://pca-cpa.org/en/news/pca-press-release-the-south-china-
sea-arbitration-the-republic-of-the-philippines-v-the-peoples-republic-of-china/
[Accessed: 9 February 2017].

Raine, S. and Small, A. (2015) *Waking Up to Geopolitics. A New Trajectory of EU-Japan
Relations*. The German Marshall Fund of the United States (GMF). Washington. Available from: www.gmfus.org/publications/waking-geopolitics-new-trajectory-japan-europe-
relations [Accessed: 5 December 2016].

Reiterer, M. (2013) The EU-Japan Relationship in Dynamic Asia. In Keck, J., Dimitri
Vanoverbeke, D. and Waldenberger, F. (eds) *EU-Japan Relations, 1970–2012: From
Confrontation to Global Partnership*, pp. 293–328. London; New York: Routledge.

Reiterer, M. (2015) *EU Security Interests in East Asia: Prospects for Comprehensive
EU–Japan Cooperation Beyond Trade and Economics*. NFG Policy Paper No. 6. NFG
Asian Perceptions of the EU.

Roman, D. (2016) France to Push for Coordinated EU Patrols in South China Sea.
Bloomberg News. 5 June. Available from: www.bloomberg.com/news/articles/2016-06-
05/france-to-push-for-coordinated-eu-patrols-in-south-china-sea [Accessed: 24 September 2016].

Tsuruoka, M. (2013) *The EU and Japan: Making the Most of Each Other*. European
Union Institute for Security Studies (EUISS). Available from: www.iss.europa.eu/
publications/detail/article/the-eu-and-japan-making-the-most-of-each-other/ [Accessed:
29 November 2016].

Tyszkiewicz, R. (2013) Towards New Political and Economic Agreements with Japan:
Bringing New Dynamism into the Strategic Partnership between the EU and Japan.
Policy Paper. No. 9(57). The Polish Institute of International Affairs (PISM). Warsaw,

Poland. Available from: www.pism.pl/files/?id_plik=13357 [Accessed: 26 October 2016].

Ueno, H. and Rich, M. (2016) Across the World, Shock and Uncertainty at Trump's Victory. *New York Times*. 9 November. Available from: www.nytimes.com/2016/11/09/world/europe/global-reaction-us-presidential-election-donald-trump.html [Accessed: 9 February 2018].

3 Abe's pro-active pacifism and values diplomacy

Implications for EU–Japan political and security cooperation[1]

Paul Midford

Introduction

Liberal Democratic Party (LDP) Prime Minister Shinzo Abe led himself and his party back into power in late 2012 by promising a more active and values-focused foreign policy. Since 2013 he has specifically promoted what he has called "pro-active pacifism" and "values diplomacy."[2] The Abe administration's 2013 National Security Strategy pledges that "Japan will further step up its cooperation with UN PKO and other international peace cooperation activities, with its determination to contribute even more proactively to peace, based on the principle of international cooperation" (GoJ NSC, 2013, pp. 1–2, p. 14, p. 30). Moreover, Europe is identified as a "partner" for Japan "in ensuring the peace and security of the international community," based on shared values: "Japan and European countries … share universal values of freedom, democracy, respect for fundamental human rights, and the rule of law." On this basis the Strategy calls for enhanced relations (GoJ NSC, 2013, pp. 26–27).

This chapter considers the implications of these claims for EU–Japan security cooperation, and for global security and stability. Specifically, do "pro-active pacifism" and "values diplomacy" mean that Japan will more actively promote common liberal values together with the EU? Under these new concepts is Japan promoting liberal and democratic values in its aid policy? Is it more proactively promoting post-conflict peace building? Is Japan under Abe promoting common conceptions of the rule of law? Finally, based on the answers to these questions, what are the implications for EU–Japan cooperation based "proactive pacifism" and "common values"? What are the consequences for China and for the US?

Pro-active pacifism

The term proactive pacifism is derived from the term "positive peace" that in turn originates with the famous Norwegian peace researcher Johan Galtung. "Proactive contribution to peace" is the Japanese government's common English translation of "*sekkyokuteki heiwashugi*" (積極的平和主義). "*Sekkyokuteki*" has the implication of "positive" as well as "proactive," allowing this word to serve as a linguistic bridge between the idea of "proactive pacifism" and Galtung's concept of "positive peace."[3]

Among Japanese foreign policy elites the term "proactive pacifism" can be traced back to at least 1991, when Ito Kenichi, President of The Japan Forum on International Relations, used the term in a book he published in reaction to the end of the Cold War, and the Gulf War from earlier that year. He did not link the term to Galtung's "positive peace," but rather defined it as the opposite of "passive pacifism" (*shokyokuteki heiwashugi:* 消極的平和主義).[4] For Ito, Article 9 of Japan's constitution embodies "passive pacifism," or the idea of "do not become an aggressor"[5] through "abstinence" and "self-control" (Ito, 1991, pp. 117–118). He contrasted this with the call for Japan to become a "contributor" to international peace that is contained in the preamble of Japan's constitution, and what he defined as "proactive pacifism." He called for maintaining "balance" and "harmony" between the passive and proactive pacifisms (Ito, 1991, pp. 117–118). Ito has actively promoted the concept of "proactive pacifism" as a guiding concept for Japanese foreign policy since 2004 (Nihon kokusai fōra-mu, 2004), and especially since 2007 (Ito, 2007; Japan Forum on International Relations, 2009), although he dropped the idea of balancing "active" and "passive" pacifisms in favor of a whole-hearted embrace of replacing "passive pacifism" with "proactive pacifism." Specifically, policy recommendations published by his institute under the banner of promoting proactive pacifism have called for rethinking Japan's three non-nuclear principles and its three principles on the non-export of weapons. Other policy recommendations include reclaiming the right to collective self-defense and revising the war-renouncing Article 9 of Japan's constitution (Nihon Kokusai Fōra-mu, 2004; Japan Forum on International Relations, 2009).[6]

Matake Kamiya, an associate of Ito, has further elaborated on "passive pacifism" and "proactive pacifism," dividing each into two parts. Passive pacifism consists of a "lack of willingness to take proactive action toward peace," and a "lack of willingness to utilize its military power for peace." Kamiya argues that "the first condition of being proactive can be seen as having progressed remarkably in the twenty-four years since the end of the Cold War," with the dispatch and active participation of the Self-Defense Forces (SDF) overseas for peacekeeping operations and humanitarian and disaster relief operations (Kamiya, 2014).[7] Thus, Japan has made significant progress toward overcoming the first form of "passive pacifism," thereby also taking a step toward "proactive pacifism."

On the other hand, Kamiya claims that the Japanese public has not made much progress toward "accepting the concept of the role of military power for peace." This involves recognizing "that military force plays an essential role in building and maintaining peace ... in reality, peace and order cannot exist without force." Consequently, the Japanese public "continue[s] to call for the international peace efforts of the Self-Defense Forces to be kept as far as possible from military affairs." Nonetheless, Kamiya claims this second form of proactive pacifism is being actively promoted by policymakers: "proactive pacifism that was recently incorporated into Japan's National Security Strategy and its Defense Program Guidelines can be read as Prime Minister Abe making it clear that his own administration will advance this second condition of becoming proactive" (Kamiya, 2014, pp. 2–3).

Ito and Kamiya's concept of proactive pacifism as normalization as a great military power does indeed appear to reflect how the term is used by the Abe administration. As such, it is not surprising that its concept of "proactive pacifism" has been criticized as a deceptive and even cynical word play that has nothing to do with Galtung's concept of "positive peace" or pacifism. Galtung himself has criticized the Abe administration's use of "proactive pacifism."[8] Indeed, it is hard not to see this relabeling exercise that renames realist concepts such as deterrence and balance of power as forms of "pacifism," rather than presenting them as the realist concepts that they are, as anything but a cynical deception. With such a permissive definition, virtually any use-of-military-force decision could be defined as "pacifist."[9]

Peace-building and Abe's passive pacifism

In the context of EU–Japan security cooperation, proactive pacifism's emphasis on the utility of military power, up to and including nuclear weapons, raises questions about whether Japan under this concept might be distancing itself from the common values it has shared with the EU up to now, especially in the area of post-conflict peace-building at the nexus of security and development, in favor of more military-centric policies. Japan and the EU have emphasized the importance of economic and social reconstruction, and the reintegration of combatants into society (EJARN and KAS, 2012). This distancing seems especially likely given that the Abe administration's promotion of "proactive pacifism" is clearly a critique of the previous policy as being "passive pacifism," including peace-building policies ranging from Cambodia to Mozambique, Rwanda, Sudan and Haiti. EU–Japan approaches up to now differ from the approach of their US ally, who has tended to emphasize identifying and killing "bad guys" in internal conflicts. A top Japanese diplomat criticized the US for having "too much of a so-called cowboy mentality by which justice can be delivered if bad guys are punished."[10]

Abe administration policy indicates a lack of interest in proactively participating in UN peacekeeping operations and peacebuilding more generally. This represents a potential setback to what had been a burgeoning area of EU–Japan security cooperation. In fact, under the Abe administration Japan has been practicing "passive pacifism" when it comes to peacekeeping and peacebuilding, as per Kamiya's first definition of "passive pacifism": a failure to make proactive contributions to peace. By comparison, the previous Democratic Party of Japan (DPJ) governments practiced greater proactive pacifism than has the LDP Abe administration, despite their significantly shorter tenure of office. During their three years and four months in power DPJ governments started two new UN peacekeeping missions, in Haiti and South Sudan, and maintained a third, the Golan Heights (started by a socialist prime minister in 1995). The DPJ also maintained a counter-piracy mission in the Gulf of Aden and waters off the

Somali coast. By comparison, the Abe administration, during its first five years in office, started no new UN peacekeeping operations (PKOs), and ended Japan's participation in all UN peacekeeping missions: those in Haiti and the Golan Heights soon after taking office, and the South Sudan mission in mid-2017. The Abe administration also failed to join any other missions, even though with fifteen UN peacekeeping missions employing 110,000 personnel (United Nations Peacekeeping, 2017), there is no shortage of UN PKOs needing Japan's contribution of troops, missions where the SDF could have closely collaborated with EU militaries. The only new overseas SDF dispatches the Abe administration has authorized are short-term deployments for disaster relief, including one large scale deployment to the Philippines in the wake of Typhoon Haiyan.

Given that the foreign policy intellectuals who form a de facto brain trust for the Abe administration, such as Ito and Kamiya, have consistently emphasized the "demands of the international community" for Japan to make greater contributions to international security, the passivity of the Abe administration in supposedly answering these "demands" is all the more striking. Notably, the Abe administration has passed up several important opportunities to deploy the SDF overseas for meaningful non-combat missions that contribute to global security. First, in 2014 the Kantei passed up an opportunity to deploy the SDF to West Africa to join the UK military, and several other European militaries, not to mention the US and Chinese militaries, in combating the Ebola epidemic then devastating the region and threatening fragile states and regional efforts to combat Islamic extremist terrorist organizations such as Boko Haram (Hornung and Midford, 2014). Second, in the wake of French military operations to free northern Mali from occupation by Islamic extremists Japan could have dispatched the SDF to provide humanitarian relief, and reconstruction and development assistance. However, Japan did ultimately help EU security efforts in Mali by providing grant aid (492 million Yen) and technical expertise to the EU Common Security and Defence Policy (CSDP) mission there, specifically for rehabilitating the national police academy (Fukushima, 2013; Pejsova, 2015, p. 4).

Finally, Japan could have deployed the SDF, especially the Maritime Self-Defense Force (MSDF) and Air Self-Defense Force (ASDF), and Japan's Coast Guard (JCG) to help deal with the Mediterranean refugee crisis, a crisis involving tens of thousands of refugees attempting to cross from Libya to Italy in unsafe boats, with thousands of deaths resulting, and another flow of refugees attempting to reach Greek islands from the nearby Turkish coast. MSDF and JCG cutters could have supported the overstretched Italian navy and maritime police, potentially saving thousands of lives in the process. Japan could have provided similar support for Greece, helping that nearly bankrupt country to deal with the crushing burden of hundreds of thousands of refugees arriving on its shores. The ASDF could have delivered supplies to refugee camps in both Italy and Greece.

In terms of human security, Japan could have made its single greatest contribution, helping to save thousands of lives and relieve suffering for hundreds of thousands more. This would also have been a great contribution to international security, as it would have reduced the destabilizing impact of massive refugee flows on Greece, Italy, and the EU overall, an impact that is threatening Japan's core security interests as the damage sustained by the EU and Western partners more generally means that Japan may find itself more alone in an East Asian crisis, with the EU and others less willing and able to come to Japan's assistance. This would be the case not only with a maritime conflict in the South or East China Seas, but even if Japan faces its own influx of boat people, say from a collapsing North Korea. In this light, the Abe administration's passivity regarding the Mediterranean refugee crisis appears short-sighted, and an exercise in passive pacifism rather than proactive pacifism (Hornung and Midford, 2015b).

In terms of peace-building, the Abe administration has appeared more interested in expanding the Rules of Engagement (ROEs) for SDF units deployed overseas than in maximizing Japan's contribution under the pre-existing legal framework. Specifically, as part of the controversial September 2015 security legislation the Abe administration pushed through the Diet was authorization for SDF units deployed to the UN mission in South Sudan to engage in combat for reasons beyond self-defense of themselves or those in their care. Specifically, the new legislation allows SDF units to defend other units participating in UN peacekeeping when they come under attack. In November 2016 the Abe administration decided, based on this new legislation, to expand the operations of the GSDF unit deployed in South Sudan beyond reconstruction and development missions (engineering work), to include, in response to an urgent request, coming to the aid of other UN peacekeepers and UN staffers who come under attack (*kaketsuke keigo:* 駆けつけ警護), and joining other UN peacekeepers to defend a UN base that is used by the GSDF and the militaries of other countries, even if the GSDF itself is not the direct target of the attack. Nevertheless, these missions could be performed only "in very limited cases," such as when South Sudan security authorities or other UN peacekeeping troops could respond by themselves (*Kyodo*, 2016a; Mie, 2016c; Jiji, 2016).

These conditions were so restrictive that the chance of GSDF units being called on to perform these combat roles was very small. With public opinion overwhelmingly opposed to the SDF engaging in overseas combat, the Abe administration apparently was only seeking to establish a new legal precedent without provoking a large public backlash (*Kyodo*, 2016a; Mie, 2016c; Jiji, 2016; and *Kyodo*, 2016b).[11] Indeed, this appeared to be the main reason for the Abe administration's continuation of the South Sudan mission. While this modest expansion of GSDF ROEs could conceivably benefit EU peacekeepers and aid workers, in practice there is likely to be little impact. Meanwhile, the Abe administration, by investing significant political capital in trying to set a new domestic precedent for the SDF neglected other SDF dispatches for peace-building that could have resulted in greater EU–Japan cooperation and a greater contribution to global security.

Finally, in spring 2017, having set a new legal, if not political, precedent, the Abe administration withdrew the GSDF even from South Sudan, leaving Japan at "PKO Zero," with no ongoing participation in any peacekeeping, peacebuilding, or humanitarian relief operations for the first time in a quarter of a century. As of early 2018, there was yet no sign that the Abe administration was planning to join any of the ongoing sixteen UN PKOs, or any other peacebuilding missions, such as the EU CSDP mission in Mali (Hornung, 2017; Kawabata, 2017).

Values diplomacy

The second major new concept promoted by the Abe administration is "values diplomacy," or *kachikan gaikō*. Values diplomacy explicitly calls for promoting "common" liberal values of democracy, human rights, and the rule of law. It is a successor to the geographically based "Arc of Freedom and Prosperity" that was promoted by Abe and his then foreign minister, Taro Aso, during Abe's first stint as prime minister in 2006–2007.[12] Designed to promote liberal values of democracy and human rights as well as prosperity, the Arc, curving from Southeast Asia through south and Central Asia, included some very illiberal states and was transparently shaped to build cooperation, if not an alliance, aimed at containing China. The Arc, although including the word "prosperity," was clearly a departure from Japan's post war regional security strategy of developmentalism, which saw the promotion of economic development, not the promotion of common democratic values, as the key to strengthening stability and resolving conflicts. After Abe resigned from office following a humiliating and personally depressing election defeat in the 2007 Upper House election, Abe's successor as prime minister, Yasuo Fukuda, dropped the concept.[13]

The day after Abe returned to power, on December 27, 2012, he proposed the concept of an "Asian Democratic Security Diamond," with the points in the diamond including Japan, Australia, India, and the US state of Hawaii. Emphasizing that this diamond was based on the universal values of democracy, human rights, and the rule of law, this concept was more clearly aimed at maritime conflicts, especially in the East and South China Seas. It called for the four democracies to safe-guard rule of law in the "maritime commons" of the Western Pacific and Indian Ocean, and in particular prevent the South China Sea from becoming "Lake Beijing." Abe has subsequently stopped explicitly promoting this concept (Abe, 2012; Hughes, 2015, p. 81; Midford, 2015b). The Arc of Freedom and Prosperity has also not been explicitly revived. Rather, except for the brief promotion of the Diamond, the Abe administration has instead promoted "values diplomacy" without applying the concept to a specific geographic region. Nonetheless, it is clear that values diplomacy is primarily intended for Southeast Asia, and secondarily for the rest of the old Arc.

Promotion of democracy and human rights

The Abe administration introduced five new principles of diplomacy, which together can be thought of as the essence of its "values diplomacy." Strikingly, these five principles retained a geographical grounding in Southeast Asia, especially first principle: "protecting freedom of thought, expression, and speech in this region where two oceans meet." Of the remaining four principles, the second and third were also directly relevant to promoting common liberal values: second, "ensuring that the seas, which are the most vital commons to us all, are governed by laws and rules, not by might;" and third, "pursuing free, open, interconnected economies as part of Japan's diplomacy" (Abe, 2013a).[14] Abe's clearest enunciation of values diplomacy came during a visit to Southeast Asia in 2013, and especially a speech in Jakarta, where he emphasized promoting "universal values, such as freedom, democracy and basic human rights" together with ASEAN nations (Abe, 2013b).

On the face of it, Abe's promotion of common liberal values through values diplomacy appears to offer the EU a promising new partner for politico-security cooperation. Nonetheless, although the geographic component has largely been dropped, it appears that values diplomacy remains primarily aimed at containing China rather than promoting common values. This reality is visible both outside and inside what was previously the Arc of Freedom and Prosperity.

Outside the Arc, and most starkly for the EU, the Abe administration has been prioritizing national interest over common values, especially the rule of law. Tokyo has been critical of EU and especially US sanctions on Russia. Japan sees these sanctions as driving Russia toward greater cooperation with China, producing new sales of advanced weaponry (such as long-range S-400 surface-to-air missiles; Dominguez, 2018) that are destabilizing and threatening to tip the military balance of power against Japan. As such the Abe administration has been deemphasizing Russia's annexation of Crimea, and its sponsorship of a separatist movement in eastern Ukraine, as an issue of the rule of law, and Abe has been assiduously attempting to improve relations with Putin.

Inside the Arc, and especially its epicenter of Southeast Asia, there is little evidence that Abe's rhetorical promotion of common liberal values is translating into actual policies promoting human rights and democracy. Long before the Abe administration, Japan was promoting liberal values on paper. ODA Charters since 1992 have emphasized "promoting democratization ... and the situation regarding the securing of basic human rights and freedoms in the recipient country" (MOFA, 1992). Yet, its actual behavior often contradicted these passages from its ODA Charters. Thus, Japan signed the Bangkok Declaration in 1993, thereby pledging not to make development assistance conditional on human rights compliance, and to emphasize the importance of state sovereignty and non-interference in the domestic affairs of Asian states (UNOHCHR, 1993).

Japan's track record regarding ODA to Southeast Asia during the first and second Abe administrations shows little evidence that aid decisions are being made so as to promote common values of human rights and democracy. The four least democratic countries in ASEAN have received the highest aid per capita from Japan, and 80 percent of all aid disbursements to ASEAN. Vietnam in particular has been a priority in Japan's aid policy. Vietnam's human rights record has been no better than China's record, and worsened as Japanese aid to Hanoi tripled between 2008 and 2011. Cambodia and Laos also made no progress, and even backslid (Asplund, 2016).[15]

Even far outside Asia, in Africa, the Abe administration has taken the initiative to begin giving significant aid to a very illiberal dictatorial regime. Since 2015 Abe has hosted Zimbabwe's president Robert Mugabe twice. Mugabe's regime was one of the most illiberal in Africa with one of that continent's worst human rights records. During his two summit meetings with Mugabe, Abe offered two significant aid packages totaling 1.8 billion Yen ($16.2 million) and 600 million Yen ($6.4 million) respectively for road and other infrastructure projects, the first time Japan had given any economic assistance to Zimbabwe in fifteen years (Mie, 2016a). The Abe administration's initiative to start funding infrastructure development in Zimbabwe reflects the goal of counter-acting Chinese influence and competing with China throughout Africa (Mie, 2016a), and a more general competition mentality with China (see below). This is also part of Japan's efforts to enlist support for its quest for a permanent seat on the UN Security Council.

Rule of law at sea

The Abe administration has been highlighting its support for the rule of law internationally. Special emphasis has been placed on maintaining the rule of law in the maritime commons and in the context of maritime conflicts, and on the inadmissibility of changing the status quo through the use of force. The last point undoubtedly represents a common value with the EU. However, it is unclear whether the EU and Japan share a common understanding of maritime law. In some respects, Japan's understanding of maritime law may be to closer to that of China.

One clear example of this regards foreign naval and intelligence activities in a littoral state's Exclusive Economic Zone (EEZ). The United Nations Convention on the Law of the Sea (UNCLOS) (Articles 56 and 58) allows foreign military activity in EEZs if these activities and other activities "have due regard for the rights and duties of the coastal State," and are "peaceful" (Article 301) (Geng, 2012, pp. 24–27). The US and most Western states define intelligence gathering as consistent with these provisions.[16] However, a growing group of twenty-seven states, including most notably China, Brazil, and India, defines foreign military activities, including intelligence gathering activities, as potentially harmful to the littoral state's rights and duties, and hence as not covered by freedom of navigation in other states' EEZs.[17] Although Japan publicly sides with the EU and its US ally on this issue, in practice Tokyo's actual position has often appeared closer to China's interpretation.[18]

Japan has often opposed foreign intelligence gathering activities in its EEZ in ways that parallel Chinese opposition to foreign intelligence gathering ships operating in its EEZ. In at least one instance (discussed in the following paragraph) Japan's response to such operations far exceeded Chinese responses to date. In the late 1990s Japan complained about Chinese intelligence gathering and maritime surveys in its claimed EEZ in the East China Sea, paralleling Chinese complaints about US intelligence gathering in its claimed South China Sea EEZ. Japanese officials insisted, very much as Chinese officials have insisted to the US, that there can be no survey or other data gathering activities in its EEZ without Tokyo's consent.[19] Later Beijing and Tokyo enacted a bilateral mutual notification regime based on a shared interpretation of UNCLOS: the two sides agreed to notify each other when they conduct survey work in each other's EEZ.[20] This bilateral Sino–Japanese regime created a regional, if not an international, norm of prior notification that undermines the more permissive US and EU interpretation of foreign data gathering in a coastal state's EEZ under UNCLOS.[21]

In an even clearer break from US and EU interpretations of UNCLOS, in December 2001 JCG vessels chased a North Korean intelligence ship found lurking in Japan's EEZ into China's EEZ (390 kilometers from Amami Oshima island, and almost equidistant to China's coast) and after a fire-fight there the North Korean ship sank (Samuels, 2007/2008, p. 96; Valencia, 2002). To date there is no record of China taking such drastic action against a foreign intelligence vessel found in its claimed EEZ. In the wake of the sinking of this North Korean spy ship then Prime Minister Junichiro Koizumi called for legislation allowing the JCG to arrest suspicious ships, including spy ships, in its EEZ, and if they resist, to open fire in order to seize these ships, an idea his administration did not subsequently pursue. If the Koizumi administration had pursued this legislation, it would have directly clashed with EU and US understandings of UNCLOS, although it would have clearly corresponded with China's interpretation (Samuels, 2007/2008, p. 96; Valencia, 2002; Yomiuri Shimbun, 2001).

Above all, Japan's armed attack on a spy ship found within its EEZ, apparently the first case of any country doing so since EEZs were created by UNCLOS, creates a precedent for China taking forceful action against US intelligence-gathering ships operating in China's EEZ. Japan's precedent-setting action might also have negative consequences for EU member spy ships and naval vessels operating in littoral states' EEZs.

On the other hand, in 2006 the Koizumi administration asserted the right to carry out a survey in an EEZ area also claimed by South Korea, but backed down when Seoul threatened to seize the JCG vessels scheduled to conduct the survey. Japan's position in this case had little to do with an interpretation of UNCLOS more consistent with EU and US interpretations, and rather was based on its assertion that the maritime space in question was in fact its own EEZ. Japan subsequently threatened to use force to stop a Korean Coast Guard survey of the same waters, but again backed down. This case also shows that Japan is not the only EU partner in East Asia that has an interpretation of UNCLOS that is in fact closer to that of China, as South Korea regards foreign maritime surveys conducted in its claimed EEZ without its express permission as illegal under UNCLOS (United States State Department, 2006; Midford, 2015a, p. 35).

More recently, in June 2016, Japan protested foreign naval vessels transiting through the "contiguous zone" (CZ) of 12 nautical miles beyond the 12-mile territorial waters (TZ) of the dispute Senkaku islands (islands claimed by China, which calls them the Diaoyu islands) by Chinese and Russian naval vessels (surprising the Russian government). Yet, the prevailing EU and US interpretation of UNCLOS essentially regards CZs as high seas as far as naval vessels are concerned, especially when those ships are simply transiting, which was the case in the instance Japan protested. Moreover, UNCLOS even allows naval vessels to transit through TZs, although with some significant restrictions (restrictions that Chinese coast guard vessels repeatedly entering the Senkaku islands' TZ appear often, if not always, to violate). By comparison, Chinese naval vessels passed through US territorial waters in Alaska in 2015 without the US registering any complaint about their passage.

Okinotorishima (沖ノ鳥島)

Finally, Japan's maritime claims surrounding a small reef it has sovereignty over in the western Pacific raises questions about its willingness to abide by UNCLOS when doing so is not seen to be to its national advantage, including in ways that have some parallels to Chinese defiance of UNCLOS. Okinotorishima is a small reef (around 10 meters square at high tide) that Japan has used to claim a 200-nautical mile EEZ in the surrounding waters, plus a continental shelf zone beyond that. In April 2012 the UN Commission on the Limits of the Continental Shelf denied Japan's claim for giving Okinotorishima a continental shelf, based on the inhabitability of this geographical feature. Article 121, of UNCLOS forbids claiming an EEZ around islands incapable of naturally sustaining human habitation, strongly suggesting that Japan's claim of a 200-nautical mile EEZ violates UNCLOS. Moreover, Tokyo has reportedly spent $600 million over three decades laying concrete and taking other artificial means to preserve this decaying reef, actions also of dubious legality under UNCLOS given that the ability of geographical features to generate EEZs are based on their "natural state" (Lee, 2015).

Japan's claim to a 200-nautical mile EEZ around a reef that is the size of a studio apartment at high tide has stoked regional tensions, most notably with Taiwan, with whom Japan otherwise has very close and friendly, if unofficial, ties. Japan seized a Taiwanese fishing vessel operating in its claimed EEZ around Okinotorishima, prompting Taiwan to dispatch Coast Guard vessels to challenge Japan's EEZ claim (*Japan Times*, 2016). Japan has justified its EEZ claim by arguing that Article 121 of the UNCLOS treaty bars uninhabitable "rocks" from having an EEZ, but does not do so in the case of uninhabitable "islands." This unusual interpretation of Article 121 is at variance with the way the EU, and indeed most countries understand this article. However, some observers have pointed out that China could profit from Japan's interpretation, as it could use Tokyo's interpretation to claim 200 mile EEZs around its several above high-tide Spratly island features, thereby realizing much of its claimed

9-dash line in the South China Sea through a process of "Okinotorishima-ization" of its claims (Lee, 2015). This reality reflects some parallels between Japan's approach to UNCLOS and China's, parallels notable for their deviation from how the EU and most Western states view UNCLOS.

However, the risk of "Okinotorishima-ization" of the South China Sea dispute was rendered moot by the decision by a Tribunal at the Permanent Court of Arbitration at the Hague, when it issued its verdict on July 12, 2016, on the maritime dispute between the Philippines and the People's Republic of China. In the course of rejecting most of China's claims in the South China Sea, this verdict interpreted Article 121 of UNCLOS in a way that clearly rejects Japan's interpretation of that article. The Tribunal rejected the distinction between "rocks" and "islands" in favor of the neutral term of geographic "features," thereby including both rocks and islands, and argued that Article 121 was written "to prevent insignificant features from generating large entitlements to maritime zones." The Tribunal further:

> interpreted Article 121 and concluded that the entitlements of a feature depend on (a) the objective capacity of a feature, (b) in its natural condition, to sustain either (c) a stable community of people or (d) economic activity that is neither dependent on outside resources nor purely extractive in nature.

As such, all the above-high-tide geographical features of the Spratlys were ruled to be incapable of sustaining human habitation, and hence not entitled to EEZs, despite the fact the one of these features, Taiping Island, controlled by Taiwan, has its own natural source of fresh water and has had people living on it since at least the 1950s. It thus becomes clear that Okinotorishima is not entitled to its own EEZ under the legal interpretation of UNCLOS established by the Tribunal (Permanent Court of Arbitration, 2016a, pp. 9–10).[22]

Though generating far less attention than China's very loud rejection of the Tribunal's ruling, Japan also challenged the ruling, claiming it did not establish a standard that applied to the Western Pacific, only to the South China Sea, as if different versions of UNCLOS applied to the South China Sea and the Western Pacific. Foreign Minister Fumio Kishida also clung to the discredited distinction between a rock and an island, saying Okinotorishima was an island simply because Japan said so: "Since 1931, when the interior ministry recognized the island (as Okinotorishima), it has been an island. The verdict does not set the standards for what constitutes rock" (Mie, 2016b). As Jeffrey Hornung has argued: "It is simply too hard to ignore the hypocrisy: Japan criticizes China for claiming islands out of low-tide elevations or rocks while Tokyo itself is doing the same thing in Okinotorishima" (Johnson, 2016).

While the scale of Tokyo's land reclamation at Okinotorishima pales in comparison with what China has recently been doing in the South China Sea, there is a parallel in behavior that reflects a parallel in underlying policy. Most significantly, like Beijing, the Abe administration has prioritized its own territorial interests over that of UNCLOS and the rule of law when the two come into conflict. While the regional tensions created by Okinotorishima remain minor compared with those generated in the South China Sea, Japan's position on Okinotorishima undermines its standing to promote rule of law in the maritime commons (just as the US failure to ratify UNCLOS undermines US standing to do the same), and raises significant questions about whether Japan and the EU share common values when it comes to UNCLOS and maritime rule of law.

Competition mentality with China

As discussed above, the Abe administration displays a strong competition mentality with China. While this need not be incompatible with the promotion of liberal values, in fact it appears that the Abe administration sees competition with China as taking precedence over, and as ultimately divorced from, the promotion of liberal values. The decision to start providing aid to Zimbabwe, one of Africa's most repressive regimes, in order to compete with China is one obvious indicator discussed above. The broader return to large-scale infrastructure development aid, and away from socially focused forms of aid is another indicator, as this involves implicitly following the Chinese model. To be fair, the EU and other donors are showing a similar tendency in terms of infrastructure aid.

What really stands out in this competition mentality, however, is the implicit belief that Japan, despite what it says publicly, cannot distinguish itself from China based on adherence to liberal values. This is a belief among conservatives that predates the launch of the second Abe administration. One case from the conservative media that illustrates both this belief and the extremes to which Japanese conservatives take competition mentality with China appeared in early 2010. At that time, DPJ Prime Minister Yukio Hatoyama was moving to end the MSDF refueling mission in the Indian Ocean in support of the naval forces of countries engaged in anti-terrorism military operations in Afghanistan, a deployment the LDP had continued (with one brief interruption) since late 2001. The MSDF was refueling US naval vessels, plus those of some EU members such as the UK, also Australia and Pakistan. The LDP unsuccessfully introduced legislation to restart this mission, and there was significant opposition to ending it in the ministries of defense and foreign affairs. It was in this context that *Yomiuri Shimbun*, the conservative leaning and pro-LDP major daily published a story "citing government sources" and "documents" claiming that the Chinese navy wanted to take over the refueling mission from the MSDF, was training for this mission, and had already approached the US government with an offer to take over this mission three years earlier when Hatoyama's DPJ briefly succeeded in suspending this mission through parliamentary maneuver. It added that the US did not react "at that time," although it left open the possibility the US would agree once Hatoyama had permanently ended the MSDF mission (*Daily Yomiuri*, 2010; *Yomiuri Shimbun*, 2010).

While this story appears to have mainly been a bureaucratic leak intended to undermine Hatoyama's policy of ending the MSDF refueling mission in the Indian Ocean, underlying this leak was the assumption that the US could quickly choose China as a naval partner to replace Japan, irrespective of the common values that Japan and the US share and that China and the US lack. A further implication of this competition mentality with China is that to compete Japan may sometimes have to pursue illiberal policies to match China, such as by supporting illiberal regimes in Zimbabwe, Vietnam, and elsewhere.

Conclusions

Although the Abe administration's foreign policy concepts of "proactive pacifism" and "values diplomacy" appear to promise more active Japanese support of common values through expanded political and security cooperation between the EU and Japan, this chapter unfortunately concludes that this apparent promise is largely a mirage. It is hard to argue that Abe's pro-active pacifism offers an opportunity for greater EU–Japan security cooperation based on shared liberal values. Proactive pacifism has turned out to be "passive pacifism" compared with the activism of previous DPJ governments. Policy toward the South Sudan mission, the sole remaining SDF overseas peace-building mission during the first four years of the Abe administration, was driven more by the domestic legal goals of loosening restrictions on the SDF's use of force overseas, an initiative that ironically produced little change in actual use-of force rules due to overwhelming domestic public opposition.

After setting a legal (but not a political) precedent, the Abe administration then withdrew from South Sudan in spring 2017, leaving Japan at PKO Zero for the first time in a quarter of a century, and reconfirming the passive pacifist nature of Abe's foreign policy in this area. The Abe administration's implementation of "values diplomacy," has quite often deviated from the proclaimed promotion of human rights, democracy, and rule of law, even in the maritime commons. Policy in these areas has often been illiberal.

A possible counter, if rather cynical, argument to these points would be that the EU and the US are also retreating from liberal values, as part of a global trend.[23] Consequently, not only is Japan not exceptional in this regard, but in the future EU–Japan cooperation could be catalyzed by converging shared illiberal values. The problem with this counter argument is that this would also attenuate, if not wipe away altogether, any values distinction between the EU and Japan on the one hand, and illiberal China and Russia on the other.

A stronger counter argument is that the Abe administration's "proactive pacifism" and "values diplomacy" can plausibly be described as "liberal clothing for a realist strategy." Certainly, Kamiya's relabeling exercise, with deterrence and balance of power policies being renamed as "proactive pacifism" is suggestive. Although the deception and cynicism inherent in this exercise can be criticized (and may be ultimately self-defeating), the substance of the Abe administration's policies can plausibly be described as a sensible realist strategy aimed at countering China's rising influence. The problem with this argument is that a traditional-realist policy based on national interest and power balancing, although perhaps of value for Japan's national security, fails to provide a solid foundation for EU–Japan security cooperation. This because if cooperation is based on narrow national interest, significant gaps emerge between the EU and Japan on policy toward China, where their interests often diverge, on Russia, where they also diverge, and even on specific rule-of-law issues, such as how to define the maritime commons and interpret UNCLOS. The only plausibly robust platform for sustaining EU–Japan political and security cooperation is through a shared commitment to liberal values. This chapter finds this lacking.

This finding is especially unfortunate in the wake of the launch of the Donald Trump administration, an administration that is ushering in an era of uncertain US leadership of the liberal order, if not an era of blatant illiberalism. The Trump administration, by creating uncertainty in US–Japan relations, might persuade the Abe administration to begin prioritizing the joint pursuit of liberal values together with the EU. We can already see early indications of this in trade, where Trump's abandonment of the Trans Pacific Partnership (TPP) has greatly increased the relative importance of the newly concluded EU–Japan Economic Partnership Agreement, as this became the largest FTA under negotiation in 2017. It remains to be seen whether a similar positive dynamic will develop in security cooperation. Finally, it is striking that China is responding to the Trump administration's latent protectionism by positioning itself as a champion of free trade, and attempting to build a coalition with the EU on this issue (Emmott, and Baczynska, 2017). Allowing China to join the EU and Japan in cooperating to promote free trade might help to cement China's adherence to at least the liberal international trading order, while offering the EU and Japan new opportunities to cooperate in engaging China and attempting to moderate its behavior in other areas.

Notes

1 This chapter only examines EU–Japan cooperation, not Japanese cooperation with individual EU members.
2 The term in English used by the Abe administration and Japan's Foreign Ministry (MOFA) is "pro-active contributions to peace." Nonetheless, this essay mostly uses the term "pro-active pacifism," which is a more accurate and direct translation of the original Japanese term *sekkyokuteki heiwashugi*. See the discussion below.
3 Of course, there is also some difference between "pacifism" versus "peace" itself.
4 Also see Kitaoka, 2014, pp. 5–6.
5 Besides meaning "aggressor," the term "*kagaisha*" (加害者) could also be translated as "assailant," or "perpetrator."
6 These themes are echoed in Ito's 1991 book (Ito, 1991, pp. 120–131).
7 For an earlier and less developed discussion by Kamiya, see 2009.
8 The author heard Galtung criticize the Abe administration's concept of "proactive pacifism" in an NHK television interview in February 2016. One observer even went so far (almost certainly too far) as to equate the Abe administration's "proactive pacifism" with a code word for "pre-emptive attack." See Hamaji, 2015.

9 For example, the 2003 US invasion of Iraq could be so labeled.

10 This statement was made by Yoshifumi Okumura, Deputy Ambassador to the UN, as quoted by Asahi Shimbun, 2016.

11 The Abe administration delayed authorizing even this modest expansion in GSDF ROEs until after the July 2016 upper house election for fear of provoking voter backlash.

12 This Arc of "Freedom and Prosperity" is highlighted in Chapter 1 of MOFA's 2007 *Diplomatic Bluebook*; indeed it is even featured in the title: *Diplomatic Bluebook 2007: "Arc of Freedom and Prosperity: Japan's Expanding Diplomatic Horizons"* (MOFA, 2007).

13 The arc of freedom was replaced with "strengthened" Asian diplomacy" (Asahi Shimbun, 2008).

14 The remaining two principles focused on promoting cultural and youth exchanges between Japan and Southeast Asian nations.

15 Regarding Vietnam's human rights record, see Freedom House, 2008; International Federation for Human Rights and Vietnam Committee on Human Rights, 2013.

16 EU member states, including Germany, Italy, the Netherlands, and the UK, have issued statements claiming that UNCLOS allows military exercises in EEZs (Geng, 2012, p. 26). However, Portugal, has adopted the opposite position, see below. The US has been the most extreme in rejecting any restrictions on military operations in EEZs, by essentially arguing: "'Freedom of navigation' is clear and easy to understand. 'Freedom of navigation in some circumstances' is more problematic, and leaves ships open to selective enforcement by the coastal state" (Schwarck, 2014).

17 The full list includes Bangladesh, Brazil, Burma, Cambodia, Cape Verde, China, Egypt, Haiti, India, Iran, Kenya, Malaysia, Maldives, Mauritius, North Korea, Pakistan, Portugal, Saudi Arabia, Somalia, Sri Lanka, Sudan, Syria, Thailand, United Arab Emirates, Uruguay, Venezuela, and Vietnam (O'Rourke, 2016, p. 11). The Philippines has also been identified as part of this list by Schwarck, 2014, p. 2. Given that many East Asian states are on this list, and that Japan and South Korea de facto have a similar view, there is arguably a de facto regional norm against military operations within another state's EEZ.

18 Another issue is that not all intelligence gathering is passive. Some involves active pinging or "tickling" of radar and communications systems in coastal states to elicit programed responses, test electronic warfare capabilities, and even disrupting maritime and onshore communications systems and computers. These invasive signals intelligence gathering operations raise questions about whether they are more likely to violate the rights of Coastal States and the Peaceful Uses Article 301 of UNCLOS (Valencia, 2011, p. 4).

19 Japanese officials stated this position at the 7th annual bilateral Sino-Japanese security dialogue (Yomiuri Shimbun, 2000).

20 The US interpretation is that no such notification is needed, a point it expressed in reaction to a dispute between Japan and South Korea. The fact that South Korea rejected this position indicates that South Korea, like Japan, has a more restrictive view of permissible EEZ activities by foreign states (United States State Department, 2006).

21 Although Article 246 of UNCLOS mandates that coastal states "have the right to regulate, authorize and conduct marine scientific research in their exclusive economic zone and on their continental shelf," the US has promoted a norm that essentially ignores the implementation of this provision, perhaps because this might restrict US intelligence gathering, including military related hydrological research in coast states' EEZs. Moreover, Article 258 of UNCLOS states that:

> The deployment and use of any type of scientific research installations or equipment in any area of the marine environment shall be subject to the same conditions

as are prescribed in this Convention for the conduct of marine scientific research in any such area,

(see Valencia, 2011, p. 5)

thereby raising bigger doubts about the US position favoring unrestricted research and data gathering in another state's EEZ.

22 For the full text of the decision see Permanent Court of Arbitration, 2016b.
23 For a general claim about the retreat of Western liberal values see Luce, 2017.

References

Abe, S. (2012) Asia's Democratic Security Diamond. *Project Syndicate*. December 27. Available from: www.project-syndicate.org/commentary/a-strategic-alliance-for- japan-and-india-by-shinzo-abe. [Accessed: July 18, 2014].

Abe, S. (2013a) *The Bounty of the Open Seas: Five New Principles for Japanese Diplomacy*. January 18. Tokyo: Kantei. Available from: http://japan.kantei.go.jp/96_abe/statement/201301/18speech_e.html. [Accessed: September 4, 2016].

Abe, S. (2013b) *Five Principles of Japan's ASEAN Diplomacy*. Available from: www.mofa.go.jp/region/asia-paci/asean/factsheet.html. [Accessed: September 4, 2016].

Asahi Shimbun. (2008) *Jiyū to hanei no yumi' kie "Ajia gaikō kyōka' e gaikō seisho."* April 1, p. 1.

Asahi Shimbun. (2016) *'Beikoku ha kaubo-iteki' hihan*. December 29, p. 4.

Asplund, A. (2016) *Aligning Policy with Practice: Japanese ODA and Normative Values*. Unpublished manuscript of June 2016.

Daily Yomiuri. (2010) *China May Take Over Refueling*. 17 January, p. 2.

Dominguez, G. (2018) *Russia Begins Delivering S-400 Air Defense Systems to China, Say Report*. HIS Jane's Defense Weekly. January 18. Available from: www.janes.com/article/77157/russia-begins-delivering-s-400-air-defence-systems-to-china-says-report [Accessed: February 2, 2018].

Emmott, R. and Baczynska, G. (2017) EU Preparing Early China Summit in Message to Trump. *Reuters*. February 16. Available from: http://uk.reuters.com/article/uk-eu-china-idUKKBN15U1RJ. [Accessed: February 18, 2017].

European Japan Advanced Research Network (EJARN) and Konrad Adenauer Stiftung (KAS). (2012) *A Proposal for a Way Forward on EU-Japan Cooperation at the Nexus of Security and Development*. Tokyo: KAS.

Freedom House. (2008) *Vietnam: Freedom in the World 2008*. New York: Freedom House. Available from: freedomhouse.org/report/freedom-world/2008/Vietnam. [Accessed: June 20, 2016].

Fukushima, A. (2013) Japan-Europe Cooperation for Stability: Pursuing Synergies on a Comprehensive Approach. *Asia Program Policy Brief*. The German Marshall Fund (April), p. 2.

Geng, J. (2012) The Legality of Foreign Military Activities in the Exclusive Economic Zone under UNCLOS. *Merkourios* 28(74), pp. 22–30.

Government of Japan, National Security Council (GoJ NSC). (2013) National Security Strategy. December 17.

Hamaji, M. (2015) The Deliberate Misuse of "Positive Peace." *Japan Quality Review* 8(August). Available from: http://jqrmag.com/en/column-en/other-eyes-and-ears/vol-8-the-d. [Accessed: November 22, 2016].

Hornung, J.W. (2017) Japan's Mistaken South Sudan Withdrawal. *The Diplomat*. June 7.

Hornung, J.W. and Midford, P. (2014) A Role for Japan in the Fight Against Ebola. *The Wall Street Journal* (global edition), November 4, p. 17.

Hornung, J.W. and Midford, P. (2015) Opening Japan's Doors to Refugees. *The Wall Street Journal* (global edition), November 4, p. A11.

Hughes, C.W. (2015) *Japan's Foreign and Security Policy Under the "Abe Doctrine": New Dynamism or New Dead End?* New York: Palgrave Macmillan.

International Federation for Human Rights and Vietnam Committee on Human Rights. (2013) *Universal Periodic Review of Vietnam, Joint Submission.* Paris: United Nations Human Rights Council.

Ito, K. (1991) *"Futatsu no shōgeki" to Nihon: Gaikō "Shōsha naki heiwa" to "Shinsekai chitsujo" wo motomete.* Tokyo: PHP.

Ito, K. (2007) *Shin sensōron-sekkyokuteki heiwashugi he no teigen.* Tokyo: Shinchosha.

Japan Forum on International Relations. (2009) *Positive Pacifism and the Future of the Japan-U.S. Alliance.* Tokyo: Japan Forum on International Relations.

Japan Times. (2016) *Taiwan Patrol Ships Enter Waters off Okinotorishima.* May 7. Available from: www.japantimes.co.jp/news/2016/05/07/national/politicsdiplomacy/taiwanpatrolshipsenterwatersoffokinotorishima/#.Vy5KfmLTIU. [Accessed: May 11, 2016].

Jiji. (2016) SDF Likely to Be Handed New Security Duties in South Sudan as Early as November. *Japan Times.* August 7. Available from: www.japantimes.co.jp/news/2016/08/07/national/politics-di. [Accessed: August 26, 2016].

Johnson, J. (2016) After South China Sea Ruling, Could Tiny Okinotorishima Be the Next Flash Point? *Japan Times.* July 13. Available from: www.japantimes.co.jp/news/2016/07/13/national/south-china-sea-ruling-tiny-okinotorishima-next-flash-point/#.WDlQjvmLTIU. [Accessed: July 17, 2016].

Kamiya, M. (2009) Sekkyokuteki heiwa kokka-21 seiki Nihon no kokka senryaku. *The Yomiuri Quarterly* (Winter), pp. 111–119.

Kamiya, M. (2014) A Nation of Proactive Pacifism-National Strategy for Twenty-first-Century Japan. *Discuss Japan: Japan Foreign Policy Forum, Diplomacy* 18(January 20), pp. 1–3. Available from: www.japanpolicyforum.jp/archives/diplomacy/pt20140120123844.html. [Accessed: November 22, 2016].

Kawabata, T. (2017) Experts Question Wisdom, Achievements of SDF South Sudan Peacekeeping Mission. *Japan Times*, May 19, p. 1.

Kitaoka, S.A. (2014) Proactive Contribution to Peace and the Right of Collective Self-Defense: The Development of Security Policy in the Abe Administration. *Asia-Pacific Review* 21(2), pp. 1–18.

Kyodo. (2016a) First Rescue-ready GSDF Troops Head to South Sudan. *Japan Times.* November 20. Available from: www.japantimes.co.jp/news/2016/11/20/national/japanese%ADtroops%ADhead%ADsouth%ADsudan%ADpeacekeeping/#.WDJ9t_mLTIU. [Accessed: November 22, 2016].

Kyodo. (2016b) Japanese Troops to Train for New Overseas Tasks Under Revised Security Laws. *Japan Times.* August 20. Available from: www.japantimes.co.jp/news/2016/08/20/national/japanese-t. [Accessed: August 26, 2016].

Lee, P. (2015) Okinotorishima-ization: South China Sea Arbitration Case Enters Middle Game. *Asia Times.* July 18. Available from: http://atimes.com/2015/07/okinotorishimaizationsouthchinaseaarbitrationcaseentersmiddlegame/ [Accessed: June 19, 2016].

Luce, E. (2017) *The Retreat of Western Liberalism.* New York: Atlantic Western Press.

Midford, P. (2015a) *Does a Democratic Peace Exist between Japan and South Korea? New Evidence. Unpublished manuscript prepared for "Legacies of World War II, Part 4."* In Osaka University International Symposium. Osaka, February 13–14, p. 35.

Midford, P. (2015b) Japan's Approach to Maritime Security in the South China Sea. *Asian Survey* 55(3, May/June), pp. 525–547.

Mie, A. (2016a) Abe Offers 600 Million Yen Grant to Zimbabwe in Bid to Counter Chinese Economic Offensive. *Japan Times*. 28 March. Available from: www.japantimes.co.jp/news/2016/03/28/national/politicsdiplomacy/abeoffers%c2%a5600milliong rantzimbabwebidcounterchineseeconomic. [Accessed: March 30, 2016].

Mie, A. (2016b) Japan Steps up Rhetoric over Okinotorishima in Wake of Hague Ruling. *Japan Times*. July 15. Available from: www.japantimes.co.jp/news/2016/07/15/national/ politicsdiplomacy/japanstepsrhetoricokinotorishimawakehagueruling/#WDlOt_mLTIU. [Accessed: November 25, 2016].

Mie, A. (2016c) Tokyo Faces Tough Decisions over Japan's Role in South Sudan. *Japan Times*. October 6. Available from: www.japantimes.co.jp/news/2016/10/06/national/ politics-di. [Accessed: October 7, 2016].

MOFA. (1992) *Official Development Assistance (ODA): Japan's Official Development Assistance Charter*. Tokyo: Ministry of Foreign Affairs of Japan.

MOFA. (2007) *Diplomatic Bluebook 2007: Arc of Freedom and Prosperity: Japan's Expanding Diplomatic Horizons*. Tokyo: MOFA. Available from: www.mofa.go.jp/ policy/other/bluebook/2007/html/index.html. [Accessed: May 16, 2008].

Nihon Kokusai Fōra-mu. (2004) *Dai-24 seisaku teigen-Atarashii sekai chitsujo to nichi- bei dōmei no shōrai-"Fusen kyōdōtai" no kōchiku ni mukete*. Tokyo: Nihon kokusai fora-mu (April).

O'Rourke, R. (2016) Maritime Territorial and Exclusive Economic Zone (EEZ) Disputes Involving China: Issues for Congress. *Congressional Research Service Report*. R42784. Washington: Congressional Research Service, p. 11.

Pejsova, E. (2015) EU and Japan: Stepping up the Game. *Brief Issue*. European Union Institute for Security Studies (May), pp. 1–4.

Permanent Court of Arbitration. (2016a) Press Release: The South China Sea Arbitration (The Republic of the Philippines v. the People's Republic of Korea). July 12.

Permanent Court of Arbitration. (2016b) Case N° 2013–19 In the Matter of the South China Sea Arbiration Before an Arbitral Tribunal Constituted Under Annex VII to the 1982 United Nations Convention on the Law of the Sea between the Republic of the Philippines and the People's Republic of China Award. July 12. Available from: https://pca-cpa.org/en/news/pca-press-release-the-south-china-sea-arbitration-the- republic-of-the-philippines-v-the-peoples-republic-of-china/. [Accessed: November 25, 2016].

Samuels, R.J. (2007/2008) "New Fighting Power!" Japan's Growing Maritime Capabil- ities and East Asian Security. *International Security* 32(3, Winter), pp. 84–112.

Schwarck, E. (2014) Freedom of Navigation and China: What Should Europe Do? *PacNet* 68(August 18), p. 3. Available from: www.csis.org/analysis/pacnet-68- freedom-navigation-and-c. [Accessed: February 20, 2017].

United Nations, Office of the High Commissioner for Human Rights (UNOHCHR). (1993) *Final Declaration of the Regional Meeting for Asia of the World Conference on Human Rights ("Bangkok Declaration")*. A/CONF.157/ASRM/8 A/CONF.157/PC/59. (April 7), sections 4, 5, 13.

United Nations Peacekeeping. (2017) Where We Operate. Available from: https://peace keeping.un.org/en/where-we-operate. [Accessed: December 19, 2017].

United States State Department. (2006) FM Ban Concerned with Japan Survey of Disputed Waters. Cable 06Seoul2212 (July 5), confidential cable Seoul 002212. as published by Wikileaks. August 30, 2011.

Valencia, M.J. (2002) Japan's Rights and Wrongs in the "Fishing Boat" Incident. *Japan Times*. January 10. Available from: www.japantimes.co.jp/opinion/2002/01/10/commentary/world-commentary/japans-rights-and-wrongs-in-the-fishing-boat-incident/#. WnlH-6hl_IU. [Accessed: February 6, 2018].

Valencia, M.J. (2011) Policy Forum 11–28: Intelligence Gathering, the South China Sea, and the Law of the Sea. *NAPSNet Policy Forum* (August 30). Available from: http://nautilus.org/napsnet/napsnet-policy-forum/intelligence-gathering-the-south-china-sea-and-the-law-of-the-sea/. [Accessed: February 6, 2018].

Yomiuri Shimbun. (2000) *Nicchu anpo taiwa kaiyō chōsa ha jizen dōi wo Nihon gawa, Chūgoku ni yōkyū*. June 20, p. 2.

Yomiuri Shimbun. (2001) *Fushinsen taiō 3tsu no kadai- "hōseibi," "seibikaizen," "jieitai-kaiho no renkei tsuyōka,"* December 25, p. 3.

Yomiuri Shimbun. (2010) *Chugoku ga indo yō kyūryu hiki tsudtsuki kentō-kako ni beigun he dashin*. January 16, p. 4.

4 Ordinary/civilian, not normative/post-modern

Lessons from the EU for Japanese security policy

Paul Bacon and Hidetoshi Nakamura

Overview

In this book we consider the shadows cast on EU–Japan relations by two great powers, the United States and China. This chapter focuses on security issues, and constructions of security identity. Two of Japan's greatest security concerns relate to these two countries: how to avoid abandonment by the US, and avoid antagonizing China. Perhaps more than at any time since WWII, if the rhetoric of US President Trump is to be believed, Japan will need to demonstrate its political and military commitment to the alliance with the US. In the shadow of a Trump Presidency, Japan will need to show commitment to the deterrence of China, to increase military expenditure, and to show that it has the legal permission and political will to fight alongside the US in regional contingencies. Japan will have to be resilient in the face of what it sees as Chinese provocation, while offering a firm defence of international law, and avoid political and military flashpoints with China. These two diplomatic imperatives will require quite a balancing act.

How relevant are EU–Japan relations to all of this? Both the EU and NATO, and individual European states have increased their activities and profiles in the region. Japan's recent 'normalization' has created opportunities with European actors for greater interoperability, arms sales, intelligence-sharing, cyber security cooperation, and cooperation through PKOs or anti-piracy operations. However, in terms of hard security, European states are not serious players in the Asia-Pacific (Nakamura, 2013).

This notwithstanding, one of the more important but under-appreciated senses in which the EU *is* relevant to the security shadows cast over Japan by the US and China lies in the realm of ideas. European debates on and conceptions of security identity are relevant to, and potentially have an impact on the way in which Japan conducts itself. In order to best manage its relations with China, we suggest that Japan needs to learn from European experience, and avoid some of the traps into which Europeans have fallen in their self-definitions and actions since the end of the Cold War. As we will see, the EU's mistakes have led to it being variously characterized as 'hubristic', 'negligent', 'self-righteous' and 'messianistic'. Japan runs the risk of repeating European mistakes, as a result of its persistent and strident references to democracy and human rights in its strategic diplomacy in the Asia-Pacific.

Security identities are important phenomena to study if we want to have a better understanding of actor behaviour. The internal dimension of EU actorness is perhaps over-researched, with long debates running about whether the EU is or could be, among other things, a civilian, normative, military or post-modern power. However, insufficient reflexive attention has been paid to the impact of these EU self-identifications on its Others (Manners and Whitman, 2003; Diez, 2005; Diez and Manners, 2007). There are two dimensions to this under-researched impact: first, how are other states impacted by Europe's self-definitions, and how do they respond? Second, do other states follow debates on European security identity, and consciously or unconsciously adapt and utilize European conceptions of security identity, to frame their own security identities?

We suggest that Manners and Whitman's 'difference engine' argument (2003) is important; according to them, complex polities can possess more than one security identity simultaneously. We also believe that there are risks and dangers associated with self-identification as a post-modern power and as a normative power respectively. Post-modern self-identification has led some European states to become involved in foreign policy failures such as Afghanistan, Iraq and Libya. Furthermore, the conception of 'normative power Europe (NPE)' is not necessarily as successful or as popular with its 'targets' or 'subjects' in the neighbourhood it is sometimes presented to be. The negative role of the EU and the 'normative power Europe' mentality in the Ukraine crisis is under-appreciated. We suggest that the EU made many mistakes in the Ukraine crisis which can arguably be traced back to this mentality and the insufficiently reflexive enlargement and association strategy that it informed.

In the final section of this chapter, we note that Japan is currently undergoing a transformation of its security and defence profile. There is public and elite contestation about what kind of power Japan is and should be. Using Manners and Whitman's 'difference engine' argument, we suggest that Japan can and should be *both* an ordinary power and a civilian power. Referring to lessons from the European theoretical and practical experience, we suggest that Japan should resist the temptation to self-identify as either a post-modern or normative power, as these self-identifications can themselves be inherently conflict-producing. We can and should give attention to concrete sectoral analysis of EU–Japan relations, in areas such as weapons exports and trade issues. But the transmission of security ideas and concepts, and the possibility of role emulation are also important dimensions of EU–Japan relations.

It is suggested that adopting a mix of ordinary and civilian power identity is best for Japan because the move towards ordinary power sends a reassuring signal to the US that Japan is a dependable ally in the Asia-Pacific, and recognizes the need to take more security responsibility. This will become still more important in the context of a Trump Presidency. And the tone and language of civilian power are a more appropriate means through which to engage China, downplaying confrontational rhetoric about Japan's superior credentials on democracy and human rights, and emphasizing a consistent, defensive commitment to the rule of international law. These two identities in combination can help Japan navigate the tricky diplomatic waters which lie ahead.

Defining civilian and normative power

In this first section of this chapter we briefly survey debates within the EU regarding how to characterize its international actorness. We offer definitions of normative power and civilian power, and note how the EU has often been thought of as the former, and Japan as the latter. We argue, following Manners and Whitman (2003) and Diez and Manners (2007), that polities such as the EU and Japan are complex, and capable of supporting more than one security identity simultaneously. We also take a critical look at post-modern EU theories which explicitly identify different types of sovereignty and sovereignty games, and identify the 'Othering' consequences of this in theory and practice. We note that a self-identification as this or that type of international actor is never innocent, and never happens in a vacuum; it involves constituting an Other. We argue that insufficient attention has been given to this crucial aspect of perennial debates about what type of actor the EU is or ought to be: the way that EU self-identification in turn impacts on its various Others.

Definitions of normative power and civilian power are now well-established, and only need to be briefly restated. For Manners (2002), not only is the EU constructed on a normative basis, but this 'predisposes it to act in a normative way in world politics ... the most important factor shaping the role of the EU is not what it does or what it says, but what it is' (p. 252). The EU possesses the 'ability to define what passes for "normal" in world politics', which is 'ultimately, the greatest power of all' (p. 236, p. 253). The broad normative basis of the EU consists of five core norms; peace, liberty, democracy, the rule of law, and respect for human rights (p. 242). This normative basis is reflected in the content of the EU treaties.

Following Diez and Manners (2007, p. 178), we define civilian power as entailing three central characteristics; 'diplomatic cooperation to solve international problems' (multilateralism), 'centrality of economic power' (non-military) and 'legally-binding supranational institutions' (international law). Although we agree that there are some similarities between normative power and civilian power, in that both involve the promotion of norms, we believe that the two concepts are distinct. As Diez and Manners (2007) note, 'the normative power approach encourages us to differentiate between the civilian nature of the EU prior to circa 1999 and the normative justification for the use of military power when appropriate, for example, in humanitarian intervention' (p. 178).

Another point of differentiation, according to Diez and Manners, is that civilian power writings emphasize the 'communitarian' nature of civilian power, which according to writers such as Maull (1990), is deployed in the service of 'national goals', 'national interest' and 'national values'. Normative power by contrast is cosmopolitan, because it refers to principles and norms which are held to be

Table 4.1 Composite definition of civilian power for Japan

Definition of civilian power for Japan (Manners and Diez, 2007, unless stated)
• Diplomatic cooperation to solve international problems (multilateralism)
• Centrality of economic power (non-military)
• Support for legally-binding international institutions (respect for international law)
• A more concrete reference to respect for international law, freedom of maritime passage, freedom of overflight, territorial integrity, non-aggression (Abe, 2014)
• Communitarian – national goals, values and interests (Maull, 1990)
• 'Westphalian' ontology
• Status quo focus, not transformative
• International society, not world society
• Civil association (Nardin, 1983), not 'mission civilisatrice' (Diez, 2005)
• More emphasis on human security relative to human rights (Hobson, Bacon and Cameron, 2014)
• Greater humility about scope for cosmopolitan norm diffusion
• Greater reflexivity about the inherent impact of 'Othering' entailed in the normative approach (Doyle, 1983)

universal, and which are embedded in UN treaties. A further point of differentiation is that civilian power possesses a more 'Westphalian' ontology (Inoguchi and Bacon, 2001) and therefore, using the *argot* of the English School, focuses more on 'the status quo' of an international society as opposed to the normative power approach, which seeks to transcend the 'normality' of international society, and move towards world society. A final point of differentiation, we suggest, is that the civilian power approach entails a greater humility about the scope for cosmopolitan norm diffusion, and a greater reflexivity about the impact of 'Othering' entailed in the normative approach, on its 'subjects' (Doyle, 1983).

Diez and Manners on self and 'Othering'

Diez and Manners (2007) argue that 'academic discussions about normative power, and political representations of the EU as a normative power ... need to develop a greater degree of reflection and reflexivity', and that 'it is such reflection and reflexivity that constitute the EU as a normative power' (p. 174). The narrative of 'normative power Europe' 'constructs the EU's identity as well as the identities of the EU's Others' (p. 183). They argue that the 'difference between the EU as a civilian power and a normative power' needs to be 'analyzed more carefully', and that the discourse of normative power 'should be analyzed more systematically, particularly regarding forms of Othering and the degree of reflexivity it entails' (p. 188). Greater reflexivity should drive us to spread norms through example rather than preaching, to accept and address our own failures, and adopt a dialogical orientation towards the Other, rather than simply trying to change it (p. 185). They suggest that the EU should be a more 'humble' power, 'attempting to construct non-hierarchical relationships' (p. 185).

It is a basic premise of post-modern thought that 'identities are seen always to require an Other against which they are constructed; an Other which they thus construct at the same time' (Walker, 1993, p. 184). Concretely, the EU has several Others against which it has sought to construct itself. As Waever (1998) famously noted, one is Europe's violent past. A second is the US, perhaps as personified by Robert Kagan's caricature, and the Bush doctrine, as a counterpoint against which the EU Security Strategy was drafted (Diez, 2005, p. 635). Turkey has also performed this function as a civilizational Other (Rumelili, 2004). Russia is arguably the Other against which the entire enlargement project is oriented, as a declining, non-democratic power which can be disregarded, as the EU extends the zone of peace and democracy into the formerly authoritarian, but now self-determining post-Soviet space (Williams, 2007). Finally, in championing the virtues of what he refers to as post-modern states, Robert Cooper (2003) securitizes and 'Others' what he refers to as 'modern' and 'pre-modern' states, as security threats which need to be addressed by what he approvingly endorses as 'liberal imperialism'.

Diez and Manners (2007) identify five strategies of constructing 'self' and 'Other' in international relations (pp. 184–185), 'in order to trace them in articulations of NPE' (p. 184).

- *Representation of the Other as an existential threat*, the practice of 'securitization' identified by the Copenhagen School.
- *Representation of the Other as inferior*, a version of Othering whereby the self is simply constructed as superior to the Other. A classic example might be that of Orientalism, where the other is feted and exoticized, but still looked down upon.
- *Representation of the Other as violating universal principles.* For Diez and Manners, this is a stronger version of the second strategy. Here, the standards of the self are not simply seen as superior, but as of universal validity, and the Other should therefore be convinced or otherwise brought to accept the principles of the self.
- *Representing the Other as different*, a strategy which differs from the previous three because it does not place an obvious value-judgment on the Other as either inferior or as a threat, but merely as different. For Diez and Manners, this practice is not innocent, as it still imposes an identity on Others, but it is preferable to the other three, in that it 'reduces the possibility to legitimize harmful interference with the Other'.
- *Representation of the Other as abject*, drawing on Julia Kristeva's notion that the Other is always part of the self, an 'abject foreigner which is part of our conscious and unconscious selves', (Diez and Manners, 2007, p. 185).

The 'difference engine', and some differences between civilian and normative power

There are four political implications of the NPE discourse (Diez and Manners, 2007 Manners and Whitman, 2003); first, the self-identification should be welcomed, because it promotes peace and justice; second, we need to be reflexive when the EU itself fails to live up to human rights standards that it imposes on others (in cases such as the Barcelona Process and Turkey); third, there is a risk that if the concept of NPE is developed in an insufficiently reflexive way, it will be undermined because force will be used to promote it, in unacceptable ways (Cooper, 2003). Finally, we should not assume that the EU possesses a single self, which is capable of a strategy:

> from the viewpoint of conventional work on identity, the notion of a differ-ence engine reflects the attempts within the EU to engineer a single, essen-tial, categorical identity which acts as a multiplier of differences between the EU and the world. However, critical-social theory encourages us to analyse the international identity of the EU as far more fluid, consisting of ongoing contestations of complex, multiple, relational identities. From this critical viewpoint, the notion of a 'difference engine' is a means to analyse these ongoing contestations as part of the international identity of the EU which does not add up to a single, integrating whole.
>
> (Manners and Whitman, 2003, p. 397)

This is a valuable insight; it is far more meaningful to conceive of the identi-ties of international actors as contested and multi-faceted. However, it is also very important to reflect on how these contestations and the settlements that occur can affect the perceptions and behaviours of Others with whom the EU interacts. This is one important way in which we can differentiate between poli-ties that self-identify as normative and civilian powers; they produce different levels of threat, and therefore different responses from the Other.

It was noted earlier that normative power and civilian power are superficially similar, in the sense that they both advocate adherence to and diffusion of uni-versal norms. However, there is an important substantive difference between the content of the universal norms that each promotes. The EU seeks to impose its universalist conceptions of human rights on Others via a variety of diffusion techniques, across a range of different mechanisms, including enlargement and neighbourhood policy. The norms that civilian power tries to uphold are also universal, but at the Westphalian or international society level, rather than at the cosmopolitan or world society level. This entails communitarian respect for international law and the status quo; civil association between states, rather than a mission civilisatrice. This distinction between the types of universalism per-sonified by civilian power and normative power becomes important later, when we argue that Japan should strive to remain a civilian power, and focus, defen-sively but legitimately, on the fact that states should respect international law, and in particular the rights to freedom of navigation, freedom of overflight, and territorial integrity.

We have suggested that civilian powers and normative powers place greater relative emphasis on different concrete universal ends, but that they also address these ends with differing degrees of humility and intensity. Civilian powers and normative powers, despite their underlying similarities, therefore produce different security *cultures*; they do not approach international relations in the same way, and as a result of projecting different self-identities, they generate different responses in their respective Others, because of the different nature of their Othering processes.

The normative power self-identification of the EU has in fact come to be dominant. The most pressing concern is therefore not with looking at the contest between different identities which are potentially in play. It is the need for greater consideration of the impacts that normative power Europe's Othering processes (the way that the EU conceives of and behaves towards other actors) have on the EU's Others, and how this can have important practical implications. This claim brings into play broader and more damning claims about the conflict-producing nature of liberal self-identification in international relations.

Cooper and Diez on liberal, post-modern and normative power 'Othering'

It has been suggested above that liberal thought can securitize non-liberal Others, and frame them as inferior and undeserving of respect, for failing to adhere to universal standards. Some go even further, and claim that liberalism itself, through its disposition towards the non-liberal Other, is therefore an *inherently* conflict-producing phenomenon (Doyle, 1983). We should be alert to this and reflexive with regard to the temptations and pathologies of the liberal mentality, in both Europe, with regard to Russia, and Japan, with regard to China. In its more extreme and explicit forms, this mentality is permissive of forcible intervention against 'inferior', non-democratic Others (Cooper, 2003). In a subtler but still damaging form, we suggest that this mentality pervades the EU enlargement process, and the self-identification of the EU as a normative power. This spills over negatively into how the EU conducts itself: the EU is insufficiently reflexive or respectful towards its Others. In the case of the Ukraine, 'hubristic' assumptions are made about all non-members wanting to join the EU (MacFarlane and Menon, 2014); dismissive assumptions are made about the status and inability of opposed regional powers to do anything about this; true intentions are not sympathetically conveyed to potential associates or members such as the Ukraine, or adequately communicated to Others with legitimate strategic concerns, such as Russia. Such states in turn feel threatened and are more likely to make strategic miscalculations (Freedman, 2014).

Robert Cooper identifies three different types of EU actor identity – post-modern, modern and pre-modern – and constructs and defends the EU as a post-modern power. He also identifies different types of inter-subjectivity, which are dependent upon context. For example, he acknowledges that states like the US and EU members can be post-modern in their dealings with other post-modern states, but that in their dealings with modern and pre-modern states, they must be prepared to operate according to the logic of the different, modern sovereignty game.

'Among ourselves, we keep the law but when we are operating in the jungle, we also must use the laws of the jungle' (Cooper, 2003).

Cooper identifies what he calls the modern and the pre-modern worlds as threats against which the post-modern world must guard itself, so in that respect he employs Diez and Manners's first strategy, that of securitization. But we would add that he is also identifying the Other as inferior and different, thereby also invoking the second and fourth strategies of 'Othering' outlined above. Cooper's securitization strategy, and sometimes his political influence, has been a permissive cause of a series of foreign policy failures, such as those which took place in Afghanistan, Iraq and Libya.

We agree with Diez that Cooper's position 'legitimizes the formation of European armed forces, and of interventions in the pre-modern world' (2005, p. 629), and also that it is unusual for advocates of normative power approaches to be quite so ready to support the use of military force. When the post-modern strategy of 'Othering' is this acutely transparent, it is not particularly in need of deconstruction or nuanced explication. But it is helpful for us to see it laid out in this way because it reveals, in admittedly starker form, the liberal pathology that is also deployed, albeit with rather more subtlety, in normative power Europe rather than post-modern European 'Othering' strategies. In both cases, non-liberal Others are not shown adequate respect, and become the victims of the transformative animus entailed in the liberal conception of the non-liberal Other.

Diez also argues that 'Othering' processes connected to normative power have a negative impact on the course of events. He suggests that normative power Europe's approach operates according to the third strategy outlined above, where Others are guilty of violating universal principles: for him 'the European standard becomes the world standard, and Europe is called upon to engage in a "mission civilisatrice"' (2005, p. 629). Importantly, Diez explicitly argues that the EU enlargement process, and the Copenhagen criteria, which set the political, economic and administrative standards for EU membership candidates, are 'a prominent example of this' (2005, p. 629). Diez also expresses concern about the danger that normative power Europe might become a 'self-righteous, messianistic project' (p. 636). Having identified what we believe are some legitimate grounds for concern with regard to self-identification as a post-modern or normative power, we now turn to a discussion of the relevance of these two theoretical constructs to debates within Japan about which security identity or identities to adopt.

Applying the 'difference engine' argument to the Japanese case: evaluating five identity constructions

We suggested above that the 'difference engine' argument advanced by Manners and Whitman (2003) is important and underappreciated. According to this argument, advanced polities like the EU are complex, and capable of simultaneously supporting various different identities. In the EU context, they suggest that it is possible for the EU to possess three identities simultaneously; civilian power Europe, normative power Europe, and military power Europe (2003, p. 388). We have three observations to make here about their work. First, in the EU, people have still tended to view debates about civilian and normative power as an either/or choice, and the idea of 'military power Europe' has not really taken off. This could change as a result of Brexit removing the British obstacle to greater EU security cooperation, and President Trump demanding that Europeans take more responsibility for their own security. But at the present writing, the idea of normative power Europe has come to dominate in both theory and practice. Second, Manners and Whitman note that the 'difference engine' argument also applies to external relations, and that the internal identity or combination of identities that a polity adopts has external implications for Others, and therefore for the EU in its dealings with its various Others. In this sense, they anticipate the later arguments by Diez (2005) and Diez and Manners (2007) that the EU has not been sufficiently reflexive about the external implications of its internal attempts at identity creation.

Last, to our knowledge Manners and Whitman's 'difference engine' argument has not been applied to other states or polities apart from the EU. In this final section of the chapter we suggest that this argument can in fact be applied to Japan in three fruitful ways: we can use it to develop a loose taxonomy of the identities claimed to be relevant for contemporary Japan; we can anticipate the responses that some of these self-identifications might draw from strategically relevant Others beyond Japan's borders, such as China; and we can tentatively use these anticipations to select and promote those identities which complement and balance each other best, and which constitute the most appropriate combination with which to address Japan's various foreign policy objectives and imperatives.

We suggest that there are five identity constructs potentially in play with regard to Japan at present: as a 'revisionist' power; as an ordinary power; as a civilian power; as a post-modern power; and as a normative power. We dismiss the first of these identities, and suggest that it would be unwise to cultivate the fourth and the fifth, and argue that the best policy advice would be to combine civilian power and ordinary power identities.

1. Japan as Revisionist Power – ✗
2. Japan as Ordinary Power – ✓
3. Japan as Civilian Power – ✓
4. Japan as Post-Modern Power – ✗
5. Japan as Normative Power – ✗

Figure 4.1 Applying the 'difference engine' argument to Japan: evaluating five identity constructions.

The recent transformation of Japan's security and defence policy

Japan has recently taken a number of significant transformative steps in its security and defence policy. These include the strengthening of the Japan–US alliance through the dispatch of Japan's Self-Defense Forces (SDF) to contingencies outside of UN command in line with special laws passed in 2001 and 2003, and the development of a missile defence system in 2004. Weapons that might be construed as offensive in character have been acquired. The Japan Defense Agency was upgraded to a full ministry in 2007, and a new National Security Council and National Security Strategy were created in 2013, all of which signals the elevation of security issues up the political agenda (Hagström, 2015). In April 2014 Japan amended and substantially relaxed restraints on weapons exports. In July 2014 the Cabinet decided to reinterpret Article 9 to permit the exercise of collective self-defence, and legislation to this effect was voted through the Diet in September 2015, and enacted in March 2016. Last, the new guidelines on Japan–US defence cooperation were introduced in April 2015.

The nature and desirability of these changes, and the type(s) of identity Japan possesses and ought to cultivate have been fiercely contested. There is a contest between the various possible identities, between different generations of diplomats, and between the security elites and the general public. We identified five possible security identities above. Key official and unofficial security documents have referred to different elements of these security identities. For example, Abe's private November 2012 opinion piece on the 'democratic diamond' could be characterized as supporting the idea of a post-modern Japan. However, his NATO speech in May 2014, as PM, could be characterized as supporting the idea of a civilian power Japan. In an interview with a senior Japanese diplomat, Bacon was told that there is an inter-generational struggle within MOFA, concerning how much Japan should both highlight its own democratic credentials, and use them as an overt (and potentially antagonistic) source of contrast, or 'Othering', when discussing and engaging with China and Russia. Generalizing somewhat, younger diplomats are more comfortable engaging in 'value-oriented diplomacy', while the older diplomats have reservations about this (Interview one, 2016).

There has also been a substantial gap between security elites and the Japanese general public on the desirability of recent security legislation. All 30 of the senior defence specialists Bacon interviewed for a recent project on NATO–Japan relations considered it to be self-evident that the security legislation mentioned above was highly necessary. Even though many were overtly critical of the PM and the current government, they welcomed the legislation. But when the security legislation was passed in September 2015, an Asahi poll found 51 per cent opposition and 30 per cent support for the bills (McCurry, 2016). About a month later, another Asahi poll found 49 per cent opposition and 36 per cent support for the legislation (McCurry, 2016). The gap had narrowed, but a clear majority of the Japanese public still opposed the new security legislation, putting them at odds with the security elites.

In October 2017, Abe won a sweeping election victory which has arguably given him a mandate for constitutional revision. His Liberal Democratic Party (LDP) and coalition partner, Komeito, secured 313 seats in the 465-seat lower house, passing the 310-seat threshold for a two-thirds majority, which is necessary for constitutional amendment. However, an October 2017 Nikkei/TV Tokyo survey showed a shrinking margin of support for Abe's proposal to revise the pacifist constitution. The poll asked about Abe's proposal to revise the war-renouncing Article 9, which would leave the two existing clauses untouched, while adding new text to explicitly recognize the SDF. Public sentiment has wavered, but remains marginally supportive of Abe's proposal, with 44 per cent of respondents in favour – down from 51 per cent in a May survey posing a similar question – and 41 per cent against, up from 36 per cent previously (*Nikkei Asian Review*, 2017). So, just as there was considerable opposition to the security legislation enacted in 2016 to allow Japan to come to the assistance of the US, there is only a marginal support for constitutional revision in recognition of the SDF in 2017. And any constitutional amendment would only be possible through a national referendum, even if a huge majority of MPs (Diet members) support it.

Revisionism

Some worry that in the past decade or so there has been a significant development in Japan's military profile, and that this will culminate in Japan revising its constitution, once again giving Japan the potential to wage war. These concerns have increased in some quarters as a result of Abe's re-election. Rightly or wrongly, many feel that Japan has not addressed various 'history issues' adequately, and that this is a symptom of the fact that Japan has not learned its lesson, fails to understand or acknowledge that it did anything wrong, and remains a potential threat to regional and international order, given the opportunity. We might say that perceptions of Japanese constitutional and historical revisionism raise concerns about geopolitical revisionism in the eyes of some (Liu, 2014; Dudden, 2015). If, as noted by Waever, Europe's warlike past has become its own principal Other, then it can sometimes seem, from the scrutiny it receives, as if Japan's past has become everybody else's Other.

However, we believe it is inaccurate to think of Japan as revisionist or revanchist. Although there has been a recent (2015) increase in defence spending to $42 billion, this figure is significantly lower (by a factor of 3.5) than the official Chinese figure of $146 billion (and many estimates place real Chinese spending at a significantly higher level than this). Japan's budget is smaller than that of the US by a factor of roughly 15; it is comparable to, but smaller than, the military budgets of France, Germany and the UK, and therefore not remotely sufficient to render it a threat to regional order. However, such simplistic realist power calculations could also be said to miss the point; as has been persuasively suggested (Berger, 1998; Katzenstein, 1998), Japan's security identity has been fundamentally transformed into that of a peace-loving nation. The new security legislation does not (yet) affect that.

The recent normalization (and any possible subsequent constitutional revision) is intended to make Japan a more credible alliance partner, not give it scope to become a revisionist rogue. In fact, as has been suggested by several commentators, much of what Prime Minister Abe has been implementing closely reflects the content of the third Armitage-Nye report (Armitage and Nye, 2012). This third report can be thought of as a kind of 'bucket list' of semi-official American requests put forward by two highly influential public intellectuals. The new security legislation permits Japan to engage in collective defence with the US in the region, but it still does not allow Japan the same general right of collective defence that is recognized under international law (Tokyo Foundation, 2008). Furthermore, under the new legislation it is only permissible to engage in peacekeeping with the support of an UN Security Council Resolution. Although there has been considerable domestic opposition to the new security legislation, the overwhelming issue of concern within Japan prior to the recent US election related more to the risk of entrapment in US missions, rather than any serious indigenous concern regarding the possibility of revisionism.

Ordinary power

Moving on from revisionism, after the end of the Cold War the concepts of ordinary power and civilian power were championed as visions for Japan. The most well-known early proponent of Japan as a more proactive military player was Ichiro Ozawa, who argued that Japan should seek to become a 'normal' or 'ordinary' state (futsu no kuni)[1] (Ozawa, 1993). Ozawa developed this idea in the context of post-Gulf War reflection on damning criticism of Japan's so-called 'chequebook diplomacy'. He argued that under the Preamble to Japan's Constitution, Japan should have been free to support the right of 'collective security' of the US and other coalition partners in the Gulf War with an authorization by UN Security Council Resolution. Ozawa also argued that Japan should support the creation of a UN standing army, and participate fully in it as its main contribution to international security. Ozawa's radical vision of a Japan operating at the hub of collective security was rejected at the time, but the idea that Japan should become an ordinary or normal power survived and became 'the central reference point for the debate on the future of Japan's security policy' (Hughes, 2004, p. 50).

Debate about the future of Japan's security policy has historically taken place in the context of possible constitutional revision. The Japanese Constitution has not been amended since 1946. Any Japanese foreign, security and defence policy should be made under Constitutional constraints. If the Constitution alone is said to determine state identity, it logically follows that Japanese identity should not change, unless the Constitution is amended. But, depending on how one interprets the Constitution, there is manoeuvring room for any government to change policy (Nakamura, H., 2015).

With the return of Prime Minister Abe in late 2012, his government has gradually revealed a relatively clear position on the form that Japanese state identity should take. Abe initially shelved his political desire to amend the Japanese Constitution itself, but has re-interpreted it, and changed Japan's foreign, security and defence policy. In 2007–2008 the first Abe Cabinet had tried but failed to carry out such a change. The Advisory Panel on Reconstruction of the Legal Basis for Security, consisting of a group of like-minded experts, issued its report in June 2008, recommending the Abe government to change the interpretation of the Constitution, in order for Japan to exercise the right of collective self-defence. However, the Abe Cabinet failed to approve that reinterpretation before his resignation. Abe has been keen to push through his foreign policy agenda in his second term in office. The 'Report of the Advisory Panel on Reconstruction of the Legal Basis for Security' was published on 15 May 2014 and paved the way for a possible 'exercise' of the right of collective self-defence. The Abe Cabinet approved the basic ideas in this report in a Cabinet Decision in July 2014. Until the publication of this Decision, the government had considered that the use of force by the Japanese state would only be permitted when an armed attack occurs against Japan. However, the 2014 Cabinet Decision of 2014 changes this:

> the Government has reached a conclusion that not only when an armed attack against Japan occurs but also when an armed attack against a country that is in a close relationship with Japan occurs and as a result threatens Japan's survival and poses a clear danger to fundamentally overturn people's right to life, liberty and the pursuit of happiness, and when there is no other appropriate means available to repel the attack and ensure Japan's survival and protect its people, use of force to the minimum extent necessary should be interpreted to be permitted under the Constitution as measures for self-defense.
>
> (MOFA, 2014)

We can see from the key paragraph above that these parameters, and the circumstances under which Japan might use force are still quite tightly drawn. This Cabinet Decision led to the new security bills. We can say that it is a significant step towards normalization, but still not perhaps full 'normality', compared to the looser restrictions that exist for nearly all other states in the world. We support this move towards the assumption of ordinary power status.

Civilian power

The concept of civilian power has received considerable attention within Japan since the early nineties (Bacon, Mayer and Nakamura, 2015). Its most influential Japanese proponent has been Yoichi Funabashi, the prominent journalist and public intellectual. Funabashi used the phrase 'global civilian power' (Funabashi, 1991). Japan has historically regarded itself, and been regarded by others, as a civilian power (Maull, 1990). Some have argued in the past that the term civilian power has faded from mainstream Japanese security discourse (Hughes, 2004, p. 57), but today it is not hard to find influential commentators who believe that Japan is a civilian power (Hosoya, 2012, p. 319; Sabathil, 2015, p. 78). These more contemporary opinions are not without resonance and relevance; Gerhard Sabathil was until recently the EU's chief negotiator with Japan on the Strategic Partnership Agreement, and Yuichi Hosoya has been a member of Abe's two most influential recent expert panels on security, and played a substantial role in the drafting of Japan's National Security Strategy.

Apart from the establishment of a right to collective self-defence discussed above, in the context of ordinary power, it is important to emphasize that other parts of the legislative package contained several developments that are consistent with, and strengthen Japan's credentials as a civilian power. For example, additional security legislation allows Japan to be involved in: support activities; international peace cooperation activities; the rescue of Japanese nationals abroad; and ship inspection operations (Funabashi, 2017). The Japanese SDF will be able to provide necessary logistics support and search and rescue to armed forces of foreign countries collectively addressing situations which threaten international peace and security, under specified conditions regarding the content of UN resolutions. The Japanese SDF will also be able to provide necessary logistics support and search and rescue to armed forces of foreign countries engaging in activities for ensuring Japan's peace and security in situations that will have an important influence on Japan's peace and security. Additional functions will be conferred upon Japanese soldiers on operations, to respond to changes in the role and responsibility of UN PKOs, including the protection of civilians. Rules of engagement will be revised to allow for a use of weapons which is better aligned with current UN standards. Finally, Japan will be able to participate in internationally coordinated operations for peace and security (outside the UN peacekeeping operation (PKO) framework) with permission from the UN, organizations established by the UN, or regional organizations such as the EU.

Ordinary power *and* civilian power

The existing literature on Japan's foreign, security and defence policy historically struggled to describe or prescribe what type of international actor Japan has been or should be. Inoguchi and Bacon (2008) have argued that Japan's foreign policy evolved through five phases since the end of the Second World War: an unstable phase of contestation between pro-alliance and anti-alliance sentiment (1945–1960); a stable phase of Yoshida doctrine (1960–1975); a third phase as a systemic supporter of the US (1975–1990); a fourth as a global civilian power (1990–2005); and the current phase as a 'global ordinary power', on the UK model (from 2005 towards 2020). Developing and supporting Inoguchi and Bacon's argument, Welch and others observe that the 'general tendency is clearly towards a pragmatic embrace of normalcy' and that this is part of Japanese 'national strategy' (Soeya, Tadokoro and Welch, 2011, p. 13).

Hidetoshi Nakamura (2015) has argued that there may be a disagreement over how to describe Japan's actorness in the current phase, whether as 'a civilian power' or an 'ordinary power', and that Japan should best be thought of as a proactive civilian power rather than a proactive military power.

Our argument is that Japan has been developing more in the direction of an ordinary power in recent years. This has generated much controversy, as can be seen in the demonstrations and disagreements that marked the passing of the security bills in 2015. However, we believe that this is a justifiable development, but with the considerable rider that this resumption/move towards ordinary power should also be accompanied by a re-affirmation of Japan's civilian power credentials. These two identities do not contradict each other, and need not be mutually exclusive; in fact, they are complementary, provide necessary balance, and can serve to mutually re-enforce each other. As we learned from Manners and Whitman, it is perfectly normal and acceptable for complex polities to have more than one security identity. In this sense, Inoguchi and Bacon (2008) were mistaken to originally think in terms of a development through a series of different identities, culminating in Japan's exclusive assumption of 'ordinary power'. Similarly, Hidetoshi Nakamura (2015) was mistaken to imagine that we face an either/or choice between Japan as a proactive ordinary power, and Japan as a proactive civilian power; Japan is in fact, and should be, both.

The traditional concept of civilian power demonstrates the effectiveness of non-military means. There has been some cooperation between Japan and the EU/Europe in the wider security field, for example Japan's cooperation with the Netherlands and Germany in the aftermath of the Iraq War, and with the EU in the Horn of Africa. The concept of making such a 'proactive contribution to peace' increases the likelihood of domestic public approval for greater Japanese burden-sharing and enhanced military capabilities. This thereby enhances the sustained commitment of traditional civilian powers to new forms of engagement in all theatres of global insecurity. In this way, a more proactive articulation of the role of civilian power gains greater credibility and public support. In its post-Cold War quest for proactivity, it is possible for Japan to be both an 'ordinary power', fulfilling legitimate and strategically proportionate obligations to its alliance partners in the Asia-Pacific, and a 'civilian power' with global (but of course UN-authorized) reach.

'Arcs of freedom' and 'democratic diamonds': Japan as a post-modern/normative power

In this section we look at some of the temptations to 'value-oriented diplomacy' of positioning Japan as a democracy which shares values with American and European partners through the Japan–US alliance, and relations with the EU and NATO. Japan periodically tries to position itself in this way, and here we suggest that it is diplomatically unwise and perhaps strategically provocative for Japan to place too much emphasis on a differentiation between democracies and non-democracies. Furthermore, although the diplomatic rhetoric about shared values between Japan and its partners is true to some degree, there is a risk that this can be overstated (Bacon and Burton, 2017).

In November 2006, during the first Abe administration, then Foreign Minister Aso gave a speech in which he stated that he wanted to develop a 'value-oriented diplomacy', and that this involved placing emphasis on 'universal values' such as democracy, freedom, human rights, the rule of law, and the market economy. The two major concepts which Japan has used to promote these values are the 'arc of freedom and prosperity' (Aso, 2006), and the 'democratic diamond' (Abe, 2012). Aso (2006) was referring to 'the successfully budding democracies that line the outer rim of the Eurasian continent, forming an arc', and noted that Japan wants to 'design an "arc of freedom and prosperity"', and that it is imperative to 'create just such an arc'.

This arc includes Cambodia, Laos and Vietnam, the three Baltic states (Estonia, Latvia and Lithuania), the four Visegrad states (the Czech Republic, Hungary, Poland and Slovakia), and the four GUAM states (Georgia, the Ukraine, Azerbaijan and Moldova), as well as Turkey and Indonesia. We can therefore see that Aso is linking together two strategic theatres, using the concept of democracy promotion; the Asia-Pacific and the former Soviet spaces in Western Eurasia. In this particular vision of its security identity, Japan is asserting a stake in the democratic transition of countries such as the GUAM states, and providing substantial aid to such countries. Although the intensity and scope of its intrusion is not as significant as that of the EU, Japan is also trying to emphasize democracy and human rights, encourage democracy, and operate on territory in which Russia imagines itself to have a sphere of influence.

Just before assuming power for a second time, in November 2012 Abe wrote an op-ed on 'Asia's Democratic Security Diamond', in which he also repeatedly emphasized Japan's democratic credentials, and singled out China for particular attention, arguing that the South China Sea was in danger of becoming a 'Lake Beijing' (Abe, 2012):

> The ongoing disputes in the East China Sea and the South China Sea mean that Japan's top foreign-policy priority must be to expand the country's strategic horizons. Japan is a mature maritime democracy, and its choice of close partners should reflect that fact. I envisage a strategy whereby Australia, India, Japan, and the US state of Hawaii *form a diamond to safeguard the maritime commons stretching from the Indian Ocean region to the western Pacific*. I am prepared to invest, to the greatest possible extent, Japan's capabilities in this security diamond.

As we have seen, this attraction to value-oriented diplomacy is often also shared by Europeans. It is characteristic of the EU's normative power approach to external relations, but also sometimes to how the Europeans imagine that Japan should engage with the world. For example, a recent project and report on EU–Japan relations by the European Council on Foreign Relations (2015), which was partly sponsored by the Japanese MOFA suggested, in our view unhelpfully, that Japan should try to construct a 'human rights and democracy alliance' in the Asia-Pacific. In this sense, there are striking potential similarities between the EU and Japan with regard to this value-oriented diplomacy. We saw from the discussion of Cooper above that adopting a post-modern approach can lead one to securitize and 'Other' modern and pre-modern states with disastrous results, thereby creating a permissive environment for antagonistic and counter-productive diplomacy, and sometimes even intervention.

The contest over Japan's security identities is not settled

In recent years the Japanese government has produced several important security-related documents. Many of these documents explicitly mention values, and contain elements that could belong to post-modern or normative or civilian conceptions. There is uncertainty and a contest as to which of the identities Japan will ultimately settle on, and this uncertainty has been intensified as a result of the US election result. It is necessary and helpful to think in terms of these the different conceptions of security identity and look for evidence of them in key government documents. It is also necessary to look for differences in relative emphasis and support for these concepts in these key documents. The documents that it is necessary to analyse include at least the following:

- Aso's (2006) 'Arc of Freedom and Prosperity' speech
- Abe's (2012) 'Democratic diamond' op-ed
- The (2013) National Security Strategy
- Abe's (2014) 'Natural partners' speech to NATO
- The (2014) Cabinet decision on 'Seamless security legislation'
- The (2015) Guidelines for Japan-US Defense Cooperation
- The annual MOFA Diplomatic 'Blue Books'
- The annual MOD 'Defense of Japan' White Papers
- The annual Japan–EU Summit Statements

Below, we have identified the type of arguments that are often used in relation to security identity constructs in the key Japanese security documents. Argument one is the most 'post-modern', argument five is the most 'civilian'.

1 Explicit advocacy of some kind of democratic alliance.
2 Self-identification as committed to democracy, human rights and the rule of law.
3 Explicit criticism of the security behaviour of China/Russia/North Korea.
4 Mention of China/Russia/North Korea by name in a security context.
5 More abstract reference to respect for international law, freedom of maritime passage, freedom of overflight, territorial integrity, non-aggression.

Although we have given separate definitions for each of the post-modern/normative/civilian power concepts above, in practice there is some overlap between them, so we can also think in terms of a continuum, ranging from post-modern through normative to civilian power. If items higher up the list are mentioned more, or are mentioned more purposively, then the document in question lends itself more to a more post-modern interpretation, and so on.

Using this preliminary framework, we can see that some of the major speeches or documents offer quite different self-identifications. For example, the Abe 'democratic diamond' piece (2012) is the most 'post-modern'. It mentions and prioritizes democratic alliance, and is fiercely critical of China, and mentions all five elements we identify. The Abe NATO 'natural partners' speech (2014), on the other hand, is the most 'civilian', in that it places most relative emphasis on items 4 and 5. As mentioned, we believe that it is best for Japan to cultivate both ordinary power and civilian power identities, but not to self-identify as post-modern or normative. It is therefore instructive to attempt to decode the various key documents to see where their relative emphases lie. Ultimately, from our perspective it is preferable if all of the key documents develop over time, to contain a series of coordinated and consistent elements that strongly support ordinary and civilian power. At the moment however, the messages from these documents are mixed and inconsistent, sometimes even within one particular document, which is in itself interesting, and reflective of the fact that the contest to establish Japan's prevalent security identity or identities remains far from settled.

We should think of Japanese discussions of 'arcs of freedom' and 'democratic diamonds', and European exhortations to create democratic alliances, as equivalent in nature to Cooper's post-modern EU theory. They entail an explicit and targeted securitization of non-democratic states. We suggest that such strident self-identification is unwise for Japan. We should think of pervasive Japanese attempts at self-identification as democratic, but without quite the same degree of explicit antagonism towards rivals and Others, as equivalent to the mentality behind the promotion of normative power in Europe. This self-identification should also be handled with great care. Going back to the five strategies of 'Othering' offered by Diez and Manners earlier in the discussion, we can see that this second approach, self-identifying as a normative power, involves the second, third and fourth strategies respectively: representing the Other as inferior, as violating universal principles such as democracy and human rights, and representing the Other as different. When this process is too aggressive or antagonistic, we are concerned that liberal, normative 'Othering' can itself be a significant factor contributing to the causes of conflict. Such liberal 'Othering' could have a significant negative impact on future Japanese relations with China.

From our perspective, since Abe came to power for a second time, (and as senior Japanese diplomats are very quick to point out in interviews) references to the arc of freedom and the democratic diamond have largely disappeared from both the public and diplomatic discourses. This is reassuring, and shows that, for the time being at least, many feel that both the repeated emphasis on Japan's own democratic credentials, and the explicit naming and framing of China and latterly Russia as potentially aggressive non-democratic Others is perhaps not the wisest strategic approach.

Furthermore, although the diplomatic rhetoric about shared values between Japan and its partners is true to some degree, there is a risk that this can be over-stated. For example, the Abe administration and its supporters have frequently criticized the Japanese Constitution as having been imposed by the US, and not adequately reflecting Japanese values. Takao Suami (2014) has argued that Euro-peans and Japanese have different understandings of the rule of law and human rights. He claims that Japanese people value some rights, such as the rights of victims of crime rather than perpetrators of crime, more than Europeans do, and are more reluctant to accept the European idea that social and economic rights are important. Paul Bacon (2015) has suggested that in recognition of Japan's resistance to the EU's 'death penalty diplomacy', the EU should adopt a more nuanced and localized approach to human rights promotion in Japan. Tamio Nakamura (2015) argued that it was neither necessary nor appropriate for the EU to insist on signing a Strategic Partnership Agreement with Japan, as well as an FTA. He also argues that the political and human rights terms and conditions of the agreement signed between the EU and South Korea, for example, should not be acceptable to Japan.

Empathy with the Other: internal balance, external reflexivity

Finally, we have to think about Japan's own particular circumstances, and also about the notion of balance and complementarity between the security identities that a country might cultivate at any particular time, and how this might be per-ceived by Others. For example, a senior Japanese editorial writer told Bacon in an interview that it would be a tactical error for Japan to position itself too stri-dently as a champion of human rights and democracy in the region, as it would leave Japan vulnerable to criticism from China, North Korea and also South Korea with regard to historical issues (Interview two, 2015).

Also, we have suggested that post-modern and normative power can often involve aggressive securitization of non-liberal states, confrontational rhetoric and a hubristic and transformational psychological animus. There is an increased risk for Japan that such aggressive self-positioning raises (unfounded) fear in Others regarding revisionism. Not choosing a post-modern or normative power identity helps to avoid this problem. Civilian power is more humble and non-threatening, and complements Japan's other commitment to a modest 'ordinary' defensive realism. As stated above, while it is true that civilian powers also promote universal values, these are universal in a more communitarian or 'West-phalian' sense; uncontroversial values such as respect for territorial integrity, freedom of the seas and freedom of overflight.

The combination of multiple security identities relative to a state's security objectives is important. There is a basic contradiction, and a lack of balance, between Japan's need to present a non-threatening face to the region, and the aggressive 'Othering' entailed in self-identification as a normative or post-modern power. If Japan gives in to the temptation to self-identify in either of these ways, it would be guilty of the same lack of reflexivity and respect for the Other that Europeans have shown in the examples we mentioned earlier, including Afghanistan, Iraq, Libya and Ukraine. It is to be hoped that similarly conflict-inducing mistakes and processes would not also be repeated in the Asia-Pacific in the event of such a development.

The advent of a Trump Presidency makes the stakes even higher, but arguably reinforces this need for Japan to recognize and bolster a complementary combination of ordinary power and civilian power. Japan can reassure the US by improving the robustness of its commitment to ordinary power and developing its self-defence profile, all the while making sure that it minimizes the risk of antagonizing China by adopting a posture more commensurate with self-identification as a civilian power. This combination of security identities is the most appropriate in a region which is likely to become more vulnerable over time to uncertainty and to the insecurity that this brings.

Note

1 Following Inoguchi and Bacon (2008) we prefer to use the term 'ordinary' to avoid confusion between use of the terms 'normal power' and 'normative power'. The term 'ordinary' is considered to be the direct equivalent of 'normal' or 'futsu' for our purposes here.

References

Abe, S. (2012) Asia's Democratic Security Diamond. *Project Syndicate.* 27 December.

Abe, S. (2014) *Japan and NATO as 'Natural Partners' – Speech by Prime Minister Abe.* Prime Minister of Japan and his Cabinet. 6 May 2014. Available from: http://japan. kantei.go.jp/96_abe/statement/201405/nato.html. [Accessed: 23 February 2016].

Armitage, R.L. and Nye, J.S. (2012) *The US-Japan Alliance: Anchoring Stability in Asia,* August. Available from: http://csis.org/files/publication/120810_Armitage_USJapan Alliance_Web.pdf. [Accessed: 11 November 2017].

Aso, T. (2006) *Arc of Freedom and Prosperity: Japan's Expanding Diplomatic Horizons.* Speech at the Japan Institute of International Affairs. 30 November.

Bacon, P. (2015) EU-Japan Relations: Civilian Power and the Domestication/Localization of Human Rights. In Bacon, P., Mayer, H. and Nakamura, H. (eds) *The European Union and Japan: A New Chapter in Civilian Power Cooperation?* New York: Routledge.

Bacon, P. and Burton, J. (2017) NATO-Japan Relations: Projecting Strategic Narratives of 'Natural Partnership' and Cooperative Security. *Asian Security,* pp. 1–13. (DOI: 10.1080/14799855.2017.1361726).

Bacon, P., Mayer, H. and Nakamura, H. (eds). (2015) *The European Union and Japan: A New Chapter in Civilian Power Cooperation?* New York: Routledge.

Berger, T. (1998) *Cultures of Antimilitarism: National Security in Germany and Japan.* Baltimore, MD: Johns Hopkins University Press.

Cooper, R. (2003) *The Breaking of Nations: Order and Chaos in the Twenty-First Century.* London: Atlantic Books.

Diez, T. (2005) Constructing the Self and Changing Others: Reconsidering 'Normative Power Europe'. *Millennium: Journal of International Studies* 33(3), pp. 613–636.

Diez, T. and Manners, I. (2007) Reflecting on Normative Power Europe. In Berenskoetter, F. and Williams, M.J. (eds) *Power in World Politics*, pp. 173–188. New York: Routledge.

Doyle, M. (1983) Kant, Liberal Legacies, and Foreign Affairs, Part 2. *Philosophy and Public Affairs* 12(4, Autumn), pp. 323–353.

Dudden, A. (2015) The Shape of Japan to Come. *New York Times*. 16 January. Available from: www.nytimes.com/2015/01/17/opinion/the-shape-of-japan-to-come.html?_r=0. [Accessed: 11 November 2017].

European Council on Foreign Relations. (2015) *Shaping the Future: Japan in Europe*, Conference Report, December, Berlin.

Freedman, L. (2014) Ukraine and the Art of Crisis Management. *Survival* 56(3, June–July 2014), pp. 7–42.

Funabashi, Y. (1991) Japan and the New World Order. *Foreign Affairs* 70(5), pp. 54–78.

Funabashi, Y. (ed.). (2017) *Galapagos Cool: 11 Programmes to Rediscover Japan*, Toyo Keizai. (In Japanese.)

Hagström, L. (2015) The 'Abnormal' State: Identity, Norm/Exception and Japan. *European Journal of International Relations* 21(1), pp. 122–145.

Hobson, C., Bacon, P. and Cameron, R. (eds). (2014) *Human Security and Natural Disasters*. New York: Routledge.

Hosoya, Y. (2012) The Evolution of the EU-Japan Relationship: Towards a 'Normative Partnership'? *Japan Forum* 24(3 September), pp. 317–337.

Hughes, C.W. (2004) Japan's Re-emergence as a 'Normal' Military Power. *Adelphi Paper*. London: The International Institute for Strategic Studies.

Inoguchi, T. and Bacon, P. (2001) Sovereignties: Westphalian, Liberal, and Anti-utopian. *International Relations of the Asia-Pacific* 1(2), pp. 285–304.

Inoguchi, T. and Bacon, P. (2008) Rethinking Japan as an Ordinary Country. In Ikenberry, G.J. and Moon, C.I. (eds) *The United States and Northeast Asia: Old Issues, New Thinking*. Lanham: Rowman & Littlefield.

Interview one, senior political representative of the Japanese Ministry of Foreign Affairs. (2016) March.

Interview two, editorial writer with a leading Japanese newspaper. (2015) September.

Katzenstein, P. (1998) *Cultural Norms and National Security: Police and Military in Postwar Japan*. Ithaca: Cornell University Press.

Liu, X. (2014) China and Britain Won the War Together. *Daily Telegraph*. 1 January. Available from: www.telegraph.co.uk/comment/10546442/Liu-Xiaoming-China-and-Britain-won-the-war-together.html. [Accessed: 11 November 2017].

Manners, I. (2002) Normative Power Europe: A Contradiction in Terms? *Journal of Common Market Studies* 40(2), pp. 234–258.

Manners, I. and Whitman, R. (2003) The 'Difference Engine': Constructing and Representing the International Identity of the European Union. *Journal of European Public Policy* 10(3), pp. 380–404.

Maull, H.W. (1990) Germany and Japan: The New Civilian Powers. *Foreign Affairs* 69(5), pp. 91–106.

McCurry, J. (2016) China Accuses Japan of Threatening Pacific Peace with Military Law. *Guardian*. 29 March. Available from: www.theguardian.com/world/2016/mar/29/china-accuses-japan-of-threatening-peace-in-pacific-with-new-law [Accessed: 11 November 2017].

MOFA. (2014) *Cabinet Decision on Development of Seamless Legislation to Ensure Japan's Survival and Protect its People*. July.

Nakamura, H. (2013) The Efficiency of European External Action and the Institutional Evolution of EU-Japan Political Relations. In Telò, M. and Ponjaert, F. (eds) *The EU's Foreign Policy: What Kind of Power and Diplomatic Action?*, pp. 189–208. Abingdon: Routledge.

Nakamura, H. (2015) Japan as a 'Proactive Civilian Power'? Domestic Constraints and Competing Priorities. In Bacon, P., Mayer, H. and Nakamura, H. (eds) *The EU and Japan: A New Chapter in Civilian Power Cooperation?* Abingdon: Routledge.

Nakamura, T. (2015) *A Comparative Analysis of the Legal Frameworks of the Canadian and Korean SPA Agreement*. In Japan Society for the Promotion of Science Workshop. Waseda University, 1 September.

Nardin, T. (1983) *Law, Morality, and the Relations of States*. Princeton: Princeton University Press.

Nikkei Asian Review. (2017) Support for Abe Cabinet Hits 54%, Steadily Climbing from Summer Nadir. 3 November. Available from: https://asia.nikkei.com/Politics-Economy/Policy-Politics/Support-for-Abe-cabinet-hits-54-steadily-climbing-from-summer-nadir. [Accessed: 11 November 2017].

Ozawa, I. (1993) *Nihon Kaizo Keikaku*. Tokyo: Kodansha.

Rumelili, B. (2004) Constructing Identity and Relating to Difference: Understanding the EU's Mode of Differentiation. *Review of International Studies* 30(1), pp. 27–47.

Sabathil, G. (2015) Making the Strategic Partnership between Japan and Europe Work. *Asia-Pacific Review* 22(2), pp. 77–81.

Soeya, Y., Tadokoro, M. and Welch, D. (2011) *Japan as a Normal Country? A Nation in Search of its Place in the World*. Toronto: Toronto University Press.

Suami, T. (2014) Rule of Law and Human Rights in the Context of the EU-Japan Relationship: Are Both the EU and Japan Really Sharing the Same Values? In Vanoverbeke, D., Maesschalck, J., Nelken, D. and Parmentier, S. (eds) *The Changing Role of Law in Japan: Empirical Studies in Culture, Society and Policy Making*. Cheltenham: Edward Elgar.

Tokyo Foundation. (2008) *New Security Strategy of Japan: Multilayered and Cooperative Security Strategy*. Available from: www.tokyofoundation.org/en/additional_info/New%20Security%20Strategy%20of%20Japan.pdf. [Accessed: 11 November 2017].

Waever, O. (1998) Insecurity, Security and Asecurity in the West European Non-war Community. In Adler, E. and Barnett, M. (eds) *Security Communities*. Cambridge: Cambridge University Press.

Walker, R.B.J. (1993) *Inside/Outside: International Relations as Political Theory*. Cambridge: Cambridge University Press.

Williams, M. (2007) *Culture and Security: Symbolic Power and the Politics of International Security*. Abingdon: Routledge.

5 Japan and EU defence production cooperation

A strategically important but nascent relationship

Christopher W. Hughes

Introduction: defence production as part of a broader strategic relationship?

Japan and Europe, comprising the European Union (EU) and its individual member states, have clear aspirations for enhanced security and defence cooperation. As many of the chapters in this volume outline, Japan–EU security cooperation is evolving in many aspects, with some substance in anti-piracy activities, post-conflict resolution, and Official Development Assistance (ODA), whilst in other areas finding it slower to gain traction. Amongst the array of potential areas for Japan–EU security cooperation the expectation is that the relationship – as with any serious set of security partners – would also extend to include defence technology collaboration, production and exports, and indeed dialogue and cooperation is now moving into this dimension. Japan has concluded bilateral agreements on joint research, development and production of defence equipment with the United Kingdom (UK), France, and Germany from 2013 onwards, with other bilateral agreements in the pipeline, and more broadly a range of government and private sector actors maintain an interest in interacting with and influencing EU defence procurement and arms export policies (MOFA, 2013, 2015, 2017b).

The question for Japan and the EU is now how far this emerging defence production relationship can develop and serve to reinforce and further broader security ties and international cooperation. As with the other areas of cooperation explored in this volume, the relationship has considerable potential and might follow on from early successes witnessed thus far, but at the same time this area of cooperation also contains considerable obstacles that might hinder its advancement and be reflective of the issues for, and even impede broader Japan–EU security cooperation.

In order to explore the potential development and pitfalls, and broader ramifications, of Japan–EU cooperation in defence production, this chapter proceeds in its analysis in four main sections. The first explores the motivations of Japan, the EU and individual member countries and their respective key governmental and private sector actors to seek new ties in defence production. These motivations encompass broad strategic and security calculations that show some convergence in response to regional and global threats but also for helping to deal with respective alliance relations with the US. They further include more technologically and commercially focussed interests, although these do feed into broader strategic considerations. As this section will point out there is indeed some compatibility and convergence amongst Japan and the EU relations that does provide a degree of dynamism behind this area of cooperation.

The second section moves on to examine actual progress to date for Japan and the EU in identifying priorities and projects for cooperation in defence production. It outlines the state of play of Japan–EU arms transfers, the nature of emerging defence technology development projects, and attempts made on both sides to promote cooperation. As the section points out, Japan and the EU have for sure identified a range of areas with promise for development, and Japan in particular has taken active steps to enhance cooperation with EU states.

The third then assesses the limitations on Japan–EU cooperation in this area. The issues for cooperation that have arisen include a continued degree of strategic dissonance between Japan and EU states over key threat priorities as well as how to prioritise the management of alliance ties with the US. In addition, Japan–EU cooperation is still hampered by more straightforward trade and commercial calculations.

The conclusion section of the chapter draws together the key findings and argues that overall, whilst the relationship is one of considerable potential, the impediments to defence production cooperation are still significant and that ties have a long way to advance before the establishment of a strong and credible relationship that can add full weight to Japan's ties with the EU and individual EU members. Hence, the conclusion identifies the areas that Japan and EU states are likely to concentrate on to attempt to more effectively realise the potential of cooperation. But until there is further progress in these areas, Japan–EU defence production may remain alongside other categories of underdeveloped security ties.

Japan–EU motivations for defence production cooperation

Japan can be thought to share with EU states a similar range of motivations, and of potential mutual advantage, for seeking to advance a relationship in defence production. On the grand strategic front, Japanese policymakers, in line with the Meiji maxim of 'rich nation, strong army' and reflecting the stance of other developed states, have long viewed an indigenous defence production capability as one means for the maintenance of national security autonomy (Samuels, 1994). Japan's post-war immediate demilitarisation and its minimalist defensive stance, reinforced by a range of anti-militaristic principles, necessarily limited the type and quantity of military production, with most particularly the eschewing of producing capabilities that form 'war potential'. In turn, Japan's utilisation of defence production and arms transfers for security ends was limited by the self-imposed 1967 and 1976 bans on the export of arms and military technology.[1] But even as Japan's defence production stance has been relatively constrained compared to other major powers in the post-war era it has remained a key element of Japanese security and international strategy (Hughes, 2017).

Japanese policymakers in the guise of the long-governing Liberal Democratic Party (LDP), main opposition Democratic Party of Japan (DPJ) (until the formation of the Democratic Party in 2016), Japan Ministry of Defense (JMOD), Ministry of Economy and Industry (METI), Ministry of Foreign Affairs (MOFA), and Defence Production Committee (DPC) of the Japan Business Federation (Nippon Keidanren) as the umbrella organisation for a variety of equipment manufacturer associations and individual enterprises – have worked to build an effective indigenous defence production base (*kokusanka*). Japan's defence production model has been characterised by attempts to nurture *kokusanka* in part through the government's direct and indirect subsidisation of the defence industry, but also in large part through attempts to harness together military and civilian technology within predominantly civilian corporations so as to draw technological 'spin-off' from the military sector, and for the smaller military sector to derive 'spin-on' from civilian industry (Hughes, 2011).

Japan has developed a particular industrial defence structure: armaments accounting for less than 1 per cent of total national industrial production; arms production itself occupying, with the exception of aircraft manufacture, small proportions of key industrial sectors such as vehicles, shipping and communications; and the concentration of arms production within a limited number of large civilian corporations with a small percentage of their sales devoted to this sector. Mitsubishi Heavy Industries (MHI), Japan's largest defence contractor, secures up to 20 per cent of all government contracts, but derives only around 10 per cent of its total sales from this activity (Bōei Nenkan Kankōkaihen, 2010, pp. 521–524). Meanwhile, outside MHI and other large contractors, a considerable number of civilian small and medium enterprises (SME) provide components and specialist technologies to the larger systems integrators and are more heavily dependent on defence work.

Japan's nurturing of an indigenous defence production base has attained important successes in the post-war era. The civilian conglomerate-led model has created a very capable defence research and development (R&D) and production base whereby much of the initial cost and technological risk of weapons development is borne by the private sector, and there has been inter-diffusion of civilian and military technologies. Japan has shown that it is able to build advanced armoured vehicles, missiles and maritime destroyers, and succeeded in rebuilding its post-war aircraft defence production. Although it should also be acknowledged that Japan has not managed to build this production base through a policy of complete technological military autarky. Japan has continued inward transfers of foreign technology when deemed necessary, and especially through Foreign Military Sales (FMS) from the US, such as the *Aegis* radar system, as they offer relatively fast and low-risk, if not always low-cost, solutions to Japan Self Defense Forces (JSDF) needs. More preferable still has been licensed production of systems such as the F-4J and F-15J fighters and engines, and P-3C patrol aircraft, to enable the learning and innovation of technologies. Japan has also in the past begun to utilise co-production with the US as in the development of the F-2 fighter, and the first tentative steps towards the transfer of military technologies through exemptions made in the arms export for thirteen different bilateral cooperation projects with the US.

Japanese policymakers in building this model of defence production have envisaged that even in its constrained form it is an important component of security and international strategy. First and most vitally, of course, the maintenance of an indigenous defence production base provides for the JSDF's core deterrent needs calibrated to providing for its 'exclusively defence-oriented' posture; and it provides for a degree of self-sufficiency in defence equipment, typically at rates of 90 per cent or more, and ability to expand procurement in a time of national emergency. Second, and increasingly important, Japan's maintenance of advanced military technologies has always been seen as a way to augment national negotiating leverage in the broader international community, and especially in the context of US–Japan alliance cooperation (Hughes, 2011).

Japan's hedging stance under the so-called 'Yoshida Doctrine' and vis-à-vis the US alliance in the post-war era has been well documented and defence production has formed part of this hedging effort. The ability to procure a high proportion of defence equipment domestically has helped to mitigate overall security dependence on the US. Similarly, Japan's possession of leading-edge technologies has meant that it stands as a potentially attractive partner for technology sharing as seen in the F-2 project and exemptions to the arms export ban in the case of US–Japan alliance cooperation. In these ways, Japanese policymakers have felt that they retain some ability to hedge against dependence on the US *within* the alliance, but also potentially to hedge *outside* the alliance by limiting reliance on the US in defence equipment and even possibly seeking additional partners for cooperation in this area to cushion dependence on the US (Heginbotham and Samuels, 2002).

In the post-Cold War period, Japan's perception of the importance of defence production as an element of grand strategy and creating hedging options has only increased. The waxing and waning of US power has enhanced alliance dilemmas over entrapment and abandonment, and China's rise has further complicated the security situation (Oros, 2017, pp. 160–162). As noted in the other chapters of this volume, this has necessitated that Japan's policymakers look to consolidate where possible the alliance relationship with the US to mitigate alliance dilemmas, but also to consider forging new security ties with other partners that can complement the US–Japan alliance or even form options for lessened dependence on the US.

In the dimension of arms production, Japan's awareness of these shifting alliance trends and the need to create hedging options for its security strategy has been greatly enhanced in recent years. Japanese policymakers have become increasingly aware that the traditional model of defence production is no longer sustainable. The first challenge is that Japan's constrained defence budget since the late 1990s. Despite recent increases under Prime Minister Abe Shinzō, with the JMOD requesting for 2018 the largest increase of 2.5 per cent in the defence budget since 1997, there has long been a declining proportion of the budget available for equipment procurement (from around 23 per cent of the budget in 1988 to around 16 per cent in 2016, with only the first increase in twenty years to 17 per cent in 2017 (Bōeishō, 2017, p. 3; Asagumo Shimbunsha, 2015, p. 285; 2017, p. 287). These trends have meant limited resources for indigenous development of weapons technologies.

Japanese administrations have looked to address these problems by supporting new *kokusanka* projects such as the P-1 patrol aircraft, C-1 transport aircraft and Advanced Technology Demonstration-X (ATD-X/F-3), stealth fighter prototype. Nevertheless, Japan's procurement of frontline platforms of main-battle tanks, destroyers and fighter aircraft has continued to decline. Japan is further attempting to stretch the defence budget with more efficient systems and competitive tenders for procurement domestically and internationally, following a series of corruption scandals in the mid-1990s, and in 2015 established an Acquisition, Technology and Logistics Agency (ATLA) (*Bōei Sōbichō*) in an attempt to integrate and manage procurement more efficiently (Kankōkai Henshūbu, 2016, pp. 8–43; Tamura, 2016; Sugai, 2016, pp. 13–20). Defence producers have also been encouraged to consolidate in order to produce economies of scale, but this has proved difficult given that most manufacturers are civilian production-oriented, and that the dual-use spin-on spin-off model cannot easily separate civilian from military production facilities, and thus have no incentive to rationalise their business to suit defence production prerogatives. The result is that the shake-out in the Japanese defence industry has taken the form of producers simply exiting the sector and switching to concentrate on more profitable civilian products. The proportion of defence equipment procured domestically has now fallen to 76 per cent by 2015 (Kankōkai Henshūbu, 2017, p. 454).

The second challenge is that Japan's techno-nationalist policies risk leaving its defence industry behind in the development of internationally competitive technologies. Japan's emphasis on the indigenisation of technologies has run into the obstacle of the increasing reluctance of the US and other states to provide FMS or licensed production of advanced weapons systems. Japanese industry estimates that the domestic content under licensed production of US systems has progressively decreased, from 85 per cent of the F-104, to 90 per cent of the F-4EJ, and 70 per cent of the F-15J, with a high black-boxed content for the F-15J, and 60 per cent for the F-2 (Chinworth, 1992, p. 127, p. 137). Japan was frustrated by the US's refusal to transfer the full or even a 'dumbed-down' less capable version of the F-22 to its ally despite intense lobbying (Sunohara, 2012, pp. 195–248). Japan's highly limited international cooperation to date, especially in terms of co-development and co-production, due to its arms export ban, have thus raised concerns of a 'Galapagos effect' as Japan is isolated from the evolution of international defence production (Kiyotani, 2010, pp. 185–188). Hence, as other states forge ahead with consolidation of their defence companies domestically and internationally, and initiating new multilateral weapons platforms to share technologies and costs through economies of scale, Japan has risked being left as a bystander and surpassed technologically, or over-dependent on its US ally (Brooks, 2005, pp. 235–237; Sato, 2015, pp. 5–6).

In this increasingly fluid strategic and technological environment, Japan has sought to modify its defence production model and international engagement policies – seeking to preserve an indigenous production base but through utilising increasing international collaboration to buttress the technological base and forge new security ties with other states. Japan's primary impulse has still been to strengthen defence production ties with the US as in the joint development and production of the SM-3 Block II-A interceptor missile for Ballistic Missile Defence (BMD) and the procurement the F-35A fighter, with some off-the-shelf procurement but also Final Assembly and Checkout (FACO) and development of elements of the fighter's engine parts, radar, and electro-optical distributed aperture systems (EODAS). However, at the same time, Japan has begun to explore additional partners for joint development, production and export of weapons technologies.

The potentially most significant of Japan's reappraisal of its options, and demonstration of its intent to seek new partners in defence production, has been the lifting since April 2014 of the ban on the exports of weapons technology in favour of the 'Three Principles on Transfer of Defence Equipment and Technology' (MOFA, 2014). The new principles somewhat return to the original 1967 original restrictions by preventing export only to states considered to impede international peace and security, such as those transgressing international treaties or under UN sanctions, but would allow export to those states contributing to international peace or Japan's security such as the US, NATO countries, and those engaged in UN peacekeeping operations (PKO), and that could prove the controls in place to prevent re-export to third countries (*Asahi Shimbun*, 2014a, 2014b). The 2013 National Security Strategy (NSS) also makes it clear that defence equipment and technology cooperation should become 'mainstream' in Japan's security activities and part of the 'proactive contribution to peace' (National Security Council, 2013). In turn, as Japan's vista for the international collaboration in arms production has begun to open up, this has meant a new space for Japan–EU cooperation in this area.

The EU in Japan's strategic calculations over defence production

Japan's desire to preserve its defence production base through enhanced international collaboration in order to preserve a degree of security autonomy, enhance its international leverage, and simultaneously strengthen ties with the US but also keep open its hedging options, should be seen to be a strategy compatible also with that of the EU and its individual states.

The EU's individual states have long similarly held to the belief that a minimum level of indigenous defence production capabilities should be maintained even in the midst of the global restructuring of the arms industry. For example, the UK's Defence Industrial Strategy formulated in 2005 sought to preserve a sovereign capability for the production of key armaments systems, even whilst acknowledging that not all systems could be procured domestically and the UK needed to preserve an arms market characterised by openness and international collaboration (Ministry of Defence, 2005). The UK has argued, very much in a similar vein to Japan, that retaining and nurturing key indigenous technologies provides the benefits of 'strategic assurance' in areas that are essential to the essential safeguarding of the state, 'defence capability' to maintain equipment performance, and 'strategic influence' militarily and diplomatically.

At the level of the EU itself, there is a similar impulse to promote domestic procurement for security reasons but also acknowledge the importance of international collaboration. The EU has sought to enhance security of supply (SoS) of defence equipment to enhance the autonomy of the region, avoid over-duplication of weapons systems, counter dependence on the US and Russia for supply of systems, and boost the political presence of the EU and the Common Foreign and Security Policy (CFSP) (IISS, 2008, pp. 99–196). The aim of the European Defence Agency's (EDA) European Defence Technological and Industrial Base (EDTIB) policy has been to encourage its major national defence producers to lessen emphasis on their own autonomy and integrate their defence industrial bases to ensure improved common security of supply (Directorate-General for External Policies Policy Department, 2013). The EU has further sought to promote a more integrated market for defence equipment across the community through the 2006 voluntary code of conduct for defence procurement and the 2011 Defence and Security Procurement Directive (Edwards, 2011).

Japan is thus presented in the EU with some considerable potential for international collaboration. The EU and its states are safe partners to collaborate with given their standing as US allies and thus pose no risk of Japan being seen to gravitate away from the US–Japan alliance. At the same time, though, the EU states offer an alternative to exclusive reliance on the US for international collaboration; and likewise, the EU states are also looking for collaborations with each other but also other technologically advanced states that may lessen dependence on the US. The EU furthermore presents a potential new set of commercial collaborations on the development of key technologies and even longer-term export markets for Japanese producers. The converse is also true for EU producers exploring the potential of the Japanese market.

Finally, for Japan attempts to enhance collaboration with the EU on defence production may be beneficial not just in regard to leverage vis-à-vis the US, but also increasingly vis-à-vis China. Japanese policymakers have long been concerned that the EU might look to lift its embargo on the exports of military technology to China imposed after the Tiananmen Square incident in 1989. Japan has regularly and actively lobbied against the lifting of the embargo as potentially destabilising to the balance of power in the Asia-Pacific (MOFA, 2005, 2010; *The Daily Telegraph*, 2010).

How significant the EU arms embargo is in practice is debatable given that it originates from an EU declaration that is non-binding on its members, does not specify the actual restrictions and leaves interpretation and enforcement of the embargo to individual members states' own national arms export policies.

In fact, France has continued to be a significant exporter of military equipment to China and other EU states export dual-use technology. All the same, Japan clearly views the embargo as an important political commitment by the EU to constraining Chinese behaviour that has helped to limit arms exports. Hence, the consideration of Japan's policymakers appears to be that by establishing collaboration with EU arms producers and establishing a presence in EU security strategy and defence procurement that they may be able to exert added influence on the maintenance of the arms embargo against China (Weitz, 2012).

Japan–EU defence production cooperation to date

Following up on the Japan–UK Defence Equipment Cooperation Framework in 2013, the two sides indicated in July 2014 the intention to work on the joint development of the *Meteor* air-to-air missile. The project is believed to involve the integration of Japanese seeker technologies into MBDA's *Meteor* missile to improve their accuracy and performance, with the eventual application of the missile to the F-35 (Allison, 2017). The UK and Japan are also thought to be keen to discuss cooperation in Nuclear, Biological and Chemical (NBC) defence technology, mine detection, helicopters, tanks and artillery. Japan was also rumoured to have attempted to pitch sales of the P-1 to the UK, which could have been its first transfer of an entire military platform, although the UK in 2015 chose instead to procure the Boeing P-8 *Poseidon* maritime patrol aircraft (*Japan Times*, 2014). In March 2017, the JMOD announced that it would conduct a joint study with the UK Ministry of Defence (MOD) on a future combat fighter system (Bōei Sōbichō, 2017). The visit of Prime Minister Theresa May to Japan in August 2017 affirmed that Japan and the UK would extend cooperation in dual-use defence items and technologies (MOFA, 2017c).

Japan has been exploring similar defence and military technology cooperation with France since 2012, and there are reports of plans for cooperation on unmanned submarine technology (Bōeishōhen, 2015, p. 268). Japan's 2017 agreement with Germany is expected to focus on the exchange of technologies for armoured vehicles – Japan having already developed its Type-90 tank barrels with assistance from Germany, and looking to utilise German engine technologies for its troop transport armoured vehicles, and Germany to benefit from the high mobility technologies of Japan (*Asahi Shimbun*, 2017).

Japan has recently signed a defence technology sharing agreement with Italy in May 2017, which is thought to concentrate on naval capabilities in naval guns, radar and patrol aircraft (MOFA, 2017a). The JMOD is further believed to be interested in a similar agreement with Sweden, revolving around cooperation on submarine technologies and Sweden's advanced air-independent propulsions systems (*Nikkei Asian Review*, 2017).

Problems and opportunities for Japan–EU defence production cooperation

Japan has thus succeeded in proliferating an array of emergent defence technology exchange and development agreements with some considerable potential
and substance. Nevertheless, this relationship is clearly in its very early days,
with arguably UK ties the most mature, and still much road to travel before the
potential can be fulfilled. There are a number of obstacles that are clearly now
and, in the future, going to hinder the development of the relationship that all
sides will need to consider.

The first consideration is that Japan, the EU and individual EU states, despite
sharing a similar outlook on security, the desire to preserve autonomy, and awareness of the need to hedge against dependence on the US and other powers, are as
yet far from fully convergent in their principal strategic orientations. On the Japanese side, the fact remains that the US–Japan alliance continues to be the chief
preoccupation of security efforts and international efforts for defence production
collaboration. Japan's largest and currently realised collaborative defence production project in political, technological and budgetary terms is BMD. The project
entails not only the joint development of components of the SM-3 BLK-IIA interceptor missile, but in due course the likely establishment of joint production facilities. Japan's participation in the F-35 project only promises to further reinforce
alliance bonds. For even if Japan has managed to negotiate a degree of build on
the F-35 through FACO and some elements of joint development, the majority of
technology remains black-boxed and Japan remains dependent on its alliance
partner for the importing of the most advanced technology. In addition, Japan's
necessary participation in the F-35 ALGS Autonomic Logistics Global Sustain-
ment (ALGS) system (Bōeishōhen, 2015, pp. 266–267) integrates its technological capabilities into a US-organised network of allies and strategic partners, all
reinforcing broader US strategic dominance. Japan might seek to mitigate dependence on the US through development of the F-3, but given its budgetary pressures
and the lack of feasibility in going it alone at this stage in stealth fighter development, this may only represent an attempt to have some technological leverage on
the US within the alliance but surely not a ready alternative.

Hence, despite Japan indicating that it wishes to seek new partners in defence
production, the EU states are aware that they will always play second fiddle to
the US, thereby limiting the scope for cooperation. An insight into the importance of alliance ties in curtailing Japan's options was provided by BAE Systems'
attempt to purvey the Typhoon/Eurofighter to Japan as the replacement for the
F-2. Although the Eurofighter was arguably an excellent fit for Japan's specified
needs of an air interceptor, at relatively lower cost, and with a high proportion of
domestic build and access to technology, in the end Japan plumped for the F-35
in part largely driven by US alliance pressures and the need to procure an aircraft that strengthened bilateral cooperation.

Meanwhile on the EU side, Japan may also find a lack of strategic coherence
or convergence that complicates the relationship. In spite of the efforts of the

EDA and EDTIB to corral individual states and their national defence producers into a more collective production and procurement, the tendency has still been for individual national security and commercial interests to take priority over collective interests. The result has been that many European defence producers whilst entering into tie-ups and consolidation have also continued to compete vigorously with each other. For Japan this might be advantageous to allow for various options for cooperation but also makes for a complex field for action, a limited integrated market for defence equipment, and difficulty to establish a broader security relationship with the EU. In turn, the limited collective unity of European states and defence producers means that this may make it harder to hold the line on the arms embargo to China, especially as there is an eagerness to develop a full strategic relationship with China including arms exports which may help to exert some leverage on its security behaviour. This is a difficulty for Japan that might only be compounded by Brexit, and the loss of the UK voice in the EU stance towards China which has generally been supportive of maintaining the overarching embargo.

Japanese defence production possibilities with EU states are further constrained currently by a lack of large-scale platforms for major collaborative projects. Japan's decision not to procure the *Eurofighter* deprived the UK and other European producers involved in the project of a major opportunity to deepen their defence relationship on the type of scale that the US and Japan are prepared to engage in with regard to the F-35 and BMD. The consequence is that Japan and European collaborators at this stage are largely limited to small-scale projects and key technologies. These can still deliver much but necessarily constrain the potential for cooperation. The technology exchange agreements will at the very least provide familiarity between Japan and its partners to extend their relationship, and the Japan–UK fighter project mooted, indicates the ambition for platform development. All the same, short of platform development, Japan–EU defence production can only progress in niche and slow steps.

Finally, Japan ties with Europe in defence production and exports are severely limited by quite straightforward commercial obstacles. Japan's policymakers and defence contractors are still comparative novices at dealing with, and often lack the motivation, to pursue effective international collaborations. The Keidanren and defence manufacturers, whilst in favour of enhanced international engagement, still appear to cling to the argument that the only way to really preserve Japan's indigenous production base is for the government to increase domestic defence spending, and are concerned that international collaboration spells simply more competition and market-opening that could jeopardise domestic producers (Keidanren, 2015; *Asahi Shimbun*, 2014c). Defence producers appear keenly aware that they lack experience of international bidding processes, even basic language skills for purveying their products, and argue that the Japanese government if it wishes to encourage international transfers for strategic reasons should provide a system of FMS, offsets and export subsidies (Keidanren, 2015, p. 3; Jo, 2016). The failure of Japan's attempt to sell *Sōryū*-class attack submarines to Australia in 2016 illustrated all these failings and appear to have heavily deterred many major Japanese defence producers from venturing into international markets. Finally, many defence producers continue to worry about the reputational costs domestically of arms exports and are simply not very motivated to follow government international strategies, still preferring more lucrative and lower-risk civilian markets (*Asahi Shimbun*, 2016).

From the perspective of EU defence producers, it is also the case that they view Japan quite simply in many cases as a difficult partner to deal with and a not entirely welcome international competitor. The European Business Council in Japan has expressed frustration that the Japanese defence market remains heavily protectionist and the JMOD subservient to the US on imports of equipment. Kawasaki Heavy Industries and Airbus Helicopters were irked by the JMOD's decision to award the order for the replacement of UH-X helicopters with a claimed 'older-generation US helicopter', and the JMOD's seeming preference from the off for the US tanker aircraft which meant that Airbus Industries chose not to tender its A-330 fearing defeat for the bid from the start (European Business Council in Japan, 2015).

Japan's sudden emergence as a competitor in international arms trade has further highlighted that there is no inherent status for Japanese and European firms as collaborators. MHI and Kawasaki Shipbuilding Corporation found themselves in fierce competition with Germany's ThyssenKrupp Marine Systems and France's DCNS, and, despite heavy political support from the Abe government as part of its attempts to strengthen Japan–Australia security ties, eventually losing out to the latter. The Australian competition thus demonstrated that Japan and European producers may readily become rivals and how this can derail broader Japanese international strategies.

Conclusion: Japan and Europe defence production next steps

As noted earlier, Japan's cooperation with the EU and individual EU states is clearly at an early stage, and teething problems are expected as the relationship develops. Japan's defence production ties with its US ally of over sixty years can be testy enough as demonstrated by the F-2, F-22, F-35A and BMD examples, so moving towards a similar level of ties with the EU would expect to encounter similar barriers to immediate progress.

The key ultimately to improved defence production will be greater strategic convergence on issues of international security cooperation. Japan's expansion of influence with Europe on defence production may assist this, but ultimately there needs to be sufficient high-level political will to prioritise and substantiate security ties which create the avenues for deeper defence-industrial linkages. This will is emerging on the bilateral level and may be furthered by the renewed Japan–EU Strategic Partnership Agreement (SPA). Although, of course, problems remain to the broader relationship as the EU's own external unity is challenged by Brexit and other issues outlined in this volume.

In turn, Japan and the EU clearly need to get right the commercial cooperation aspect of defence production. Japan will need to accept that seeking to internationalise much of its defence industry will also imply opening up its domestic markets to expanded European imports. Japan's own market reforms will need to be mirrored by the EU's own in pushing forward pan-European defence procurement. Key to this effort will be the Japan–EU Economic Partnership Agreement (EPA) but as far as can be seen at present it does not cover defence equipment. Hence, more work and expansion will be required on the SPA and EPA to further Japan's cooperation with Europe in this area. The conclusion is thus that at present defence production sits more in the 'work in progress' aspects of security cooperation with far more potential to be realised, although the potential is perhaps very substantial indeed.

Note

1 In 1967, Prime Minister Satoō Eisaku's administration first enunciated restrictions on arms exports to communist states, countries under UN sanctions, and parties to international disputes. In 1976, Prime Minister Miki Takeo's administration ordered restraint in the case of all states, and prohibited the export of weapon-related technology.

References

Allison, G. (2017) Details of Joint Missile Project with Japan Emerge. *UK Defence Journal*. 15 January. Available from: https://ukdefencejournal.org.uk/details-of-joint-missile-project-with-japan-emerge/.

Asagumo Shimbunsha. (2015) *Bōei Handobukku 2015*. Tokyo: Asagumo Shimbunsha.

Asagumo Shimbunsha. (2017) *Bōei Handobukku 2017*. Tokyo: Asagumo Shimbunsha.

Asahi Shimbun. (2014a) Buki yushutsu shingensoku o shogiron. 13 March, p. 3.

Asahi Shimbun. (2014b) Buki yushutsu 'shinsangensoku' o kakugi kettei, gensoku kinshi o motomeru. 1 April. Available from: http://digital.asahi.com/articles/ASG41033ZG 30UTFK00T.html.

Asahi Shimbun. (2014c) Kokunai 13sha, buki mihon ichi ni: yushutsu sangensoku kanwa shinchō ni shōki narau. 17 June, p. 4.

Asahi Shimbun. (2016) Buki yushutsu ōte kigyō shirigomi kinyu kanwa 2nen seifu to ondansa. 1 May, p. 4.

Asahi Shimbun. (2017) Japan Quietly Inks Deal with Germany on Defense Sharing. *Asahi Shimbun*. 19 July. Available from: www.asahi.com/ajw/articles/AJ2017071 90028.html.

Bōei Nenkan Kankōkaihen. (2010). *Bōei Nenkan 2010*. Tokyo: DMC.

Bōeishō. (2017). Waga Kuni no bōei to yosan: Heisei 30nendo gaisan yōkyū no gaiyō. Available from: www.mod.go.jp/j/yosan/2017/gaisan.pdf.

Bōeishōhen. (2015) *Bōei Hakusho 2015*. Tokyo: Zaimushō Insatsukyoku.

Bōei Sōbichō. (2017) Shōrai Sentōki ni okeru Eikoku to no kyōryoku no kanōsei ni kakawaru Niichiei kyōdō sutadei ni kansuru torikime no teiketsu ni tsuite. 16 March. Available from: www.mod.go.jp/atla/pinup/pinup290316.pdf.

Brooks, S.G. (2005) *Producing Security: Multinational Corporations, Globalization, and the Changing Calculus of Conflict*. Princeton, NJ: Princeton University Press.

Chinworth, M.W. (1992) *Inside Japan's Defense: Technology, Economics and Strategy*. New York: Brassey's.

Directorate-General for External Policies Policy Department. (2013) *The Development of a European Defence Technological and Industrial Base (EDTIB)*. June. Available from: www.europarl.europa.eu/RegData/etudes/etudes/join/2013/433838/EXPO-SEDE_ET%282013%29433838_EN.pdf, pp. 8–12.

Edwards, J. (2011) The EU Defence and Security Procurement Directive: A Step Towards Affordability? *International Security Programme Paper*. 2011/05. August. Available from: www.chathamhouse.org/sites/files/chathamhouse/0811pp_edwards.pdf.

European Business Council in Japan. (2015) *Golden Opportunity: The EBC Report on the Japanese Business Environment 2015*. Tokyo. Available from: www.ebc-jp.com/images/stories/2015_EBC_White_Paper_E.pdf.

Heginbotham, E. and Samuels, R.J. (2002) Japan's Dual Hedge. *Foreign Affairs* 81(5), pp. 110–121.

Hughes, C.W. (2011) The Slow Death of Japanese Techno-nationalism? Emerging Comparative Lessons for China's Defence Production. *The Journal of Strategic Studies* 34(3), pp. 51–479.

Hughes, C.W. (2017) Japan's Emerging Arms Transfer Strategy: Diversifying to Recentre on the US-Japan Alliance. *The Pacific Review*. Forthcoming.

IISS. (2008) *European Military Capabilities: Building Armed Forces for Modern Operations*. London: IISS.

Japan Times. (2014) Japan Wants UK to Buy Sub-hunter Jet. 8 January. Available from: www.japantimes.co.jp/news/2015/01/08/national/japan-wants-u-k-buy-sub-hunter-jet/#.VK7BQRaqzFI.

Jo, B.Y. (2016) Japan Inc.'s Remilitairization? A Firm-centric Analysis of Mitsubishi Heavy Industries and Japan's Defense Industry in the New TPAE Regime. *International Relations of Asia-Pacific* 16(1), pp. 137–166.

Kankōkai Henshūbu. (2016) *Bōei Nenkan 2016*. Tokyo: Kankōkai Henshūbu.

Kankōkai Henshūbu. (2017) *Bōei Nenkan 2017*. Tokyo: Kankōkai Henshūbu.

Keidanren. (2015) Proposal for Execution of Defense Industry Policy. 15 September. Available from: www.keidanren.or.jp/en/policy/2015/080_proposal.pdf.

Kiyotani, S. (2010) *Bōei Hatan: Garapagosuka Suru Jieitai Sōbi*. Tokyo: Chūō Shinsho Rakure.

Ministry of Defence. (2005) *Defence Industrial Strategy*. December. Available from: www.gov.uk/government/uploads/system/uploads/attachment_data/file/272203/6697.pdf, pp. 6–7.

MOFA. (2005) 14th Japan-EU Summit, Joint Press Statement. 14 May. Available from: www.mofa.go.jp/region/europe/eu/summit/joint0505.pdf.

MOFA. (2010) 19th Japan-EU Summit, Joint Statement. 28 April. Available from: www.mofa.go.jp/region/europe/eu/summit/joint1004.html.

MOFA. (2013) Agreement Between the Government of Japan and the Government of the United Kingdom of Great Britain and Northern Ireland Concerning the Transfer of Arms and Military Technologies Necessary to Implement Joint Research, Development and Production of Defense Equipment and Other Related Items. 4 July 2013. Available from: www.mofa.go.jp/mofaj/files/000016357.pdf.

MOFA. (2014) The Three Principles on Transfer or Defense Equipment and Technology. 1 April. Available from: www.mofa.go.jp/press/release/press22e_000010.html.

MOFA. (2015) *Bōei Sōbihin oyobi Gijutsu no Iten ni kansuru Nipponkoku Seifu to Furansu Kyōwakoku Seifu to no aida Kyōteo no Shomei*. 17 March 2015. Available from: www.mofa.go.jp/mofaj/erp/we/fr/page22_001880.html.

MOFA. (2017a) Agreement between the Government of Japan and the Government of the Italian Republic Concerning the Transfer of Defence Equipment and Technology. 22 May. Available from: www.mofa.go.jp/mofaj/files/000262376.pdf.

MOFA. (2017b). Agreement Between the Government of Japan and the Government of the Federal Republic of Germany Concerning the Transfer of Defense Equipment and Technology. 17 July. Available from: www.mofa.go.jp/mofaj/files/000273509.pdf.

MOFA. (2017c) Japan-UK Joint Declaration on Security Cooperation. 31 August. Available from: www.mofa.go.jp/mofaj/files/000285569.pdf.

National Security Council. (2013) *National Security Strategy*. 17 December. Available from: www.cas.go.jp/jp/siryou/131217anzenhoshou/nss-e.pdf.

Nikkei Asian Review. (2017) Japan Bolsters Defense-technology Cooperation with Europe. 11 May. Available from: https://asia.nikkei.com/Politics-Economy/International-Relations/Japan-bolsters-defense-technology-cooperation-with-Europe.

Oros, A.L. (2017) *Japan's Security Renaissance: New Policies and Politics for the Twenty-First Century*. New York: Columbia University Press.

Samuels, R.J. (1994) *Rich Nation, Strong Army: National Security and the Technological Transformation of Japan*. Ithaca, NY: Cornell University Press.

Sato, H. (2015) Japan's Arms Export and Defense Production Policy. *CSIS Strategic Japan Working Papers*. Available from: http://csis.org/files/publication/150331_Sato_JapanArmsExport.pdf: 1–13.

Sugai, H. (2016) *Japan's Future Defence Equipment Policy*, Washington D.C., Brookings Institution. Available from: www.brookings.edu/wp-content/uploads/2016/10/201610_japan_future_defense_hiroyuki_sugai.pdf.

Sunohara, T. (2012) *Rei no Idenshi: Nijūisseki 'Nihon no Maru Sentōki' to Nihon no Bōei*. Tokyo: Shinchō Bunko.

Tamura, S. (2016) *Bōei Sōbicho to Sōbi Seisaku no Kaisetsu*. Tokyo: Naigai Shuppan.

The Daily Telegraph. (2010) Japan Warns West Against Lifting China Arms Embargo. 18 November. Available from: www.telegraph.co.uk/news/worldnews/asia/china/8144383/Japans-warns-West-against-lifting-China-arms-embargo.html.

Weitz, R. (2012) EU Should Keep China Arms Embargo. *The Diplomat*. 18 April. Available from: http://thediplomat.com/2012/04/eu-should-keep-china-arms-embargo/.

Part II

Political economy, development, and normative issues

6 EU–Japan relations in the age of competitive economic governance in Asia

Maaike Okano-Heijmans and Takashi Terada

Introduction

As the second and fourth biggest economies in the world, the EU and Japan share a profound interest in maintaining the open, rules-based system of global economic and financial governance that has been developed since 1945. While the US has generally been the staunchest defender of the status quo in this so-called Bretton Woods system, China is undoubtedly its key challenger – even if it does not attempt to overthrow the system, from which it still has much to gain. The EU and Japan are more mixed in their approaches, although by no means aligned on their preferred outcomes or the ways to get there. In recent years, however, the EU and Japan have reshaped their bilateral relationship also to better fulfil shared objectives in the realm of global economic governance. Long based on trade and investment, EU–Japan relations now include political, security and social dimensions as well. In addition, cooperation has taken up normative elements, with explicit references to shared commitment to fundamental values like democracy, human rights and the rule of law (Hosoya, 2012). Real cooperation between the EU and Japan has been scant, however, symbolism – indicating the status of the EU and Japan in international relations – is the driving force behind EU–Japan summits (Morii, 2015). Stated intentions have often not been translated into joint policy action. The agreement in principle on the EU–Japan Economic Partnership Agreement (EPA), symbolically signed on the eve of the G20-meeting in Hamburg in July 2017, signals political willingness to move on this front.

Even if explicit reference to China (or the United States, for that matter) is unusual in bilateral interactions between the EU and Japan, there can be little doubt that China's efforts to reshape global economic governance are having a profound effect on both economic giants. Uncertainties about the post-Obama era, in which Donald Trump leads the United States with a strong 'America-first' policy, add to concerns about what the system will look like. Albeit in diverging ways, the EU and Japan are also affected by Chinese attempts of further reform in existing institutions – notably the World Bank, the International Monetary Fund (IMF), the World Trade Organization (WTO) and the Asian Development Bank (ADB). In addition, both are searching for proper responses to Chinese initiatives to create new parallel institutions of global economic and financial governance – especially the Asian Infrastructure Investment Bank (AIIB), but also the New Development Bank (NDB) and the Contingent Reserve Arrangement (CRA) – and to establish new cooperative networks – notably, via China's Belt and Road Initiative (BRI, also referred to as One Belt One Road (OBOR) and New Silk Road) and through trade diplomacy (the negotiation of regional and bilateral economic agreements).

Both the EU – and its Member States[1] – and Japan play an important role in each of the aforementioned levels of Beijing's global economic governance action, as well as in Washington's attempts to (re)shape global economic governance. Their indirect power of influence suggests that cooperative efforts to steer either of the two major powers in a certain direction could have a more substantial impact – at least in theory. This is important, as China's activism is certainly not about to diminish, and the EU and Japan may expect, in the coming years, to be increasingly invited by Beijing to join other institutions or informal frameworks. At the same time, Washington may pressure them to resist such invitations, as it did with the AIIB, and Chinese calls for reform of existing institutions.

The enthusiasm with which European and other developed countries decided to join the Bank in March 2015 surprised many – not only the United States and Japan, which decided to stay out, but also Beijing itself. Uncertainty about the standards of the AIIB was one important reason why Washington put pressure on European capitals to reject the opportunity to join the AIIB as prospective founding members. However, several European countries believed that exerting pressure on standards would be more effective from within, rather than from the outside, and discussions in Brussels centred around how to have most influence on the AIIB's standards and procedures.[2]

Given this context, this chapter explores recent policies of the EU and Japan in the field of economic governance in Asia. In addition, it asks to what extent the EU and Japan have set out to coordinate their foreign economic policies to support their respective and shared strategic and geo-economic interests in the context of competitive economic governance in East Asia, and with what results so far. In doing so, it seeks so unveil the perceived and potential added value of increased EU–Japan cooperation. As negotiations on the Economic Partnership Agreement (EPA) and the EU–Japan Strategic Partnership Agreement (SPA) drew to a close in 2017, the EU and Japan now have an opportunity to strengthen their partnership also for this purpose. Will they live up to this potential? Or do their divergent approaches to managing the rise of China and the protectionist course of the new US Administration distract from the greater benefits of cooperation and from their shared interest in a similar preferred outcome? Answers to these questions require, first of all, a better understanding of the key initiatives in the field of global economic governance; the perceived key interests on the European and Japanese sides; and of how these converge or diverge with Chinese and US proposals and (in)activities, respectively. The following section starts out by establishing this broader context.

Competitive economic governance in Asia

The great power competitions between China and the US – stretching to regional security, trade and financial spheres – and the strengthened efforts of past US Administrations to garner support from like-minded countries as a response to China's ascendance, have profoundly shaped developments in multilateral governance in East Asia. Japan under Prime Minister Shinzo Abe, since 2012, has largely taken a zero-sum style approach – resisting Chinese moves and showing itself to be a loyal US-ally. For their part, Europeans have generally been welcoming of a greater role for China in the global economy and in global (economic) governance (Okano-Heijmans and Lanting, 2015). More than other established powers – Japan and the United States in particular – European actors have been and want to continue to be positive engagers of China, in principle.

Chinese initiatives for development and financing

The upsurge in new economic regionalism in Asia and the Pacific, as evident in the Trans-Pacific Partnership (TPP), the AIIB, and BRI, conceivably constitutes a major toolkit in US and Chinese struggles to form a new regional economic order in Asia. Policies on the part of the EU and Japan towards these initiatives are telling of their divergent approaches. Ever since newly appointed President Trump withdrew the US from the TPP in January 2017, on his first working day in office, the Japanese government is urging Washington to rethink its opposition to the agreement – which excludes China. By contrast, Tokyo has not committed to the AIIB or engaged much on the BRI despite persistent requests by China for its participation. With an estimated spending figure of US$1.3 trillion and covering 68 countries, the BRI has become a pivotal component of the Chinese version of the 'rebalance Asia' strategy. The AIIB, capitalized with US$100 billion, exemplifies China's success in multilateralizing and institutionalizing its effort, at least in part.

Japan's unaccommodating stance is illustrative of its increasingly assertive balancing behaviour with the United States vis-à-vis China amidst the ongoing Sino–US power struggle. Japanese concerns are based on a view that China pursues to further (development) rules of its own preference through building an institution from scratch – where it can be in the driver's seat – rather than merely relying on the existing institutions, which it seeks to reform. Such concerns are not unheard in Europe, as illustrated by the characterization of an EU-diplomat of Chinese foreign policy under Xi's rule as: (1) bilateralism, as evident in its emphasis on 'partnerships' rather than more multilateral alliance structures; (2) multilateralism 'when it suits', meaning Beijing's willingness to rely on multilateral initiatives only when it is able to initiate and therefore control the process, as embodied by the growing role played by the AIIB; and (3) *fait accompli*, meaning that China tends to present other countries with 'ready-for implementation' initiatives, without providing preliminary information or involving them in the earlier stages of the decision-making process (Parton, 2016).

This understanding of China's diplomacy today serves as a reminder that, even if the AIIB is a welcome multilateral effort on the part of China, the Bank is relatively small in scope compared with other instruments held by Beijing. Of the so-called Chinese policy-banks – such as the China Development Bank (CDB) and the Export-Import Bank of China – the CDB alone held US$95 billion in base capital and over $1 trillion in assets in 2016, compared to less than $600 billion in assets of the entire World Bank Group. More than European countries, Japan understands that Beijing's activism in the field of global economic governance should be considered in its full scope and proper context. This also means avoiding the risk of being preoccupied with its multilateral elements alone.

While sharing key elements of Japan's concerns about Chinese practices in the field of development cooperation, most European governments judge that they stand a greater chance of steering Chinese action in their preferred direction by engaging with China rather than by isolating it. This helps to explain why 14 EU Member States (MS) became founding members of the AIIB, with more waiting to join already in 2017. Even if most policymakers and observers in Europe today admit to the 2015-response being faulty, lagging and lacking in coordination, the general consensus is that European capitals were ultimately right to join the Bank. China's growing presence and influence in the world – especially in the field of global economic governance – cannot be stopped, but others can help to shape its decisions. As a prospective member, the Netherlands has 'direct influence on the drafting of policies', argued Dutch Finance Minister Jeroen Dijsselbloem in a Letter to Parliament in June 2015 wherein he expressed his government's intention to join the AIIB. In other words, it is better to act from within than to stay outside. A similar perspective is reflected in the comment by former US Treasury Secretary Larry Summers that the lead-up to the establishment of the AIIB 'may be remembered as the moment the United States lost its role as the underwriter of the global economic system' (Summers, 2015).

There should be little doubt that economic opportunism also featured large in the decision of many EU Member States to join the AIIB. It is indeed worrying that instead of binding forces early on to increase their power of influence – for example, in negotiations about good governance and (environmental) standards of the new infrastructure bank's projects – European countries competed against one another in courting Beijing. Just as with attracting Chinese investments, European capitals tumbled over one another to woo China. The main goal of each individual country appeared to be to achieve more economic gain than their European neighbours. Fixated on the economic opportunities that the AIIB may provide their domestic private sector, the governments of European countries paid scant attention to the fact that the AIIB also serves Beijing's geostrategic purposes, which do not always align with EU interests.

Many European capitals and companies are keen to engage China also on the New Silk Road. The EU is slightly more restrained in this regard, with its emphasis on rules and regulations that China should comply with when operating in the EU and its immediate neighbourhood. Finally, the EU is a player in East Asia's competitive trade multilateralism by way of its trade and/or investment agreements with individual Asian states, including South Korea, Singapore and Vietnam (concluded); and Japan, China, Indonesia and Myanmar (under negotiation). Importantly, however, these are bilateral deals and the EU is not offering a value-proposition of its own to rival the mega-trade deals that are being negotiated in the region.

Although European countries are thus far from the generally confrontational stance taken by the United States and Japan towards China, also in Europe voices are becoming stronger that the EU and its Member States should be less naïve in their relationship with China. Specifically, the European Commission's in-house think tank urges them to 'keep a close eye on wider geopolitical and geostrategic trends, which suggest that China may use its economic and financial prowess to pursue its unilateral political and security interests' (EPSC, 2015, p. 5).

Some have observed that European countries should recognize the benefits of potential Japanese participation in the AIIB as a regional member, which would dilute China's stronghold, albeit less so if it would join now than before the Articles of Agreement were signed in June 2015. This is an argument to actively engage with Japan on the matter. For the time being, however, Tokyo remains on a strategic par with Washington – displaying a great sense of strategic ambivalence towards Beijing, which is increasingly challenging Japanese interests in the region, including in the security field.

Competitive mega-trade deals

Representing three of the four biggest economies in the world, trade and investment negotiations involving the US, Japan and the EU will have global effects, as they will set the tone for future deals. Key initiatives towards this purpose have been the TPP (effectively, a US–Japan bilateral plus), the Transatlantic Trade and Investment Partnership (TTIP) and the EU–Japan EPA. The ultimate aim of these agreements has been to agree on new common standards, including in new areas such as worker protection, anti-corruption, government procurement, sustainable development and investment. Failing to agree to such new agreements that include significant groups of countries will also contribute to the patchwork of regional and bilateral agreements. This would result not only in a furthering of the famous rules-of-origin noodle bowl, but also in a noodle bowl of varying rules and regulations in different places.

In recent years, Prime Minister Abe has made it clear that he views the inter-regional TPP as essential for not only its economic benefits, but also its geopolitical impact – stressing the TPP's role in sustaining US regional engagement towards promoting regional security. In order to attain an early conclusion of the TPP negotiations, for instance, Akira Amari, Minister in charge of the TPP negotiations, often told his US counterpart Michael Froman 'We come to negotiate despite opposition back home because we think U.S. involvement is crucial for the stability of East Asia. We are doing this for our common values which go beyond the tariff issue' (*Nihon Keizai Shimbun*, 2015a). Chinese policy circles recognized this strategic element of the TPP, as illustrated by comments by official state press news agency Xinhua that Japan's entry into the TPP negotiations contributed to the US taking a step forward in encircling China (Sohn, 2015, p. 471).

The US–Japanese commitment to the TPP conclusion in 2015–2016 illustrated the countries' direct concern for China's economic and strategic moves in the region, especially regarding the AIIB establishment and the South China Sea dispute. The TPP agreement was eventually signed in February 2016, and ratified by the Japanese Diet (House of Representatives) later that year in November. The protectionist backlash in the US under President Trump put the future of the Trans-Pacific pact in doubt, although Japan and Australia have since taken the lead to push for an 11-member TPP 2.0 – i.e. without the US but leaving the door open for future US engagement. Against this context, the Japanese government from mid-November 2016 redoubled its efforts to conclude the EU–Japan EPA swiftly. Tokyo now regards the EU–Japan EPA and sectoral plurilaterals as key instruments to set the next-generation standards in international trade and investment and – with the TTIP in the freezer for now – much the same goes for the EU. This strong political push enabled the EU and Japan to sign an agreement in principle on the EPA on the eve of the G20-meeting in Hamburg in July 2017, sending a powerful signal that the two partners reject protectionism.

Clearly, the early conclusion the EU–Japan EPA is of relevance also in the relationship with China, which is putting forward value-propositions of its own. In China's 5th Plenum Communiqué issued in November 2015, the buzzword 'institutional voice' emerged and was later incorporated into guidelines for the 13th Five-Year Plan (2016–2020). It clarified China's intention to further its preferences upon systems of international governance. On the heels of the Transatlantic crisis triggered by the 2008 bankruptcy of Lehman Brothers, China began to view the existing global financial architecture – based largely on the US dollar – as 'a product of the past', to quote then-President Hu Jintao (*Wall Street Journal*, 2011). By extension, current President Xi Jinping has since called for the realization of the so-called Chinese Dream, involving both societal prosperity and national rejuvenation. The Free Trade Area of the Asia-Pacific (FTAAP, covering the 21 economies of the Asia Pacific Economic Community, APEC) is promoted as the ultimate aim of the grand design for Asian-Pacific integration.

China's proposed action has been broadly regarded as a counter-offer to the TPP, which previous US Administrations have sought to promote as an economic pillar of their rebalancing strategy, with China as its primary target (the so-called US 'pivot to Asia'). Unsurprisingly, President Xi implicitly criticized the TPP in the 2015 APEC meeting in Manila, stating that 'with various new regional free trade frameworks cropping up, fragmentation is becoming a concern' (*Nikkei Asia Review*, 2015). Presidents Hu and Xi are clearly offering alternatives to the institutions of the US-led global and regional economic orders – with some success since 2015.

Confronted with the TPP's development, especially after Japan showed an initial interest in the participation in September 2010, China accelerated the establishment of a regional free trade agreement (FTA) framework in which it could set its own standards for regional integration according to its own schedule (Terada, 2012). Protectionist tendencies in China make it difficult, however, for the country to play a leading role in trade regionalism, which primarily aims to promote economic liberalization and deregulation. The treatment of SOEs (State Owned Enterprises) poses another major obstacle to China's prospects for joining the TPP, whose policy seeks to ensure a level playing field for SOEs, or competitive neutrality between SOEs and private companies, despite exceptions for local SOEs and sovereign wealth funds, given the dominance of state capital in some of China's key sectors, including petrochemicals, finance, and steel. China thus identifies development regionalism as more suitable than trade regionalism, for it can now capitalise on both having the world's largest foreign reserves (US$4 trillion) and being its largest developing economy. Its regional trade deals of choice – next to the FTAAP, also the Regional Comprehensive Economic Partnership (RCEP, covering 16 countries in East Asia) – portray a much lower level of ambition for trade liberalization than the TPP or any agreement that the EU is negotiating.

Amid the growing competitive multilateralism in trade diplomacy in the Asia-Pacific, China's strategy of establishing more bilateral FTAs, especially with TPP members, is effectively deepening the dependency of countries in the region that can be mobilized to help China's political and strategic interests. Chinese activism on this front may not be so different from past Japanese and US strategy in the region, but it does go against the best interests of these established powers. For instance, in 2015 China signed FTAs with two key US allies – namely, Australia and South Korea – whose substantial export dependence upon China (at roughly 33 per cent and 25 per cent, respectively) has motivated their enthusiasm for the establishment of preferential trading relations with China. This political-economic vulnerability stemming from excessive trade reliance on the Chinese market also explains why Australia and South Korea dispelled US pressure not to participate in the AIIB.

The power of such influence was demonstrated also by China's massive flows of economic assistance to Laos and Cambodia, which in turn has been instrumental in dividing ASEAN members on the South China Sea dispute. Trump's policies may accelerate this process, forcing most countries in East Asia to lean more towards China by lack of an alternative. That being said, the fact that the Trump administration may be handing Beijing a strategic opportunity to strengthen its role in regional economic and financial governance does not mean that China can effectively take advantage of it. Considering the domestic challenges it faces – such as lower economic growth, ballooning national debt and winnowing returns on investment – the opportunity may indeed present itself just a decade or so too early. Against this background, Japan and the EU, together with like-minded middle-power countries like South Korea, Australia, and Singapore have to step up their efforts to protect the liberal norms and values that have guided global economic governance and practice over the past 70 years.

EU–Japan: interests and actions in the political-economic field

Against a background of growing Chinese activism in the field of economic and financial governance, the EU and Japan started negotiations on an economic agreement in 2013. In that same year, the EU commenced similar talks with the US on TTIP, while the TPP negotiations continued to develop. Japan had signed more than 30 investment treaties including a trilateral one with China and South Korea, while the EU concluded economic agreements with key partners, including South Korea, Canada, Vietnam and Singapore. The late start of the EU–Japan EPA negotiations represents a lack of strong impetus on both sides over years.

Given that the EU is Japan's third largest trading partner, contributing to approximately 10 per cent of its total trade, it has become imperative for Japan to deepen its business and economic links with the EU by signing the EPA, which also contains an investment chapter. The establishment of the EU–Japan EPA signifies their economic balancing with the United States in terms of promoting economic governance with more advanced and deeper trade and investment rules. In sum, Japan's overarching interest in strengthening links with the EU is driven by expected economic benefits to be gained from market expansion, as well as by the strategic calculation of the benefits of a deeper partnership with like-minded countries that share common values such as democracy and rules of law. As became apparent from Prime Minister Abe's reaction, Japan thus found it frustrating that the UK and other EU members decided to join the AIIB, judging that these countries became succumbed to China's economic and financial power and apparently sacrificed the shared values element in the partnership-building with Japan. From the European perspective, however, the decision to engage China was one of tactics, rather than of strategy or desired outcome – and as such did not constitute a step away from the values shared by European countries and Japan. Unquestionably, the different attitudes towards the AIIB between Japan and the EU remained obscure because of the absence of a policy-coordination platform to facilitate communications and consultations.

Europe's response to China's rise

In the eyes of most Europeans, resisting China's efforts and not joining its new initiatives – the AIIB, but also BRI – is not an option, as it may result in missed opportunities for both potential funders and entrepreneurs, and eventual beneficiaries in Europe. Other factors that help explain the relatively more welcoming stance of Europeans to China's rise include the geographical distance; the lack of deep and comprehensive security links with countries in the Asia-Pacific;

and preoccupation with more immediate crises within Europe and in its neighbourhood. China is just not a strategic priority in Brussels or in European capitals.

This is not to say that Europe is oblivious to the potential downsides of the greater influence China is gaining through its increasingly activist approach to global economic governance – as well as through its growing investments in Europe, for that matter. There is growing concern amongst government officials and business representatives about the sustainability of China's economic model (and the impact on Europe if the system were to falter); the lack of reciprocity in openness for foreign investment; and the potential lowering of established international standards on development cooperation (and – although less so – financing), including on government procurement, anti-corruption, national debt of lenders, labour rights, the environment, and the rule of law. This is all the more worrying when seen in the context of China's hierarchical view of the regional – and perhaps global – order and the growing repression of civil liberties in China.

Having failed to show a united front vis-à-vis the China-proposed AIIB in spring 2015, the EU and European capitals are now stepping up the ante. There is widespread agreement among observers and officials in Europe that the uncoordinated response to China's invitation to join the AIIB was unwanted – in the sense that it went against the shared interests of the EU and its Member States. This in turn contributed to the acceptance of coordination of an EU joint approach, led by the European Commission's Directorate-General for Economic and Financial Affairs, towards designing the rules governing the AIIB during the negotiations of its Articles of Agreement (Mackoki, 2016). The Global Strategy as well as the China Strategy aim to contribute to a more coherent framework in dealing with China and other key partners (European Commission, 2016a, 2016b). Also, engaging with BRI will, once again, put under scrutiny whether the EU and its Member States can be more than a collection of individualistic entities. As Beijing's BRI-branding machinery was kicking into gear, most EU MS significantly increased their activism towards China, eagerly trying to win the prize of 'foremost gateway' for the implementation of China's New Silk Road in Europe. Although some are more responsive than others, using BRI as a way to promote better ties with Beijing, actions hardly surpass the rhetorical level. All in all, Europe's response to BRI has so far been characterized by a relative cautious, wait-and-see approach of most governments.

More capable than in other sub-fields of economic governance, the EU is able to speak with one voice on trade – as it is the European Commission that negotiates such deals on behalf of the Member States. The lack of competition between EU MS thereby serves as an important explanation for why the EU is taking a tougher stance on China in trade policy than in other fields. Negotiations on the EU–China Comprehensive Agreement on Investment are very much about market access – that is, about investment liberalization. The existing bilateral investment deals that most EU MS have with China are about investment protection, and the new agreement should clearly deliver more. The standard-setting value of this first stand-alone investment treaty for the EU obviously adds to its importance. China is thus challenged to show a significant level of ambition, also because only then will the EU positively answer its calls for the negotiation of a wider trade agreement.

Japan's response to China's rise

Following American views on the AIIB, Japan under Prime Minister Abe did not join the AIIB, which it conceives as a challenge to the prominence of both Japan and the United States in the region's economic order-creating. Abe sceptically described the Bank in the following manner: 'a company that borrows money from a so-called bad loan shark may overcome immediate problems, but will end up losing its future. The [AIIB] should not turn into something like that' (*Asahi Shimbun*, 2015). More profoundly, AIIB's status as the first multilateral lender where China can play a dominant role through its 26 per cent of the voting rights – giving it a de facto veto over important decisions – is another reason why Japan found it difficult to support. Japan's negative approach to the AIIB was partly based on the lingering view within Japanese policy circles that China could use the new bank to increase its economic influence in both regional and global settings.

The AIIB's ascendance with the participation of major EU MS surprised Abe, who was eager to strengthen the US–Japan alliance. This is exemplified in his efforts to pass new security legislation in the Diet in September 2015, promising to widen the role and scope of the overseas activities of SDFs and allowing Japan to exercise the right to collective self-defense based on the reinterpreted Constitution. Abe reportedly condemned his policy aides, blaming the Finance and Foreign Ministries for not informing him that the United Kingdom and Germany would join the AIIB (Toshikawa, 2015). For its part, the US condemned UK determination as saying there had been virtually no consultation with the US and that it is 'wary about a trend toward constant accommodation of China, which is not the best way to engage a rising power' (Dyer and Parker, 2015).

As the second biggest economy in Asia, Japan is China's most direct competitor. The countries are often at odds – including over territorial issues – and the strategic rivalry for influence in the region between them is intensifying. As long as the United States does not join the AIIB and remains uncommitted to the AIIB – Abe, loyal to the US–Japan alliance – will not consider Japan's participation. Japan thus choses to confront the AIIB, rather than welcome the move. This competitive reflex is illustrated by Tokyo's pledge of US$110 billion for 'quality infrastructure investment' in the region (a 30 per cent increase during the 2016–2020 period) as well as its support the Association of Southeast Asian Nations (ASEAN) integration efforts, only two months after the launch by China of the AIIB and the Silk Road Fund. Moreover, Japan promised US$6.2 billion of new Official Development Assistance (ODA) to the Mekong region – where China's economic and political presence is dominant – by expanding the financial basis of domestic agencies, including the JICA and the Japan Bank of

International Cooperation (JBIC), by supplying funds from the private sector (*Nihon Keizai Shimbun*, 2015c). In terms of fiscal investment and loan programs in 2016, JICA has committed US$4.1 billion and JBIC US$11 billion, up 20 per cent and 70 per cent, respectively, compared to the previous year (*Nihon Keizai Shimbun*, 2015b).

Japan and the United States, both non-members of the AIIB, have increasingly used the phrase 'Indo-Pacific', as a potentially counterbalancing regional concept against the BRI with a different set of economic rules, based on freedom, openness, transparency and fairness. Yet, a concrete policy or institutional body has yet to emerge within the Indo-Pacific concept, while more than 50 Chinese state-owned enterprises have invested in 1700 BRI projects. A shared concern among the Indo-Pacific concept users – including Australia and the United States – is that the BRI has been viewed in the Chinese military circle as instrumental in supporting Chinese military strategy. through the provision of easy access to foreign ports, especially in the Indian Ocean, management of which is relegated to Chinese SOEs by the local governments.

Whither greater EU–Japan coordination?

Neither Japan nor the EU initially saw a bilateral economic agreement as an urgent matter. Indeed, the momentum was always provided by outside movements – mainly a concern about trade diversion. It was South Korea that spurred Japan to initially develop an interest in an agreement with the EU in the late 2000s: its initiation of talks on bilateral FTAs with the United States and the EU resulted in a situation where Japan – which competes in major export goods, particularly automobiles and electric appliances – was forced to follow suit in order to remain competitive. South Korea's trade diplomacy strategy targets its large export markets. Having FTAs with 45 countries including the United States and the EU, 'the economic territory of South Korea is the best in the world', (*Nihon Keizai Shimbun*, 2010), according to former President Lee Myung-bak.

Japanese companies have yet to establish extensive production bases in the EU, where the tariff rate on competing products was relatively high (LCD TVs at 14 per cent, automobiles at 10 per cent). Preventing price disadvantages with South Korean competitors was a major motivation for Japan to seek a similar trade agreement with the EU. The day after negotiations began between South Korea and the EU in May 2007 the Japanese Business Federation (Nippon Keidanren) called for a Japan–EU EPA (Nippon Keidanren, 2007). However, the EU judged that a trade agreement with Japan would not be advantageous, and so did not respond to Japan's requests for a long period of time. Of the automobiles exported to the EU in 2009, Korean ones made up 12 per cent of the total, while Japanese were 36 per cent. It was felt that if tariffs were eliminated for Japanese automobiles, which had advanced green technology such as hybrid vehicles, it would be a threat to similar types of European cars. Also, along with the normalization of then EU trade deficit with Japan (€32.8 billion in 2008, €19.9 billion in 2009), about 70 per cent of EU exports were already tariff-free.

As a result, the EU considered the benefits of an FTA with Japan to be small (Terada, 2014, p. 174).

The EU's attitude began to change, however, after Japan showed an interest in the TPP in October 2010. The EU was interested in regulatory easing of non-tariff barriers, seen as the cause of low levels of European investment in Japan and of not being able to bid in government procurement. Easing or eliminating domestic regulations was a major aim of the US-led TPP, heightening EU expectations that it could also put the elimination of non-tariff barriers for exports and investment on the negotiating table. The EU has chosen potential Asian FTA partners who have participated in TPP talks – such as Singapore, Malaysia, and Vietnam – or signed an FTA with the United States – such as South Korea – leading some to characterize EU trade strategy as chasing the US (Heydon and Woolcock, 2009, p. 165). Accordingly, Japanese participation in TPP opened the path to an agreement with both the United States and the EU, signifying responsiveness to the requests made by exporting industries in Japan to catch up to Korea's aggressive trade diplomacy. Yet, this move gave the United States a key tool in the competition with China for the possible formation of a de facto trade agreement among the United States, Japan and EU through the potential establishments of TPP and TTIP. The EU–Japan EPA is crucial for this US consideration.

By the end of 2016, the EU–Japan EPA stood as the only side of the triangle that appeared feasible in the time ahead. TTIP negotiations had become sluggish in prior years due to growing civil opposition to the Investor-State Dispute Settlement (ISDS) clause among social movement activists across Europe. In the Asia-Pacific context President Trump's decision to withdraw from the TPP dashed any remaining hopes of ratification of the TPP in its initial form. As a result, the Japanese government stepped-up the momentum to conclude negotiations on the EU–Japan EPA.

In November 2016 a newly created Task-force on the EU–Japan EPA brought together for the first time the 'Main Ministers' on the Japan–EU Economic Partnership Agreement (EPA) to facilitate close coordination among the relevant ministries, considering comprehensive policies towards early conclusion of negotiations. As argued earlier, Japan's chief interest in the economic agreement with the EU stemmed from the potential expansion into European markets of its globally competitive automobiles and automobile parts. While the TPP failed to sufficiently open the US market to Japan's automobile sectors (Terada, 2015), the EU has been more forthcoming to open this market, notwithstanding strong opposition from Italy, France and even Germany – key automobile producing states in Europe. In return, the EU asked for greater concessions on the part of Japan in the field of agriculture, which the *norin-zoku* (the 'agricultural tribe' of the ruling party in Japan) strongly opposes. Even after the agreement in principle on the EU–Japan EPA, this contentious issue remained to be solved.

But there is more about global economic/financial governance than the EPA. In this context, it is worth recalling the argument made by the European Political Strategy Centre that European capitals and companies alike should not inadvertently help to lay the grounds for a world in which Chinese or AIIB finance will be preferred in emerging markets (EPSC, 2015, p. 5). This is especially the case because little is known about the extent to which the new bank will subscribe to the economic prescriptions and economic and social standards that are upheld by other multilateral development banks. If European non-governmental organizations and parliaments were worried about standards (not being) upheld by the ADB before – as illustrated by a Parliamentary debate in the Netherlands in February 2014 – current Chinese practices warrant even more scrutiny of the AIIB's future projects.

Similarly, by subscribing all too easily to the new trade opportunities that are offered by BRI, European countries run the risk of further marginalizing the multilateral, non-discriminatory and rules-based system centred on the WTO. This risks (further) undermining the cohesion of global trade governance and increasing the level of friction between the leading world economies, which is clearly not in Europe's interest. The Japanese government is more aware than EU Member States of these challenges and the need to confront them, but has failed to convince European capitals of the need also to provide substantial counterweight to Chinese activism. This is partly explained by the fact that more than a few in Europe view Tokyo as apparently stuck in its zero-sum, containment mentality – amplified by its image of an always obedient follower of the US. Clearly, more efforts need to be made to bridge the existing gaps. This includes broadening and deepening practical cooperation as well as lines of communication between European and Japanese policymakers and researchers.

Linking politics and economics

Paralleling negotiations on the EU–Japan EPA are negotiations on a bilateral political agreement, the so-called SPA. A key characteristic of EU trade diplomacy, the EU commonly requires that third countries sign such an agreement as a prerequisite to a free trade agreement (Okano-Heijmans, 2014, pp. 15–17). To the EU, these political agreements are a vehicle for developing broad-based and mutually beneficial cooperation in fields such as non-proliferation, security, energy, maritime transport, air services, science and technology. They include political clauses related to human rights; democracy and the rule of law; non-proliferation of weapons of mass destruction; counter-terrorism; the International Criminal Court; and small arms and light weapons. In essence, the political agreements thereby constitute a formal way by which the EU tries to use the attraction of access to its big market as economic leverage to gain political concessions, including commitments to human rights and international law.

Not all negotiating partners agree to this rather legalistic approach to political cooperation – even if they agree on the benefit of more cooperation in principle. Like a few other countries – including Canada and Singapore – the Japanese government long resisted the legally binding character of the document and the inclusion of 'essential' political clauses, including on human rights. Indeed, the EU wishes to complement the human rights clause by a suspension mechanism providing for the possibility to suspend the agreement or parts thereof, including without prior consultation in cases of special urgency. While the suspension mechanism, from the EU's standpoint, offers clarity and legal certainty about the right to suspend and the procedure to be followed, it is regarded as discriminating and patronizing by more than a few counterparts.

Notwithstanding its reservations about the SPA, the Japanese side is reportedly more committed to the SPA negotiations. This is important because, ultimately, the conclusion of negotiations and signing of the document is a matter of political will. The final result will reflect Japanese push-back on the agreement in the sense that will be more general in nature, while the EU would have preferred more specifics – for example, specifying cooperation in the field of environment to clean air and water, and endangered species.

A question that is of key relevance for the purposes of this chapter is whether cooperation on global economic and financial governance features in the SPA negotiations – and eventually, in the agreement. This would seem logical considering China's growing activism in this field and the accordingly decreasing European, Japanese and US influence. Clearly, this is an issue of vast importance to the future of the East Asian region and globally.

If political agreements that the EU signed with other partners are any indication, there should be little hope for strategic engagement on the topic, however. The EU–Canada SPA, for example, is characterized as deepening and broadening the scope of bilateral cooperation 'on a wide range of issues such as international peace and security, counter-terrorism, human rights and nuclear non-proliferation, clean energy and climate change, migration and peaceful pluralism, sustainable development, and innovation' (Council of the European Union, 2016). Global economic and financial governance goes unmentioned in this summary – which is at the same time quite extensive. A closer look at the various titles and chapters of the EU–South Korea agreement also suggests that hopes for enhanced cooperation on economic/financial governance should not run high. Title III on Cooperation in regional and international organizations consists of just one article, which makes very broad reference to cooperation in a variety of institutions – but fails to mention strategic dialogue on the future regional or global order. Title IV on Cooperation in the area of economic development is more specific – including chapters on economic policy dialogue, business cooperation and development cooperation. Narrowly focusing on bilateral cooperation, however, these articles also fail to mention a joint effort to address the bigger challenges that come with shifting power balances and initiatives to create new institutions (EU, EEAS).

For all their potential benefit, the political agreements thereby appear reflective of yesterday and today's world, rather than offering visionary ideas on how to address the strategic challenges of tomorrow. The EU–Japan SPA should address this flaw by way of a chapter global economic and financial governance that aims to further a more coordinated strategic approach between the EU and Japan in this field. For its part, the EPA should also take into account the strategic context in which the EU and Japan operate – including the China-factor and the role of the US. Setting an example on far-reaching elimination of non-tariff barriers is essential, and more straightforward tariff reduction should also be regarded as a welcome opportunity to further domestic reforms, including in the field of agriculture. But the real value of the EU–Japan EPA should be sought in its potential to promote norms that the EU and Japan share, including on sustainable development (protecting the environment, furthering green growth), labour rights, freedom of movement, agriculture (including non-genetically modified goods), protection of intellectual property rights, government procurement and perhaps even state-owned enterprises. Delivering on this front will serve both sides' long-term economic and political interests by setting standards for others to aspire to – and, ultimately, to follow. Eventually, Trump's economic nationalism upped the momentum in the EU and Japan to finalize the agreement. The timing of the announcement of the agreement in principle – just hours before the start of the G20 Summit in Hamburg in July 2017 – was thus no coincidence, but a clear signal that two of the world's biggest economies would stand against the protectionist tide.

What has Brexit got to do with it?

As the UK government in March 2017 invoked Article 50 of the Treaty of the European Union, it officially started the process towards the departure of the UK from the EU. Uncertainty about the future trade relationship of the EU and the UK and the rest of the world – most importantly, about whether the UK will remain part of the EU single market and/or of its customs union – is causing considerable concern for foreign investors, trade partners and governments involved.[3] For example, uncertainty triggered questions with negotiating partners on the 'balance of concessions'.

The Japanese government, in close coordination with the country's big business federation Keidanren, was quicker and more outspoken than any other country in its response to the referendum result. The Cabinet Office created a Special Task Force on Brexit in August 2016, which published a 15-page-long message to UK and EU on Brexit (MOFA, 2016), reflecting the concerns and interests of the Japanese business community, as well as the demands Japanese businesses made for the conditions of Brexit. While the British media described the message as an 'unprecedented' and 'dire' warning, a 'stark' threat, or dismissed as 'doom-mongering', the impact was immense given the UK was Japan's second-largest FDI destination following the US in 2015; more than 1400 Japanese firms have established offices in the UK, some as European headquarters. The previous UK government led by David Cameron invested heavily in the promotion of economic ties with China, with former British Chancellor of the Exchequer, George Osborne, symbolically vowing to make Britain Beijing's 'best friend in the west' (*Guardian*, 2015). Yet, after the Brexit-vote, the new government intensified its efforts to maintain Japanese companies in the UK.

As shown in the chart below, Chinese investment towards the UK is much lower than that of Japan, illustrating Japan's direct contribution to UK employment. The importance of Japanese investment in the UK is symbolized by Prime

Table 6.1 FDI international investment positions in the UK by area and main country, 2006 to 2015 (£ million)

	2006	2007	2008	2009	2010	2011	2012	2013	2014	2015
EU	299,906	290,801	317,375	344,344	347,469	366,400	452,276	462,342	490,245	431,174
USA	170,880	143,297	170,369	159,900	185,458	205,925	255,169	217,950	242,070	252,144
China	99	196	199	607	367	767	1,118		1,100	1,844
Hong Kong			6,979	5,884	7,527	16,972	10,253	11,622	12,799	11,090
Japan	14,766	20,321	24,801	19,263	22,501	26,071	36,036	36,194	39,756	40,518

Source: ONS (Office for National Statistics).

Minister Theresa May's direct meetings with executives from large Japanese investment companies – such as Hitachi's Nakanishi and Nissan's Ghosn – who worry about Brexit's negative impact on their business operation. Nissan sells 80 per cent of the vehicles made in the UK to customers in the EU's internal market, while purchasing about half of the parts and components from the continent. Haruki Hayashi, then-President of the Japanese Chamber of Commerce in the UK and Mitsubishi's chief executive in the EU, cautioned that Japanese companies 'have already started receiving offers to relocate elsewhere in the EU' (*The Independent*, 2016). Indeed, French and German campaigns to attract businesses from the UK to the continent are actively targeting Japanese financial institutions and manufacturers based in the UK (*Nikkei Asia Review*, 2016). The UK has expressed its interest in establishing a bilateral FTA with Japan as Prime Minister Terresa May stated in her visit to Japan in August 2017. A possible UK–Japan FTA is expected to help maintain Japanese business in UK, invite new investments from Japan, and appeal to British citizens as a benefit of Brexit. Yet, Japan's general response was less enthusiastic as uncertainties remain until the UK's departure negotiations with the EU are finalized.

Conclusion

Japanese and EU leaders tend to stress their shared values whenever they meet, but hardly did they take action to translate these into policy practice. Japan–EU relations, even against the context of China's rise, may be characterized by 'functional distance'. The agreement in principle of the EPA on the eve of the G20 in July 2017 does little to change this, although it does signal the intention to change on this front. While European capitals tend to prioritize political and security relations with immediate neighbour, Russia over those with China, the opposite goes for Japan in its relationship with both powers. This is reflective of the fact that relations with direct neighbours tend to be more problematic and immediate. The influence of China's trade, investment and financial strong hand factors in on Europe's softer stance on China's maritime aggressiveness in East and South China Seas, acting as a major hurdle to the development of Japan's partnership with the EU. The EU's preoccupation with its intra-regional problems and conflicts – in particular the Brexit issue and migration – further adds to this. For its part, Japan is walking its own trajectory in its relations with Russia, as reflected also by Prime Minister Abe's frequent meetings with the Russian President. The functional distance between the two powers has thereby become more conspicuous.

While US alliances in the region have long contributed to stability in the region – including for European companies and governments that need to preserve their economic interests – the future is uncertain. On the positive side, the US commitment to the security of allies in the Asian region appears in the end to be maintained under the Trump Administration, as Defence Secretary James Mattis confirmed in his first overseas trip to South Korea and Japan in February 2017. The summit meeting between Trump and Abe held that same month in

Washington DC and Florida reconfirmed America's security commitment, as illustrated by the fact that Article 5 of the Japan–US Security Treaty's application to the Senkaku Islands was mentioned in the joint statement launched by two leaders, the first time in history. More worrying is Trump's withdrawal from the TPP, which former President Barack Obama pushed as a way of securing American influence in Asia – opening up space for China to take the lead in establishing a free trade area in Asia (and perhaps the Pacific) and to increase its economic and geopolitical influence in the region. This is adding to the challenge that an increasingly strong and assertive China has posed in recent years to the status quo. Changes in the policy of the United States towards China and the region require more well-thought strategies for how not only Japan, but also the EU and its Member States can protect their economic and political interests. As a way of strengthening regional economic cooperation which Trump shows no interest in, Japan attempted to alter the previous strained political atmosphere with China. Toshihiro Nikai, the Secretary General of the ruling Liberal Democratic Party and Takaya Imai, an executive secretary to the prime minister became pivotal in persuading Abe to take a softer turn on China's infrastructure initiatives. Nikai, a well-known pro-China politician, attended the BRF (Belt and Road Forum) in May 2017 as the Japanese representative and, on the side-line, delivered a letter from Prime Minister Abe (drafted by Imai) to President Xi, calling for more visits to Tokyo by key Chinese figures. China seemed to accept it, allowing Abe to unusually meet with two top Chinese leaders in a single overseas visit: President Xi in the APEC Summit in Danang, Vietnam and Premier Li in the East Asian Summit in Manila, the Philippines in November 2017. The Nikai-Imai faction that prioritizes economic ties with China seemed to gain more prominence in Abe's foreign policy.

Other than by improving on their own strategy and action, European actors are realizing the potential benefits of the indirect approach to dealing with China. This is pointing to the need to work with key partners in the region – including Japan, as well as ASEAN and India. Clearly, there is a need also to invest in Transatlantic relations, which were given a serious blow by the decision of several key US-allies in Europe to join the AIIB. Europe's defiance of US wishes about joining the AIIB can be seen as an example of the diverging interests of European capitals and Washington. Also, it is important for the EU and its Member States to approach relations with Japan in a strategic manner, so as to serve European interests in the region best.

Japan stands on the opposite end – now remaining as the only US-ally not to join the AIIB. This is illustrative of Japan's greater loyalty to the US in general terms, explained at least in part by geographical closeness and thus Japan's greater stakes in the issue. While Japan is keeping a strategic distance from Chinese initiatives in the field of global economic governance, it does cooperate in more muted ways – as is illustrated clearly by the (now formalized) cooperation between the Japan-led ADB and the China-led AIIB. At the same time, the demise of the TPP in its initial form and broader uncertainties about the new Trump administration are reasons for Japan to strengthen relations with other partners, including the EU. In recent years, Japan has indeed broadened its almost exclusive focus on the United States to now also engage European counterparts more regularly.

Effectively, Europe and Japan still fail to coordinate on a strategic vision of a world in which China is more influential – both at the EU Member State and at the EU level. The early conclusion of the EU–Japan EPA and SPA would constitute an important acknowledgement of the growing importance of relations between the two sides. The SPA should provide impetus to create a platform to discuss present and upcoming issues of global economic/financial governance, including the AIIB, BRI and competitive trade multilateralism. Even if Europe and Japan are unlikely to arrive at a shared understanding of China's rise and of the evolving role of the US in global and regional affairs – including of the urgency of the issue and of the strategy to take – Europe stands to benefit from the profound knowledge and larger number of communication lines between Japan and China. For its part, Japan could gain from a stronger Europe that would engage China without being naïve about the fact that, for now and some years to come, the Chinese government's pursuit of its own interest is not necessarily in line with (long-term) European interests. A stronger EU–Japan partnership could also serve the purpose of softening the hard edges of the traditional US approach and to convince the new Trump Administration of the importance of maintaining – and ideally, deepening – the rules-based international system of global economic governance. Japan's unilateral approach to the Trump administration without consultation with the EU was primarily aimed to realize its national interests, including the continued US commitment to Japan's defence and the retention of the TPP. Any type of policy coordination platform, including the EPA and SPA, is urgently needed to secure their shared interest in the field of global economic and financial governance by jointly dealing both with the unpredictable Trump administration and with the growing activism of the Xi administration.

Notes

1 Throughout this chapter, references to the EU should be interpreted to also include EU Member States. 'Europe' is generally used to refer to this same group of countries, when the EU is not so much involved.
2 Interview with officials of DG ECFIN and DG TRADE, Brussels, June 2015.
3 The EU single market facilitates the free movement of goods, persons, services and capital amongst member states. The EU customs union establishes a single external customs tariff for the EU and the abolition of duties between member states. Since the EU has exclusive competence regarding the 'common commercial policy (as per the Treaty of Lisbon), the UK cannot sign trade deals with countries outside the EU until it has left the EU.

References

Asahi Shimbun. (2015) *Shushō: Saido kakuhitsuyōnai, Muratama Danwa, Shinryaku Owabi Mongon* [Prime Minister Abe: No Need to Mention Again about the Murayama Discourse and Apologies about the Past Aggression]. 21 April.

Dyer, G. and Parker, G. (2015) US Attacks UK's 'Constant Accommodation' with China. *Financial Times*. 12 March.

European Political Strategy Centre (EPSC). (2015) The Asian Infrastructure Investment Bank: A New Multilateral Financial Institution or a Vehicle for China's Geostrategic Goals. *ESPC Strategic Notes*. No. 1. 24 April. Available from: http://ec.europa.eu/epsc/pdf/publications/strategic_note_issue_1.pdf. [Accessed: 30 April 2015].

European Union, Council of the European Union. (2016) *Strategic Partnership Agreement between Canada, of the One Part, and the European Union and its Member States, of the Other Part*. 30 October (date of signature). Available from: http://data.consilium.europa.eu/doc/document/ST-5368-2016-REV-2/en/pdf. [Accessed: 10 March 2017].

European Union, European Commission. (2016a) *Elements for a New EU Strategy on China*. Joint communication to the European Parliament and Council. Brussels. 22 June. Available from: http://eeas.europa.eu/archives/docs/china/docs/joint_communication_to_the_european_parliament_and_the_council_-_elements_for_a_new_eu_strategy_on_china.pdf. [Accessed: 4 July 2016].

European Union, European Commission. (2016b) *Shared Vision, Common Action: A Stronger Europe*. A Global Strategy for the European Union's Foreign and Security Policy. Brussels. June 2016. Available from: https://europa.eu/globalstrategy/en/global-strategy-foreign-and-security-policy-european-union. [Accessed: 4 July 2017].

European Union, European External Action Service (EU, EEAS). (2010) *Framework Agreement between the European Union and its Member States, on the One Part, and the Republic of Korea, on the Other Part*. 10 May (date of signature). Available from: https://eeas.europa.eu/sites/eeas/files/framework_agreement_final_en.pdf. [Accessed: 17 October 2016].

Guardian. (2015) Osborne Kicks off China Visit Vowing to be Beijing's Best Friend. 20 September.

Heydon, K. and Woolcock, S. (2009) *The Rise of Bilateralism: Comparing American, European and Asian Approaches to Preferential Trade Agreements*. Tokyo: United Nations University Press.

Hosoya, Y. (2012) The Evolution of the EU-Japan Relationship: Towards a 'Normative Partnership'? *Japan Forum* 24(3), pp. 317–337.

Mackoki, M. (2016) The EU Level: 'Belt and Road' Initiative Slowly Coming to Terms with the EU Rules-based Approach. In Van der Putten, F.P., Seaman, J., Huotari, M., Ekman, A., Otero-Iglesias, M. (eds) *Europe and China's New Silk Roads*. ETNC Report. December. Available from: www.clingendael.nl/sites/default/files/Europe_and_Chinas_New_Silk_Roads_0.pdf. [Accessed: 3 January 2017].

MOFA. (2016) *Japan's Message to the United Kingdom and the European Union*. 2 September. Available from: www.mofa.go.jp/files/000185466.pdf. [Accessed: 21 September 2016].

Morii, A. (2015) Dialogue without Cooperation? Diplomatic Implications of EU-Japan Summits. *Asia-Europe Journal* 13, pp. 413–424.

Nihon Keizai Shimbun. (2010) Kankoku Daitoryō Keizairyōdo-ha Sekaiichi: Beikan FTA Goi [Korean President Declaring His Nation's Economic Territory as World No. 1: KORUS Was Concluded]. 7 December.

Nihon Keizai Shimbun. (2015a) Wareware-ga Rūru-wo Tsukuru: Ishikisubekiwa Chūgoku [We Make Rules, What Should Be Aware is China]. 14 October.

Nihon Keizai Shimbun. (2015b) JICA, Ajiakaigin, Kaigai Infuramuke Kyōdo Shussi [JICA and ADB Work for Joint Investment for Overseas Infrastructure]. 4 September.

Nihon Keizai Shimbun. (2015c) Mekon Nanshin Isogu Chūgoku: Nihon-ha Bohateizukuri Hongoshi [China Make a Quick Move to South for Mekong Region, While Japan Becomes Eager for Protecting Its Own Vested Interest]. 10 July.

Nikkei Asia Review. (2015) China, Russia Protest Trade Pact as Philippines Eyes Entry. 19 November.

Nikkei Asia Review. (2016) Moves to Lure Companies from UK Gather Steam. 5 December.

Nippon Keidanren. (2007) *Nichi EU keizai renkei kyōtei ni kansuru kyōdo kenkyū wo motomeru* [A Call for Joint Research on a Japan-EU Economic Partnership Agreement]. 12 June.

Okano-Heijmans, M. (2014) Trade Diplomacy in EU-Asia Relations. *Clingendael Report* (September). Available from: www.clingendael.org/sites/default/files/pdfs/Trade%20 Diplomacy%20in%20EU-Asia%20Relations%20-%20Clingendael%20Report%20 (Sept%202014).pdf. [Accessed: 4 December 2016].

Okano-Heijmans, M. and Lanting, D. (2015) Global Economic Governance in Transition: China's Activism and its Impact on Europe. *Clingendael Report* (October). The Hague: Clingendael Institute. Available from: www.clingendael.org/sites/default/files/pdfs/ 2015%20-%20Europe's%20Response%20to%20China's%20Activism%20-%20Clingendael%20Report%20MOH-DL.pdf. [Accessed: 4 December 2017].

Parton, C. (2016) *Unpublished Paper Presented at Chatham House.* 29 September. London.

Sohn, Y. (2015) The Abe Effect on South Korea's Trade Policy. *Asian Perspective* 39, pp. 461–482.

Summers, L. (2015) Blogpost. 5 April. Available from: http://larrysummers.com/2015/ 04/05/time-us-leadership-woke-up-to-neweconomic-era/. [Accessed: 17 August 2015].

Terada, T. (2012) Trade Winds: Big Power Politics and Asia-Pacific Economic Integration. *Global Asia* 7(1), pp. 90–95.

Terada, T. (2014) Japan and Regional Integration Dominoes: Golden Opportunity or Another Political Failure? In Rozman, G. (ed.) *Joint US-Korea Academic Studies – Asia's Slippery Slope: Triangular Tensions, Identity Gaps, Conflicting Regionalism, and Diplomatic Impasse toward North Korea*, pp. 171–184. Korea Economic Institute.

Terada, T. (2015) Japan and the TPP Conclusion: Regional Order, Negotiations, and Domestic Adjustment. *Asan Forum.* (October). Available from: www.theasanforum. org/japan-and-the-tpp-conclusion-regional-order-negotiations-and-domestic-adjustment/. [Accessed: 15 November 2016].

The Independent. (2016) Brexit: Japanese Companies 'Have Already Started Receiving Offers to Relocate Elsewhere in the EU'. 1 November.

Toshikawa, T. (2015) AIIB-wa Chūgoku Gaikō-no Shōri [Triumph of Chinese Diplomacy over the AIIB]. *Gendai Business.* 4 April. Available from: http://gendai.ismedia. jp/articles/-/42761. [Accessed: 10 May 2015].

Wall Street Journal. (2011) China's President Lays Groundwork for Obama Talks. 17 January.

7 Taking the lead in current and future trade relationships

Patricia A. Nelson

Towards an agreement

Movement towards negotiating an economic partnership agreement (EPA) or free trade agreement (FTA) between Japan and the European Union gained significant momentum after 2010 for two reasons. The first was Korea's aggressive trade strategy with the EU and the United States that resulted in two large and comprehensive trade agreements. The momentum, felt acutely in Tokyo, led to the second, the creation of a 'golden moment' when Japan was open to creating its own Japan–EU comprehensive trade agreement.

In 2006, South Korea began negotiations with the US first and then the EU on free trade deals. The FTA negotiations with the USA, Korea–United States Free Trade Agreement (KORUS FTA), progressed rapidly with both sides signing on 30 June 2007. But it foundered thereafter going into effect nearly five years later on 15 March 2012. The EU–Korea FTA negotiations progressed rapidly, largely piggy-backing off the KORUS FTA, and was signed on 15 October 2009. After some adjustments, it went into effect on 1 July 2011.

The market access granted to Korean firms in the EU under the new EU–Korea FTA posed challenges to powerful Japanese business interests, in particular those competing directly with Korean firms in European markets in electronics and automobiles where EU tariffs were highest, up to 22 per cent (METI, n.d.). Many Japanese electronics and automobile companies faced significant market barriers in Europe in the post-WWII era and had fought hard over the decades to gain market access (Nelson, 2012). They had built solid trade relationships with their European partners, ranging from direct investments to complex local supply networks that satisfied the EU's local content laws. Key business leaders (and the organizations that represented them) expressed concerns that the very comprehensive EU–Korea FTA represented a direct threat to their hard-won European markets and they were loath to give that up.

These leaders of Japanese industry (especially the electronics, automobile and related industries) were key members of the business lobby, Keidanren, or the Japan Business Federation, which is commonly referred to as the 'boss' of Japanese business.[1] Once Keidanren's leadership understood the potential negative impact of the EU–Korea FTA on many of their top companies' profits in the EU, it opened up the possibility of negotiating to improve market access for EU firms in Japan. In short, South Korea's active pursuit of free trade agreements created a so-called 'golden moment' for the EU and Japan.[2] For the EU, an agreement with Japan would bolster its 'Global Europe' strategy aimed at stimulating growth in the EU and improving competitiveness.[3]

The pressure of the EU–Korea FTA brought the Keidanren and Japanese government to the table creating a true, unparalleled golden opportunity to push forward with a deep free trade agreement that would open markets and reduce non-tariff barriers (NTBs) to European companies in Japan (Nelson, 2012). This was something the EU had sought for decades without success. The lack of success was partly due to the linkage of tariff barriers and NTBs to non-economic or non-trade issues. The EU, until this point, had a strategy of linking cultural and social issues such as human rights with economic and trade issues: if there were no progress in human rights, there could be no progress in trade. Linkage proved to be a rather ineffective strategy as nothing happened despite both sides having agreed to the EU–Japan Action Plan of 2001 in a concerted effort to forge stronger relations (Berkofsky, 2012). The primary outcome of a decade of no activity was frustration, apathy and, in some cases, increased distrust.

Because the EU had only a few remaining tariffs on Japanese goods (primarily in the electronics and automobile sectors) there was not much wiggle room to force Japanese businesses to reckon with difficult-to-remove NTBs – or the broader, more inclusive term non-tariff measures (NTMs) – which are typically embedded in cultural norms and in accepted (although unwritten) business practices. Japan also wrestled with NTMs in Europe. Among the NTMs were testing requirements and/or procedures which seemed to employ delay as a tactic. This was seen as an effort to allow competitors time to catch up with market leaders. The EU, for example, complained that some Japanese medical and pharmaceutical requirements forced repetitive testing that in its view served no logical scientific purpose. Instead, it caused delay by forcing replication of the thorough testing which had already been completed. Copenhagen Economics, a consulting firm that studied the impact of NTMs, found that Japan had an especially high number of NTMs in pharmaceuticals as compared to other sectors, and estimated them to be the equivalent of a 22 per cent tariff (Sunesen *et al.*, 2009, p. 187). This and other NTMs could be avoided if the EU and Japan harmonized their systems through a comprehensive free trade agreement or economic partnership agreement. No agreement could result in unhappy and costly outcomes for both Japan and the EU, especially if other countries set potentially disadvantageous rules first.

With economic pressure on leading Japanese companies mounting due to the threat of Korea's FTA with the EU, momentum towards an EU–Japan EPA grew. It was amplified by the unprecedented economic impact of the 2011 triple disasters: the earthquake, tsunami and nuclear reactor meltdowns in Fukushima. The negotiations were divided into two: economic and trade on the one hand and policy cooperation including climate change, development, disaster relief and security on the other. The latter is known as the EU–Japan Strategic Partnership Agreement (for more details, see Chapter 2).

Japan and the EU comprised *c.*10 per cent of the world's population and *c.*30 per cent of global GDP. The EU accounted for 10 per cent of Japan's total import and export value, which according to METI (n.d.) placed it third behind China and the USA. The EU was Japan's largest investor while Japan's investment in the EU ranked number two. Japan sought to: eliminate EU tariffs on Japanese automobiles, general machinery, electric machinery and chemical goods (ranging from 3 to 22 per cent, see Table 7.1); remove barriers such as on the movement of persons; and improve transparency and the operation of regulations. On the EU side, the priorities were to: remove non-tariff barriers/measures

Table 7.1 The EU–Korea FTA compared to Japan without an FTA with the EU, 2012

Sectors	EU–Korea FTA	Japan, MFN tax rate (%)
Passenger Cars		
Gasoline	Under 1500cc: Duty Free in 5 years	10
	Over 1500cc: Duty Free in 3 years	
Diesel	Under 5t or over 20t gross: Duty Free in 5 years	10–22
	Others: Duty Free in 3 years	
Auto Parts	Duty Free	3–4.5
General Machinery		
Bearings	Duty Free in 3 years	7.7–8
Outboard Motors	Duty Free Immediately	4.2–6.2
Electric Machinery		
Colour TVs	Duty Free in 5 years	14
Video Recorders	*Magnetic Tape:* Duty Free Immediately	8–14
	Other: Duty Free in 5 years	
Chemical Goods		
Ink	Duty Free Immediately	6.5
Photochemical backup stock	Duty Free Immediately	6

Source: WTO–IDB, 2012 as cited at METI (n.d.) www.meti.go.jp/policy/trade_policy/epa/epa_en/eu/.

Note
MFN = Most Favoured Nation.

on specific items (e.g. automobiles, pharmaceuticals, medical devices and food additives); improve access to public procurement, notably to railways, electricity and gas; and implement Geographical Indication (GI).[4]

Once the EPA negotiation process was launched, it proceeded very quickly. The scoping exercise began on 28 May 2011, the EU Council gave the EU Commission the 'green light' to proceed on 29 November 2012 and then formal negotiations began on 23 March 2013 (EC, 2013). The negotiations were completed on 8 December 2017 (EC, 2017a). The EPA was then subject to ratification by parliaments in Japan and Europe in 2018, and possibly beyond, depending on the pace with which EU member states' parliaments are able and willing to ratify the agreement.

The EU–Japan EPA negotiations produced a so-called 'Mega-FTA' on trade and investment issues, such as market access and improving the environment for business (METI, n.d.). The parties agreed to codify, or record in detail, rules for e.g. testing, monitoring, amending and managing infringements to the agreement. They established rules beyond market access to include regulatory harmonization, NTMs, intellectual property, government procurement, the environment and labour. The deal was expected to generate benefits to the EU and Japan, contribute to economic growth in their respective regions and create spill-over effects for the world. By codifying the rules and expectations through tough negotiations, Japan and the EU set standards to which other countries could aspire. It sent a strong signal that two of the world's largest economies reject protectionism (EC, 2017a).

The EU Commissioner for Trade Cecilia Malmström (2017, p. 4) summed up the purpose of the negotiations in a speech saying:

> The EU is the largest market in the world; we have a lot to offer our partners, but also expect things in return in negotiations. But trade agreements do not deal with market access alone; trade must be responsible, and consistent with EU and universal values; this is at the core of our negotiations. We can create incentives for change and improve the living and working conditions of the poorest. And it works!

The next section reviews Korea's FTAs with the US and the EU, and why they created so much pressure on Japan to negotiate the EU–Japan EPA. Insistence from the Trump administration to renegotiate the KORUS agreement hit home with Korean leaders in late 2017. Meanwhile the EU–Korea agreement has stabilized with benefits to both parties. Next, the chapter analyses the progress and completion of the EU–Japan deal. The final section reviews other related issues including the anti-multilateral trade stance of the UK and especially the US, mega-trade deals in Asia and implications for the future.

Impact of Korea's FTA strategy

Many Japanese and Korean multinational enterprises compete with each other globally in the same sectors. When Korea swiftly concluded two major FTAs, one with the US and one with the EU, the Japanese business community was shocked. Major companies in Japan, represented by three major business organizations, Keidanren, Keizai Doyukai and the Chamber of Commerce, made it clear that it was time for Japan to adopt a deep, comprehensive trade agreement with the EU. Table 7.1 demonstrates why. With only Most Favoured Nation tax rates in EU markets, Japanese companies were at a distinct disadvantage to Korean firms that would enjoy no duties whatsoever on their passenger cars, auto parts, general machinery, electric machinery and chemical goods by 2016. Japanese goods faced duties on those goods ranging from 3 per cent to 22 per cent. This section outlines how the two agreements, KORUS and the EU–Korea FTA came about and their impact.

KORUS

South Korea took a bold approach to free trade, pursuing an FTA strategy that would make it what the government at the time referred to as an 'economic hub' in Northeast Asia (Kim, 2015; Park, 2014). It took the initiative with the US to create a bilateral FTA starting in February 2006. The primary negotiations were completed in just fifteen months and the agreement signed on 30 June 2007 (USTR, n.d.). Thereafter, it stalled due to the US demands for "wider access to Korea's auto market" (Yim, 2010).

Adjustments were completed and signed on 3 December 2010 to achieve the goal of 95 per cent free trade in the first three years of the agreement and 100 per cent free trade in ten years (see Table 7.2). It gained US Congressional approval on 12 October 2011 and that same year was approved by Korea's National Assembly on 22 November. The following February, both countries formally agreed that the FTA would go into effect on 15 March 2012. In all, from the start of negotiations to the implementation of the agreement, it took slightly more than six years.

KORUS was the most significant FTA negotiated by the US since the North American Free Trade Agreement (NAFTA). Both sides found the FTA beneficial for four main reasons. First, it would bring benefits to Korea for economic development and new opportunities for Korean companies. Second, it would bring benefits to the US through agricultural exports, service sector exports and direct investment. These would further President Obama's National Export Initiative goal to double US exports over five years or by 2015 (ITA, n.d.). Third, the agreement would help maintain US competitive advantage through the relatively quick ratification process granted the president under the so-called fast-track trade authority.[5] Fourth, the FTA would strengthen the two partners' geostrategic relationship.

In 2009, US trade with South Korea amounted to $66.7 billion. US exports to South Korea were $10 billion while Korean exporters to the US faced on average

Table 7.2 KORUS Free Trade Agreement and the EU–Korea Free Trade Agreement

	KORUS FTA *15 March 2012*	*EU–Korea FTA*[1] *1 July 2011*
Expected economic benefits	US GDP annual increase: $10–12 billion US exports to reach $11 billion per year on average benefitting thousands of US workers. South Korea's exports plus employment to reach 46 per cent of GDP	EU: EUR19.1 billion in new trade Korea: EUR12.8 billion in new trade
General provisions	US visas for Koreans in the US to increase from one year to five years Trade remedies put in place including a binational consultative committee to review bilateral trade remedy decisions	Strong competition rules Intellectual property rights protection Horizontal transparency Effective and quick dispute settlement Framework for cooperation on trade and sustainable development
Tariff reductions, economy-wide	*After the agreement enters into force:* a a 3-year tariff phase out of 95 per cent of trade in goods b a 10-year phase out of most of the remaining tariffs	99 per cent duty free immediately Remainder duty free by 2016 EUR1.6 billion per year Korean tariffs eliminated EUR1.1 billion per year EU tariffs eliminated
Agriculture and meat	*Korea agreed to:* a the elimination of nearly two-thirds of tariffs (on grains, hides, cotton, almonds, pistachios, bourbon, wine, grape juice, orange juice, etc.) b a 2-year tariff phase out on avocados, lemons, dried prunes and sunflower seeds c a 5-year tariff phase out on chocolate, sweet corn, sauces, alfalfa, breads, dried mushrooms d a 20-year phase out on apples and pears e a 15-year phase out on beef f a 10-year phase out on fresh and chilled pork products g a 12-year phase out on frozen chicken breasts and wings h an increase in quotas on skim and whole milk powder, whey, cheese, starches, barley, popcorn, and feed-grade soybeans i exclude rice; the quota remains on rice imports	
Textiles and apparel	61 per cent duty free immediately Injury clause allowing 24-month restrictions in imports, extendable up to 48 months in total	
Autos	Both agreed to implement a special dispute settlement mechanism *US agreed to:* a eliminate the 2.5 per cent tariff on Korean autos (engines up to 3,000 ccs) b a 5-year tariff phase out on the rest of Korean autos c in year eight, begin a 2-year phase out of the 25 per cent tariff on light trucks *Korea agreed to:* a a tariff shift from 8 per cent to 4 per cent b a 5-year tariff phase out, including on electric cars c soften safety and emissions standards for US cars	*EU agreed to:* eliminate the 8 per cent tariff on autos valued at EUR25,000 and up
Services	Korea committed to market access across major service sectors, for example: a international delivery services b foreign legal consulting services c financial services – specifically, Korea to provide market access, greater transparency and investor protection	Improved market access for EU service suppliers
Public procurement	Korea to grant market access	Korea to expand access

continued

Table 7.2 Continued

Electronics, pharm-aceuticals, medical devices	Korea agreed to make medical equipment imports 90 per cent tariff free	On EU exports, Korea agreed to: a no duplication of tests and certification b increased transparency and predictability
Simultaneous and related agreements		*EU–Korea Framework Agreement –* comprehensive cooperation in human rights, transnational crime, climate change, energy security, etc.

Sources: Bilaterals.org (2011); Cooper and Manyin (2007); European Commission (2010b); Shim (2011); and USTR (n.d.).

Note:
1 Because the EU–Korea FTA is based on KORUS FTA, the column is limited to specific differences only.

a 3.5 per cent tariff. The reduction in tariffs resulting from the KORUS agreement would add roughly $10 to 12 billion per year to the US GDP and US exports to South Korea were expected to average $11 billion per year. In addition, the agreement was expected to support tens of thousands of US jobs and the $560 billion Korean services market would be opened to US companies (ITA, n.d.). For South Korea, the FTA was expected to increase exports to the US of midsize cars, flat display colour TVs, textiles and shoes. Growth and employment from Korean exports was expected to reach *c*.46 per cent of GDP.

EU–Korea FTA

The EU and South Korea began exploring an FTA in the summer of 2006, notably while the KORUS agreement was in the early stages of negotiation. They launched formal FTA negotiations in May 2007, and after eight negotiation rounds signed the agreement on 15 October 2009. The EU–Korea FTA entered into force (provisional application) on 1 July 2011 (Lee, 2010).[6] As it was completed before KORUS, it became the world's second largest after NAFTA and the most comprehensive trade agreement to be successfully concluded by the EU (EC, 2010a). The entire process took just over four years. Thus, the EU–Korea FTA negotiations began *after* the KORUS negotiations, yet it was concluded and ratified *before* the KORUS FTA.

The unusually speedy conclusion of the EU–Korea FTA can be attributed to the progress achieved by the KORUS negotiations, especially in the agriculture sector, before the EU–Korea negotiations began. Again, South Korea's bold approach to free trade played a role, and this allowed the EU to piggy-back off the KORUS negotiations while continuing to pursue its Global Europe strategy of stimulating trade, innovation and investment (Schott, 2009). The EU Council successfully reigned in myopic, parochial views, notably the Italian auto industry. Other motivations of the EU–Korea FTA were: European concerns over trade diversion without an FTA; the potential of South Korea as a springboard for EU companies into the rapidly growing Asian market; and concerns on both sides of the risk of consolidation of US dominance in Northeast Asian economies and business.

The EU–Korea agreement's goal was 99 per cent duty free trade within three years (see Table 7.2). South Korea's second largest export market in 2009 was the EU at $78.8 billion. Exports from the EU to Korea grew at an average annual rate of 7.5 per cent from 2004 to 2008 yet the EU had persistent trade deficits with Korea. To control the rate of goods flowing into the EU, Korea faced tariffs of on average 5.6 per cent. After concluding the FTA, South Korean exports to the EU were expected to rise in midsize cars, flat display colour TVs, textiles and shoes. New trade in goods and services for the EU was expected to be $24.5 billion and for South Korea $16.7 billion (Lee, 2010). Alongside the comprehensive trade agreement, a cooperative agreement on anti-competitive activities was also put into force in 2009. Then in 2014, the EU and Korea ratified a political and security cooperation agreement legally linked to the FTA called the EU–Korea Framework Agreement that entered into force on 1 June 2014 covering human rights, non-proliferation of weapons of mass destruction, counterterrorism, climate change, and energy security (EC, 2010c).

Assessing the FTAs

The KORUS FTA was a relatively insignificant agreement from the perspective of US trade and the economy, but not from a security perspective. Both sides expected – until the election of President Trump in the US – that the Trans-Pacific Partnership Agreement (TPP) would become the main trade instrument in Asia for the US. This meant that the KORUS agreement (as well as NAFTA) would be folded into the TPP, making it an important but also an adjunct agreement to the main FTA agreement in Asia, that is, the TPP. KORUS may become even more important to both parties given that the TPP without the US, i.e. the TPP11, was signed on 8 March 2018. Furthermore, it could fulfil the long-term Korean objective of being a trade hub in Asia, and a launching pad for US companies entering Asia.

The actual performance of the KORUS FTA during its first five years showed that US exports in goods fared very well while Korea's exports in services fared even better (Fatheree, 2016). The trade and services balance put the US in (continued) deficit despite the enormity of the gains from the FTA since 2012. Despite the continued challenges of the service sector in Korea, US exporters reported to the US Chamber of Commerce that the environment in Korea is improving and they are optimistic for broader benefits in the coming years.

By 2015, bilateral trade in goods had grown significantly according to Korean Customs Service statistics (US–Korea Connect, n.d.). In total bilateral trade, the US jumped two places to become Korea's number two trading partner (after China) at $113.9 billion while Korea's total trade with the US at $115.3 billion meant a rise from number seven to number six. Trade in services continued to be dominated by US exports at $22.4 billion while trade in goods was dominated by Korea at $69.8 billion. Cross-border investment flows in 2015 showed that Korea's investment in the US was about twice the investment of the US in Korea. Cumulative totals, or investment stock, over the period 1968 to 2015 also put Korea's investment in the US higher than US investment in Korea at $89.9 billion compared to $62.4 billion.

The Trump administration was not happy with the deal, however, placing the blame on its inability to resolve the imbalance in trade in goods. The US Trade Representative put the trade in goods deficit in 2016 at $27.7 billion (USTR, n.d.). Looking at total trade in *goods and services*, the deficit was significantly lower at $1.4 billion. Renegotiation of the deal was expected to occur throughout 2018.

The EU–Korea FTA deepened trade linkages between the two since its implementation in 2011, and in general, the EU benefited more than South Korea (Amighini and ISPI, 2016). According to the FTA, trade was 99 per cent duty free within the first year with the remaining tariffs removed in the summer of 2016 (EC, n.d.a). The EU had a persistent deficit in its trade in goods with South Korea – over EUR10 billion throughout much of the 2000s and peaking at EUR18 billion in 2006 – was turned into a trade surplus of nearly EUR3.1 billion in 2016 (EC, 2017b).[7] Korea was the EU's ninth largest export market for goods while the EU had become relatively less important for Korean goods exporters, dropping from second to its third largest export market after China and the US (EC, n.d.a). The EU had a significant surplus in trade in services with South Korea and is South Korea's largest inward foreign direct investor. The first six years of the FTA brought the EU a significantly improved trade picture, yet, it was not complete.

Korea's overall performance with its third largest trading partner was dampened relative to the EU's impact on the Korean market due to several macroeconomic factors (Amighini and ISPI, 2016). First, there was sluggish growth in the EU coupled with a depreciation of the Euro to the Korean Won. Global overcapacity also affected a slowdown in Korean production in key exports to EU markets in specific sectors, namely transport equipment and electronics. In automobiles, Korea was the largest single exporter of cars to the EU and accounted for 21 per cent of all imports. In contrast, EU automakers accounted for only 8 per cent of the Korean market primarily in the premium automobile market, and they continued to consider the market difficult.

Yet from an overall competitiveness position, the bilateral FTA was not the key for either party. Garikipati (2015) noted that Korean exporting companies needed to increase their use of tariff preferences in order to continue to reap benefits from the FTA. Kang and Kim (2013) observed that as globalization progressed, and Korean companies continued to move production overseas (mainly to China) Korea's relative advantage of being an early comprehensive FTA-er would run its course. In the long run, Korea needed to address its industrial competitiveness by improving its business environment, increasing its productivity and adjusting its industrial structure.

To conclude, both FTAs provided specific and substantial gains, such as market access, to the parties in each agreement due to the deepening of their trade and economic ties since ratification. The disappointment from the US regarding goods trade seems misplaced as the US excelled in services where trade with Korea was performing very well. In the wider context of trade in Asia, Europe and the US, these bilateral agreements between the EU and Korea and the US and Korea were important, but they were – potentially – relatively small parts of a large economic picture.

Achieving the EU–Japan EPA

Ratification of the EU–Korea FTA and then the KORUS FTA sent "major shock waves through Japan and other countries in Asia" (Amighini and ISPI, 2016 p. 35). It created the 'golden moment' the EU and Japan had been waiting for as already discussed. The EU was expected to increase its imports of Korean autos and electronics now that they were duty free, which would directly – negatively – affect its trade with Japanese companies in those same sectors. Jong-yong Yim (2010), currently head of South Korea's Financial Services Commission and in 2010 First Vice Minister of Ministry of Strategy and Finance, summed it up nicely in piece for the *Maeil Business Newspaper*, South Korea's top business daily, when he wrote:

> Japan and China seem to feel uncomfortable watching Korea signing free trade deals with the United States and the European Union. When revision to the KORUS FTA was completed, Japan's major media outlets reported extensively on Korea's FTA initiatives and raised concern that Japanese companies would be put in a disadvantageous position. These circumstances seem to validate why we have to speed up free trade deals.

Japan's competitive position had already absorbed two significant financial blows. First was the pension scandal affecting 18.4 million individual pension holders and some 51 million pension accounts (Ryall, 2008). Second was the impact of the US subprime mortgage crisis that suddenly made the Japanese yen one of the 'safe' global currencies to hold. The first resulted in people holding down their spending in expectation of having to increase their personal saving and investment in the absence of a pension. The second caused the Japanese yen to appreciate to new levels reaching a fifteen-year high against the US dollar in September 2010, exerting extreme pressure on Japan's top corporations operating in global markets (*BBC News*, 2010). Many companies found it impossible to operate in the black, putting pressure across the economy and raising fears that some major corporations would again be plunged into years of zero profits resulting in layoffs or an inability to hire new graduates.

The triple shocks of 3/11 dwarfed the impact of the two financial blows. The 3/11 earthquake, tsunami and nuclear power disasters – the most expensive combined disaster in human history at $360 billion in economic losses (Ferris and

Solís, 2013) – were felt across Japan. They raised questions about the ability of Japan, not to mention Japanese companies, to recover quickly. The impact was felt around the world when critical parts produced in Japan were in danger of being in short supply. The popular impression that many high-tech products made in China, without any Japanese company involvement, was quickly shattered. The new iPad 2, which was about to be released worldwide, was reported – shortly after the triple disasters – to have at least five key parts sourced from Japan (Williams, 2011). It was critical to get Japanese business up and running using non-nuclear energy sources. The desperate situation took its toll on over a quarter of a million people directly affected and millions more through economic challenges that followed. Aid from around the world came into Japan. At the government level, there was a renewed understanding of the importance of building and strengthening international connections which could aid with recovery through, for example, international trade agreements.[8]

In the wake of all these shocks to the economy and people, the path was clear for Japanese leaders to push forward on negotiations with the EU as well as Asia-Pacific neighbours, namely the Trans-Pacific Partnership Agreement (TPP), the Regional Comprehensive Economic Partnership (RCEP) and an FTA with China and South Korea. Moreover, major Japanese corporations, analysts, government officials and business leaders understood that Japan needed to use FTAs – as it used foreign pressure (or *gaiatsu* in Japanese) in the past – to force through difficult structural changes in the Japanese economy such as removing NTMs.

Brief chronology of the negotiations

Japan's 'boss' of industry, Keidanren or Japan Business Federation, urged the Japanese government to enter negotiations for an EU–Japan trade deal as early as 2006. They called for broader and deeper economic partnership agreements in an effort to resolve global issues while at the same time urged leaders to save the WTO Doha Round (Keidanren, 2007).[9] By 2009, major Japanese companies and Keidanren recommended even more urgently that Japan initiate talks with the EU (Keidanren, 2009). After the 3/11 disasters, pressure from business organizations increased regarding the pace and number of trade agreements Japan was involved in with an eye to creating new opportunities for the recovery of the economy and their members (Keizai Doyukai, 2011). Schott (2009) observed that Japanese business interests showed more enthusiasm for negotiating an EU deal than they had shown over the previous two decades towards proposals for a Japan–USA agreement.

The EU, on the other hand, was concerned it was losing ground in the world's third largest consumer market and fourth largest national economy (EC 2016a; EC, n.d.b). The EU–Japan Action Plan of 2001 had resulted in almost nothing, or a great deal of talk, but not much action (Berkofsky, 2012). The two had stated that within the decade, they would jointly agree to promote peace and security, strengthen the economic and trade partnership, cope with global and societal challenges, and bring together people and cultures (MOFA, 2001).

One of the stumbling blocks to economic and trade progress was that the EU had long linked trade with non-trade issues which effectively bogged down any potential for progress in the trade area (Nelson, 2012) as noted above. The EU was reluctant to remove tariffs on Japanese goods without substantial progress in other areas that were difficult to quantify including NTMs as well as cultural and/or social norms and practices that stood in the way of EU businesses operating in Japan.[10] At the 2010 EU–Japan Summit, the European Business Council in Japan joined Keidanren in calling for an economic integration agreement (Keidanren and EBC, 2010). Then the following year at the 20th Japan–EU Summit, a critical decision was made to separate trade from other issues and to proceed with parallel negotiations on a Strategic Partnership Agreement (SPA) and an Economic Partnership Agreement (MOFA, 2016). This significantly stepped up the pace of progress on trade.

The EU free trade agreement process begins with an agreement to start negotiations, which is then followed by a scoping exercise to ensure that both sides understand and agree to the scope of issues that will be negotiated. The next phase is the formal negotiation phase followed by ratification and implementation.[11] The EU and Japan reached agreement and began the scoping exercise in May 2011. An impact assessment was released in July 2012 and after both parties approved it, the formal negotiations began on 23 March 2013 (EC, n.d.b; Council of the European Union, 2012).[12]

Although the parties agreed to negotiate, there were deep suspicions that the negotiations would move very slowly and become yet another delay tactic especially in Japan with regard to NTMs. With this in mind, both parties agreed to set an unusual one-year deadline to confirm – or not – that there had been enough progress to merit continuing the negotiations (De Gucht, 2013). Japanese business organizations and companies deeply engaged in the global economy were eager to conclude trade deals despite the potential for discomfort among small and medium sized enterprises (SMEs) with the removal of NTMs. This was partly because deeply unfavourable exchange rates had caused much pain and consternation on top of the increased competition in Europe from Korean competitors.

The urgency shown by the Japanese side eventually eased European apprehensions over whether Japan was truly serious about removing NTMs and improving market access under a free trade agreement. After the one year deadline, both parties agreed to continue the negotiation process. The negotiation phase had been predicted to take a minimum of two to three years after the completion of the scoping exercise. It took over four years to announce the agreement in principle on 6 July 2017 and five months more to finalize the negotiations on 8 December.

The eighteenth and final round of negotiations was held in Tokyo on 3–5 April 2017. It was followed by a ministerial meeting from 30 June to 1 July during which the two parties resolved many of the important issues that remained to be negotiated. On 5 July, Minister of Foreign Affairs Fumio Kishida and European Commissioner for Trade Cecilia Malmström acknowledged that they had a shared duty to promote free trade while remaining considerate of "respective domestic sensitivities" (MOFA, 2017a).

At the 24th Japan–EU Summit on 6 July, the leaders formally announced the agreement in principle in Brussels. Minister Kishida commented after the announcement (*NHK*, 2017): "The EPA between Japan and the EU will be the first of its kind among large and advanced economies. I believe it's a comprehensive, high-level and balanced agreement that can be a model for the world". The announcement of the agreement in principle was met with enthusiasm in the EU and Japan. Both sides see the accord as "striking a blow against a feared increase in nationalistic protectionism in world trade" (*Japan Times*, 2017). On 15 November, the European Commissioner for Trade Cecilia Malmström and Japan's newly appointed Minister of Foreign Affairs of Japan Taro Kono talked by telephone and reaffirmed their commitment to concluding the agreement swiftly (MOFA, 2017b). They spoke again on 8 December reaffirming their commitment. This was followed later the same day by an EU–Japan telephone summit between the Prime Minister of Japan Shinzo Abe and the President of the European Commission Jean-Claude Juncker at which the finalization of the negotiations was confirmed. In their joint statement, they wrote in part (EC, 2017d):

> Amid widening protectionist movements, the finalization of the negotiations on the EU-Japan EPA demonstrates to the world the firm political will of Japan and the EU to keep the flag of free trade waving high and powerfully advance free trade. [...] The EU-Japan EPA will be the model of high standard, free, open and fair trade and investment rules in the 21st century.

The Japan–EU EPA is one of the largest and most comprehensive economic agreements concluded by either party so far. The negotiated agreement comprised twenty-one chapters plus appendices. The agreement in principle of July 2017 set out what the agreement covers and is summarized in the Appendix (pp. 138–144) (EC, 2017c). The complete agreement by chapter was made public on the Commission's dedicated web pages with the proviso that it could be modified during the process of 'legal scrubbing' or legal revision (EC, 2017e).

While most of the agreement was ready, investment protection was not yet completed (Saeed, 2017). Investment liberalization had been agreed in principle, but the investment dispute resolution issue was still open. The EU would like to see the new (reformed) Investment Court System, not the old-style investor state dispute settlement (ISDS) provisions. However, Japan prefers the ISDS mechanism. To move forward, the parties agreed to separate the investment protection deal from the rest of the EPA to advance the negotiations to their conclusion. Both sides recognized that achieving agreement on investment protection will require a bit more time.

Estimated benefits of the EU–Japan EPA

Once the EU and Japan agreed to launch negotiations, they set the stage for the largest, most comprehensive trade negotiation that either party had ever engaged in to date (Denková, 2016). The *New York Times* characterized the deal as more exports of Japanese cars to the EU and more EU cheese to Japan (Kanter, 2017). While those might be the flashy, headline-making sectors in the agreement, the deal is certainly a bit more complicated than that. And in the current environment, the strategic value of the agreement could be more important than the economic impact (Jungbluth *et al.*, 2017).

The 28 nations of the EU (27 after the British exit) and Japan together constitute nearly 640 million people and account for *c.* one-third of the world's economic activity (Kurtenbach, 2017). Japan is the EU's number two trading partner in Asia after China, and number six overall. The EU is Japan's third largest trading partner. The EU–Japan EPA was expected to deliver more benefits to the EU than Japan, yet still substantially benefit both. EU exports to Japan, according to EC estimates, were expected to rise by 32.7 per cent, while Japanese exports to the EU were likely to increase by 23.5 per cent (Denková, 2016).

A number of studies have attempted to assess the benefits and disadvantages of concluding an economic partnership agreement between Japan and the EU. One early study looked at the bilateral barriers to trade and investment (Suneson *et al.*, 2009). With regard to the pharmaceutical industry as noted above, the estimated the impact of Japan's NTMs on EU trade was 22 per cent. Another study developed scenarios analysing the impact of the deal on each of the EU member states (Jungbluth *et al.*, 2017). One scenario was a very ambitious agreement that reduced NTMs substantially and the other was a conservative scenario similar to the EU–Korea FTA. A more recent IFO Institute study considered the impact of the EPA on the EU without the UK (Felbermayr *et al.*, 2017).

All studies shared the same conclusion: with a reduction in NTMs, there will be welfare gains from the EPA. The Felbermayr *et al.* (2017, pp. 14–16) summarized the gain and losses succinctly using what was known about the impact of the EU–Korea FTA. They noted that Japan's structure of trade and production is quite different from most of the EU. This is because Japan's exports faced relatively high levels of protection and so opened production sites in Europe, the US and Asia. The EU countries rely more on exports than local production to serve its markets. The authors wrote that Japan spent 14 per cent in 2011 on foreign value added. This was under the Organisation for Economic Co-operation and Development (OECD) average of 18 per cent, so there is potential for growth. They noted that the EU–Korea FTA lowered South Korea's NTMs substantially, which is similar to the potential for the EU–Japan EPA. The authors very conservatively estimated that Japan's welfare gains at *c.*EUR9 billion per year for the first ten years. The figure for the EU28 is *c.*EUR11 billion with Germany gaining the most, followed by the UK, France and the Netherlands and peripheral countries gaining as well. The losses, albeit minor, would affect China,

Korea and Taiwan and the total losses in the rest of the world would be *c*.EUR2 billion. Brexit would reduce the economic gains for Japan by 14 per cent.

In terms of GDP gains, Felbermayr, *et al.* continued, Japan's GDP could rise by 1.6 per cent and Germany's by 0.7 per cent. The EU sectors that would benefit are pharmaceuticals, food/beverages/tobacco and motor vehicles. In EU services, wholesale trade would benefit. There would be slight negatives for the EU in machinery, computer programming and entertainment. For Japan, the greatest gains would be in the computer and electronics sectors with some gains in the motor vehicle and machinery sectors. Losses are likely in pharmaceuticals and wholesale trade with some moderate losses in the agri-food sector. Overall, the welfare gains are substantial. The agreement also signals that both parties have agreed on the importance of "an open, global trade order based on rules and cooperation" (Felbermayr, *et al.*, 2017, p. 16).

Other issues affecting the EPA

The UK, Brexit and Trump's USA

Recent events in the UK and the US have revealed deep, protectionist fears routed in suspicions that globalization and the free trade regime as it exists today is unfair. Some have been quick to blame the outsized role of multinational corporations in our economies and in our international trade. Stoking such fears, protectionist politicians with anti-trade rhetoric swept into power in Britain and the USA in 2016. First was Brexit, Britain's decision to leave the EU, and then came the election of Donald Trump to the presidency of the US, who campaigned against multilateral trade agreements including the TPP, NAFTA and KORUS.

The UK held a referendum on whether the country should stay or leave the EU on 23 June 2016. A slight majority of the British public voted to leave; the numbers were 51.9 per cent to leave and 48.1 per cent to stay (Hunt and Wheeler, 2017). With such a close vote by 71.8 per cent of voters, the result was highly controversial. And the controversy delayed the UK's negotiations with the EU over how to proceed with Brexit, scheduled for 29 March 2019. According to some experts, the leave coalition believed that the UK could become an off-shore tax haven such as a 'Singapore-on-the-Thames', but as such it would simply become a huge money laundering machine (Shaxson, 2017). The EU – aware of these ideas, which were clearly expressed by Philip Hammond, Chancellor of the Exchequer, as a Brexit bargaining position in January 2017 – is expected to make it impossible for Britain to attain such an outcome. Some expert observers suggested that the EU's pre-occupation with hammering out a deal on Brexit would divert its attention from the EU–Japan trade deal (Leigh, 2017). Instead, the EU focused on finalizing the negotiations for the EU–Japan trade agreement on 8 December 2017.

In the US, Donald Trump, a flashy, controversial, New York real estate developer who had become famous through his own reality TV show, was elected to become president in November 2016. His popular appeal was that he would come to the aid of neglected Americans who lost out from, for example, unfair trade deals that had wreaked havoc on their lives. He provided little evidence to support his claims that he would bring back jobs in coal mining or prevent companies from moving manufacturing elsewhere (such as Mexico or Canada due to NAFTA). Nonetheless, many wanted a change from the Democrats who had held the presidency for eight years and many disliked the Democratic candidate, Hillary Clinton. Trump won, not through the popular vote, which was won by Clinton, but because of what was generally agreed to be an imperfection in the electoral college system.

Upon becoming president in January 2017, Trump immediately fulfilled one of his campaign promises to put America first in its bilateral trade deals and immediately pulled the US out of the TPP. He then insisted that the US renegotiate the twenty-three-year-old NAFTA in order to bring it into the digital and e-commerce age and to improve the US trade in goods deficit. Not finished, Trump criticized the KORUS FTA for not delivering on its promises, namely reducing the trade in goods deficit that the US had with Korea. As noted above, the US had robust trade in services with Korea, making the overall trade deficit considerably smaller than the deficit in goods trade alone.

NAFTA, the TPP and other deals

NAFTA renegotiations progressed rapidly in 2017. The fifth round of the NAFTA negotiations began on 15 November 2017 at twenty-eight separate bargaining tables (Blanchfield, 2017). The US wanted deficit reduction and to 'fix' NAFTA, according to Lori Wallach, Director of Public Citizen's Global Trade Watch, and that meant dealing with issues that have been problematic for decades. One was removing the ISDS system – the EU did not want it in the EU–Japan EPA either – which allows companies to sue governments before a panel of three corporate lawyers and then demand unlimited compensation from taxpayers for violations (Public Citizen, n.d.). Fixing NAFTA also meant acknowledging that an estimated 930,000 jobs were lost in the US through offshoring employment in Canada and Mexico. From Canada's viewpoint, the US brought five 'poison pills' from the TPP into the NAFTA renegotiation: (1) raising the American content in automobiles; (2) attacking Canada's agriculture supply management system; (3) imposing a five-year sunset clause if NAFTA does not perform; (4) lowering Canada and Mexico's access to bidding on US procurement projects; and (5) removing the ISDS (Blanchfield, 2017).

Three months after the election of Prime Minister Shinzo Abe in December 2012, Japan entered the TPP as part of the third arrow of the so-called 'Abenomics'. Without the US, Japan and Canada were the two leading economies in the TPP. The *Economist* (2016) argued that if the TPP did not go ahead without the US, the vested interests that resisted reform will be vindicated, and that the ten years of work to win political battles over market access issues will have been lost. The TPP offered, among others, harmonization of standards and the removal of NTBs, labour standards reform in Vietnam, and reform of environmental protections and intellectual property. The TPP would support Abe's 'third arrow' and the deal offered more substance than the other mega trade deal in Asia including India and China, the Regional Comprehensive Economic Partnership (RCEP), which was a much shallower deal than the TPP having tariff reduction as its primary goal (Petri *et al.*, 2017). The TPP and RCEP were originally complementary agreements that arose out of different circumstances, yet they are widely seen as competitive agreements. yet it is a shallower agreement than the original TPP.

Pressure on Canada and Mexico from the NAFTA negotiations spilled over into the November TPP11 meeting at the Asia-Pacific Economic Cooperation (APEC) forum when the two countries decided they were not yet ready to push forward with the TPP11. Canada's Prime Minister Justin Trudeau said, "We are not going to be rushed into a deal" (Blatchford, 2017). Of issue are three provisions that were affected by the US withdrawal from the TPP and the renegotiation of NAFTA: cultural industries; automobiles; and intellectual property provisions. All three were a reflection of US demands in the original TPP negotiations. Without the US presence, they could be renegotiated to better reflect the interests of Canada and Mexico.

The TPP11 countries (the original grouping without the USA) have renamed the deal the Comprehensive and Progressive Agreement for Trans-Pacific Partnership or CPTPP (Geist, 2017). There is still some uncertainty over the TPP11, or CPTPP, and if it will expand to include another five countries that expressed interest in joining. The TPP11 plus South Korea, the Philippines, Indonesia, Thailand, and Taiwan would become the TPP16 (Petri *et al.*, 2017). Japan, Canada, Mexico and the others led the TPP11 to a conclusion with the possibility that the US could join at a later date.

Table 7.3 presents some of the FTAs currently under discussion or awaiting ratification that may affect Japan or the EU (EC, n.d.c; Petri *et al.*, 2017). The long-term goal of many is the creation of FTA of the Asia Pacific (FTAAP) that would bring together the economies of the region. In addition to the agreements already mentioned, those under consideration include: the Canada–Japan Economic Partnership Agreement (C–J EPA), and the Japan–South Korea–China FTA. In 2014, Canada and Japan agreed to continue the C–J EPA negotiations in parallel with the TPP; it was a kind of 'back-up' in case the TPP, or the later CPTPP, was not ratified. The Japan–South Korea–China FTA could become a path for China into the TPP11 and/or the FTAAP. The EU–J EPA and the TTIP balance each other with the CPTPP or RCEP as a third leg of the stool. An FTAAP deal would supersede the CPTPP and/or RCEP in the future.

The Trans-Atlantic Trade and Investment Partnership (TTIP) between the EU and the US, which had been discussed for decades, found itself on uncertain ground with the Trump administration's aversion to mega trade deals. Commissioner Malmström (2017) characterized the TTIP deal as being 'on ice'. Denková (2016) reported that the EU–Japan free trade deal would be more beneficial to the EU than the TTIP: the EU–Japan deal would increase the EU's GDP by

Table 7.3 Selected FTAs affecting Japan and the EU

FTA	Year initiated	No. of partners	Current state of play	Objective	Longer-term objectives
TPP11 or CPTPP	2008	11	Renegotiated and signed	Ratify (option for US to join later)	FTAAP
TPP16	2017	16	TPP11 or CPTPP with five new members	Strength and breadth with more countries	FTAAP
RCEP	2011; 2012	16 (ASEAN+6)	Negotiating	Beyond ASEAN+1 FTAs, Link Asia Pacific partners	FTAAP
CJEPA	2012	2	Negotiating in parallel with TPP	Market access, Setting trade rules	FTAAP
J-SK-C	2012	3	Negotiating	Trilateral, benefits to all parties	FTAAP
EUJEPA	2013[1]	2 (EU28 and 1)	Agreement in Principle	Market access, Setting trade rules, Ratification	Balance TTIP and FTAAP
TTIP	2013	2 (EU28 and 1)	On Hold	Bilateral economic benefits	Balance FTAAP and EUJEPA

Sources: see text.

Notes

1 The impact assessment was completed after the scoping process which took place between May 2011 and July 2012.

TPP: Trans-Pacific Partnership Agreement.
TPP11 or CPTPP: Comprehensive and Progressive Agreement for Trans-Pacific Partnership.
TPP16: TPP11 including 5 more countries.
FTAAP: Free Trade Agreement of the Asia Pacific.
RCEP: Regional Comprehensive Economic Partnership.
CJEPA: Canada–Japan Economic Partnership Agreement.
J-SK-C: Japan–South Korea–China free trade agreement.
EUJEPA: EU–Japan Economic Partnership Agreement.
TTIP: Transatlantic Trade and Investment Partnership Agreement.

about 0.8 per cent while the TTIP would increase it by 0.5 per cent. Thus, it would appear that while the TTIP's benefits to the EU would be great, they would not be as significant as the EPA with Japan.

Asia in the context of global trade

A WTO and IDE-JETRO (2012) study on trade patterns and global value chains found that most of world trade was in intermediate goods, and that regions – in particular Asia and Europe – had well developed production networks integrated with value-added chains. In automobiles, rules of origin – the basis upon which customs officials determine which goods are entitled to preferential treatment – are likely to change under a renegotiated NAFTA. This is because, as noted above, the US wanted a larger percentage of its own input in automobiles. US pressure on the NAFTA renegotiation has the potential to disrupt "or at least negatively affect" North America automobile production networks. Such an outcome might make the prospect of adjusting the TPP11 agreement – to allow Canada and Mexico to deepen their integration into Asia's production networks and associated value-added chains – quite promising.

Japan and the EU declared their support for free trade at the announcement of the agreement in principle in July and again at the conclusion of the negotiations in December. They clarified their position as quite the opposite of the UK and the US, ironically the two countries that were the staunchest defenders of free trade in the post-war era until 2016. It would seem that their promotion of free trade had reached an unsustainable extreme, an economically unpalatable extreme, hitting a breaking point in 2016 and 2017. The problem is not globalization or FTAs but an inability of the UK and US to pursue a fair and just distribution of the gains from trade and of the economic wealth associated with globalization which has disproportionately benefited the financial sector over most others in those countries.

The EU Commission President Jean-Claude Juncker expressed his commitment to listen and respond to the concerns of EU citizens about the dangers of globalization including populist anxiety about the sustainability of the EU and its continued integration into the world economy (EC, 2016b). In response, Commissioner Malmström and her team revised the EU's trade agenda in 2015 calling it *Trade for All*. The EU and Japan have worked throughout their FTA negotiations to assure SMEs in particular that a trade agreement will not exclude them or force them out of business via the creative destruction process of free market capitalism. A chapter of the agreement in principle summarized in the Appendix (p. 144) is devoted to SME concerns.

Malmström (2017, p. 2) noted that it is popular to believe that globalization, and thereby free trade agreements, caused various dislocations in recent years, such as lost income and increased uncertainty. However, she stated, the reality is that automation is replacing people at work. She argued that we are experiencing a fast-paced 'Fifth Industrial Revolution'. Much of this is connected to the rise in Europe of trade in intermediate goods – not finished goods – that may cross the same national border several times during the production process. It is coupled with the rise of highly integrated production in Asia driven by leading Japanese and other companies (WTO and IDE-JETRO, 2012). Malmström (2017) stressed that blaming trade deals for changes that are inevitable is folly; government leaders and businesses need to work together to adapt rapidly to change while making sure that social systems function well and act as an integral element in the system. In short, free trade deals are a key to the future of a sound economic, political and social system.

Conclusion

This chapter provided an analysis of the forces that led Japan and the EU to enter negotiations – and finalize them – on a Japan–EU EPA. After 2010, Korea's aggressive FTA strategy with the US and especially the EU deeply shocked Japan, especially the Japanese business community. The potential gains for Korean businesses in the EU meant potential losses for Japanese businesses that competed directly with them in the EU. Japanese companies that had worked for as many as four decades to build markets in Europe did not want their efforts to be for naught. The EU, realizing the threat to Japanese businesses in Europe, understood that there was an opening to negotiate market access in Japan, especially to negotiate NTMs in Japan, a matter that had been a sticking point for decades. Korea's bold FTA strategy created an opportunity, a 'golden moment', for both the EU and Japan to investigate a deal.

Keidanren, the Keizai Doyukai and other business interest groups were behind a trade deal with the EU since at least the mid-2000s. They understood the need to integrate Japan further into the world economy. In the 2000s, the economy absorbed two significant financial blows: the Japanese government's pension scandal and the US subprime mortgage crisis. Japanese businesses were severely negatively affected by the yen-dollar exchange rate which reached a fifteen-year high in September 2010. Then came the earthquake, tsunami and nuclear power disasters of 3/11, which were the costliest combined disaster in human history. As business leaders' concerns grew and the depth of Japan's reliance on the world economy was made clear, the path towards an EU–Japan deal opened, leading up to the finalization of the negotiations on 8 December 2017.

This chapter also examined the context of the populist anti-trade stance felt in the UK, namely Brexit – Britain's decision to leave the EU – and the US. The irony is that the two countries that were the staunchest supporters of the capitalist free trade system have abandoned it, at least for the moment. Populist views in both countries instead perceived globalization and free trade as having robbed them of their wealth and standing in the world while the fundamental issue at stake is that their governments failed to redistribute the gains from trade fairly and equitably to their citizens.

The anti-trade, anti-globalization sentiment expressed by the Trump administration created a vacuum in Asia that provided both opportunities and uncertainty. There was a good deal of momentum among the signatories of the TPP11 or CPTPP, and there was the possibility that the US would join. Given all the hard work that went into the CPTPP and the EU–Japan EPA, the outlook for further integration in Asia was positive. Proactively moving forward and quickly ratifying the CPTPP and the EU–Japan EPA could provide a strong boost to the Japanese economy. Mikitani (2016) wrote that Japan should say 'Sayonara' to insularity. It could do this by opening up remote areas of the countryside to international tourists, building out the medical system to cater to tourists and non-resident foreign nationals, and promoting Tokyo as Asia's innovation hub.

Trade in Asia (and Europe) was organized in well-developed production networks integrated with value-added chains, and most of the trade was in intermediate goods. The KORUS deal, which the US wants to renegotiate, could prove quite important to US business interests in Asia participating in production networks. Assessments of the EU–Korea FTA found that it offered more benefits for the EU than Korea mainly due to exogenous forces. Although Korea could benefit from it more in future, many Korean companies have been drawn further and further into regional networks in Asia, and so were not taking advantage of all that the deal offered. Given Korea's strong pro-trade stance, it is likely that the EU deal will be one of many. For the EU, the Japanese and Korean deals could offer foundations from which European companies can expand their presence in Asia.

The EU–Japan EPA is a major achievement. It is subject to ratification by the parliaments in Japan and the EU member states, which could take a year or more depending on the pace of the ratification process in Europe. The investor-state dispute resolution (ISDS) mechanism remains to be negotiated yet. Japan's position to stick with the ISDS system is practical, but without the US in the TPP11 and with NAFTA's ISDS system under attack, Japan could soften its position on the Investment Court System preferred by the EU. It remains to be seen how long that negotiation will take. Given that the EPA was separated from investment protection, the deal could go into force during 2018 or soon thereafter.

The EPA conveyed strong leadership and signalled the commitment of Japan and the EU to powerfully advance free trade while striking a blow to protectionism. The deal was a high-level, balanced agreement that could serve as a model for both fair and free trade and – once the investment protection rules are finalized – investment. It might well become a new model of trade and investment rules for an emerging trade order.

Appendix

EU–Japan EPA – The Agreement in Principle 6 July 2017 (European Commission, 2017c, abridged by the author)

1   The chapter on **Tariffs: Trade in Goods Market Access** details the extent of market liberalization. Japan will liberalize 91 per cent of its imports from the EU at the start of the FTA and then to 99 per cent at the end of the staging period. The remaining 1 per cent will be partly liberalized through tariff and quota reductions. The EU will liberalize to 99 per cent with automobiles fully liberalized in seven

years with Japan eliminating non-tariff barriers (NTBs) to EU exports. The two parties will have virtually total alignment on international standards in the automobile sector. The only full exclusions are the mutual exclusion of rice and seaweeds. EU agricultural and processed agricultural goods including agri-food products exported to Japan will be duty-free over time roughly corresponding to 85 per cent of tariff lines. Details included in the chapter cover pork, wine and aromatized wines, most alcoholic beverages, EU additives and processing aids used in wines, cheese and dairy products, whey and whey products, skimmed milk powder, butter and condensed milk, bovine meats including veal, processed agricultural products including pasta, chocolate, confectionary, prepared tomato sauce, gelatine, etc. In industrial goods, the chapter details full liberalization in all sectors including chemicals, plastics, cosmetics, textiles, clothing while leather including shoes and handbags and sports shoes and ski boots will be liberalized over ten years. Tariffs on wood and fish products will be fully eliminated with five or seven years staging for some items that are not immediately liberalized. An anti-fraud clause is included in the chapter; it is a necessary pre-condition for the EU to grant tariff preference to any third country. Cooperation in agriculture, forestry, fisheries and food is to enable the two parties to promote trade through exchange of technical information and best practices and cooperation on regulatory issues to for example improve farm management, cooperation in production and technology, productivity and competitiveness.

2   The **Non-Tariff Measures** (NTMs) chapter contains finalized technical work on the NTMs identified by both parties at the start of the negotiating process. By the end of 2017 most solutions that were identified should be implemented. There are four areas that may remain in the Sanitary and Phytosanitary measures area. The NTM auto annex has solved all issues in close consultation with industry associations and covers a substantial part of the United National Economic Commission for Europe Regulations. The NTM work concluded should lead to the removal of all regulatory barriers for accessing the Japanese car market and includes robust cooperation procedures and obligations to ensure this can be continued. Robust compliance provisions that are similar to the EU–Korea FTA were agreed. Special provisions are included on the EU approved hydrogen fuelled car. The chapter includes substantial progress on the approval process for food additives including transparency and predictability regarding standard processing time. A major achievement is the work by both parties on expanding the coverage of the Mutual Recognition Agreement on Good Manufacturing Practice for new pharmaceutical products.

3   The **Rules of Origin and Origin Procedures** chapter is comprised of three sections and a number of annexes. The Rules of Origin section includes provisions of the absorption rule and the principle of territoriality. The Origin Procedures section includes that a claim for preferential tariff treatment is to be based on either a statement of origin by the exporter/producer or the importer's knowledge. The third section covers miscellaneous items. The chapter details the Product Specific

Rules of Origin (PSR) including industrial and agricultural products. For the entire automotive section, the PSR includes the same provisions as in the EU–Korea FTA. Footwear, leather items, textiles and clothing provisions are detailed as are processed agricultural products, sugar and sugar products and dairy.

4   The **Investment, Trade in Services and E-Commerce** chapter contains many provisions that apply horizontally to all trade covered in this chapter including: (a) reaffirming the parties' right to regulate; (b) definitions of all concepts used; (c) rules on a Specialised Committee for Trade in Services, Investment and E-Commerce; (d) general exceptions to the chapter. For public services, the EU follows previous FTAs by maintaining the right of EU member states to keep public services public; there is no requirement for governments to privatize or deregulate any public service at a national or local level. Europeans will continue to decide for themselves how their healthcare, education, water services and other public services are delivered. For cross-border services, some sectors and issues are excluded, while including articles on Market Access, National Treatment, Most-Favoured-Nation Treatment, and Denial of Benefits. Negative listing is included in Annexes of existing and future measures that do not conform with the obligations in the articles. Additionally, the chapter includes: (i) provisions on movement of natural persons for business purposes ('mode 4'); (ii) regulations by sector as well as horizontally such as making public and easily understandable licensing and qualification requirements and procedures so they do not act as an unfair barrier; (iii) a two-tier track of mutual recognition with joint recommendations first, followed by assessment and negotiation of a Mutual Recognition Agreement; (iv) regulations on postal and courier services; (v) provisions on telecommunications services; (vi) obligations on international maritime transport services; (vii) regulatory cooperation on financial services establishing the Financial Regulatory Forum; (viii) text on all trade conducted electronically including customs duties; (ix) agreement to maintain a dialogue on regulatory issues and best practices regarding electronic commerce. There are no substantive provisions on flows of personal data, but the parties agreed to revisit this after three years after the FTA goes into force.

5   The chapter on **Corporate Governance** – included for the first time in an EU FTA – was derived from the OECD Code on corporate governance reflecting best practices and rules in the EU and Japan. The chapter includes a commitment to adhere to, for example, transparency and information disclosure regarding publicly listed companies, accountability of management to shareholders, effective and fair exercise of shareholders' rights, transparency and fairness in takeovers, responsible decision making based on objective and independent information.

6   The chapter on **Procurement** builds on the WTO Government Procurement Agreement with a new set of disciplines including: (a) one single point for electronic publication of notices; (b) fair treatment of EU construction businesses under Japan's *keishin* – construction business evaluation – system; (c) recognition

of test reports; (d) using environment standards as selection criteria. Regarding new market access, Japan agreed to a non-discrimination procurement regime for so-called 'core cities' (forty-eight cities of *c*.300,000 inhabitants or *c*.15 per cent of total population) and the EU agreed to reciprocate via a similar commitment at the sub-central level. The chapter includes a procurement agreement on hospitals and academic institutions by both parties. Japan agreed to withdraw the 'operational safety clause' on railways which opens it up above the value of 400,000 SDR (1 special drawing right is roughly equal to 1 euro). A transition period of one year, maximum, will apply after the FTA enters into force. The EU agreed to open procurement of: (i) railways facilities in the overland railways sector; and (ii) rolling stock in the urban railways sector (to be the equivalent of the estimated value of Japanese contracts freed up by removing the operational safety clause).

7   The **Intellectual Property Rights** (IPR) chapter builds on the WTO Agreement on Trade-Related Aspects of Intellectual Property Rights (TRIPS) and is strongly based on existing IPR protection and enforcement by the EU. The chapter includes detailed protection on copyright, providing for improved copyright protection. In a first for a major agreement, the chapter provides rules on trade secrets. Additional elements of the chapter are: (a) minimum common rules for patent term extension for plant protection products and pharmaceutical patents; (b) minimum common rules for regulatory test data protection for pharmaceuticals; (c) protection of regulatory test data for plant protection products. Regarding IPR enforcement, the chapter includes is a high standard of civil enforcement rules.

8   The **Geographic Indications** (GI) chapter provides for: (a) high level protections for EU GIs for more than 200 foodstuffs and wines and spirits; (b) direct protection of GIs and removal of all associated charges or taxes for user registration; (c) protection of GIs in relationship to trademarks (TMs); (d) administrative enforcement of protection plus enforcement on request and civil remedies; (e) phasing out of prior uses identifies in the Japanese market within five years for alcoholic beverages and within seven years for foodstuffs after entry into force of the FTA; (f) possibility of adding new GIs to the list of GIs protected under the FTA.

9   The chapter on **Competition, Subsidies, State Owned Enterprises** (SOEs) establishes principles so that both sides commit to maintaining comprehensive competition rules and the necessary authorities to implement competition laws in a transparent and non-discriminatory manner. Continued cooperation between competition agencies is foreseen in this chapter. The chapter ensures that both parties commit to promoting competition to the benefit of all market participants and especially the consumers and private citizens. Specifically, the chapter includes commitments to: (a) laws that address anti-competitive practices in a non-discriminatory manner on all enterprises and when exceptions are allowed they are to be transparent and limited to the public interest; (b) competent

enforcement of competition laws; (c) respect for principles of procedural fairness and transparency of procedures; (d) continued cooperation between competition agencies. Japan agreed to provide more information on subsidies for goods and services at all levels of government. Provisions for consultation allow both parties to raise issues and request information. Two types of subsidies are prohibited which do not apply to sub-central levels of government: (i) unlimited guarantees and (ii) subsidies for restructuring ailing enterprises without having prepared a credible restructuring plan. The chapter specifies that transparency rules apply to subsidies in agriculture and fisheries; the audio-visual services sector is excluded. Both parties will be allowed to continue providing aid to public services. The chapter ensures that SOEs, enterprises granted special rights or privileges and designated monopolies, may not discriminate between EU and Japanese goods, services and enterprises. They may not benefit from undue favourable treatment on commercial markets.

10 The **Trade Remedies** chapter confirmed the right of both parties to apply trade defence instruments in accordance with WTO rules and defined additional rules to ensure transparency and right of defence during investigations of trade remedies. The chapter provides for a bilateral safeguard clause such that preferences can be temporarily suspended to allow a domestic industry to adjust when there is a reduction or elimination of custom duties.

11 The chapter on **Technical Barriers to Trade** (TBT) follows other FTAs with the distinction of naming international standard setting bodies. The chapter in combination with the NTM list of solutions addresses quite effectively issues on electronics, pharmaceuticals, textiles, chemicals and refers to the Codex Alimentarius as well as the ICAO for aeronautical products. The parties are open to including further annexes.

12 The **Customs and Trade Facilitation** (CTF) chapter has two purposes: to facilitate trade and promote customs cooperation on a bilateral and multilateral basis. It aims to modernize and simplify the various rules and procedures related to trade recognizing international rules and standards such as WTO provisions and instruments. Customs controls are to be more efficient, safe and secure. Limitations regarding inconsistencies for TBT and SPS are included in their chapters. The chapter ensures transparency of legislation and procedures; transparency of fees and charges is included (where not included in the Trade in Goods Chapter). The chapter establishes a specialized committee for all customs related issues to ensure coherence with the already existing Joint Customs Cooperation Committee established under the EU–Japan Custom Cooperation and Mutual Administrative Agreement (CCMAAA) and foresees that these two committees will hold joint meetings. Under the existing CCMAAA, the Protocol on Mutual Administrative Assistance in Customs Matters will allow exchanges of information which in turn will ensure a correct application of customs legislation and prevent customs violations.

13 The chapter on **Dispute Settlement** ensures that the rights and obligations under the FTA are fully observed and provides a transparent, efficient, and effective mechanism for avoiding and solving disputes. The chapter is accompanied by the Rules of Procedure for the Panel, the Code of Conduct for the Panellists, and the Mediation Mechanism. The panellists are to be appointed from a pre-established list of highly qualified, experienced and independent panellists. There is not appellate review stage. The mediation mechanism is designed to encourage the parties to reach a solution using less formalized proceedings.

14 The chapter on **Sanitary and Phytosanitary** (SPS) **Measures** aimed to improve predictability for all agricultural products without lowering safety standards or requiring the parties to change domestic policy choices (e.g. use of hormones or genetically modified organisms (GMOs)). Import procedures are to be simplified, expedited and completed without undue delays. Both parties shave agreed to on procedures for listing exporters who are eligible to export meat and meat products. Agreement was reached on how to handle audits, outbreaks of animal disease, and how to establish and maintain mutual recognition of such issues. Both parties agreed on the recognition of pest free areas/production sites and low pest prevalence areas and protected zones and to ensure without undue delay the establishment or maintenance of phytosanitary conditions. Transparency in food additives regarding the approval process and assessment has improved and both parties committed to publishing timelines for food additives' approval. Both parties committed to ensuring transparency on import conditions and procedures including details on mandatory administrative steps and expected timelines to prevent them from becoming de facto barriers. To avoid blocking trade for unnecessarily long periods, both parties agreed to provide scientific evidence in cases when emergency measures are needed. The chapter provides for a specialized committee on SPS measures to enhance communication and cooperation and serve as a forum to solve trade irritants if technical consultations have not resolved the issue. The chapter also promotes an auditing system for promoting confidence in each party's system. In cases where a dispute escalates, the chapter provides for a dispute settlement mechanism and retains the possibility of raising the issue in the WTO.

15 The **Trade and Sustainable Development** chapter included the key elements of the EU approach to FTAs. It provides for: (a) commitments to international instruments on labour and the environment, including International Labour Organisation (ILO) provisions and the Paris Agreement; (b) sustained progress towards other fundamental ILO conventions; (c) prohibition of relaxation of labour or environmental laws to attract investment and trade; (d) commitments to conservation and sustainable natural resource management addressing biodiversity, illegal logging, and illegal, unreported and unregulated fishing; (e) promotion of trade and investment practices that support sustainable development including corporate social responsibility; (f) an institutional set-up to involve civil society in the implementation of this chapter; (g) a mechanism for dispute resolution.

16   The chapter on **Small and Medium Sized Enterprises** (SMEs) aimed to activate SMEs in Japan and the EU and in each other's markets and make it easier to do business. Each party is committed to transparency regarding market access, which for SMEs can represent trade barriers, through information sharing via websites. The interactions will be managed by the SME Contact Points under the SME chapter, and are responsible for addressing issues in other committees of the FTA affecting SMEs.

Notes

1   The other main business lobbies are Keizai Doyukai and the Chamber of Commerce.
2   Interviews with Alison Murray, Jacob Edberg and Bjorn Kongstad, European Business Council in Japan, Tokyo, 2009 and 2011.
3   The Global Europe strategy of 2006, reinforced by the 2010 Trade, Growth and World Affairs, states that the EU welcomes free trade deals to be competitive on an international scale and to stimulate growth through investment and innovation within the EU (2016a).
4   Japan's Geographical Indication Law (Act No. 84, 2014) was promulgated on 25 June 2014 to take effect one year later (Umeda, 2014). The law protects producers of certain agricultural products, protects consumers and promotes local agriculture and food brands.
5   Fast-track trade authority, granted to the President by Congress under the Bipartisan Trade Promotion Act of 2002, allowed the President to negotiate agreements to either be approved or denied by Congress. No amendments or filibusters were allowed. It was renewed as the Bipartisan Congressional Trade Priorities and Accountability Act of 2015.
6   Provisional application is applied to practical agreements with foreign governments so that the agreement does not have to wait for lengthy parliamentary approval process of each EU member country.
7   At the end of year two, the EU posted a trade surplus, the first time in fifteen years that the EU had recorded a trade surplus with South Korea (EC, 2014; Kang and Kim, 2013).
8   Although radically different circumstances, Japan's outward shift shared some similarities with South Korea. Lee (2014, p. 61) analysed how Korea's trade policy was essential to creating "capacity to overcome the external economic shocks caused by the global financial crisis".
9   The EU employs the term free trade agreement or FTA for its deep, comprehensive trade agreements. Yet in Japan, the term FTA has a slightly narrower, less comprehensive connotation. Because the scoping exercise resulted in a very deep and wide negotiation for a trade agreement, the Japanese side prefers the term economic partnership agreement or EPA. The agreement was sometimes called the FTA/EPA. Since 8 December 2017, it seemed both sides have settled on using Japan–EU EPA or EU–Japan EPA.
10   These barriers were deterrents to all new entrants to old markets regardless of nationality.
11   The scoping exercise is not meant to completely delimit the landscape of the negotiations as economic conditions do change and therefore might alter the landscape prior to the finalization of the negotiation phase.
12   The SPA negotiations began on the same date.

References

Amighini, A. and ISPI. (2016) *In Depth Analysis: Implementation of the EU-ROK FTA.* European Parliament Directorate General of External Policies of the European Union, Directorate B, Policy Department, p. 40. Available from: http://ispionline.it/DOC/EU_Parl_EU-ROK_3.pdf. [Accessed: 22 February 2017].

BBC News. (2010) *Q&A: What's Moving the Japanese Yen?* 10 September. Available from: www.bbc.com/news/business-11297402. [Accessed: 3 November 2017].

Berkofsky, A. (2012) EU-Japan Relations from 2001 to Today: Achievements, Failures and Prospects. *Japan Forum* 24(3), pp. 265–288.

Bilaterals.org. (2011) *EU-South Korea Free Trade Agreement: Green Light a Step Away.* European Parliament Newsletter. 14–17 February. Strasbourg plenary session. Available from: www.bilaterals.org/spip.php?article19026. [Accessed: 20 February 2017].

Blanchfield, M. (2017) Canada and Mexico Cold to US Using TPP to Make Progress on NAFTA. *National Post.* 14 November. Available from: http://nationalpost.com/pmn/news-pmn/canada-news-pmn/canada-and-mexico-cold-to-u-s-using-tpp-to-make-progress-in-nafta. [Accessed: 15 November 2017].

Blatchford, A. (2017) How Canada Allied with Mexico to Fend off TPP Pressure from Japan and Australia. *The Globe and Mail.* 11 November. Available from: www.theglobeandmail.com/news/politics/how-canada-allied-with-mexico-to-fend-off-tpp-pressure-from-japan-australia/article36931639/. [Accessed: 15 November 2017].

Cooper, W.H. and Manyin, M.E. (2007) *The Proposed South Korea-U.S. Free Trade Agreement (KORUS FTA).* Congressional Research Service Report for Congress. 23 April. Available from: fpc.state.gov/documents/organization/84284.pdf. [Accessed: 20 February 2017].

Council of the European Union. (2012) Directives for the Negotiation of a Free Trade Agreement with Japan. 15864/12, Brussels. 29 November. Declassified on 14 September 2017. Available from: http://trade.ec.europa.eu/doclib/docs/2017/september/tradoc_156051.en12.pdf. [Accessed: 13 November 2017].

De Gucht, K. (2013) *Challenge and Opportunity: Starting the Negotiations for Free Trade Agreement between the EU and Japan.* Speech by the European Commissioner for Trade. EU-Japan Business Summit. Tokyo, 25 March. Available from: http://trade.ec.europa.eu/doclib/docs/2013/march/tradoc_150791.pdf. [Accessed: 15 November 2017].

Denková, A. (2016) EU-Japan FTA Would Boost Growth More Than TTIP, EURACTIV. 17 June. Available from: www.euractiv.com/section/trade-society/news/eu-japan-fta-would-boost-growth-more-than-ttip/. [Accessed: 22 February 2017].

Economist. (2016) Try, Persist, Persevere! 19 November, pp. 11–12.

European Commission. (2010a) *EU-Korea Free Trade Agreement: A Quick Reading Guide.* October. Available from: http://trade.ec.europa.eu/doclib/docs/2009/october/tradoc_145203.pdf. [Accessed: 23 December 2017].

European Commission. (2010b) *EU-Korean Free Trade Agreement: 10 Key Benefits for the European Union.* Press Release. Memo/10/423, Brussels. 17 September. Available from: http://europa.eu/rapid/pressReleasesAction.do?reference=MEMO/10/423&format=HTML&aged=0&language=EN&guiLanguage=en. [Accessed: 20 February 2017].

European Commission. (2010c) *Framework Agreement between the European Union and Its Member States, on the One Part, and the Republic of Korea, on the Other Part.* 10 May. Available from: http://eeas.europa.eu/archives/docs/korea_south/docs/framework_agreement_final_en.pdf. [Accessed: 20 December 2017].

European Commission. (2013) *A Free Trade Agreement between the EU and Japan.* Memo/13/572. 17 June. Available from: http://europa.eu/rapid/press-release_MEMO-13-572_en.htm. [Accessed: 27 February 2017].

European Commission. (2014) *Report from the Commission to the European Parliament and the Council: Annual Report on the Implementation of the EU-Korea Free Trade Agreement.* COM(2014) 109 final. Brussels. 28 February.

European Commission. (2016a) *Trade Sustainability Impact Assessment of the Free Trade Agreement between the European Union and Japan: Final Report.* Directorate-General for Trade. Luxembourg: Publications Office of the European Union, p. 314. Available from: http://trade.ec.europa.eu/doclib/docs/2016/may/tradoc_154522.pdf. [Accessed: 27 February 2017].

European Commission. (2016b) *Trade for All: Towards a More Responsible Trade and Investment Policy.* Luxembourg: Publications Office of the European Union. p. 40. Available from: http://trade.ec.europa.eu/doclib/docs/2015/october/tradoc_153846.pdf. [Accessed: 1 March 2017].

European Commission. (2017a) *Trade Policy in Focus: EU-Japan Economic Partnership Agreement.* Available from: http://ec.europa.eu/trade/policy/in-focus/eu-japan-economic-partnership-agreement/. [Accessed: 22 December 2017].

European Commission. (2017b) *European Union Trade in Goods with South Korea.* 17 November. Available from: http://trade.ec.europa.eu/doclib/docs/2006/september/tradoc_113448.pdf. [Accessed 23 December 2017].

European Commission. (2017c) *EU-Japan EPA – Agreement in Principle.* 6 July, p. 15. Available from: http://trade.ec.europa.eu/doclib/docs/2017/july/tradoc_155693.doc.pdf. [Accessed 12 November 2017].

European Commission. (2017d) *Joint Statement by the President of the European Commission Jean-Claude Juncker and the Prime Minister of Japan Shinzo Abe.* 8 December. Available from: http://europa.eu/rapid/press-release_STATEMENT-17-5182_en.htm. [Accessed: 24 December 2017].

European Commission. (2017e) *EU-Japan Trade Agreement: Texts of the Agreement.* 8 December. Available from: http://trade.ec.europa.eu/doclib/press/index.cfm?id=1684. [Accessed: 24 December 2017].

European Commission. (n.d.a) *South Korea.* Trade Policy public information pages. Available from: http://ec.europa.eu/trade/policy/countries-and-regions/countries/south-korea/. [Accessed: 20 February 2017].

European Commission. (n.d.b) *Japan.* Trade Policy public information pages. Available from: http://ec.europa.eu/trade/policy/countries-and-regions/countries/japan/. [Accessed: 20 February 2017].

European Commission. (n.d.c) *Trade: Countries and Regions, Public Information Database of Trade Agreements.* Available from: http://ec.europa.eu/trade/policy/countries-and-regions/. [Accessed: 14 March 2017].

Fatheree, J.W. (2016) *Here's the Real Picture of KORUS: The United States is Selling More to Korea than Ever Before.* US Chamber of Commerce. 12 May. Available from: www.uschamber.com/article/here-s-the-real-picture-korus-the-united-states-selling-more-korea-ever. [Accessed: 20 February 2017].

Felbermayr, G., Kimura, F., Okubo, T., Steininger, M. and Yalcin, E. (2017) *GED Study: On the Economics of an EU-Japan Free Trade Agreement.* Study of the Ifo Institute on behalf of the Bertelsmann Foundation. Final Report. 3 March. Available from: www.bertelsmann-stiftung.de/fileadmin/files/BSt/Publikationen/GrauePublikationen/NW_EU-Japan_FTA.pdf. [Accessed: 15 February 2018].

Ferris, E. and Solís, M. (2013) *Earthquake, Tsunami, Meltdown: The Triple Disaster's Impact on Japan, Impact on the World.* Brookings. 11 March. Available from: www. brookings.edu/blog/up-front/2013/03/11/earthquake-tsunami-meltdown-the-triple-disasters-impact-on-japan-impact-on-the-world/. [Accessed: 27 February 2017].

Garikipati, R. (2015) Does Korea Benefit from FTA with EU? *The Korea Herald.* 27 July. Available from: www.koreaherald.com/view.php?ud=20150727001080. [Accessed: 14 March 2017].

Geist, M. (2017) No Deal is Better than a Bad Deal: Why Canada Won the TPP Stand-off. *The Globe and Mail.* 11 November. Available from: https://beta.theglobeandmail. com/report-on-business/rob-commentary/no-deal-is-better-than-a-bad-deal-why-canada-won-the-tpp-stand-off/article36931537/. [Accessed: 12 November 2017].

Hunt, A. and Wheeler, B. (2017) Brexit: All You Need to Know About the UK Leaving the EU. *BBC News.* 23 December. Available from: www.bbc.com/news/uk-politics-32810887. [Accessed: 27 December 2017].

International Trade Administration (ITA). (n.d.) *Why a US-Korea Trade Agreement?* US Department of Commerce. ITA public information pages. Available from: http://trade. gov/fta/korea/. [Accessed: 20 February 2017].

Japan Times. (2017) Japan and EU Reach Free Trade Accord in Blow against Protection-ism. 6 July. Available from: www.japantimes.co.jp/news/2017/07/06/business/eu-commissioner-says-free-trade-agreement-japan-reached-kishida-visit/#.WhPIYZP5iHo. [Accessed: 12 November 2017].

Jungbluth, C., Felbermayr, G., Kimura, F., Okubo, T., Steininger, M. and Yalcin, E. (2017) EU-Japan: Free Trade Agreement a Sign of Commitment to Economic Cooperation. Future Social Market Economy Policy Brief #2017/01. Bertelsmann Stif-tung. Available from: www.bertelsmann-stiftung.de/fileadmin/files/BSt/Publikationen/ GrauePublikationen/NW_Policy_Brief_FTA_EU-Japan.pdf. [Accessed: 15 February 2018].

Kang, Y-D. and Kim, J.Y. (2013). Trade and Investment between Korea and the EU after the Korea-EU FTA and Its Prospect. *World Economy Update.* Korea Institute for Inter-national Economic Policy (KIEP). 3(44). 27 September.

Kanter, J. (2017) The EU-Japan Trade Deal: What's in It and Why It Matters. *New York Times.* 6 July. Available from: www.nytimes.com/2017/07/06/business/economy/ japan-eu-trade-agreement.html. [Accessed: 12 November 2017].

Keidanren. (2007) *Call for the Start of Joint Study for a Japan-EU Economic Partnership Agreement.* Nippon Keidanren. 12 June. Available from: www.keidanren.or.jp/english/ policy/2007/050.html. [Accessed: 27 February 2017].

Keidanren. (2009) *Call for the Start of Negotiations on Japan-EU Economic Integration Agreement: Third Proposal for Japan-EU Economic Partnership Agreement.* Nippon Keidanren. 17 November. Available from: www.keidanren.or.jp/english/policy/2009/ 099.html. [Accessed: 27 February 2017].

Keidanren and EBC. (2010) *Japan-EU Summit: Time for an EIA.* Nippon Keidanren and European Business Council in Japan/EU Chamber of Commerce in Japan. 20 April. Available from: www.keidanren.or.jp/english/policy/2010/036.pdf. [Accessed: 27 Feb-ruary 2017].

Keizai Doyukai. (2011) *Economic Partnership Strategy as the Core of Economic Growth: Turning Early Participation in the TPP Negotiations into an Economic Breakthrough.* Japan Association of Corporate Executives. August, p. 5. Available from: www. doyukai.or.jp/en/policyproposals/2011/pdf/110831a.pdf. [Accessed: 27 February 2017].

Kim, Y.G. (2015) Evaluation of a Decade of Korea's FTA Policy. *World Economy Update*. Korea Institute for International Economic Policy (KIEP). 5(22). 6 November.

Kurtenbach, E. (2017) Cheese Please: Japan, EU Said to be Near Agreement on Trade Pact. *AP News*, 30 June. Available from: www.apnews.com/de6601e4a5724b83822 52be6d5b0d869/Cheese,-please:-Japan,-EU-said-near-agreement-on-trade-pact. [Accessed: 12 November 2017].

Lee, H-J. (2010) The EU-Korea FTA: A Boost to Economic Recovery and a Challenge to the U.S. *Brookings Northeast Asia Commentary*. (No. 42, October). Available from: www.brookings.edu/opinions/the-eu-korea-fta-a-boost-to-economic-recovery-and-a-challenge-to-the-u-s/. [Accessed: 22 February 2017].

Leigh, M. (2017) *Brexit Scenarios: An Exercise in Damage Limitation*. David P. Calleo Seminar Series, SAIS. Washington DC. 17 October.

Malmström, C. (2017) *The Future of EU Trade Policy*. Bruegel Lunch Talk. Speech by the EU Trade Commissioner. Brussels. 24 January. Available from: http://trade.ec. europa.eu/doclib/docs/2017/january/tradoc_155261.pdf. [Accessed: 10 March 2017].

METI. (n.d.) *Japan-EU Economic Partnership Agreement under Negotiation*. Ministry of Economy, Trade and Industry. Public web pages. Available from: www.meti.go.jp/policy/trade_policy/epa/epa_en/eu/. [Accessed: 6 March 2017].

Mikitani, H. (2016) Open up, Japan – The World in 2017. *Economist*. (November), p. 53.

MOFA. (2001) *An Action Plan for EU-Japan Cooperation, EU-Japan Summit, Brussels*. Ministry of Foreign Affairs of Japan. Available from: www.mofa.go.jp/region/europe/eu/summit/action0112.html. [Accessed: 6 March 2017].

MOFA. (2016) *Japan-EU Strategic Partnership Agreement*. Ministry of Foreign Affairs of Japan. 16 December. Available from: www.mofa.go.jp/erp/ep/page22e_000707. html. [Accessed: 6 March 2017].

MOFA. (2017a) *Economic Diplomacy: Foreign Minister Fumio Kishida Holds a Working Lunch with Dr. Cecilia Malmström, European Commissioner for Trade*. 5 July. Available from: www.mofa.go.jp/ecm/ie/page4e_000631.html. [Accessed: 12 November 2017].

MOFA. (2017b) *Japan-EU Economic Partnership Agreement, Japan-EU EPA (Outline)*. Available from: www.mofa.go.jp/policy/economy/page6e_000013.html. [Accessed: 27 December 2017].

Nelson, P.A. (2012) The Lisbon Treaty Effect: Toward a New EU-Japan Economic and Trade Partnership? *Japan Forum* 24(3), pp. 339–368.

NHK. (2017) 'Quotes of the Day' NHK Newsline from Tokyo, 6 July. Available from: www3.nhk.or.jp/nhkworld/nhknewsline/quotesoftheday/2017070601/. [Accessed: 12 November 2017].

Park, S.C. (2014) South Korean Trade Strategies in the Post-global Financial Crisis. *Contemporary Issues in Business and Government* 20(1), pp. 59–76.

Petri, P.A., Plummer, M.G., Urata, S. and Zhai, F. (2017) *Going it Alone in the Asia-Pacific: Regional Trade Agreements without the United States*. Working Paper 17–10. Peterson Institute for International Economics. Available from: https://piie.com/publications/working-papers/going-it-alone-asia-pacific-regional-trade-agreements-without-united. [Accessed: 12 November 2017].

Public Citizen. (n.d.) More Job Offshoring, More Inequality and Investor State Dispute Settlement (ISDS): Extraordinary Corporate Power in Trade Deals. Public web pages. Available from: www.citizen.org/our-work/globalization-and-trade. [Accessed: 12 November 2017].

Ryall, J. (2008) 'Missing Pensions' Scandal Engulfs Japan's PM Candidates. *Telegraph.* 10 September. Available from: www.telegraph.co.uk/news/worldnews/asia/japan/2776768/Missing-pensions-scandal-engulfs-Japans-PM-candidates.html. [Accessed: 18 October 2017].

Saeed, S. (2017) EU Closes Mammoth Trade Deal with Japan: 'Biggest Trade Deal We Have Ever Negotiated', Commissioner Malmström Said. *Politico.* 8 December. Available from: www.politico.eu/article/eu-closes-mammoth-trade-deal-with-japan/. [Accessed: 24 December 2017].

Schott, J.J. (2009) *Free Trade Agreements and the Future of US-Korean Trade Relations.* Proceedings from the Academic Symposium, *Navigating Turbulence in Northeast Asia: The Future of the US-ROK Alliance* sponsored by Korea Economic Institute, Korea Institute for International Economic Policy and East West Center. 23–24 October. Available from: www.keia.org/sites/default/files/publications/JAS-Schott_Final.pdf. [Accessed: 25 February 2017].

Shaxson, N. (2017) Opinion: Britain Can't Prosper as a Tax Haven. It Has to Stop these Hollow Threats. *Guardian.* 24 October. Available from: www.theguardian.com/commentisfree/2017/oct/24/britain-cant-prosper-tax-haven-hollow-threats-brexiteers-offshore-eu. [Accessed: 12 November 2017].

Shim, S. (2011) Gov't, Ruling Party Discuss Ratification of S. Korea-U.S. FTA. *Yonhap News Agency.* 9 February. Available from: http://english.yonhapnews.co.kr/national/2011/02/09/19/0301000000AEN20110209006300315F.HTML. [Accessed: 20 February 2017].

Sunesen, E.R., Francois, J.F. and Thelle, M.H. (2009) *Assessment of Barriers to Trade and Investment between the EU and Japan: Final Report.* Copenhagen Economics. Available from: http://trade.ec.europa.eu/doclib/docs/2010/february/tradoc_145772.pdf. [Accessed: 15 February 2018].

Umeda, S. (2014) Japan: Geographic Indication Act Promulgated. *Global Legal Monitor.* 24 September. Available from: www.loc.gov/law/foreign-news/article/japan-geographical-indication-act-promulgated/. [Accessed: 10 March 2017].

United States Trade Representative (USTR) (n.d.) *Korea-US Free Trade Agreement: New Opportunities for U.S. Exporters Under the U.S.-Korea Trade Agreement.* Office of the President. USTR public information pages. Available from: www.ustr.gov/trade-agreements/free-trade-agreements/korus-fta. [Accessed: 20 February 2017].

US-Korea Connect. (n.d.) *Issues and Answers KORUS FTA Trade Figures.* Embassy of the Republic of Korea in the USA. Available from: www.uskoreaconnect.org/facts-figures/issues-answers/korus-trade-figures.html. [Accessed: 22 December 2017].

Williams, C. (2011) Apple iPad2 Supplies 'Threatened by Japan Disaster'. *Telegraph.* 18 March. Available from: www.telegraph.co.uk/technology/apple/8390562/Apple-iPad-2-supplies-threatened-by-Japan-disaster.html. [Accessed: 25 February 2017].

WTO and IDE-JETRO. (2012) *Trade Patterns and Global Value Chains in East Asia: From Trade in Goods to Trade in Tasks,* World Trade Organisation and the Institute of Developing Economies. Available from: www.wto.org/english/res_e/booksp_e/stat_tradepat_globvalchains_e.pdf. [Accessed: 3 November 2017].

Yim, J-Y. (2010) Benefits of KORUS FTA. *Korea Focus,* reprinted from *Maeil Business Newspaper.* 14 December. Available from: www.koreafocus.or.kr/design2/layout/content_print.asp?group_id=103363. [Accessed: 20 February 2017].

8 Negative interest rate policy by the Bank of Japan from the perspective of monetary policy in Europe

Markus Heckel[1]

Introduction

In response to the financial crisis, central banks around the globe implemented a range of unconventional monetary policies. Central banks in Europe and the Bank of Japan have even introduced negative interest rates (NIR). The main incentives for the implementation of new monetary policy frameworks were to obtain higher inflation rates in order to meet price stability objectives and to support economic growth. This chapter analyses the introduction of NIR in Japan from the perspective of central banks in Europe by taking into account important international events such as the Brexit referendum and the US election of 2016. International implications show that monetary policy is intertwined, and enhanced coordination and cooperation between central banks is preferable to avoid global financial instability and future crises. In addition, this chapter summarizes some positive, but mainly focuses on the negative side effects of quantitative easing and NIR which include declining bank profitability, risks to financial stability, balance sheet risks, distributional effects and global imbalances through currency depreciation. In sum, NIR have a place in the toolkit of central banks, but, given their negative domestic and global implications, the benefits of these policies occur simultaneously with uncertainties and risks which might threaten the credibility and independence of central banks.

Negative interest rates

Since the financial crisis of 2008, major central banks have frequently dropped their policy rates, reaching very low levels or even zero which is usually regarded as the lower bound. Moreover, additional monetary policy strategies were implemented, including forward guidance and asset purchase programs, in order to stimulate output growth and to raise inflation expectations. This policy mix resulted in a considerable drop in nominal and real interest rates. However, in some countries central bank policies did not have the desired effects. From 2014 onwards, some central banks ignored the zero lower bound and dropped interest rates into negative territory, including the European Central Bank (ECB), the Swedish Riksbank (SR), the Danmarks Nationalbank (DNB), the Swiss National Bank (SNB), and the Bank of Japan (BoJ).[2]

In fact, nominal negative interest rates are a new experience for central banks. Up to that point, the zero lower bound and negative nominal interest rates were regarded as theoretical curiosities. They were not relevant to monetary policy-makers because interest rates typically stayed above zero, and central bankers could just drop interest rates to stimulate the economy (Ball *et al.*, 2016, p. 5). The unprecedented use of negative rates has generated a highly polarized debate on the implications of this policy. Proponents argue that negative interest rates have supported the goal of lower lending prices and real interest rates. Critics, however, highlight the risks such as financial instability (Hannoun, 2015). Central bankers have divided opinions about negative rates as well. Mark Carney, Governor of the Bank of England (BoE), belongs to the critics, stating that he is "not a fan of negative interest rates" and that the Monetary Policy Committee of the BoE, "is very clear that we see the effective lower bound as a positive number" (Bank of England, 2016a). On the other hand, there are some central bankers who argue in favour of negative rates. Thomas Jordan (2016), president of the Swiss National Bank, has confirmed that NIR is necessary and effective and Mario Draghi (2016) concluded that "all in all the [NIR] experience has been positive". Aside from the central bankers who introduced NIR, Janet Yellen, Chair of the US Federal Reserve, also argued that she is not ruling out negative interest rates (Udland, 2016). Despite these highly polarized discussions, the body of academic literature on NIR is still rather small.[3]

There is the valid question of why central banks implemented negative rates in the first place. It is claimed that there are some (theoretical) advantages of NIR, including the stabilization of inflation expectations, the support of output growth, and the reduction of currency appreciation pressures. On the other side, there are many risks and disadvantages of low (and negative) interest rates. Stanley Fischer (2016), former Vice Chairman of the US Federal Reserve, lists three disadvantages. First, low and negative interest rates are a signal that the economy's long-term prospects are weak (despite the fact that, in theory, lower interest rates should generate higher levels of investment). Second, low interest rates make the economy more susceptible to shocks. Because of the lower bound, central banks are forced to implement unconventional policy measures such as asset purchases and forward guidance. These limitations of monetary policy could thus result in longer recessions. US Federal Reserve Governor Powell (2016) confirms this view by stating that, "with interest rates so low, we are not well positioned to respond to negative shocks". Third, low (and negative) interest rates pressurize financial stability. Due to the reduced profitability of banks, excessive risk-taking might follow, which may result in (wild) inflation and/or even asset price bubbles (Hannoun, 2015; Palley, 2016). Arteta *et al.* (2016) stress that the risks to financial stability are particularly high if interest rates go considerably below zero or if NIR are implemented for a prolonged period of time.[4] Additional risks of NIR include problems of increased cash holding, including ongoing costs of safe storage (Witmer and Yang, 2015), and the negative effects on pensions which might lead to higher savings rates and less growth output. Effects on pensions have political implications and policy debates have started putting pressure on central banks to adjust monetary policy. Bean *et al.* (2015, p. 95) speak of an "*irrational component* that comes into play when going from zero to negative rates" [italics added].

Negative interest rates in Europe

Euro-area

In June 2014, the European Central Bank adopted a negative interest rate policy of minus 0.1 per cent, at which banks must pay for holding excess cash at the ECB. The aim was to achieve the price stability objective of below, but close to, 2 per cent annual inflation. Following the "no limits" of monetary policy statement by ECB President Mario Draghi in January 2016, the ECB set depositary rates at minus 0.4 per cent in March 2016. Complementary to NIR, the ECB purchased government bonds and since April 2016, it began purchasing corporate bonds by individual non-financial corporations at a current amount of more than seven billion euro every month. One reason for this new policy tool is that the supply of suitable government bonds is becoming lower and the yields are already quite low. However, corporate bond purchases by the central bank are problematic because market distortions cannot be ruled out. There is one important point for the euro area which has to be taken into account. With negative rates, it is easier for highly indebted countries (such as Italy and Greece) to finance themselves, and, if inflation rises, to lower the debt burden. Subsequently, current monetary policy is a highly political issue.

Sweden

In February 2015, the Swedish Riksbank cut the repo rate from 0 per cent to minus 0.1 per cent. The repo rate is the interest rate at which banks can deposit funds at the central bank. Similar to the ECB, the Riksbank wanted to safeguard "the role of the inflation target as a nominal anchor for price setting and wage formation" (Sveriges Riksbank, 2015). In February 2016, a further cut followed, to minus 0.5 per cent (Figure 8.1). This policy decision was associated with an immediate depreciation of the Swedish krona (Ball *et al.*, 2016, p. 22). Strictly speaking, the Riksbank set the largest negative policy rate of minus 0.125 per cent for overnight deposits, but usually Swedish banks only make a few deposits at this rate, preferring instead to park excess deposits in one-week reverse repos. In addition to NIR, the Swedish central bank purchased a higher amount of government bonds. With an inflation rate of approximately 1 per cent in 2016, Sweden's monetary policy seems to be on the right track (Ball *et al.*, 2016, p. 16; Bech and Malkhozov, 2016).

Denmark

In July 2012, the Danmarks Nationalbank lowered the deposit rate to minus 0.2 per cent. The interest rate cuts by the ECB caused upward pressure on the Danish currency. Denmark's interest rates are closely related to that of the ECB, and in fact Rohde (2017) labelled Denmark an "ECB copycat". While the rate was temporarily raised to 0.05 per cent in April 2014, the DNB cut it again to negative territory in September 2014. In 2015, the rate cut reached unprecedented levels of minus 0.75 per cent (Figure 8.1). Together with the SNB this constituted the furthest cut into negative territory by a central bank. There were two reasons for this move. First, there was some speculations that the central bank would terminate the fixed exchange rate to the euro (similar to the Swiss National Bank), resulting in large-scale purchase of the Danish Krona. Second, the asset purchase programme of the ECB caused a loss of the euro's value, resulting in higher upward pressure on the Danish currency. In 2016, the Danish central bank slightly corrected its interest rate to minus 0.65 per cent (Arteta *et al.*, 2016; Bech and Malkhozov, 2016).

Switzerland

Parallel to Denmark, the Swiss currency was constantly accompanied by upward pressures. As a response to the economic crisis in Greece, investors viewed the Swiss franc as a "safe haven" (similar to the Japanese yen) which increased the demand for the franc. The SNB cut interest rates to minus 0.25 per cent in December 2014. In response to further appreciation of the Swiss franc, the central bank was obliged to cut the rate to minus 0.75 per cent in 2015 (Figure 8.1). The SNB installed a two-tier system for banks which stored their deposits

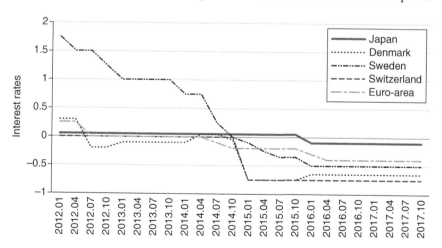

Figure 8.1 Development of interest rates in selected countries since 2012.

Source: Bank of Japan, Danmarks Nationalbank, European Central Bank, Swedish Riksbank, Swiss Nationalbank.

at the central bank. In the case of banks exceeding the allowance of 10 million francs, a penalty interest of minus 0.75 per cent was introduced. Fritz Zurbruegg from the Swiss National Bank argued that due to the introduction of negative rates, mortgage rates and the rates for firm loans were increasing, hinting at the fact that most Swiss banks were reluctant to pass on negative rates to depositors (in Bean *et al.*, 2015: 95). Due to exchange rate pressures, it is difficult for the SNB to raise the interest rate higher than the ECB and if the ECB lowers the interest rate the SNB would be forced to do so as well, meaning that (like Denmark) it had become highly dependent on its neighbour in Frankfurt.

Negative interest rates in Japan

In January 2016, the BoJ announced a new policy framework called "Quant-itative and Qualitative Monetary Easing with a Negative Interest Rate". The decision to pursue this policy was influenced by central banks in Europe. Deputy Governor Iwata (2016) stated clearly that the BoJ introduced negative interest rates after analysing the experiences of European economies. However, the deci-sion to adopt NIR by the BoJ was totally unexpected by the markets and central bank watchers.[5] Prior to this, Bank of Japan Governor Haruhiko Kuroda had fre-quently stated that the Bank of Japan would not adopt negative interest rates. The BoJ's surprise move turned out to be a problem for the markets[6] and "resulted in market upheaval, which may have increased risk aversion and safe haven pressures" (Ball *et al.*, 2016, p. 22).

However, this policy was not the last step taken by the BoJ. On 21 September 2016, the central bank announced changes that moved it towards a "Quantitative and Qualitative Monetary Easing with Yield Curve Control", with the aim of con-trolling long-term interest rates, i.e. the interest-rate level for government bonds with a 10-year maturity was to be kept near zero. In addition, the BoJ was now heading towards a higher price stability target than the 2 per cent ("overshooting"). More cautious is the BoJ's timing of reaching the goal. Instead of giving a precise date, the BoJ argued for achieving the 2 per cent price stability target at the "earliest possible time" (Bank of Japan, 2016c). The policy adjustment showed that the BoJ viewed the flattening of the yield curve as a main problem. However, as, *inter alia*, Di Maggio and Kacperczyk (2017) argue, a flat yield curve could also be interpreted as a boost for investment and output growth, i.e. the effects are far from clear. The move towards yield curve control might be interpreted as a response to criticism against the negative interest rate by commercial banks, policymakers, and the media. Thus, some economists have spoken of "tapering" or a "stealth taper" by the BoJ (Uhlig, 2016). However, the move to steepen the yield curve can be seen as an action that took the position of financial institutions into account. Complementary to this policy, the BoJ now conducted equity purchases through Exchange Traded Funds (ETF) currently at the rate of 6 trillion yen per year, in order to support a stimulation of the equity market. ETF purchases may have some short-term effects on the economy; however, the increase in the balance sheet might also create substantial risks to the capital of the central bank.

Since Kuroda became Governor in 2013, the aggressive monetary easing actions by the BoJ had consisted of three main actions: (1) increasing of the quantity and duration of its Japanese government bond (JGB) purchases, (2) purchasing riskier assets such as ETF, and (3) the interest rate cut into negative territory. An urgent question is whether this aggressive monetary policy is sustainable. Similar to Draghi's well-known "no limits" statement, Kuroda (2013) announced that the BoJ was doing "whatever is necessary" to reach the target of 2 per cent inflation. Kuroda (2016) repeated his strong determination with the statement that "there is no doubt that *ample space* for additional easing in each of these three dimensions is available to the Bank" [italics added]. However, regardless of these strongly stated intentions, it seems that the BoJ is running out of ammunition for further easing with the inflation remaining at low levels.

International implications

Central bank policies are connected to each other and it seems that central banks around the globe followed strategies of quantitative easing which were first introduced by the Bank of Japan. The three arrows of *Abenomics* found their counterpart in *Draghinomics* with a similar focus on aggressive monetary policy (De Prado, 2014; Roubini, 2014). With negative interest rates it went vice versa, the Bank of Japan followed strategies which were introduced by central banks in Europe.

NIR have international implications, for example, through a beggar-thy-neighbour policy. Because quantitative easing and negative rates have a tendency to lead to exchange rate depreciation, it might have negative effects on other countries. If many countries decide to depreciate the value of their currencies "currency manipulations" or even "currency wars" might result (Borio and Zabai, 2016, p. 28; Eichengreen, 2013; Rajan, 2015, pp. 11–12). The opinions voiced by the Monetary Policy Meeting of the BoJ show that one member was concerned that exactly this might happen: "the Bank's introduction of a negative interest rate could lead to a competition with central banks in other countries, which already have adopted negative interest rates, to lower interest rates deeper into negative territory" (Bank of Japan, 2016a).[7]

Due to strong global entanglements, many international aspects exert an influence on monetary policy in Japan and Europe. The rise of emerging economies, especially China, is viewed as one aspect that has led to sluggish economic growth and global low inflation rates (Bean *et al.*, 2015). If the economy of China follows a downward trend then the economies in other countries also face trouble, especially Japan as the yen is viewed as a "safe haven" resulting in upward pressures even in times of economic recessions. The UK referendum on 23 June 2016 is another example. After the decision for Brexit, on 3 August 2016 the BoE decided to adopt an easing framework across the three dimensions of quantity, quality and interest rates. The scale of the new programme surpassed the anticipation of the market and central bank watchers. The move included

(1) an interest rate cut to 0.25 per cent (2) asset purchases of corporate bonds of 10 billion pounds and (3) an expansion of the amount of purchases of government bonds to 435 billion pounds (Bank of England, 2016b).

The Brexit decision had strong effects on Japan. On the day following the referendum, the Japanese currency spiked to slightly above 99 yen/US dollar. A stronger yen is a burden for many export-oriented Japanese firms. The Bank of Japan clearly saw substantial uncertainties for economic activity due to the developments in Europe and acted quickly in adjusting its monetary policy. In the Monetary Policy Meeting on 29 July, the BoJ clearly referred to the UK referendum as a reason for its monetary easing:

> Against the backdrop of the *United Kingdom's vote to leave the European Union* and the slowdown in emerging economies, uncertainties surrounding overseas economies have increased and volatile developments have continued in the global financial markets. In order to prevent these uncertainties from leading to a deterioration in business confidence and consumer sentiment as well as to ensure smooth funding in foreign currencies by Japanese firms and financial institutions, thereby supporting their proactive economic activities, at the Monetary Policy Meeting (MPM) held today, the Policy Board of the Bank of Japan decided [...] [a]n *increase in purchases of exchange-traded funds* [...].
>
> (Bank of Japan, 2016b, italics added)

The BoJ almost doubled its purchases of ETF from 3.3 trillion to about 6 trillion yen. Deputy Governor Hiroshi Nakaso (2016b) explained the decision by arguing that Japan's markets were the first to be affected by the results of the Brexit referendum. Due to the rapid appreciation of the yen and the sharp fall of stock prices, the BoJ considered it necessary to support globally operating Japanese firms and financial institutions with ample liquidity in foreign currencies, in particular in the US dollar. The United States presidential election of 2016 is another example. The ECB commented on its decision by issuing the following statement:

> There is high *uncertainty* about the results of the November 2016 US election. The ECB is cautious towards the expected economic policy. If – as announced – fiscal policy will be expansionary, higher fiscal deficit and inflation expectation will follow. Higher uncertainty is accompanied by higher volatility in the markets and, therefore, *risk aversion of the investors might increase.*
>
> (European Central Bank, 2016, italics added)

After the election, the value of the US dollar went up, which can be interpreted as investors understanding Trump's victory as a signal for more investment. The result of a stronger dollar was a depreciation of the yen to 112 yen/US dollar and an increase in the Nikkei index to over 18.000 points. This development meant higher profits for Japanese export-oriented firms. Thus, a German newspaper heralded Trump as the "saviour of Abenomics" (Welter, 2016). As a consequence of the weaker yen, the Policy Board of the Bank of Japan raised the projections for growth in the fiscal year 2017 to 1.5 per cent (from 1.3 per cent in October 2016) and for 2018 to 1.1 per cent (from 0.9 per cent in October 2016) in its *Outlook* from January 2017 (Bank of Japan, 2017a).

These international implications show that monetary policy is intertwined and cannot be viewed separately. For most countries, an internationally functioning monetary market is a necessary condition. The implementation of unconventional monetary policies, including negative interest rates, has raised concerns about the transmission between countries with different levels of quantitative easing. In 2013, the Group of Seven (G-7) had already issued a statement setting basic rules to deal with potential exchange rate effects caused by monetary policy (Brainard, 2017). BoJ Governor Kuroda argued that aggressive monetary easing by major central banks needed to be complemented with "measures developed through international cooperation". Further, he stressed the positive effects of international cooperation:

> the robustness of the global financial system has been greatly enhanced by, for example, higher capital and liquidity reserve levels at financial institutions, more options for liquidity provisioning by central banks, better legal frameworks for resolving financial institutions, and enhanced communications and cooperation among authorities.
>
> (Kuroda, 2017)

The president of the Bundesbank Jens Weidmann (2017) has added that the aspect of uncertainty which increased after the financial crisis necessitates a high degree of international cooperation.[8] Central banks are in need of international cooperation with respect to international financial regulations. The experiences of the financial crisis were met by the adoption of the Basel III framework, an international regulatory accord that set rules for financial institutions, including higher capital requirements. Furthermore, the Ministers of Finance of the G20 and central bank governors agreed a commitment to international economic and financial cooperation during their meeting in Baden-Baden in March 2017. Regarding the exchange market, they made a committed avoiding competitive depreciations of their respective currencies (Bundesbank, 2017).

Discussions concerning negative interest rates

Quantitative monetary easing with negative interest rates might impose some costs and benefits on the economy. Potential benefits of NIR can include the expansion of investments through lower lending costs and a stronger aggregate demand. Potential side effects include (1) a decline in the profitability of the financial sector which might lead to enhanced financial stability risks, (2) balance sheet risks, (3) loss of credibility due to the ineffectiveness of monetary policy, and (4) the risk of rising inequality regarding the distribution of wealth.

An event study assessed the immediate market reaction to NIR and indicated that money market rates and sovereign bond yields have fallen on the day of the policy announcement (Arteta *et al.*, 2016). Ball *et al.* (2016, p. 25) show that credit growth has picked up in the Eurozone after implementing negative interest rates. Currencies of countries implementing NIR have on average depreciated with the exception of the Swiss franc and Japanese yen (Arteta *et al.*, 2016). However, over time, effects of NIR on output, inflation, and inflation expectations are marginal or have weakened in some countries (Borio and Zabai, 2016). Honda and Inoue (2017) find that NIR of the BoJ has encouraged investment and supported stock prices.[9] The Bank of Japan claims that its monetary policy and NIR has been a success:

> [W]ith regard to the effects and impact of the negative interest rate, it had been confirmed that the combination of the negative interest rate policy and JGB purchases was an effective means to push down short-term and long-term interest rates. The decline in JGB yields brought about by these policy measures had translated firmly into a decline in lending rates as well as interest rates on corporate bonds and CP.
>
> (Bank of Japan, 2016c, p. 13)

In sum, unconventional monetary policies have resulted in a considerable drop in nominal and real interest rates. The recent experiences of the central banks considered here suggest that interest rate cuts into negative territory generally did transmit to bank lending rates. However, cross-country comparisons show some differences. In the Eurozone, the average interest rate on new short-term bank loans fell by substantially more than policy and market-based rates following the ECB's decision to implement negative interest rates in 2014, with declines in almost all the member states (European Central Bank, 2016). In Denmark and Sweden, bank lending rates dropped as well, but at a slower pace (Ball *et al.*, 2016, p. 20). As a result, low or negative rates threaten the profits of banks which are highly dependent on interest rate margins. The Bundesbank has warned against the risks of diminishing bank profitability (Thiele, 2017).

Consequently, banks have had to find strategies to avoid shrinking profitability, for example, through higher fees for customers. In general, there is strong resistance from banks against negative interest rates, because they are confronted by many difficulties in passing negative rates on to small depositors. However, as costs increase, commercial banks try to find ways to pass the costs on to their retail customers in order to remain profitable. Faced with negative rates, customers may start to shift their deposits into cash at a certain point. However, it is unclear at which level that point is, and it probably varies between countries and is dependent on various costs such as storage and insurance costs as well as on psychological and institutional aspects (Borio and Zabai, 2016, p. 19; Rognlie, 2016). In Germany, some banks started to charge customers with negative rates or taxes. These banks include the *V-Bank*, the *Postbank*, the *Stadtsparkasse München* and the *Hamburger Volksbank.* Since September 2016, the German savings bank *Raiffeisenbank Gmund am Tegernsee* decided to charge penalty interest for savings in excess of 100,000 euro. The *Postbank* abolished free-of-charge current accounts. In Switzerland, the *Alternative Bank Schweiz* (ABS) charges negative rates of minus 0.125 to their customers. The result is that retail customers will cancel their bank accounts and instead rely on cash. *Julius Bär* attempted another strategy by dividing the costs of NIR between the bank, customers and customer consultants.[10]

Most central banks have introduced complementary policy measures to protect banks' shrinking profitability. For example, in the case of the ECB, the implementation of NIR was part of a package of measures including exceptionally favourable refinancing conditions for banks as well as expanded asset purchases. The BoJ, DNB, and SNB charged only a certain fraction of bank deposits with negative rates, for example through a multiple-tier system in order to protect banks from negative impacts (Arteta *et al.*, 2016; Bank of Japan, 2016a; Borio and Zabai, 2016, p. 21).[11] A bigger problem might be experienced by investors including banks, pension funds, and insurance companies. Government bonds, which are usually viewed as safe investments, dropped significantly and even moving into negative territory in some countries such as Germany, Japan and Switzerland. As a result, in order to make profits, investors had to enhance risks through either buying titles with longer maturities or taking riskier investments, which could de-stabilize the financial system. The BoJ admitted that there are side effects of NIR, such as reduced bank profitability, which impose negative effects on the economy:

> [...] the decline in lending rates had been brought about by reducing financial institutions' profits. A decline in long-term and super-long-term interest rates lowered the rates of return on insurance and pension products, and attention needed to be paid to the possibility that this could have a negative impact on economic activity through a deterioration in people's sentiment.
>
> (Bank of Japan, 2016c, pp. 13–14)

Regarding inflation in Japan, it has been rising rather slowly and the BoJ has postponed the achievement of its inflation target of 2 per cent several times. Also concerning inflation expectations, it can be argued that the BoJ did not obtain its goal as inflation expectations have continued on a downward trend since 2015 (Nishino *et al.*, 2016).

Due to negative interest rate policies followed by central banks, the share of government bonds with negative yields has risen strongly in Europe and Japan. This increases the probability of losses by central banks which could become a critical political problem resulting in harmful effects on central bank independence. Since the financial crisis, the balance sheets of central banks have increased to a high extent due to large-scale government bond buying programmes. For instance, the BoJ carries 39 per cent of government bonds (Figure 8.2). This and

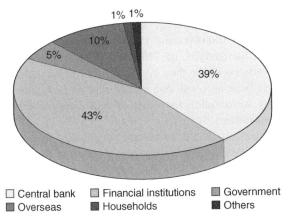

Figure 8.2 Holders of Japanese government bonds (as of December 2016).

Source: Ministry of Finance, 2017.

the purchases of other assets have led to higher risks of financial instability in Japan. The amount outstanding of the monetary base reached levels of over 470 trillion yen with a year-on-year rate of growth at around 25 per cent (Bank of Japan, 2017b). If the increase in the monetary base continues at the current pace it will reach the overall nominal output by the end of 2017. A serious issue includes the risk of purchasing the majority share of private corporate securities by the central bank. One might think of "backdoor nationalisation" in the case of a central bank possessing more than 50 per cent of corporate bonds and/or equity. So far, no central bank has ever owned a majority of private corporate securities. However, the higher the ownership share of a central bank is the more problems arise regarding voting rights and control of corporations, an area that does not belong to the responsibilities of a central bank (Ball *et al.*, 2016, p. 41). In response to enhanced asset purchases, the amount of the balance sheet is increasing in many central banks. However, the magnitude is quite different: whereas the ECB's balance sheet reached a level of around 40 per cent in 2017, the size of the BoJ's balance sheet is at an alarming level of around 90 per cent of GDP.

Increases in central banks' balance sheets are problematic because they have fiscal implications and exert influence on the balance sheets of the respective governments. This might result in central banks financing government debt (Borio and Zabai, 2016, pp. 33–34; Lombardi and Moschella, 2016). If central banks are involved in large-scale government bond purchases it can be viewed as a means of support for a government's financing of its own debts. In addition, in the case of central banks purchasing corporate bonds or equities, some borrowers benefit at the cost of others. It can be argued that both aspects are spheres central banks should not interfere in, but these are becoming serious concerns in European countries and Japan. Former Policy Board member Sayuri Shirai (2017, p. 96) has warned of the risks of buying government bonds and states:

[a]s long as the BOJ continues to purchase a large amount of JGBs in an extremely low interest environment, the interest adjustment amount will continue to grow. The resulting declining income from holdings of JGBs is one factor amplifying the balance sheet risk, suggesting that a continuation of massive JGB purchases is likely to become a challenge in the near future.

The last aspect of whether, and if so in what way, unconventional monetary policy affects the economy is the recent discussion in academic literature regarding the distribution of wealth, although a lot of research still has to be done to derive more significant results. Regarding the distributional effects of wealth, it can be argued that aggressive monetary policies leads to financial transfers between generations. Middle-aged and middle-class households, which proportionally save more, can be counted as being on the losing side of negative interest rates, because their savings diminish over time. Older generations in high income households, who own a higher proportion of financial assets, feel the advantages of expansionary monetary policies. Saiki and Frost (2014) argue that unconventional monetary policy leads to proportionally higher bond prices in comparison to wages with the result that higher income households gain profits. They found that between 2008 and 2013 the difference between the highest and lowest income increased in Japan. In addition, shareholders profited from a higher Nikkei 225 index. However, a final conclusion is difficult to reach. Unconventional monetary policies have a tendency to lift equity prices which also increases inequality. On the other hand, lower rates on loans and mortgages might support the majority of the population. However, the beneficiaries of unconventional monetary policies will probably spend less of their income and, eventually aggregate consumption will decline (Ball *et al.*, 2016, p. 42; Borio and Zabai, 2016., p. 32). Research from the Bank of England confirms that quantitative easing with low or negative interest rates tend to result in more inequality (Bank of England, 2012).[12]

El-Erian (2016) argues that the "results so far suggest that BOJ policy has not only been ineffective but also potentially counterproductive" referring to the risk of losing credibility. Therefore, the critique against unconventional monetary policy is rising. In particular, arguments highlighting the ineffectiveness and limits of monetary policy are increasing (Goodhart, 2015; Nishimura, 2016b; Yoshino and Miyamoto, 2017; Yoshino and Taghizadeh-Hesary, 2015). For instance, Mervyn King, former Governor of the Bank of England, stated that "[t] here are clearly limits" as to what monetary policy can achieve (Ward, 2016). With the NIR, it seems that the ECB is losing trust not only in the financial sector, but also in the public in certain member states. Based on data from the Eurobarometer, Ehrmann, Soudan and Stracca (2013) show that the level of trust in the ECB has followed a declining trend since 2008. Especially, in Germany and Southern European countries such as Greece and Spain dissatisfaction with the ECB is rising. According to the Eurobarometer, 53 per cent of German and 62 per cent of Spanish citizens mistrust the ECB (Standard Eurobarometer,

2017). In 2011, this value was at 39 per cent for Germany and 47 per cent for Spain (Standard Eurobarometer, 2011). As a consequence, a considerable amount of criticism has been formulated, for example by Deutsche Bank CEO John Cryan and Volker Wieland, member of the German Council of Experts, based on the argument that the current monetary policy of the ECB counteracts its objectives of strengthening the economies and banking system in Europe (*Handelsblatt*, 2016), with the result that current monetary policy is regarded as part of the problem rather than its remedy. The ECB usually responds to such criticism by hinting that without accommodative monetary policies the result would be even worse. US Federal Reserve Governor Brainard also sees that monetary policy can become less effective and warns against following the example of Europe and Japan:

> Indeed, it is striking that despite active and creative monetary policies in both the euro area and Japan, inflation remains below target levels. The experiences of these economies highlight the risk of becoming trapped in a low-growth, low-inflation, low-inflation-expectations environment and suggest that policy should be oriented toward minimizing the risk of the U.S. economy slipping into such a situation.
>
> (Brainard, 2016, p. 5)

As a result, the US Federal Reserve started to raise rates from 2015. In the end, it is difficult to judge at what point monetary policy is becoming ineffective. However, it seems that central banks have reached a dangerous point at which they might overstep their responsibilities. Indeed, there are certainly limits to what monetary policy can and should do. In order to create or maintain economic stability, the responsibility must be shared with fiscal policy (Williams, 2016).

Regarding the final point of the issue of independent agencies, there might be pressure to justify recent monetary policies by central banks. Decision-makers in the central banks are not democratically elected, but have a lot of influence on many aspects of the economy. Assuming that central bank policy is against the will of the general public and elected policymakers, how can we justify having independent central banks? Ball *et al.* (2016, pp. 28–29) argue that central bank policies can have negative effects on the credibility and efficiency of monetary policy if the general public does not accept or understand what the central bank is doing, and why. BoJ Deputy Governor Hiroshi Nakaso (2016a) admitted that he:

> cannot deny that some aspects of this policy [NIR] may be counterintuitive to the public. Therefore, we need to carefully listen to criticisms. […] In other words, it is essential to explain more persuasively that these policy measures are necessary for the economy to revert to a sustainable growth path. This seems to be a challenge the Bank of Japan and the ECB have in common.

As a consequence, central banks have been challenged to explain their monetary policy more efficiently and to increase communication as part of the need for greater central bank transparency. As a result, if the people (or politicians as representatives of the public) do not support NIR, it is difficult for a central bank to implement or maintain it. Under these circumstances, it can be argued that a non-elected independent central bank is a reduction to the absurd as it does not represent the general public in order to protect them against politicians maximizing their self-interest. In the end, the credibility of central banks might be under threat.

Conclusion

It is not clear in which direction the setting of interest-rates will proceed in the future. On the one hand, the US Federal Reserve started to raise interest rates in 2015, which puts pressure on central banks in Europe and the Bank of Japan. On the other hand, inflation figures in Europe and Japan impose some difficulties for the central banks to increase interest rates. Some academics discuss higher negative interest rates. For example, Ball *et al.* (2016, p. 28) argue that higher negative interest rates can be preferable as deeper rate cuts might shorten a recession. To repeat, the public's adherence to NIR is a strong argument that puts up barriers against such kind of drastic measures (even if they are effective). Referring to the results of NIR so far, the argument that monetary policy in the current environment is ineffective in stimulating the economy and that fiscal policy should be employed to tackle the problem of sluggish growth gains momentum. As regards to monetary policy, central banks learn from each other, a fact demonstrated by the implementation of similar policies during the crisis. Central banks have developed stronger ties and established a relationship of cooperation (Nakaso, 2017). An end to negative interest rates can be a future strategy to be followed by the Bank of Japan and the European Central Bank which will affect interest rate setting in other central banks in Europe. Enhanced coordination and cooperation between the central banks is needed in order to maintain global financial stability and to prevent future crises.

Notes

1 The author gratefully acknowledges the generous funding support of this research by the Volkswagen Foundation, issued within its initiative "Key Issues for Research and Society" for the research project "Protecting the Weak: Entangled processes of framing, mobilization and institutionalization in East Asia" (AZ 87 382) at the Interdisciplinary Centre for East Asian Studies (IZO), Goethe University, Frankfurt/Main.
2 Central banks in Norway and Hungary introduced NIR for excess bank reserves in September 2015 and March 2016 respectively.
3 Exceptions are, *inter alia*, Brunnermaier and Koby (2016) and Rognlie (2016). By applying a New Keynesian model, Dennis (2016) shows that negative nominal interest rates shorten the average durations of the zero lower bound.
4 However, there is little evidence so far that bank lending has been reduced. Arteta *et al.* (2016) argue that bank lending margins are at a similar level as after the crisis, although some surveys suggest that NIR has negative effects on bank profitability.

5 Good communication and transparency by a central bank are important before implementing NIR (see, for example, Ball *et al.*, 2016, p. 28). With its surprise decision, the Bank of Japan clearly followed a different strategy.

6 Negative interest rates are discussed quite controversially in Japan. In a volume by the Japan Center for Economic Research, leading economists discussed the pros and cons of negative interest rates. See, for example, Ryutaro Kono (chief economist at BNP Paribas) and Masazumi Wakatabe (Waseda University) (Japan Center for Economic Research, 2016).

7 However, Ball *et al.* (2016, p. 22) argue that "[m]onetary policy with negative interest rates is no more a beggar-thy-neighbour policy, and has no more international spillovers, than monetary policy in normal times".

8 Nishimura (2016a) argues that the global economy is faced by three "seismic shifts" and asset-inflated bubbles in Japan, the US, and Europe are one set of them. These bubbles have increased uncertainty in the economy.

9 Some research about monetary policy in Japan finds positive results. For instance, Iwatsubo and Taishi (2017) find that quantitative and qualitative monetary easing (QQE) contributed significantly to improving market liquidity. They identified three reasons: (1) an increased frequency of purchases, (2) a decrease in the purchase amount per transaction and (3) a reduced variability in the purchase amounts. These results helped to lessen uncertainty in the markets which can be interpreted as a positive effect of QQE. By using vector autoregression and forecast-based counterfactuals, Hausman and Wieland (2014) find that QQE contributed to 1 per cent output growth and reduced the yield of ten-year government bonds by 11.4 per cent.

10 There is an ongoing debate about the abolition of cash in order for central banks to drop interest rates further to higher negative zones (see, for example, Rogoff, 2016 and Shirakawa, 2017).

11 According to Jobst and Lin (2016), there is so far only limited evidence that NIR have a direct detrimental effect on bank profitability in the euro area.

12 In contrast, the Bundesbank (2016) raises some doubts about the relation between the increase of inequality and non-standard monetary policies.

References

Arteta, C., Kose, A., Stocker, M. and Taskin, T. (2016) Negative Interest Rate Policies: Sources and Implications. *CEPR Discussion Paper Series*. DP11433.

Ball, L., Gagnon, J., Honohan, P. and Krogstrup, S. (2016) What Else Can Central Banks Do? *Geneva Reports on the World Economy*. 18. International Center for Monetary and Banking Studies, CEPR Press.

Bank of England. (2012) The Distributional Effects of Asset Purchases. *Quarterly Bulletin* Q3.

Bank of England. (2016a) *Inflation Report Q&A*. 4 August.

Bank of England. (2016b) *Monetary Policy Summary*. Bank of England. 4 August.

Bank of Japan. (2016a) *Summary of Opinions at the Monetary Policy Meeting*. 28–29 January.

Bank of Japan. (2016b) *Minutes of the Monetary Policy Meeting*. 28–29 July.

Bank of Japan. (2016c) *Minutes of the Monetary Policy Meeting*. 20–21 September.

Bank of Japan. (2017a) *Outlook for Economic Activity and Prices*. January.

Bank of Japan. (2017b) *Monetary Base. Bank of Japan*. Available from: www.boj.or.jp/en/statistics/boj/other/mb/index.htm/. [Accessed: 13 November 2017].

Bean, C., Broda, C., Itō, T. and Kroszner, R. (2015) Low for Long? Causes and Consequences of Persistently Low Interest Rates. *Geneva Reports on the World Economy*. 17. International Center for Monetary and Banking Studies, CEPR Press.

Bech, M.L. and Malkhozov, A. (2016) How Have Central Banks Implemented Negative Policy Rates? *BIS Quarterly Review* March 2016, pp. 31–44.

Borio, C. and Zabai, A. (2016) Unconventional Monetary Policies: A Re-appraisal. *BIS Working Papers* 570.

Brainard, L. (2016) *The "New Normal" and What It Means for Monetary Policy*. Remarks at "The Chicago Council on Global Affairs". Chicago, IL. 12 September.

Brainard, L. (2017) *Cross-Border Spillovers of Balance Sheet Normalization*. Speech at the National Bureau of Economic Research's Monetary Economics Summer Institute. New York. 13 July. Available from: www.federalreserve.gov/newsevents/speech/brainard 20170713a.htm. [Accessed: 13 November 2017].

Brunnermeier, M.K. and Koby, Y. (2016) *The "Reversal Interest Rate": An Effective Lower Bound on Monetary Policy*. Unpublished manuscript.

Bundesbank. (2016) *Monthly Report*. September. Frankfurt: Deutsche Bundesbank.

Bundesbank. (2017) *G20 Finance Track Underscores Importance of International Cooperation*. 20 March. Available from: www.bundesbank.de/Redaktion/EN/Topics/ 2017/2017_03_18_g20_baden_baden.html. [Accessed: 12 November 2017].

De Prado, C. (2014) *Prospects for the EU-Japan Strategic Partnership: A Global Multi-Level and SWOT Analysis*. EU-Japan Centre for Industrial Cooperation, Florence and Tokyo.

Dennis, R. (2016) Durations at the Zero Lower Bound. *IMES Discussion Paper Series*. 2016-E-11. Institute for Monetary and Economic Studies, Bank of Japan.

Di Maggio, M. and Kacperczyk, M. (2017) The Unintended Consequences of the Zero Lower Bound Policy. *Journal of Financial Economics* 123(1), pp. 59–80.

Draghi, M. (2016) Introductory Statement to the Press Conference. 21 April. Available from: www.ecb.europa.eu/press/pressconf/2016/html/is160421.en.html. [Accessed: 12 November 2017].

Ehrmann, M., Soudan, M. and Stracca, L. (2013) Explaining European Union Citizens' Trust in the European Central Bank in Normal and Crisis Times. *Scandinavian Journal of Economics* 115(3), pp. 781–807.

Eichengreen, B. (2013) Currency War or International Policy Coordination? *Journal of Policy Modeling* 3(35), pp. 425–433.

El-Erian, M.A. (2016) Japan's Central Bank Experiments at the Wrong Time. *Bloomberg*. 21 September. Available from: www.bloomberg.com/view/articles/2016-09-21/japans-central-bank-experiments-at-the-wrong-time. [Accessed: 14 November 2017].

European Central Bank. (2016) *Financial Stability Review*. November 2016.

Fischer, S. (2016) *Why Are Interest Rates So Low? Causes and Implications*. Remarks at the Economic Club of New York. 17 October. Available from: www.federalreserve. gov/newsevents/speech/fischer20161017a.htm. [Accessed: 14 November 2017].

Goodhart, C. (2015) Why Monetary Policy has Been Comparatively Ineffective? *The Manchester School* 83(S1), pp. 20–29.

Handelsblatt. (2016) Deutsche-Bank-Chef kritisiert EZB-Präsidenten: Cryan kontra Draghi. 23 August. Available from: www.handelsblatt.com/my/finanzen/geldpolitik/ deutsche-bank-chef-kritisiert-ezb-praesidenten-cryan-kontra-draghi/14445688.html. [Accessed: 14 November 2017].

Hannoun, H. (2015) *Ultra-Low or Negative Interest Rates: What They Mean for Financial Stability and Growth*. Speech at the Eurofi High-Level Seminar. Riga. 22 April.

Hausman, J.K. and Wieland, J.F. (2014) Abenomics: Preliminary Analysis and Outlook. *Brookings Papers on Economic Activity* 48(1), pp. 1–76.

Honda, Y. and Inoue, H. (2017) The Effectiveness of the Negative Interest Rate Policy in Japan: An Early Assessment. Osaka University, Discussion Papers in Economics And Business, 17–02.

Iwata, K. (2016) *Japan's Economy and Monetary Policy*. Speech at a Meeting with Business Leaders in Nagasaki. Bank of Japan. 7 December. Available from: www.boj.or.jp/en/index.htm/. [Accessed: 13 November 2017].

Iwatsubo, K. and Taishi, T. (2017) Quantitative Easing and Liquidity in the Japanese Government Bond Market. *International Review of Finance*. Available from: https://onlinelibrary.wiley.com/doi/full/10.1111/irfi.12134. [Accessed: 22 April 2018].

Japan Center for Economic Research (Nihon Keizai Kenkyū Sentâ). (2016) *Gekiron: Mainasu Kinri Seisaku* [Heated Discussion: Negative Interest Rate Policy] Tokyo: Nihon Keizai Shimbunsha.

Jobst, A. and Lin, H. (2016) Negative Interest Rate Policy (NIRP): Implications for Monetary Transmission and Bank Profitability in the Euro Area. *Working Paper*. No. WP/16/172. Washington, DC: International Monetary Fund.

Jordan, T. (2016) *Monetary Policy Using Negative Interest Rates: A Status Report*. Speech, 24 October. Available from: www.bis.org/review/r161025c.htm. [Accessed: 13 November 2017].

Kuroda, H. (2013) *Quantitative and Qualitative Monetary Easing*. Speech at a Meeting Held by the Yomiuri International Economic Society in Tokyo. 12 April. Bank of Japan. Available from: www.boj.or.jp/en/index.htm/. [Accessed: 13 November 2017].

Kuroda, H. (2016) *Re-anchoring Inflation Expectations via "Quantitative and Qualitative Monetary Easing with a Negative Interest Rate"*. Remarks at the Economic Policy Symposium held by the Federal Reserve Bank of Kansas City. 27August. Bank of Japan. Available from: www.boj.or.jp/en/index.htm/. [Accessed: 13 November 2017].

Kuroda, H. (2017) *Building a More Robust Financial System: Where Are We after the Global Financial Crisis and Where Do We Go from Here?* Speech at the DICJ-IADI International Conference. 16 February. Bank of Japan. Available from: www.boj.or.jp/en/index.htm/. [Accessed: 13 November 2017].

Lombardi, D. and Moschella, M. (2016) The Government Bond Buying Programmes of the European Central Bank: An Analysis of Their Policy Settings. *Journal of European Public Policy* 23(6), pp. 851–870.

Ministry of Finance. (2017) *Debt Management Report*. Available from: www.mof.go.jp/english/jgbs/publication/debt_management_report/index.htm. [Accessed: 14 November 2017].

Nakaso, H. (2016a) *Japan's Economy and the Bank of Japan: Yesterday, Today, and Tomorrow*. Speech at the Economic Conference in Tokyo. Bank of Japan. 23 May. Available from: www.boj.or.jp/en/index.htm/. [Accessed: 13 November 2017].

Nakaso, H. (2016b) *Toward a "Comprehensive Assessment" of the Monetary Easing*. Speech at a Meeting Hosted by the American Chamber of Commerce in Japan (ACCJ). Bank of Japan. 8 September. Available from: www.boj.or.jp/en/index.htm/. [Accessed: 13 November 2017].

Nakaso, H. (2017) *Evolving Monetary Policy: The Bank of Japan's Experience*. Speech at the Central Banking Seminar Hosted by the Federal Reserve Bank of New York. Bank of Japan.19 October. Available from: www.boj.or.jp/en/index.htm/. [Accessed: 13 November 2017].

Nishimura, K.G. (2016a) Three "Seismic Shifts" in the Global Economy and the Policy Challenges They Pose. *International Finance* 19(2), pp. 219–229.

Nishimura, K.G. (2016b) Central Banks Face Monetary Policy Exhaustion. *Nikkei Asian Review*. 13 September. Available from: https://asia.nikkei.com/Viewpoints-archive/ Viewpoints/Kiyohiko-G.-Nishimura-Central-banks-face-monetary-policy-exhaustion. [Accessed: 12 November 2017].

Nishino, K., Yamamoto, H., Kitahara, J. and Nagahata, T. (2016) Developments in Inflation Expectations over the Three Years since the Introduction of Quantitative and Qualitative Monetary Easing (QQE). *Bank of Japan Review*. 2016-E-13.

Palley, T.I. (2016) Why Negative Interest Rate Policy (NIRP) is Ineffective and Dangerous. *Real-World Economics Review* 76, pp. 5–15.

Powell, J.H. (2016) *Recent Economic Developments and Longer-Run Challenges.* Remarks at "The Economic Club of Indiana Indianapolis". Indiana. 29 November. Available from: www.federalreserve.gov/newsevents/speech/powell20161129a.htm. [Accessed: 14 November 2017].

Rajan, R. (2015) Competitive Monetary Easing: Is It Yesterday Once More? *Macroeconomics and Finance in Emerging Market Economies* 8(1–2), pp. 5–16.

Rognlie, M. (2016) *What Lower Bound? Monetary Policy with Negative Interest Rates.* Unpublished manuscript.

Rogoff, K. (2016) *The Curse of Cash.* Princeton. NJ: Princeton University Press.

Rohde, L. (2017) Speech at the ECB Central Bank Communications Conference. 15 November. Danmarks Nationalbank. Available from: www.nationalbanken.dk/da/ Sider/default.aspx. [Accessed: 16 November 2017].

Roubini, N. (2014) *Abenomics, European-Style.* 31 August. Available from: www. project-syndicate.org/commentary/nouriel-roubini-supports-ecb-president-mario-draghi-s-plan-to-revive-eurozone-growth. [Accessed: 12 December 2017].

Saiki, A. and Frost, J. (2014) Does Unconventional Monetary Policy Affect Inequality? Evidence from Japan. *Applied Economics* 46(36), pp. 4445–4454.

Shirai, S. (2017) *Mission Incomplete: Reflating Japan's Economy.* Tokyo: Asian Development Bank.

Shirakawa, M. (2017) The Use of Cash in Europe and East Asia. In Rövekamp, F., Bälz, M. and Hilpert, H.G. (eds) *Cash in East Asia.* Financial and Monetary Policy Studies 44. Cham: Springer International Publishing.

Standard Eurobarometer. (2011) Eurobarometer 75, Public Opinion in the European Union. *European Commission.* May. Available from: http://ec.europa.eu/commfront office/publicopinion/archives/eb/eb75/eb75_en.htm. [Accessed: 11 November 2017].

Standard Eurobarometer. (2017) Eurobarometer 87, Public Opinion in the European Union. *European Commission.* May. Available from: http://ec.europa.eu/commfront office/publicopinion/index.cfm/Survey/getSurveyDetail/instruments/STANDARD/ surveyKy/2142. [Accessed: 11 November 2017].

Sveriges Riksbank. (2015) *Riksbank Cuts Repo Rate to −0.25 Per Cent and Buys Government Bonds for SEK 30 Billion.* Press release. 18 March. Available from: www. riksbank.se/en/Press-and-published/Press-Releases/2015/Riksbank-cuts-repo-rate-to-025-per-cent-and-buys-government-bonds-for-SEK-30-billion/. [Accessed: 14 November 2017].

Thiele, C.L. (2017) *Wohin geht die Reise? Die Zukunft des Bankensektors im Niedrigzinsumfeld, Vortrag bei der Handelsblatt Jahrestagung "Privatkundengeschäft".* Deutsche Bundesbank. 16 February. Available from: www.bundesbank.de/Redaktion/ DE/Reden/2017/2017_02_16_thiele.html. [Accessed: 14 November 2017].

Udland, M. (2016) Janet Yellen: I Won't Completely Rule out Negative Interest Rates. *Business Insider*. 12 May. Available from: www.businessinsider.de/janet-yellen-doesnt-rule-out-negative-interest-rates-2016-5?r=US&IR=T. [Accessed: 13 November 2017].

Uhlig, H. (2016) Geringe Erfolgsaussichten. *Neue Zürcher Zeitung*. 26 September. Available from: www.nzz.ch/finanzen/anleihen/bank-of-japan-geringe-erfolgsaussichten-ld.118732. [Accessed: 13 November 2017].

Ward, J. (2016) ECB, BOJ Seeking to Push Down Exchange Rates, Mervyn King Says. *Bloomberg*. 21 March. Available from Bloomberg.com. [Accessed: 11 November 2017].

Weidmann, J. (2017) *The G20 Agenda Under the German Presidency*. Welcome remarks at the 9th Annual IIF G20 Conference. Deutsche Bundesbank. 15 March. Available from: www.bundesbank.de/Redaktion/EN/Reden/2017/2017_03_15_weidmann.html. [Accessed: 14 November 2017].

Welter, P. (2016) Donald Trump als Retter der Abenomics. *Frankfurter Allgemeine Zeitung*. 29 November. Available from: www.faz.net/aktuell/finanzen/aktien/japan-donald-trump-als-retter-der-abenomics-14549635.html. [Accessed: 14 November 2017].

Williams, J.C. (2016) Monetary Policy in a Low R-star World. *FRBSF Economic Letter*. 2016–23.

Witmer, J. and Yang, J. (2015) Estimating Canada's Effective Lower Bound. *Bank of Canada Staff Analytical Note*. 2015–2.

Yoshino, N. and Mitamoto, H. (2017) Declined Effectiveness of Fiscal and Monetary Policies Faced with Aging Population in Japan. *Japan and the World Economy* 42, pp. 32–44.

Yoshino, N. and Taghizadeh-Hesary, F. (2015) Effectiveness of the Easing of Monetary Policy in the Japanese Economy, Incorporating Energy Prices. *Journal of Comparative Asian Development* 14(2), pp. 227–248.

9 EU and Japanese aid and trade

Legitimising "Chinese democracy" in ASEAN

André Asplund

Introduction

The European Union (EU) and Japan share the notion that human rights and democracy are concepts that need to be integral parts in developing successful and sustainable societies (EU Commission, 2017). According to Tokyo, 'quality growth', a term used by the incumbent government with regards to its development cooperation (previously 'Official Development Assistance', ODA) or simply, foreign aid, in for example Southeast Asia, is even dependent on the consolidation of such values (MOFA, 2015a). In recent years, and in the wake of a rising China, the notion that Japan and the EU are partners sharing universal values has been increasingly highlighted in Japanese foreign policy and diplomacy.

The new National Security Strategy (NSS) adopted by the Shinzo Abe administration in 2013, notes that Japan "[a]t a time when the power balance of the international community is changing" will strengthen its relationship with the EU, in order to establish an international order based on universal values and rules (Kantei, 2013a). One is hard pressed not to make the connection to China as the source for such a changing power balance.

While the EU is a long-time promoter of universal values, perhaps most successfully through the Easter European enlargement of the EU and the flaunting of liberal democracy, Japan has traditionally been more cautious to engage in similar practices, particularly in its immediate neighbourhood (East and Southeast Asia). And whereas the EU has used 'Partnership Agreements' on trade and investments as a means to export norms and values to 'third party' partners, Japan has chosen to instead link its foreign aid to human rights and democracy promotion. Yet, neither have been strangers to using its economic leverage to pressure human rights-violating governments or governments suspending democracy (in Asia) – the most striking example being sanctions levied against Myanmar until 2011. 'Political conditionality', or positive and negative linkage, of trade and aid respectively constitutes as such the (main) modes through which the two actors have sought to address human rights adherence and democracy promotion in relations with third party states.

Recent developments in EU trade policy and the newly concluded Free Trade Agreement (FTA) with Vietnam, as well as Japanese increased attention to providing foreign aid to Vietnam, suggests that policy obligations regarding principles on democracy and human rights in third party states are being side-stepped, for one reason or another. For example, after three years of negotiations the EU Commission concluded a FTA with Vietnam in December of 2015, despite a fair amount of criticism coming from the EU Parliament on the human rights situation in the region and despite the Commission neglecting to carry out a prior human rights impact assessment, as called for by the Lisbon Treaty. Japan on its side – a long-time provider of aid to Southeast Asian countries – has been ramping up its disbursements considerably to the region making its strategic partner, Vietnam, the number one recipient of Japanese aid in the twenty-first century (Asplund, 2017). Yet, priority of foreign aid should, according to Tokyo, be given to countries actively engaging in efforts to democratise and strengthen human rights. In the case of Vietnam, it is highly debatable whether or not such efforts have in fact been made at all during this past 20-odd years.

This chapter suggests that in the case of the EU free trade agreement with Vietnam, as well as in Japanese implementation of foreign aid in the Mekong region, there is evident a disconnect between policy and practice regarding the very principles emphasised as fundamental for sustainable development, and principles identified as guiding their very own foreign affairs (through trade and aid respectively). It is furthermore proposed that the rise of China incentivises the EU and Japan to promote universal values as a means to demarcate 'friend from foe'. But, the very need to do so, without necessarily being willing to 'enforce' the normative policy obligations in bilateral relations with key members of Association of South East Asian Nations (ASEAN), in effect allows China, or the 'rise of China' to lower the bar of normative commitments that ASEAN members actually need to comply with in order for them to earn the EU's and Japan's good grace as partners 'sharing values' – which in the long term might spell the devaluation of universal values as we know them today.

Sharing a belief in 'universal values'

The EU has long been heralded as an intergovernmental benchmark. As an organisation 'by democracies for democracies' (Moravcsik, 2000) the EU has successfully co-opted Eastern European nations. Notably however, such success has largely reflected the EU's leveraged position vis-à-vis non-EU Europe, through 'accession-driven conditionality', epitomised by states adopting EU norms upon accession. For non-European nations without the option of accession, Brussels 'Europeanising' mechanisms have not been as successful (Kavalski, 2013), but the appeal of the organisational and economic features of the union have still been strong. In the wake of 'Brexit', the financial crisis and Syrian refugee situation, such appeal is diminishing. Nonetheless, as a 'civilian power' without 'traditional' power projection capabilities or ability to wield global influence, the EU pushes 'democracy mainstreaming' alongside its economic interests. Trade can be considered the main vehicle through which the EU tries to export norms and values, for example to countries in sub-regions like

Southeast Asia. According to the current EU Commissioner for Trade, Cecilia Malmström, trade is the harbinger of any successful development strategy, and it is through trade she argues, that the EU can have the strongest positive influence on human rights situations in countries like Vietnam (Malmström, 2015).

While Tokyo frequently invokes the shared belief in 'universal values' or 'fundamental values' as the very thing interlinking Japan and Europe, instead of linking democracy and human rights promotion with trade, foreign aid has constituted the seemingly only tool through which Japan, has even tried to approach such concerns. Following the logic of infrastructure as a *"prerequisite to socio-economic development"* (MOFA, 1992),

Tokyo has come to subscribe to modernisation theory in the sense that it sees democracy as naturally following modernisation and economic development of a society (Personal communication, October 2015).[1] However, The Ministry of Foreign Affairs (MOFA) has noted that Japan should revise its aid commitments to a recipient country in the event of 'undesirable behaviour' like suspension of democracy and/or human rights violations (MOFA 1996, 8 § 4). MOFA also stresses that changes of governments as a result of political turmoil, crackdowns on anti-government protests, and other forms of violations of basic human rights should render the Japanese government to leave "no room for the governments of recipient countries to doubt Japan's strong interest in democracy and human rights" (MOFA, 2015c, p. 143).

Political conditionality: 'sticks' and 'carrots'

'Political conditionality' – either 'positive conditionality' ('positive linkage') or 'negative conditionality' ('negative linkage') – is a frequent method to influence 'undesirable behaviour' in other countries. Positive conditionality entails the promise of a benefit (e.g. foreign aid) in return for the fulfilment of a predetermined condition. The promised 'benefit' is a 'carrot' as it incentivises behaviour change. Negative conditionality involves the infliction of a punishment – hence the expression 'sticks' – in the event of the violation of a specified obligation. Sticks often refer to diplomatic and economic sanctions, or suspension of ODA (Tocci, 2008).

While the EU (and the US) has used negative linked and levied sanctions and arms embargoes against Myanmar, Indonesia, and Thailand, Japan has more often than not chosen not to join in on the West-sponsored embargoes. Nonetheless, Tokyo did cut its ODA to Myanmar (then Burma) when the military junta seized power in the 1988 coup. The Japanese ODA at the time constituted some 20 per cent of the Burmese national budget and about 70 per cent of the total foreign aid that the country received. In practice, infrastructural development projects initiated before 1988 were resumed, and new projects (that according to Tokyo were classified as: 'small-scale') would continue, sometimes creatively labelled as 'humanitarian assistance' – an example being an ODA loan for repairing the runway of Yangon Airport (Edström, 2009, p. 36; Seekins, 1999, p. 6). Following Myanmar's accession to ASEAN in 1997, the EU suspended the ministerial-level talks (an integral part of the EU–ASEAN relationship since its introduction in 1978).

When the EU started negotiations for a region-to-region FTA with ASEAN in 2007, there were particularly two issues that were identified as obstacles or spoilers for a future trade deal: the "situation" in Myanmar and the vast discrepancies regarding economic development among ASEAN members. Javier Solana, at the time EU High Representative for Common Foreign and Security Policies (CFSP) even insisted that the human rights record of Myanmar should render it non-eligible for the inter-regional trade deal (Doan, 2012). Belgian Foreign Minister Karel De Gucht noted that "there are many EU member states that doubt they can come to an agreement with ASEAN unless there are some signs of evolution in Burma and political change there" (Ganjanakhundee, 2008). While it is uncertain if was the political situation in the military-led Myanmar that in 2010 led to the negotiations being abandoned – with the EU instead approaching ASEAN members individually for FTAs – it was at least likely part of the equations for some of the European constituencies.

In Cambodia when Hun Sen seized power in 1997 while incumbent Prime Minister Prince Ranariddh was out of the country, the US government decided to freeze all Cambodian aid indefinitely. Germany followed suit, as did the World Bank (Oishi and Furuoka, 2003, pp. 894–895). As a result, Japan came to serve as the sole source for economic assistance for the Hun Sen regime. With such economic clout, Japan managed negotiate 'the Japanese Proposal' which led to new elections. Held in 1998, the election was sponsored by among others, Japan and the EU (EU Commission, 1998; Oishi and Furuoka, 2003).

ASEAN and Vietnam: in the interest of the EU and Japan

In the wake of the re-emerging regional power China, both Japan and the EU have come to pay increased attention ASEAN. That is perhaps not surprising given the fact that ASEAN has a combined population of 600 million, a GDP of US$2.6 trillion, offering promising sources of economic growth. Growing middle, and urban, classes in countries like Vietnam, and Thailand and Malaysia, and a continued strong economy of Singapore, are identified as huge market potentials for EU exports of goods and services, exports that would be facilitated by FTAs, according to the European Parliament (Vandewalle and Mendonca, 2015). In particular, the Mekong region, comprising Cambodia, Laos, Myanmar, Thailand and Vietnam, located in the juncture between major emerging markets like China, India, and other ASEAN members, is identified as a potential future global growth centre (MOFA, 2015a). But it is not only economic aspects that draw European and Japanese attention to ASEAN. In recent years ASEAN and its members have come to constitute an important arena in the changing power balance of East Asia. Strategically located in and around vital trade routes and sea lanes, some of ASEAN's members have been drawn into tense territorial disputes with China over control of islands located in the South China Sea. Vietnam is one key member of ASEAN that holds huge strategic and economic potential for both the EU and Japan, as well as China and the US.

Vietnam: rapid economic development, non-existing political reform

Lauded as a development success Vietnam has in a quarter of a century gone from being one of the poorest countries in the world to a lower-middle-income country. During the 1990s per capita GDP growth was among the fastest in the world, on average 5.5 per cent per year, and during the 2000s on average 6.4 per cent per year (World Bank, 2016). Extreme poverty has been close to eradicated, maternal mortality ratio has dropped to below that of upper-middle-income countries, and the Vietnamese population is not only better educated than most other countries with similar per capita income but has also a higher life expectancy (World Bank, 2016). Still, political reforms have been largely absent. Since the EU and Vietnam decided to base its future cooperative relationship on the mutual respect for human rights and democratic principles in 1996, not much has changed politically in the country. This has been duly noted by for example Freedom House which in its ranking of freedom in the world has had Vietnam scoring seven (on a scale from one to seven with seven being the absolute worst) in terms of political rights. That is a worse score than the score of countries like for example Iran, Cambodia, Qatar, Russia and Egypt, and a score on par with countries such as China, North Korea, Saudi Arabia, and Turkmenistan (Freedom House, 2016).

EU–Vietnam: moving towards a Free Trade Agreement

Since 1996, when the Framework Cooperation Agreement (FCA) between the EU and Vietnam entered into force, the EU–Vietnam partnership has evolved, through a new Framework Agreement on Comprehensive Partnership and Cooperation (PCA) in 2012, to the recently concluded FTA signed in December 2015. This is the first FTA with a developing nation in Southeast Asia.[2]

With the FCA of 1996, Vietnam had accepted, in principle, a legally binding human rights provision, although the document did not provide for any suspension clause in the case of non-compliance, as such making it toothless with regard to enforcing the human rights or democracy principle. Some have nonetheless argued that the signing constituted a significant political show of will on the Vietnamese side to strengthen cooperation, including on politics and not only economically, with the EU (Sicurelli, 2015). The fact that the EU Parliament adopted at the very least, five major resolutions (EU Parliament, 2004, 2005, 2007, 2008 and 2009) concerning human rights violations in Vietnam and the lack of democratic progress between the 1996 FCA and the signing of PCA in 2012 suggests that the Vietnamese side likely was not overly interested in discussing politics with the EU. The resolutions and the lack of incremental changes to Vietnam's one-party system likely contributed to the somewhat 'tougher' tone of the PCA.

When the PCA was negotiated and drafted by the EU Commission in 2010, it read that both parties would confirm their commitments to democratic principles and human rights, as well as such commitments constituting an essential element of the agreement. More importantly, the document also noted that a violation of an essential clause should be considered a material breach of the agreement. The type of measures to be taken in the case of a material breach however were not specified other than that a Joint Committee would hold consultations and examine the aspects of what measures to take. But for observers of the EU and its human rights policies, a hint to what such measures could entail was given two days prior to the signing of the PCA, when the EU Council made clear what it considered appropriate actions to take when faced with human rights violations in partner countries. The Council noted, in the EU Strategic Framework and Action Plan on Human Rights, and Democracy, that:

> [t]he EU will place human rights at the very centre of its relationships with all third countries, [and] when faced with violations of human rights, the EU will make use of the full range of instruments at its disposal, including sanctions ...
>
> (EU Council, 2012)

Before the negotiations being concluded for the FTA in December 2015, the European Parliament had adopted two more resolutions concerning human rights issues in Vietnam, one in 2014 calling for the Commission to carry out a Human Rights Impact Assessment prior to concluding the FTA with Vietnam. As the Lisbon Treaty of 2009 formally compelled the EU Commission to take a human rights dimension into account when negotiating trade agreements, the Commission has tended to take to heart the recommendations of the European Parliament on carrying out impact assessments before concluding trade agreements with third parties. In the case of Vietnam, the Commission defied both the Parliament and the EU Ombudsman's call for such an assessment to be undertaken. The Ombudsman went as far as accusing the Commission of maladministration and stated on 26 March 2015, that: "The Commission wrongly refuses to carry out a human rights impact assessment as part of the preparations for an EU free trade agreement with Vietnam", and demanded the Commission to conduct a comprehensive and participatory human rights impact assessment. The Commission argued that since negotiations with Vietnam was in principle an extension of the negotiations for a trade agreement with ASEAN, which had started before the Lisbon Treaty entered into force, the Commission was not compelled to carry out a human rights impact assessment concerning Vietnam. Hence, it did not.

In October 2015, a report commissioned by the European Parliament highlighted that: "Vietnam remains a one-party state with no plans to introduce a multi-party democracy. Political dissidence is repressed" (Vandewalle and Mendonca, 2015, p. 4). The report went on to conclude that "[n]o independent civil society organisations, political parties or trade unions are allowed. Civil society activists ... face harassment, assaults, arbitrary detentions and lengthy prison sentences ...." (Vandewalle and Mendonca, 2015, p. 12). Yet, the EU Commission has indicated that monitoring of some of the commitments under the FTA regarding for example labour rights and Vietnamese commitments to core conventions of the International Labour Organization (ILO) will be left to civil society in Vietnam. In a blog post from December 2015 Commissioner for the Trade, Cecilia Malmström noted that: "Civil society will have an important role in monitoring these commitments" (Malmström, 2015). How civil society will be able monitor, not to say effectively monitor, whether or not Vietnam lives up to the commitments remains unclear.[3]

In a new resolution on Vietnam from 9 June 2016, the EU parliament lambasts Vietnam, point after point, for its continued and increasingly frequent human rights violations, crackdown on peaceful demonstrations, imprisonment of human rights activists and lack of democratic reform with continued ban on political parties and the refusal to let independent candidates run in the 22 May legislative elections to the general assembly. The resolution notes that democracy is in no way, shape or form present in Vietnam, and has never been so during the now 25 years of EU–Vietnam relations and it is seemingly not headed towards that direction in any near future: "Vietnam has been a one-party state since 1975, with the Communist Party of Vietnam (CPV) allowing no challenge to its leadership and having control of the National Assembly and the court" (EU Parliament, 2016). Meanwhile, the EU–Vietnam Free Trade Agreement (EVFTA) is currently being translated into the many EU languages. The agreement is expected to become effective by early 2018 and is hoped to increase two-way trade by 30 per cent against the 2015 figure of $57 billion (VBN, 2016).

Spreading universal values: in Japan's national interest?

The NSS of 2013 outlines the national interests of Japan, after maintaining sovereignty and security over its territories, as achieving economic prosperity for the country and its citizens through economic development. To do so, the Strategy notes that it is in the national interest of Japan to maintain and protect an international order that is governed by rules and based on values such as freedom, democracy, human rights and rule of law (VBN, 2016). It also suggests one way to approach such issues: "Japan will actively utilize its ODA in supporting democratization ... human rights, and contribute to the enhancement of the growing international trend towards the protection of human rights..." (Kantei, 2013a, p. 32).

Linking Japanese ODA with universal values in ASEAN

Japan contributes trillions of yen in foreign aid, through concessional loans, yearly, to members of ASEAN. A significant share of that money goes into building infrastructure so as to improve connectivity in the Mekong region – Tokyo's new "global growth centre" (MOFA, 2015a). During the Seventh Mekong-Japan Summit in 2015 the New Tokyo Strategy 2015 for Mekong – Japan Cooperation was adopted, in which Tokyo pledged 750 billion yen (approx. US$7 billion) in new aid allocations over the following three years (MOFA, 2015a), while China recently announced a package for infrastructure to the Mekong worth US$11.5 billion (Pongsudhirak, 2016). This should be added to Japan's 600+ billion yen ODA package already provided to the region through the previous three-year plan – the Tokyo Strategy 2012 (MOFA, 2012).

The 2015 Strategy also declares that in order to achieve 'quality growth' and elevate the region to a higher development stage, the Mekong governments, in cooperation with Japan, need to consolidate democracy, the rule of law, and respect for human rights (MOFA, 2015a). A majority of these governments constitute some of the least democratic within ASEAN, many of whom are also frequently accused of systematic human rights violations (Asplund, 2015). In other words, Tokyo frames the success of the partnership for enhancing connectivity among the Mekong Five as partly premised on the region's ability to, in cooperation with Japan, consolidate democracy, rule of law and respect for human rights. On paper these values have, for more than 20 years, constituted a cornerstone for Japanese ODA implementation – in the newly adopted Development Cooperation Charter of 2015; the preceding ODA Charters of 1992 and 2003, as well as in numerous White Papers published by the Ministry of Foreign affairs (MOFA) since the turn of the millennium (MOFA, 1992, 2003, 2015b). Specifically, how Japan is seeking to consolidate these values and norms, and what type of aid contributes to such ambitions is far from clear, at least in the case of consolidating democracy and human rights.

In terms of using aid for the purpose, at least officially, of strengthening the rule of law, Japanese aid has been directed towards strengthening maritime capabilities of coastal states in the South China Sea. By provided patrol vessels and capacity development for, among others, the Philippine and Vietnamese coast guards, Japan aims to help them, together with Japan, to uphold the rule of law at sea. In the case of promoting democracy and human rights there is not really any specific type of Japanese aid that necessarily caters directly to such intended purposes. When asked about aid and democracy promotion the Japanese answer is that democracy follows economic development, that modernisation theory will prevail. For example, the *Action Plan* outlining how the objectives of the Mekong-Japan Cooperation are to be achieved, is void of any measures specifically geared towards consolidation of democracy and/or respect for human rights (MOFA, 2015d). Somewhat odd since the *Strategy* outlines such issues as the number one challenge for the Mekong countries to overcome, in cooperation with Japan, in order for economic development to be successful in the first place.

As outlined above, numerous resolutions have been adopted by the EU regarding democracy and human rights 'issues' in Vietnam, and also in Laos and Cambodia, which should not have been able to pass unnoticed by MOFA. Yet, Japan has not used any negative linkage of its foreign aid to any Mekong nation during the past decade. Aid to some African nations however has been suspended as a result of similar negative trends concerning democracy: to Guinea in 2008 following a coup d'état as well as in Madagascar in 2009 as a result of extra-constitutional regime change.[4] In Thailand, Japan's response to the 2014 coup only amounted to Abe, in meeting with self-installed Prime Minister General Prayuth Chan-o-cha, expressing his expectation for an "early restoration of democracy", while at the same time conveying his "interest in infrastructure development, including high-speed train, in Thailand" (MOFA, 2014).

With regard to Vietnam, or the other Mekong countries, no official remarks have been made concerning stalled, or even absent, democratisation process. It is perfectly possible that such remarks could be made through unofficial cables. Akiko Fukushima, a member of Prime Minister Abe's Advisory Panel on National Security and Defence Capabilities, and one of the contributing authors of the NSS, when asked about the reason ODA to Vietnam has drastically increased although the country is not "performing" in line with the spirit of the ODA Charter, noted that a stable Vietnam is very important to Japan but that Japan "always mentions human rights when dealing with Vietnam … always complains about human rights in Vietnam" (Personal communication, October 2015).[5] The Vietnamese side however seems to be of a different opinion. According to a high ranking member of the Central Institute for Economic Management – an institute working with infrastructure and foreign aid directly under the Vietnamese Politburo (the highest body of the Communist Party of Vietnam) – the reason why the relationship with Japan excels that of Vietnam's relationship with any other donor operating in the country is the fact that Japan not only builds quality infrastructure, but that Tokyo refrains from, raising issues of democracy and human rights when dealing with Hanoi (Personal Communication, October 2016),[6] at least in public. The EU however is obliged (by its parliament members) to do so, to the growing dismay of the Vietnamese government, and oftentimes even to the dismay of the EU delegations operating in ASEAN, which experience first-hand how such complaints can sometimes set back their partnerships a notch or two (Personal communication, October 2016).[7]

Universal values as competitive advantage?

Japan never has been particularly consistent in living up to the 'democracy and human rights principles' of its ODA Charter(s), at least not in Asia (Asplund, 2017). During the past decade Japan has completely refrained from using negative linkage in its foreign aid to Southeast Asian nations. Yet, while seemingly moving away from using negative linkage in Asia, Tokyo has at the same time moved from a position of not criticising Asian nations for democratic or human rights shortcomings, to that of depicting the region as needing to consolidate and internalise democracy principles and respect human rights.

In the 'New Principles of Japanese Diplomacy', announced by Prime Minister Abe whilst touring ASEAN in 2013, "protecting freedom of thought, expression, and speech in this [ASEAN] region" was ranked first among five new principles guiding Japan's diplomacy (MOFA, 2013a). Other principles included upholding the rule of law at sea and enhance economic cooperation by improving connectivity, which happens to be the two absolute main features of Japanese ODA commitments to countries in ASEAN. When Abe later would address Japan's principles of diplomacy specifically with regard to ASEAN members, he stated, as the first of five principles the need to protect and promote with ASEAN members "universal values, such as freedom, democracy and basic human rights". Again, other principles included upholding and ensuring the rule of law at sea, and promoting trade and investment trough economic partnerships in the region (MOFA, 2013b).

One should likely not make too much of the fact that Abe chose to place human rights and democracy above other objectives like making sure that the "seas are government by law and not might" (arguably a reference to China and its actions in the East and South China Seas). It is not particularly likely that Japan considers the spread of democracy and protection of human rights in Southeast Asia to be more important than fortifying the rule of law at sea.

However, Abe included the 'promotion and protection of universal values' as one of five objectives for its ASEAN diplomacy when addressing lawmakers from countries for which these values are so sensitive that during negotiations for the ASEAN Charter – the document that was going to turn ASEAN into a legal entity in 2008 – their mere mentioning in the document nearly capsized the whole project (Asplund, 2014). At the very least, that suggests that, for one reason or another, having ASEAN members sharing these universal values, as part and parcel of their very political institutions, matters for Tokyo, particularly under Abe. In fact, during Abe's first, short, stint as Prime Minister back in 2006, his then Foreign Minister Taro Aso promoted the creation of an 'arc of freedom and prosperity' by spreading universal values such as democracy, freedom, human rights, rule of law and market economy. Such an arc, it was argued, would sweep across the budding and young democracies of Southeast Asia, Central Asia and further on into the Caucasus (MOFA, 2006). It would as such have effectively encircled China, which now, as then, is closely linked to what Tokyo sees as an eminent threat to Japan's national security and interest.

When addressing the Japanese Parliament (Diet) in his yearly policy declarations Prime Minister Abe has consistently highlighted that Japan will enhance and elevate partnerships with countries that Japan 'share values of freedom, democracy, human rights and rule of law' (cf. Kantei, 2013b, 2014a 2014b 2015 and 2016). However, in the 2015 and 2016 'ASEAN' was explicitly mentioned among the very partners that share those exact values with Japan – the others being the EU, the US, Australia, and India. This assertion might not sit well with those who follow the political developments in ASEAN, but from a Japanese perspective it makes sense in that this statement, at relatively low cost, could potentially drive a wedge between ASEAN and China.

Conclusion: the demise of 'universal values'

The EU and Japan build their identities around showcasing their own 'development success' built on what they consider universal values: liberal democracy, respect for human rights, rule of law and market economy. And while it is debatable whether or not negative linkage is the best means to influence undesirable political behaviour – different cases in Southeast Asia would provide different answers – it clear that both Japan and the EU have regarded the use of sticks an appropriate measure, not long ago, in Southeast Asia as well as more recently in Africa. Yet, in the case of Vietnam any such considerations have been conspicuously absent. One reason might be found in that the EU and Japan have always found themselves in a relatively leveraged position vis-à-vis the partner state in question when utilising negative linkage. With rapid economic development of ASEAN members, the perceived notion of China (at least in Tokyo) as aggressive and bent on expansionism, as well as lingering economic and looming political problems in Europe, the EU and Japan are no longer enjoying the same previously held elevated positions, at least not in relations with Vietnam.

For the EU, the EVFTA would become the second FTA between the EU and an ASEAN partner (after Singapore). However, it would mean the first concluded agreement with a developing country in the region, and as such provide a model for other ASEAN members' negotiations with the EU, and a crucial step in establishing a framework for a future region-to-region EU–ASEAN FTA, which remains the ultimate goal for the EU. Therefore, even though the EU is compelled by its Lisbon Treaty, and EU Parliamentarians by their constituencies, to consider democracy and human rights in foreign relations, emerging markets, like that of Vietnam, seems to offer too much in terms of economic opportunities to impose conditionality. A heavily debt ridden and politically struggling European Union simply cannot afford 'gambling' with threatening to cancel trade deals with partners like Vietnam, particularly in the wake of the breakdown of the EU–US Transatlantic Trade and Investment Partnership (TTIP) negotiations. On paper, however, the EU is still tough on human rights and democracy to the extent that it would jeopardise its own businesses. One of the strongest voices against the FTA with Vietnam, on account of poor labour and human rights standards in Vietnam, were the textile and footwear industries in Europe. Whether their opposition was derived from a general concern for the rights of Vietnamese workers however is not evident. For them, an FTA with Vietnam, a country that together with China make up 60 per cent of EU imports of footwear, would mean having to compete with Vietnam's massive, cheap-labour, textile and footwear industry (Sicurelli, 2015, p. 238).

For Japan, competition with its main infrastructure rival – China, which never links aid or trade with political conditions – is intensifying in Asia. While Japan has an enormous presence in Southeast Asia as a constructor of high quality infrastructure, China is catching up. Even though Chinese aid, for example in Vietnam, is growing and likely soon will quantitatively overtake Japanese aid in most Southeast Asian nations, particularly among the Vietnamese, qualitatively Japanese aid is preferred over Chinese aid. According to Hanoi officials, Japanese foreign aid projects, like that of building the sky-train in East Hanoi, creates much added value for the Vietnamese, not only through the benefits of the finished products (in this case a commuter rail system) but throughout the whole construction phase. By being allowed to actively engage in the construction, knowledge transfer and capacity development benefit Vietnamese contractors and subcontractors, in a way they claim is not the case with Chinese projects, where instead only Chinese subcontractors benefit from the construction phase

(Personal communication, October 2016). Even so, Hanoi feels it necessary to balance ODA in order to not become too heavily dependent on the Japanese for cooperation, which Tokyo is well aware of (Personal communication, October 2016).

In the case of Vietnam, Japan, just like the EU, now finds itself in a peculiar position. Hanoi is sourcing ODA from China even though it prefers ODA from Japan, and Vietnamese leaders are forging closer relations with a China that does not conform to the liberal economic playbook preferred by Western liberal democracies, particularly given the US presidency of Donald Trump and his decision to scrap the Trans-Pacific Partnership (TPP). Even if Tokyo and Brussels would want to raise the lack of democratic reforms and human rights issues, their leaders would find it difficult to risk forsaking the relationship with a highly valued partner like Vietnam. With a huge stake in the future world economy as well as in the South China Sea dispute Vietnam does not provide much leeway for the use of negative linkage without it potentially costing Brussels and Tokyo dearly.

At the same time, having countries like Vietnam joining the group of 'like-minded' states, those who share the values of the EU and Japan, would effectively demarcate that of the 'others'– those who do not share such values, those who are on the other side, those who are (with) China. Prime Minister Abe propping up ASEAN as sharing 'universal values' – an EU-enlargement policy á la Japan and Asia – in effect includes ASEAN in the 'in-group', as opposed to the 'out-group' or China. In that sense China is encircled, from India, through ASEAN, and all the way around to Japan with members of a group that identify by sharing values such as democracy, human rights and rule of law, but more importantly, by seeking, albeit to varying degrees, some sort of containment of, or hedge against, a rising China. Ironically, by ascribing ASEAN as sharing universal values, in attempts to 'other' China, it effectively legitimises 'Chinese Democracy' in that it allows China, or the 'threat' of China, to set the threshold by which states can be included in this 'in-group', literally accepting 'Chinese levels of democracy' as part of the 'shared values' concept. This does not mean that the EU and Japan are not also driven by a genuine wish to see true universal values to be internalised in ASEAN members for the sake of the merit of such values in and of themselves, it means that the extent to which they are willing (allowed) to use their bargaining chips (aid and trade) for such purpose is dependent at least in part on the implications a rising China pose, economically and for security in the region.

Notes

1 Information to such regard was given to this author through personal communications with Akihito Tanaka, the former director for Japan International Cooperation Agency (JICA).
2 In 2014, the EU and Singapore signed a FTA. However, Singapore does not count as a developing nation.

3 In fact, Vietnam has not even ratified the ILO Freedom of Association and Protection of the Right to Organise Convention, 1948 (No. 87) nor the Right to Organise and Collective Bargaining Convention, 1949 (No. 98).

4 For information about suspension of aid, all *White Papers* from 2001 to 2016 are available in English at: www.mofa.go.jp/policy/oda/page_000017.html.

5 Personal communication 2015 October Tokyo, Japan.

6 Information to such regard was given to this author through personal communications with a member of the Central Institute for Economic Management – a government institute working with infrastructure and foreign aid directly under the Vietnamese Politburo – in Hanoi, Vietnam.

7 Information to such regard was given to this author through personal communications with a member of the Central Institute for Economic Management, and representatives at the EU Delegation in Hanoi, Vietnam.

References

Asplund, A. (2014) ASEAN Intergovernmental Commission on Human Rights: Civil Society Organizations' Limited Influence on ASEAN. *Journal of Asian Public Policy* 7(2), pp. 191–199.

Asplund, A. (2015) Values vs. Interest: Strategic Use of Japanese Foreign Aid in Southeast Asia. *EIJS Working Paper Series*. No. 241. European Institute of Japanese Studies, Stockholm School of Economics.

Asplund, A. (2017) Aligning Policy with Practice: Japanese ODA and Normative Values. In Asplund, A. and Söderberg, M. (eds) *Japanese Development Cooperation: The Making of an Aid Architecture Pivoting to Asia*. London: Routledge.

Doan, X.L. (2012) *Opportunities and Challenges in EU-ASEAN Trade Relations*. EU Asia Centre. 2 July.

Edström, B. (2009) *Japan and the Myanmar Conundrum*. Stockholm: Institute for Security and Development Policy

EU Commission. (1998) *European Union Funds Democratic Elections in Cambodia*. 16 January. Brussels: IP/98/43. Available from: http://europa.eu/rapid/press-release_IP-98-43_en.htm. [Accessed: 19 February 2017].

EU Commission. (2017) *International Cooperation and Development*. Available from: http://ec.europa.eu/europeaid/sectors/human-rights-and-governance/democracy-and-human-rights_en. [Accessed: 19 February 2017].

EU Council. (2012) *EU Strategic Framework on Human Rights and Democracy*. 25 June. Luxemburg: 11855/12.

European Parliament. (2004) *European Parliament Resolution on the Annual Report on Human Rights in the World 2004 and the EU's Policy on the Matter*. Brussels: 2004/2151(INI). Adopted 28 April 2005.

European Parliament. (2005) *European Parliament Resolution on the Human Rights Situation in Cambodia, Laos and Vietnam*. Brussels. Adopted 1 December 2005.

European Parliament. (2007) *European Parliament Resolution of 12 July 2007 on Human Rights in Vietnam*. Strasbourg. Adopted 12 July 2007.

European Parliament. (2008) *European Parliament Resolution of 22 October 2008 on Democracy, Human Rights and the New EU-Vietnam Partnership and Cooperation Agreement*. Strasbourg. Adopted 22 October 2008.

European Parliament. (2009) *European Parliament Resolution of 26 November 2009 on the Situation in Laos and Vietnam*. Strasbourg. Adopted 26 November 2009.

European Parliament. (2016) *European Parliament Resolution of 9 June 2016 on Vietnam*. Strasbourg: 2016/2755(RSP). Adopted 9 June 2016.

Freedom House. (2016) *Freedom House Country Report 2016*. Available from: https://freedomhouse.org/sites/default/files/FH_FITW_Report_2016.pdf. [Accessed: 21 April 2018].

Ganjanakhundee, S. (2008) Obstacles to EU-Asean FTA. *The Nation*. 13 June.

Kantei. (2013a) *National Security Strategy of Japan 2013*. Available from: www.cas.go.jp/jp/siryou/131217anzenhoshou/nss-e.pdf. [Accessed: 26 December 2016].

Kantei. (2013b) *Policy Speech by Prime Minister Shinzo Abe to the 185th Session of the Diet*. 15 October 2013. Available from: http://japan.kantei.go.jp/96_abe/statement/2013 10/15shoshin_e.html. [Accessed: 26 December 2016].

Kantei. (2014a) *Policy Speech by Prime Minister Shinzo Abe to the 185th Session of the Diet*. 24 January 2014. Available from: http://japan.kantei.go.jp/96_abe/statement/201 401/24siseihousin_e.html. [Accessed: 26 December 2016].

Kantei. (2014b) *Policy Speech by Prime Minister to the 187th Session of the Diet*. 29 September 2014. Available from: http://japan.kantei.go.jp/96_abe/statement/201409/policyspch.html [Accessed: 26 December 2016].

Kantei. (2015) *Policy Speech by Prime Minister Shinzo Abe to the 189th Session of the Diet*. February 2015. Available from: http://japan.kantei.go.jp/97_abe/statement/201 502/policy.html. [Accessed: 26 December 2016].

Kantei. (2016) *Policy Speech by Prime Minister Shinzo Abe to the 190th Session of the Diet*. 22 January 2016. Available from: http://japan.kantei.go.jp/97_abe/statement/2016 01/1215627_10999.html. [Accessed: 26 December 2016].

Kavalski, E. (2013) The Struggle for Recognition of Normative Powers: Normative Power Europe and Normative Power China in Context. *Cooperation and Conflict* 48(2), pp. 247–267.

Malmström, C. (2015) *Done Deal with Vietnam*. Web blog post. 2 December. Available from: https://ec.europa.eu/commission/commissioners/2014-2019/malmstrom/blog/done-deal-vietnam_en. [Accessed: 21 April 2018].

MOFA. (1992) *Japan's Official Development Assistance Charter*. Tokyo: Ministry of Foreign Affairs of Japan.

MOFA. (1996) *Japan's ODA Annual Report (Summary) 1996*. Tokyo: Ministry of Foreign Affairs of Japan, 8 § 4.

MOFA. (2003) *Japan's Official Development Assistance Charter*. Tokyo: Ministry of Foreign Affairs of Japan.

MOFA. (2006) *Speech by Mr. Taro Aso*. 30 November. Available from: www.mofa.go.jp/announce/fm/aso/speech0611.html. [Accessed: 19 February 2017].

MOFA. (2012) *Tokyo Strategy 2012 for Mekong-Japan Cooperation*. 21 April 2012. Available from: www.mofa.go.jp/region/asia-paci/mekong/summit04/joint_statement_en.html. [Accessed: 26 December 2016].

MOFA. (2013a) *The Bounty of the Open Seas: Five New Principles for Japanese Diplomacy*. Available from: http://japan.kantei.go.jp/96_abe/statement/201301/18speech_e.html. [Accessed: 26 December 2016].

MOFA. (2013b) *Prime Minister Abe's Visit to Southeast Asia (Overview & Evaluation)*. Available from: www.mofa.go.jp/region/asia-paci/pmv_1301/overview.html. [Accessed: 26 December 2016].

MOFA. (2014) *Japan-Thailand Summit Meeting*. 13 November 2014. Available from: www.mofa.go.jp/s_sa/sea1/th/page24e_000064.html. [Accessed: 19 February 2017].

MOFA. (2015a). *New Tokyo Strategy 2015 for Mekong-Japan Cooperation*. (MJC2015) Mekong Summit. 4 July 2015. Available from: www.mofa.go.jp/s_sa/sea1/page1e_000044.html. [Accessed: 26 December 2016].

MOFA. (2015b) *Cabinet Decision on the Development Cooperation Charter*. 10 February 2015. Available from: www.mofa.go.jp/files/000067701.pdf. [Accessed: 26 December 2016].

MOFA. (2015c) *Japan's Official Development Assistance White Paper 2014: Japan's International Cooperation*. Ministry of Foreign Affairs of Japan.

MOFA. (2015d) *Mekong-Japan Action Plan for Realization of the New Tokyo Strategy 2015*. 5 August 2015. Available from: www.mofa.go.jp/files/000093571.pdf. [Accessed: 26 December 2016].

Moravcsik, A. (2000) The Origins of Human Rights Regimes: Democratic Delegation in Postwar Europe. *International Organization* 54(2), pp. 217–252.

Oishi, M. and Furuoka, F. (2003) Can Japanese Aid Be an Effective Tool of Influence? Case Studies of Cambodia and Burma. *Asian Survey* 43(6), pp. 890–907.

Pongsudhirak, T. (2016) China's Its Own Worst Enemy in Regional Relations. *East Asia Forum*. 31 March.

Seekins, D.M. (1999) The North Wind and the Sun: Japan's Response to the Political Crisis in Burma, 1988–1998. *The Journal of Burma Studies* 4, pp. 1–33.

Sicurelli, D. (2015) The EU as a Promotor of Human Rights in the Bilateral Trade Agreements: The Case of the Negotiations with Vietnam. *Journal of Contemporary European Research* 11(2), pp. 230–245.

Tocci, N. (2008) EU Incentives for Promoting Peace. In Griffiths, A. and Barnes, C. (eds) *Conciliation Resources Accord: An International Review of Peace Initiatives*. Issue 19. Conciliation Resources. London. Available from: www.c-r.org/our-work/accord/incentives/eu-incentives.php. [Accessed: 29 December 2008].

Vandewalle, L. and Mendonca, S. (2015) *In-Depth Analysis Vietnam: Despite Human Rights Concerns, a Promising Partner for the EU in Asia*. Directorate-General for External Policies Policy Department. Available from: www.europarl.europa.eu/Reg Data/etudes/IDAN/2015/570449/EXPO_IDA(2015)570449_EN.pdf. [Accessed: 21 April 2018].

VBN. (2016) EU-Vietnam FTA Still on Track Despite Brexit. 30 June, Available from: www.vietnambreakingnews.com/2016/06/eu-vietnam-fta-still-on-track-despite-brexit/. [Accessed: 19 February 2017].

World Bank. (2016) Available from: www.worldbank.org/en/country/vietnam/overview. [Accessed: 21 April 2018].

10 Japan and the EU

SDGs and changing patterns of development cooperation

Marie Söderberg

Introduction

With the UN adoption of the Sustainable Development Goals (SDG) (UN, 2016) substantial changes are ongoing in the field of development cooperation. The new goals are different in character and much wider ranging than the old Millennium Development Goals (MDGs) (UN, 2015b). In connection with this, the Organisation for Economic Co-operation and Development's (OECD's) Development Assistance Committee (DAC) is issuing new guidelines for how development assistance should be conducted and what is to be calculated as foreign aid. European countries and Japan have all had DAC standards and guidelines as the basis for their foreign aid policy. Japan has always been seen as the odd man out within DAC, having their own views on what development cooperation should be like. Compared to other countries they have had a heavy emphasis on infrastructure development and assistance through loan aid as well as a close cooperation between public and private. European donors have had more "soft aid" aimed at social development financed by grants. This chapter analyses how the new SDGs and the changes in the global environment affect development cooperation in general, but in particular Japanese and EU development assistance and the patterns for cooperation between the two. It also touches on US and Chinese influences. The order of the chapter is as follows. It starts with some methodological reflections concerning research on development cooperation. This is followed by an analysis of changes in development cooperation resulting from a changing world order. The status of EU aid policy as well as Japanese aid policy is reviewed. We research the character of both as well as cooperation in the field. Finally, the conclusion analyses the implications of this chapter's findings for the ongoing changes for the EU, its member states, and Japanese development cooperation.

How to study development cooperation – some methodological issues

Development cooperation, or Official Development Assistance (ODA),[1] can be researched with different methods and in many different ways. When aid agencies evaluate their assistance they most often look at the results. What was the purpose, and did the policies or projects achieve the expected results? Did the project lead to poverty reduction, or did new policies lead to increased health, better living conditions or improved living standards etc.? In these cases, we can look at the results from a recipient's point of view and whether the assistance leads to development or not. Measuring effectiveness of ODA is, however, not addressed in this chapter.

Another way of researching ODA is to study policy formation. Most often policies are formed to meet specific needs. Malnutrition or hunger can be eased with development in the agriculture field to produce more food, or simply to provide storage, so that it can be kept longer. Poverty reduction can be achieved through education, reduced mortality rates through better health facilities, and peace and security through initiatives such as disarming of mines. Domestic policy actors in donor countries are important as it is taxpayers' money that is used. Preferences of taxpayers vary depending on country. In Sweden, women in development would be important as the country has a feminist foreign policy.

ODA can be used for many different purposes. In this chapter we will focus on development cooperation as a type of policy tool in international relations. There are several theoretical traditions in this field, such as realism, liberalism and constructivism. Realists pay attention to material forces of a state as well as the structure of the international system in seeking to explain behaviour. States are rational actors that pursue national interests through power politics, including the use of military force, or otherwise through economic power. Liberalism on the other hand, widens the scope and takes into account not only the state, but also the role of non-state and private actors, such as companies and Non-Governmental Organisations (NGOs) (Hook, 2005, pp. 41–43).

Constructivists claim that political actors are socialised into patterns of behaviour through mutual interaction. This shapes their definitions of interests and rationality. Recently the importance of identity for political decision-making has been stressed. Actors are socialised into expectations, norms and identities which define how they will behave internationally. In this study an eclectic approach will be used drawing on the collective insights and strength from all three perspectives to overcome shortcoming and weaknesses that exists in all (Hook, 2005, pp. 41–43).

Priority issues, what ODA is used for, are important for the way we should analyse it. Is it for poverty reduction, or for peace and security or for economic concerns, or is it to promote specific normative values such as democracy and human rights? This will vary with the donor and recipients/partners. At the same time, the regions and countries that are prioritised will effect what type of ODA can be used. In this chapter both EU and its members' assistance as well as that of Japan will be analysed.

The new global environment for development cooperation

At certain points in history dramatic changes happen. 2015 can be seen as such a year in the field of development assistance: The Millennium Development Goals (MDGs) were concluded. On a global basis, extreme poverty had been halved.

So, had child mortality, as well as the proportion of people without access to safe water. Many problems still remained, however, and that was why 193 member nations of the United Nations adopted the Sustainable Development Goals (UN, 2016). These should be achieved by 2030. They are much broader in scope than the MDGs, encompassing 17 different goals and 169 different targets. Included this time are goals on economic growth (Goal 8: Decent work and economic growth) and industrialisation and infrastructure (Goal 9: Industry innovation and infrastructure). None of these were included in the MDGs (Shimomura, 2017, pp. 60–62). It is an ambitious agenda and the resources needed every year to achieve the SDGs are, according to the OECD, about ten times larger than the current levels of ODA. Another difference from before is that all countries – be they upper, middle or low income – should make tangible improvements to the lives of their citizens. It is not only the developed countries (that is the members of the so called "rich donors club" DAC) that should provide assistance.[2]

At the July 2015 Conference on Financing for Development in Addis Ababa, Ethiopia, a new comprehensive approach of financing for sustainable development was agreed upon. According to the Addis Ababa Action Agenda (AAAA), (UN, 2015a) all countries should strengthen the mobilisation and use of domestic resources. Such resources should be created by developing countries' own economic growth in an effective way, which should only be supplemented by international assistance when appropriate. There was a consensus that new resources must be tapped, but also that the developed countries should live up to their commitments of assisting the poor. In following up the agenda criticism has been raised that the developed countries are not doing that. (UN, Indepthnews, 2016). A key role in filling the financing gap will be played through the disbursement of government resources in conjunction with private investment, which is partly a new initiative.

This is triggered by a new situation where ODA has actually decreased in importance for poor countries. At over US$135 billion in 2013, ODA represented only 28 per cent of all official and private flows from the 29 member countries of DAC. Private Development Assistance (PDA), which is assistance undertaken by private actors (foundations, corporations, voluntary and non-profit organisations), provided at concessional financial terms where commodities and loans are concerned, has now reached a level roughly equivalent to net ODA (Desai, 2015). Private commercial flows, in the form of trade and investment, have grown tremendously and have overtaken ODA in amount as well as importance for development in many countries. The largest inflow for many developing countries today is actually remittances. That is money sent home to family and friends from people working abroad, a clear indication of the globalisation.

We now also have a number of giant private foundations such as the Bill and Melinda Gates Foundation, The Welcome Trust,[3] Warren Buffet and the Sasakawa Peace Foundation, some with the same budget size as European states' aid-budgets. Maybe even more important is that there are a number of newly emerging (or re-emerging) donors such as China, India, Brazil and South Africa. They have been pushing for a shift from the Paris declaration of 2005 when the

DAC countries adopted an agenda of aid effectiveness, dealt with desirable aid modalities and the relationship between themselves and partner countries (that is recipient) without even mentioning the emerging donors.

This was in strong contrast to the Busan Declaration six years later (2011), where "South-South partners", in other words emerging donors, actually took centre stage. The role of non-DAC members and private sector actors were considered crucial for tackling poverty and inequality. They should be considered complimentary to existing assistance. The Busan declaration clearly stated that all actors should promote "human rights, democracy and good governance", something that had not been mentioned in the Paris declaration (Shimomura, 2017, pp. 60–62). This kind of thinking became the basis for the 30 member Open Working Group established by the UN in 2013 to work out a new policy after 2015 (that is the SDGs). The SDGs came to embrace a lot of the traditional rhetoric of the South, in particular the principle of Common But Differentiated Responsibilities (CBDR), and the right to development.

The Paris Conference on climate change was successfully concluded in December 2015, with the Paris agreement on the reduction of climate change. The text of the agreement represented a consensus of the representatives of the 196 parties that attended the conference. They agreed on limiting global warming to below 2 degrees C. The developed countries promised to assist the developing countries to reduce their greenhouse gas emissions, and there is a common goal to raise US$100 billion for this end. This is likely to put further pressure on the development assistance budget of developed countries (OECD DAC, 2016b). American President Donald Trump has, however, stated that the US will withdraw from the Paris agreement. The effect this could have might be detrimental, but remains to be seen (Business Insider, 2016).

New patterns of aid

The Development Assistance Committee of OECD (DAC) has been the dominant player in the field of foreign aid during the post-war period. Since its establishment in 1961, this so called "rich donor's club" consisting of most of the West European countries as well as the US, Japan, and recently also South Korea, has been the place where the rules and regulations concerning foreign aid, including how to define foreign aid has been decided. Recently, DAC has lost some of its importance due to several reasons, including changing patterns of development and economic growth on a worldwide basis.

To reach the SDGs other sources besides traditional ODA must be found. DAC is very well aware of this fact and there is a redefinition of ODA ongoing, and substantial administrative changes to match with the SDGs. A new aid architecture, or rather development cooperation architecture, is being formed that implies wider and deeper cooperation with non-DAC members and with other sources such as private corporations. This is very much in line with what Japan has always been proposing, but has up until today been heavily criticised for by other DAC members.

Aid, although it might be crucial in itself, should also according to DAC now be used as a multiplier to mobilise the full range of resources needed to finance the broad, interlinked SDGs. In the future it is expected to be used strategically and "smartly" to make investment attractive in high-risk situations by spreading and sharing risk with private entities and by creating incentives (OECD DAC, 2016b). The European Commission is voicing the same message to its member countries (European Commission, 2014).

The measure of Total Official Support for Sustainable Development (TOSSD) has been proposed to complement ODA as a measurement of support from all official sources. A proposal for a comprehensive definition of TOSSD as well as a measurement and monitoring mechanism is at present being developed.

Situation in EU and member countries

The EU often refers to itself as the world's largest donor of ODA. If you add the total aid provided by the 28 Member States to the amount of ODA provided through EU institutions it represents more than 50 per cent of all ODA. Since the beginning of European integration, development policy has played a central role for the European Union, given the colonial legacy of its founding members and, after decolonisation started in the early 1960s, the drive to support their former overseas territories and sustain political and economic links with them has been strong. EU and its member states have frequently been described as ambitious exporters of norms and values, seeking to promote global governance through multilateralism, and by advocating peace, liberty, democracy, human rights and the rule of law. Many EU member countries were founding members of the DAC in 1964, and have since then played an important role and provided the ideological basis (based on Christianity) for how foreign aid has been defined and executed (Owa, 2014).

Today the EU's inclination to transfer its norms and values still persists. Especially in its immediate neighbourhood, the EU has aimed to transfer norms (as well as rules) through incentives such as conditionality linked to market access. In other, more geographically distant regions including Asia, however, the EU necessarily had to resort to support, persuasion, dialogue, communication and socialisation, as the case of the EU–ASEAN dialogue illustrates.[4]

EU aid usually refers to funds disbursed through EU institutions, such as the European Commission's Europe Aid department, and through programmes such as the Development Cooperation Instrument (for Asia and Latin America) and the European Development Fund (for Africa, the Caribbean and the Pacific).[5] For EU member states it is mandatory to allocate 20 per cent of their ODA to the EU level. The EU seeks to coordinate the aid policies of its member states. Nevertheless, EU members also conduct their individual aid policies, often in order to make full use of cooperative networks in recipient countries and here there is a much more varied picture with different geographical preferences as well as modalities of aid, although ideally, EU member state policies are complementary and mutually reinforcing. Development aid is also seen as an instrument to increase the EU's influence in global affairs in general, and to boost its norm-setting power in particular.

As a way to contribute to the SDGs, the European Commission on 16 September 2016 announced a European External Investment Plan (EIP) (European Commission, 2016) for the boosting of investments in Africa and EU Neighbourhood countries, in particular to support social and economic infrastructure and SMEs, by addressing obstacles to private investment. With a contribution of €3.35 billion from the EU budget and the European Development Fund, the EIP will provide guarantees and other support to assist private investment, enabling the EIP to mobilise up to €44 billion of investment funds. If Member States and other partners match the EU's contribution, the total amount could reach €88 billion.

The EIP, which builds on a similar internal program, Investment Plan for Europe, ongoing since November 2014, consists of three complementary pillars:

- Mobilising investment by combining existing investment facilities with a new guarantee within the new European Fund for Sustainable Development (EFSD). The EFSD will be composed of two regional investment platforms for Africa and the Neighbourhood.
- Stepping up technical assistance with the aim to help partner countries to better prepare and promote projects and attract more investment.
- Improving the general business environment by fostering good governance, fighting corruption, removing barriers to investment and market distortions.

The European Investment Bank (EIB)'s lending operations will be an integral part of the European External Investment Plan and the Commission will expand the EU budget guarantee by a total of €5.3 billion. In total, the EIB will thus lend up to €32.3 billion under the EU guarantee between 2014 and 2020.

The EIP is a framework for cooperation among the EU, Member States, partner countries, international financial institutions, donors and the private sector. The purpose is to improve the way in which scarce public funds are used and the way public authorities and private investors work together. The EIP gets a double assignment of contributing both to development and management of migration.

As a result of the crisis in Syria and other places in the Middle East, aid to refugees more than doubled, from €3.3 billion in 2014 to €8.6 billion in 2015 (Agence Europe, 14 April 2016). Counting these contributions as ODA remains controversial, as they are not seen as addressing the main objective of ODA, namely to promote the sustainable economic development and welfare of developing countries, which in turn would prevent future refugee flows. In 2015 in nine EU member states so-called in-donor refugee costs were between 10 and 34 per cent of total ODA expenditure (DAC Secretariat, 2016), and in countries such as Greece, Sweden, Germany, and the Netherlands ODA surged due to the mass influx of refugees. As such these countries are the recipients of their own aid, "dramatically inflating" the figures for ODA (*Guardian*, 13 April 2016).

This also underscore the fact that ODA is focused on strategically important regions and issues for the EU, and that the fight against poverty in least developed countries (LDCs), as stated in the EU policy documents, is not always the priority.

In the 1990s the link between security and development was firmly established and the DAC Network on Conflict, Peace and Development Cooperation was formed. In 2004 the Security System Reform (SSR) was endorsed with a number of recommendations in order to promote peace and security. In the EU an aid discourse under the banner of a "comprehensive approach" reflects the link between security and development. Lately this has also been closely connected to migration issues in Europe.

Under the European Agenda on Migration the Commission on 7 June 2016 adopted a new Partnership Framework with third countries to increase its support to partner countries for managing migration and refugees. A €1.8 billion EU Emergency Trust Fund for Africa has been launched and up to €930 million have been approved for projects to better manage migrant and refugee flows, and for more long-term support addressing resilience, stability and job creation with a particular focus on youth. The EU has also set up a regional Trust Fund in response to the Syrian crises (European Commission, 2016).

In Europe there is a perception that the global centre of gravity has been shifting away from Europe, and that Europe's own power is gradually eroding. This is especially obvious in Africa where the European countries used to be the dominant development cooperation partners, but where China today is gaining more influence and power. The global financial crisis and the awareness of an "Asian Century" have without doubt strongly affected Europe's self-confidence. Exacerbated by the ongoing refugee crisis and the Brexit referendum has resulted in a process of deep introspection in order to overcome internal economic, political, and security-related challenges. The election of President Donald Trump in the US has further deepened this process.

Japanese ODA and the New Development Cooperation Charter

In 1954 Japan became a donor by contributing US$50,000 to the Colombo Plan. Otherwise it is war reparations that are presented as the origin of its "aid". Burma received such reparations in 1954, the Philippines in 1956 and Indonesia in 1958. The reparations were mainly given to repair infrastructure damaged by the war. Money was tied to Japanese companies or products, and rather than aid, it can besides war reparations be regarded as the promotion of exports from Japanese industry. Major government economic co-operation started with the so called "yen loans" of 1957, which all came from the Export-Import Bank of Japan and were based on interest rates that would not have qualified them as ODA within the present definition. In March 1960, Japan joined the Development Assistance Group (DAG), and in 1961, when DAG was reorganised and became the Development Assistance Committee of the Organization of Economic Co-operation and Development (OECD–DAC), Japan joined as one of the founding member countries. This was before Japan joined the OECD itself in 1964.

During the 1960s almost all Japanese aid was confined to Asia, and overwhelmingly served commercial purposes. This changed with the oil crises of 1973. Aid became politicised and a stable supply of natural resources became another ingredient of Japanese aid policy. By the end of the 1970s the Japanese Ministry of Foreign Affairs (MOFA) had two justifications for aid. One was that Japan should contribute to peace and stability in the world. As a country without military power[6] the only means to do this was through economic aid. The second motive was related to the first and had to do with Japan's image as a country poor in natural resources. Trade was a prerequisite to obtain such resources. To get such resources a certain amount of infrastructure was needed and that was what Japanese aid-money should be spent on. Humanitarian consideration were not mentioned as a reason for aid until 1978, when MOFA mentioned it as one out of five main considerations: the others being, international economic security, Japan's duty as an economic power, economic self-interest and what was called "normal diplomatic necessity" (Söderberg, 1996, pp. 33–35).

In 1989, Japan became the world's largest donor of ODA, and with the exception of one year, was going to continue to be so during the coming decade. Japan appeared to be a responsible country with a strong social conscience. A statistical analysis however, reveals another picture. Despite being the largest donor in absolute terms, Japan's assistance was well below the average of DAC countries, hovering between 0.35 and 0.15 as a percentage of Gross National Income (Kato, 2016, p. 278). This was far below the UN target of 0.7 per cent. Quality of aid, not measured by DAC through success of projects, but solely in economic terms, had Japan at the bottom of the list as most Japanese aid consisted of loans rather than grants (Söderberg, 1996). Most of it went to Asia for building infrastructure in the form of roads, railways, ports and power plants.

Japan has since the introduction of it foreign aid programme encouraged the use of ODA to mobilise additional private sector resources for development. In the beginning Japanese foreign aid was placed within the broader concept of Economic Cooperation. A concept that besides ODA also encompassed Other Official Flows (OOF), credits that were below market rates but not concessional enough to be calculated as aid, as well as Private Flows (PF). These three combined were seen as the Japanese approach to the developing countries. During the process of streamlining the assistance among donor countries within DAC this Japanese approach was toned down. Japan started publishing ODA White Papers every year that were dedicated only to the ODA part of its assistance. Other parts were not considered to be development cooperation, but rather what in Japan was termed economic cooperation or commercial initiatives (Söderberg, 1996).

In 1992 Japan announced its first ODA Charter. With this Japanese ODA became more politicised and more environmentally friendly. This followed the trend at the time. The Gulf Crises had called attention to the question of armaments in developing countries, and the charter had a number of principles against

dispersing ODA for military purposes, promoting democratisation and the introduction of a market-oriented economy, and securing basic human rights and
freedoms in the recipient countries (MOFA, 1999).

The US increased its foreign aid after the 9/11 terrorist attacks in 2001.
Quickly following suit were the EU and several other donors. The Millennium
Development Goals and its promise to reduce poverty by half by 2015 were
adopted by the UN and signed by more than 190 nations at the turn of the
century. With this the international donor community seemed to be moving more
towards a coordinated approach (Sunaga, 2005).

Meanwhile, Japanese citizens had become increasingly sensitive concerning
their own security. This can partly be attributed to the threat from North Korea
as well as the terrorist attack in the US and the Iraq war. Nationalism started to
surface, in particular in relation to China, where the economy was rapidly
growing. It is in this light that the Japanese government's revised ODA Charter
of August 2003 should be seen. The Second ODA Charter states the objectives
of ODA in the first section as follows: "The objectives of Japan's ODA are to
contribute to peace and development of the international community and thereby
to help ensure Japan's own security and prosperity" (MOFA, 2003). In February
2015 a new revision of the Charter was announced. In the title of this third
charter the word "ODA" has been removed and Japan is turning to a broader
concept for development cooperation, no longer limiting it to the definition of
foreign aid by DAC members. Development cooperation in the new Charter
refers to: "International cooperation activities that are conducted by the government and its affiliated agencies for the main purpose of development in the
developing regions" (MOFA, 2015). Such development cooperation in the
coming years will strengthen collaboration with other funding from the Japanese
government and affiliated agencies, as well as funding from the private sector,
local governments and NGOs. In a sense, Japan is returning to its old concept of
"economic co-operation" through which not only the developing countries, but
also Japan and Japanese companies should gain. Development cooperation
should *"ensure Japan's national interests"*, the new Charter states. Priority
issues of Japanese development cooperation now includes: "quality growth"
(referring to economic growth as inclusive, sustainable and resilient), "sharing
universal values", and "building a sustainable international community by
addressing global challenges".

What is new in moving away from the concept of ODA, and instead calling
the new Charter a Development Cooperation Charter, is that this also opens up
opportunities for broader cooperation with new donors who are not DAC
members, something DAC itself seems to be in the process of doing. It also
opens up opportunities for cooperation with other recipients or partner countries.
Although the 2015 Japanese Development Cooperation Charter was adopted in
February, well ahead of the SDGs, it seems to fit with the new agenda. Japan
declares in its charter that there are other considerations beyond income level
that have to be taken into account. Assistance will be provided to countries that
have already achieved a certain level of economic growth to keep them from

being caught in the "middle income trap". This specifically covers many ASEAN countries where Japan has a strategic interest in cooperating.

The new Charter states that Japan will enhance synergies between ODA and non-ODA finance/cooperation to achieve as much effectiveness as possible in its development assistance. Private-led growth, including investment from small- and medium-sized Japanese companies, will be promoted in developing countries. Besides expanding their own business these companies will in this way be part of a Japanese cooperative action to support developing countries. At the same time this is presumed to contribute to growth of the Japanese economy as well.

Another significant change is strengthening the linkage between development and national security. The principles against providing ODA to countries that would use it for military purposes is still there, but according to the new charter, Japan should take a more active approach. The country shall make a "Proactive Contribution to Peace", and Japanese development assistance shall be implemented bearing the country's new National Security Strategy (NSS) in mind.

The US–Japan security alliance and ODA

Japan's National Security Strategy puts an emphasis on strengthening the US–Japan alliance. Here ODA has for a long time played the role stated above. Already in the 1980s there was talk of burden sharing involving ODA, where the US was to take military responsibility in wars and Japan would thereafter assist in peacebuilding by providing ODA (Yasutomo, 1986). In the twenty-first century there have so far been two major interventions, with strong US leadership, one in Iraq and one in Afghanistan. In 2005–2006 Iraq became the top recipient of Japanese ODA, indicating that peacebuilding and/or the fight against terrorism was given considerable space within the budget. Japan was, however, not alone, as nine other DAC countries, many of them EU members, also had Iraq as a top recipient. Japan's contribution was second in size only to the US.

Concerning Afghanistan, Japan's Self Defense Forces in 2001 conducted refueling operations for US vessels (and later also allied naval vessels) conducting anti-terrorism activities outside Afghanistan in the Indian Ocean (Midford, 2010, pp. 46–67). Japan hosted the International Conference on Reconstruction Assistance (ICRA) for Afghanistan in 2002, and yet another donor conference in 2012. At first Japan's ODA for Afghanistan was quite small in amount, but when the SDF was withdrawn from refueling operations in 2010, Japan pledged US$5 billion in ODA to Afghanistan and became a major donor. Thus, using ODA for national defence purposes, and as a tool for burden sharing with the US, is actually not new, although it has not been explicitly spelled out before.

Another objective stated in Japan's new National Security Strategy is to improve the security environment of the Asia Pacific region. North Korea, with growing WMD (Weapons of Mass Destruction) capabilities, including nuclear weapons and delivery systems, most noted ballistic missiles, is seen as a threat. So is China's rapid advance in military capability, and intensified activities in various areas in the East China Sea, including around the Senkaku/Diaoyu islands and China's imposition of an Air Defense Identification Zone (ADIZ) announced in November 2013. The South China Sea is deemed important, especially the sea-lanes that are vital for transportation of goods, including oil from the Middle East to Japan. As China is strengthening its presence in the South China Sea Japan has felt that it should cooperate with the ASEAN countries that also have territorial disputes with China to promote law-based solutions. A major goal is to protect freedom of navigation in the region.

Japan has been promoting multilateral regional security cooperation when it comes to maritime safety and antipiracy activities. It has played a vital role in the formation of RECAAP (Regional Cooperation Agreement on Combating Piracy and Armed Robbery) through which information exchange is conducted regarding crimes at sea. Besides multilateral arrangements Japan is also working bilaterally concerning maritime security with many of the ASEAN countries. Here ODA packages are part of the deal. In 2006 Japan announced that it would provide Indonesia with three patrol boats financed through ODA. Although officials in charge of ODA were averse, aid has gradually been used more often for 'non-traditional' security issues such as anti-terrorism and piracy. Labeled as law enforcement issues, these 'grey zones' have become eligible for Japanese ODA (Midford, 2015; Pajon, 2013). The Japanese Coast Guard has, through aid money, provided antipiracy education and training for Southeast Asian countries, and in 2013 the Philippine Coast Guard received a pledge of 10 patrol boats financed by Japanese ODA. This kind of assistance has become an important tool in Japan's balancing strategy towards China. It assists the countries to build capacity for early warning and patrolling (Midford, 2015). For Japan it is also a way to build a network of security partners among countries facing China and is partly designed to make up for relative US decline. It is no coincidence that three of Japan's top four recipients of ODA 2004–2015 (Vietnam, Indonesia and the Philippines) have territorial disputes with China (Asplund, 2017). Although the patrol boats are meant for antipiracy and safety of navigation and not for challenging other states on territorial issues it still sends a political signal. The impetus given to "strategic use" of ODA in Japan's new national security strategy makes it likely that we will see more of this kind of aid in the future. Since the 2015 reinterpretation of Article 9 in the constitution, which now allows Japan to participate in collective defence if Japan's survival is threatened, this is no longer a grey zone either.

Strategic use of ODA has an old history and can be seen in Japanese relations with Myanmar. Since 2011 Japan has been proactively taking a leadership role in preparing for other donors to enter Myanmar again. To be able to be eligible for foreign aid again, Myanmar needed to clear old payment arrears. This was done in a series of operations in which the Japanese government played a major role (Rieffel and Fox, 2013, pp. 46–47).

EU–Japan cooperation – narrowing the gap in development cooperation

In the Paris Declaration of 2005 promoting aid effectiveness was a common theme. DAC members were to enhance and streamline their ODA cooperation. There was an emphasis on aid to the social sector and grant aid. Elements of harmonisation and budget support were contrary to traditional Japanese ODA that emphasised project assistance. Japan participated in various cooperative initiatives, but only reluctantly. At this time, it was European perspectives, and especially British ideas that were the dominant ones within DAC (Owa, 2017, pp. 124–140). With the 2008 establishment of the new JICA (Japan International Cooperation Agency) Japan that used to have a number of agencies handling ODA disbursement now got loan aid, grant aid and technical cooperation under the same roof and Japanese ODA started to converge towards that of other DAC donors.

Besides cooperation with other DAC members, an EU–Japan policy dialogue was set up for the first time in 2010; a second round was held in 2013, and since then such a dialogue has been held annually, alternating between Brussels and Tokyo. The focus has been, among other themes, the post MDG agenda, financing for development and policy coordination. There has been discussion on enhanced coordination between the EU and Japan on aid for Africa as well as in the peace and security field.

The European Union has pursued a multi-faceted approach using economic, security and cultural instruments in assisting fragile states. This approach has come to be known as the "comprehensive approach". Japan, although using another concept, namely "Human Security", is taking a similar approach. At the summit meeting in 2014 it was agreed to promote closer cooperation between the EU's Common Security and Defence Policy (CSDP) and Japanese security cooperation initiatives (Fukushima, 2015). The EU and Japan have cooperated in combating piracy in the Gulf of Arden and at the same time they are also providing development assistance to Somalia, helping to train local maritime security officials and enhance local governance capabilities.

There was a civilian CSDP mission dispatched to provide training and advice to Niger's security sector in August 2012. To assist this mission, Japan provide grant aid through the UN Development Program to facilitate coordination by providing wireless communication devices to connect regional government offices with bureaus under their jurisdiction, and provided wireless-equipped vehicles for patrolling outlying locations. Another CSDP mission was dispatched to help improve Mali's security capabilities. In March 2015, Japan agreed to provide grant aid for the rehabilitation of Mali's national police school, provision of information technology and other equipment. (Fukushima, 2015).

Traditionally Japan's bilateral aid has been overwhelmingly oriented towards the economic sector (infrastructure in the fields of transport, communications, and energy), whereas the EU institutions as well as individual EU member states displayed the opposite tendency, giving priority to social and administrative infrastructure. However, as shown in Table 10.1, in recent years there is a clear

Table 10.1 Major purpose of aid (in per cent of total bilateral ODA (2015))

	Japan	EU institutions
Economic infrastructure	51	28
Other social infrastructure	11	20
Production	8	9
Multisector	9	16
Program assistance	4	6
Debt relief	0	0
Humanitarian aid	6	10
Unspecified	4	4

Source: OECD Development Cooperation Report 2017.

shift discernible in EU aid towards a focus on more economic infrastructure (Comparable OECD figure in 2010 was 10.1, the figure has almost tripled).

Another difference in disbursement of ODA between the EU and its member countries and Japan is the geographical location. Japan's bilateral assistance is heavily focused on South and Central Asia as well as the Far East. In 2015, 69 per cent of the ODA went there. As for EU assistance 30 per cent went to Eastern Europe and 27 per cent to Sub-Saharan Africa (OECD Development Cooperation Report 2017).

The EU has usually been spending more on the poorest countries, although this has somewhat changed during recent years. 22.4 per cent of EU institutions' bilateral aid was allocated to LDCs in 2015, which constitutes a significant drop compared to 2010 (35 per cent). Due to pre-accession aid[7] to other European countries, ODA to upper middle-income countries has significantly increased (37.2 per cent of bilateral aid in 2015) (OECD, 2015, p. 200; OECD, 2017).

Japan has had a preference for Lower Middle Income Countries (LMIC). In 2015, 19.2 per cent of bilateral ODA from Japan was provided to LDCs and 44.8 per cent to Lower Middle Income Countries. The 2015 DAC country average for LDC was 24.3 per cent (OECD, 2017).

The SDG's as well as DAC's new development policy guidelines put more focus on the private sector, as well as on public–private cooperation. The EU countries now aim to focus more on "blending", by combining grants with loans or equity from other public and private financers. This shows convergence with the traditional Japanese ODA model. DAC's new definition of development assistance and its decision to develop new statistical measures can be seen as a step in the Japanese direction. It is also a proof of the fact that the other DAC members (most of them EU members) are changing their policies, adjusting to the new realities where their members' ODA is losing importance, and where it, to a much larger extent, will be used in combination with private flows or flows from non-DAC members.

China's entry on the scene

Another force to count on are now also a number of emerging donors such as China (although it is not really a new donor) who play an increasingly important role. According to JICA, China's (JICA, 2014) foreign assistance budget is now the sixth largest in the world. Its growing foreign aid has been having a significant impact on the landscape of the global development aid community. The Chinese way of development assistance builds on China's own experience as a recipient of development assistance where Japan was by far the largest donor. Chinese foreign aid, with conditions and characteristics different from that of DAC donors has become an alternative to existing aid. Ironically, just as Japanese aid was restructured to align more with general ODA constitutive and regulative norms, donor competition with China in Africa and elsewhere has forced Japan to refocus on recipient expectations for more aid targeting industrial growth, trade, and investment stimulated by Chinese aid rhetoric and practices.

Chinese "South–South cooperation" is attractive to African governments. Chinese aid procedures are relatively simple, and projects are quickly implemented. It has no political conditionality and partly due to that appeals to African leaders. Chinese aid has had a strong focus on infrastructure development and it offers an alternative to DAC aid flows in Africa, but not only there. The new Chinese Asian Infrastructure Investment Bank (AIIB) reflects Chinese strong interests in Asia as well. More than 50 other countries joined the bank, among them many from Europe, but not the US and Japan. China's success as an aid donor is forcing Japan and other Western donors to adjust their policies to remain relevant and influential. Donor competition opens up the possibility of choice for developing countries, which may lead to better results in the long run.

For the Europeans this might be most obvious in Africa. Many EU countries have backgrounds as colonisers on the continent, and they have often kept strong ties with their former colonies. Africa has been the "home ground" of European donors that have focused their assistance there. Until the twenty-first century Europe was the dominant donor on the continent. Today China has become a major donor as well.

It is ironic that no sooner had the institutional creation of New JICA in 2008 demonstrated Japan's convergence towards Western ODA norms, than it confronted the challenge of Chinese foreign aid in Africa modelled after Japan's own original style of development assistance from the 1950s, i.e. "win-win" economic cooperation that boosted the donor's own industrialisation, trade expansion, and investment penetration agendas in developing countries while also providing recipient governments with the opportunity to negotiate reciprocal benefits. The appeal of Chinese foreign aid, as well as the brand image and lessons of the East Asian miracle, are sufficient to affect the trajectory of development assistance policy in the post-2015 era in Africa and elsewhere. Japan is now adjusting to this shift and positioning itself to take advantage of its own considerable experience and donor capacity in these respects. In the 2015 Development Cooperation Charter it states that its assistance for economic growth should be sustainable, inclusive and resilient. Japan profiles itself against China by providing "quality growth". JICA is adapting its newly centralised and integrated capacities as an ODA agency to recall the lessons of Japan's own experience as a developing country as well as its half century of experience as an ODA donor to create a distinctive role for itself and meet the expectations of African states for high quality and effective development assistance (Arase, 2017, pp. 104–123).

Conclusion

Japan is going back to its old model for development assistance, but the EU and its member countries are turning in a similar direction with a mixture of loans and grants, public and private cooperation. The goals of the SDGs and the amount of money needed to achieve them are changing the rules of the game. Traditional ODA as it used to be practised by the DAC members is losing in importance and even the definition of what is to be calculated as ODA is now under revision. Under the SDGs expectations are that all countries, upper as well as middle or low income, should aim to improve the lives of their citizens with goals that encompass social, and environmental, as well as economic, goals.

It will no longer be Western norms and standards that govern the process. There is a definite pivot to Asia in development cooperation. The new Chinese established AIIB, where more than 50 other countries have joined, among them many European nations, but not US and Japan, is a case in point. How this bank, which has huge ambitions, will affect existing institutions, including the World Bank and Asian Development Bank, remains to be seen.

Notes

1 That is foreign aid as defined by OECDs Development Assistance Committee. Meaning that aid should (1) be made for development purposes (2) have a grant element of at least 25 per cent (3) be government to government.

2 Like all developing countries, they should now also be monitored themselves to see if they are making progress on the SDGs goals.

3 A Britain-based foundation that has an endowment of £18bn – about half the size of the Gates Foundation. The Wellcome Trust disburses about £700m a year towards global health and science: a figure on a par with the Gates Foundation's annual spending on global health, which fluctuates between about £800m and £1bn each year.

4 The EU has for example provided assistance in the drafting of the ASEAN Charter in 2006 and 2007, and counselling to the ASEAN Eminent Persons Group and the High Level Task Force during visits to Brussels. EU-sponsored programs to enhance ASEAN integration and increase the institutional capacity of its secretariat include the Institutional Development Programme for the ASEAN Secretariat (IDPAS), the ASEAN Programme for Regional Integration Support (APRIS), and most recently the ASEAN Regional Integration Support from the EU (ARISE) 2013–2016.

5 In 2014 additional new external financing instruments started, including the European Neighbourhood Instrument, the Instrument for Pre-Accession Assistance, the Instrument Contributing to Stability and Peace, the European Instrument for Democracy and Human Rights, and the Partnership Instrument.

6 In Article 9 (the so-called peace article) of the post war constitution Japan renounces the right to wage war or solve international disputes by military means. The country theoretically had no military force after the war, but has gradually been building up Self Defence Forces (SDF), which although not labelled a military, can be seen as essentially military forces. They are strictly for defensive defence and cannot be sent abroad to engage in combat. Japan has been relying on the US for its military security. In July 2014 Article 9 was reinterpreted so that the SDF will be able to participate in collective self-defence abroad (i.e. engage in overseas combat) in case Japan's survival is threatened.

7 Countries receiving that are Albania, Bosnia and Herzegovina, the former Yugoslav Republic of Macedonia, Kosovo, Montenegro, Serbia, and Turkey. Available from: https://ec.europa.eu/neighbourhood-enlargement/instruments/overview_en. [Accessed: 22 May 2017].

References

Arase, D. (2017) Japanese ODA and the Challenge of Chinese Aid in Africa. In Asplund, A. and Söderberg, M. (eds) *Japanese Development Cooperation: The Making of an Aid Architecture Pivoting to Asia*. London and New York: Routledge.

Asplund, A. (2017) Aligning Policy with Practice: Japanese ODA and Normative Values. In Asplund, A. and Söderberg, M. (eds) *Japanese Development Cooperation: The Making of an Aid Architecture Pivoting to Asia*. London and New York: Routledge.

Agence Europe, Bulletin Quotidien (14 April 2016).

Business Insider. (9 November 2016) *President-elect Donald Trump Doesn't Believe in Climate Change. Here's His Platform on the Environment.* Available from: www.businessinsider.com/donald-trump-climate-change-global-warming-environment-policies-plans-platforms-2016-10. [Accessed: 6 December 2016].

DAC Secretariat. (2016) *2016 Development Cooperation Report.* Available from: www.keepeek.com/Digital-Asset-Management/oecd/development/development-co-operation-report-2016/japan_dcr-2016-29-en#.WEVCqrLhCpo#page1. [Accessed: 5 December 2016].

Desai, R. (2015) *Private Aid and the Financing of Development.* Development Day. Stockholm School of Economics, Stockholm, 11 May 2015.

European Commission. (2014) Available from: http://eur-lex.europa.eu/legal-content/EN/TXT/PDF/?uri=CELEX%3A52014DC0263&qid=1400681732387&from=EN. [Accessed: 2 December 2016].

European Commission. (2016) Available from: http://europa.eu/rapid/press-release_IP-16-3002_en.htm. [Accessed: 6 December 2016].

Fukushima, A. (2015) Japan-Europe Cooperation for Peace and Stability: Pursuing Synergies on a Comprehensive Approach in the German Marshall Fund of the United States. *Policy Brief.* Available from: www.gmfus.org/publications/japan-europe-cooperation-peace-and-stability. [Accessed: 22 March 2017].

Guardian. (13 April 2016) Available from: http://jica-ri.jica.go.jp/publication/assets/JICA-RI_WP_No. 78_2014.pdf. [Accessed: 14 May 2016].

Hook, G.D. (ed.). (2005) *Japan's International Relations: Politics, Economics and Security*. 2nd ed. London: Routledge.

JICA. (2014) Available from: http://jica-ri.jica.go.jp/publication/assets/JICA-RI_WP_No. 78_2014.pdf. [Accessed: 14 May 2016].

Kato, H., Page, J. and Shimomura, Y. (2016) *Japan's Development Assistance, Foreign Aid and the Post-2015 Agenda*. Basingstoke and New York: Palgrave.

Midford, P. (2010) Japan: Balancing between a Hegemon and a Would Be Hegemon. In Söderberg, M. and Nelson, P.A. (eds) *Japan's Politics and Economy; Perspectives on Change*. London and New York: Routledge.

Midford, P. (May/June 2015) Japan's Approach to Maritime Security in the South China Sea. *Asian Survey* 55(3), pp. 525–547.

MOFA. (1999) Available from: www.mofa.go.jp/policy/oda/summary/1999/refl.html. [Accessed: 8 May 2017].

MOFA. (2003) Available from: www.mofa.go.jp/policy/oda/reform/revision0308.pdf. [Accessed: 15 May 2016].

MOFA. (2015) Japan's Development Cooperation Charter. Available from: www.mofa. go.jp/files/000067701.pdf.

OECD. (2015) Development Cooperation Report, 2015, Making Partnership Effective Coalitions for Actions. Available from: www.oecd-ilibrary.org/docserver/dcr-2015-en. pdf?expires=1524381032&id=id&accname=guest&checksum=4308A42908F0327B3E BC42B676F8A7C6. [Accessed: 22 April 2017].

OECD. (2017) Development Cooperation Report 2017 Data for Development. Available from: www.oecd.org/dac/development-co-operation-report-20747721.htm. [Accessed: 12 November 2017].

OECD DAC. (2016a) Available from: www.oecd.org/dac/financing-sustainable-development/Concept%20note%20TOSSD%20workshop%20Lisbon.pdf. [Accessed: 2 November 2016].

OECD DAC. (2016b) Available from: www.oecd.org/dac/dacnewsjanuary2016.htm. [Accessed: 7 March 2016].

Owa, M. (2014) *Collective Action in Global Governance: The Case of the OECD Development Assistance Committee*. PhD thesis. University of Warwick.

Owa, M. (2017) The Changing Global Aid Architecture: An Opportunity for Japan to Play a Proactive Global Role?' In Asplund, A. and Söderberg, M. (eds) *Japanese Development Cooperation: The Making of an Aid Architecture Pivoting to Asia*. London and New York: Routledge.

Pajon, C. (2013) *Japan's 'Smart' Strategic Engagement in Southeast Asia*. Conference paper presented at the Asan Forum, 6 December 2013. Available from: www.the asanforum.org/japans-smart-strategic-engagement-insoutheast-asia/. [Accessed: 11 August 2016].

Rieffel, L. and Fox, J. (2013) *Too Much/Too Soon, the Dilemma of Foreign Aid to Myanmar/Burma*. Report. Washington DC: Brookings Institution.

Shimomura, Y. (2017) The Development Cooperation Paradigm Under the 'New Partnership' and its Implication for Japan's Aid. In Asplund, A. and Söderberg, M. (eds) *Japanese Development Cooperation, the Making of an Aid architecture Pivoting to Asia*. London and New York: Routledge.

Söderberg, M. (1996) *The Business of Japanese Foreign Aid: Five Case Studies from Asia*. London: Routledge.

Sunaga, K. (2005) The Reshaping of Japan's Official Development Assistance (ODA) Charter. Discussion Paper No. 36, Discussion Paper Series, APEC Study Center, Columbia University.

UN. (2015a) Addis Ababa Action Agenda. Available from: www.un.org/esa/ffd/wp-content/uploads/2015/08/AAAA_Outcome.pdf. [Accessed: 5 December 2016].

UN. (2015b) The MDG Report. Available from: www.un.org/millenniumgoals/2015_ MDG_Report/pdf/MDG%202015%20rev%20(July%201).pdf. [Accessed: 20 March 2017].

UN. (2016) Available from: https://sustainabledevelopment.un.org/topics/sustainable developmentgoals. [Accessed: 5 December 2016].

UN Indepthnews. (2016) Available from: www.indepthnews.net/index.php/global-governance/un-insider/362-g77-and-china-disappointed-at-outcome-document-of-addis-ababa-follow-up. [Accessed: 3 December 2016].

Yasutomo, D.T. (1986) *The Manner of Giving: Strategic Aid and Japanese Foreign Policy*. Lexington, MA: Lexington Books.

Part III

Reflections by the two superpowers

11 The evolution of America's implicit support of EU–Japan security relations

Jeffrey W. Hornung

Nearly everything written about the European Union (EU) and Japan emphasizes their commonalities. Be it fundamental values and norms, their embrace of democracy and free markets, respect for human rights, and their support for a rules-based international system, they are often described as natural partners. Additionally, they both enjoy strategic alliances with the U.S., making them strategic partners by association. Yet, while their economic ties are deep, their security ties are shallow, leading scholars to characterize their relationship as untapped potential (Atanassova-Cornelis, 2010; Midford, 2012, 2013; Raine and Small, 2015; Tsuruoka, 2013). The EU and Japan are simply not cooperating in security-related areas as much as they could, or should. From the perspective of their common ally, the U.S., it is critical that its European and Japanese allies turn their "potential" cooperation into "actual" cooperation. The threats facing the U.S. are simply too complicated to handle by itself. This is particularly true in an era of constrained resources. Greater EU–Japan security cooperation would aid their mutual strategic ally by reinforcing similar efforts the U.S. is already pursuing as well as act as force multipliers for U.S. efforts. But U.S. views of EU–Japan security cooperation are often unstated. This chapter attempts to make America's implicit support explicit.

The chapter is organized as follows. After a brief history of the development of security cooperation between the EU and Japan, I examine U.S. strategic documents to uncover implicit support for EU–Japan security cooperation. I argue that over the past two and a half decades the U.S. has gradually come to support a greater security role for Brussels and Tokyo and many of the activities they seek to perform. This is because it is in U.S. interest for "potential" EU–Japan security cooperation to become "actual". While aiding U.S. interests, greater EU–Japan security cooperation has the potential to adversely affect China as it promises to be a target of joint efforts. I close with a consideration of potential obstacles preventing the EU and Japan turning their "potential" into "actual".

EU–Japan security cooperation: heavy on rhetoric

Throughout the Cold War, security issues were not a focus of Europe–Japan relations. This is because "their mutual partnership was secondary to their respective strategic partnerships with the United States" (Watanabe, 2016, p. 4). With foreign policies emphasizing relations with the U.S., relations between Europe and Japan were defined by economic issues and increasingly filled with friction as trade between Japan and the European Community was marked by a persistent surplus on the Japanese side (Watanabe, 2016, pp. 2–3). Glimpses of a security relationship occasionally emerged, such as when Japanese Prime Minister Yasuhiro Nakasone told the G7 gathering in 1983 that the security of Japan and Western Europe was "indivisible" (MOFA, 1984). However, because the U.S. guaranteed the security of Europe and Japan, interaction between Japan and Europe was limited to economics. This changed with the end of the Cold War. Emerging regional threats led them to confront a new spectrum of challenges that required cooperation with new international actors. The origin of today's EU–Japan security partnership is the 18 July 1991 *Joint Declaration* (European Community and Japan, 1991). This landmark declaration marked a qualitative change as they attempted to move beyond economics towards political and security dialogue. Affirming their common attachment to values like freedom, democracy, rule of law and human rights, the *Joint Declaration* stated their common interest in security, peace and stability in the world and set out their commitment to strengthen dialogue and cooperation on various international issues that may affect it. Little practical cooperation emerged from it, however, leaving the *Joint Declaration* stand as an ambitious list of non-military areas of security cooperation. In the decade that followed, both Europe and Japan undertook a review of their strategies with external powers, leading to the recognition of the need for closer security ties.

The culmination of their efforts was the 2001 *Action Plan for EU-Japan Cooperation* (hereafter: *Action Plan*). It listed more than 100 potential areas of cooperation with one of the four primary categories dedicated to promoting peace and security (European Union and Japan, 2001). With a reaffirmation of their shared responsibility to contribute non-combat means to international peace, security and prosperity, the *Action Plan* intended to serve as a guide for cooperation. But it provided no realistic action plan on how to achieve its objectives.

The *Joint Declaration* and *Action Plan* are significant in helping shift the EU–Japan relationship towards political and security issues. Subsequent summits further fleshed out areas to cooperate. This included counterterrorism, North Korea, climate change, anti-piracy, and reconstruction in Afghanistan. Still, even after another decade of summits and agreements, there was no real action to realize their stated initiatives. And despite starting negotiations in March 2013 for a binding agreement called the Strategic Partnership Agreement (SPA), it took until April 2018 for negotiations to be concluded.

Thus, despite strengthened security dialogue between Brussels and Tokyo, real-world security cooperation remains in the realm of "potential". This is evident if we consider some of the major security challenges that have emerged since the *Joint Declaration* and the lack of any significant cooperative efforts to meet those challenges. While their non-combat efforts help alleviate human suffering brought on by war in places such as Africa, the former Yugoslavia, the Balkans, Aceh, Mindanao, Afghanistan and Iraq, despite working together on similar issues and dispatching personnel on similar missions, their efforts are largely in parallel, not joint. Instead, military cooperation between Japanese and EU troops relies largely on ad-hoc coordination and cooperation on the ground (Tsuruoka, 2011, p. 40).

The exception is their anti-piracy efforts near the coast of Somalia, which stands as the best case of EU–Japan security cooperation to date. Although never officially part of the EU Naval Force (EU NAVFOR Operation Atalanta), the European and Japanese operations closely cooperate via information sharing, coordination of patrol flights, and coordination of naval vessel escorts of civilian shipping through the Gulf of Aden. Importantly, Brussels and Tokyo also jointly support regional capacity building via the establishment of the Djibouti counter-piracy regional training centre and information-sharing centres in Kenya, Tanzania, and Yemen (Midford, 2012, pp. 302–303; Midford, 2013, p. 45; Council of the European Union, 2010).

Growing U.S. implicit support

The EU and Japan have a unique role to play in global security affairs. Both are "relatively pessimistic about the utility of military force and military intervention in resolving conflicts" (Midford, 2012, p. 291). They are civilian powers that adopt similar approaches to security that stress the comprehensive nature of security threats (Atanassova-Cornelis, 2010, p. 482; Mykal, 2011). Additionally, both emphasize the role of non-combat approaches to peace building, have restrictive rules of engagement for their militaries, and share a common liberal belief that non-combat focused post-conflict reconstruction and long-term socio-economic development are the best ways to addresses the underlying sources of conflict and insecurity (Midford, 2013, p. 44). While these approaches are fundamentally different than those taken by the U.S., this does not mean the U.S. does not support their efforts.

The U.S., however, has never explicitly stated it supports EU–Japan security cooperation. Yet, U.S. strategic documents reveal its hand. National Security Strategies, Quadrennial Defense Reviews and various agreements and statements over the past two-and-a-half decades show that, while the U.S. sees itself as the global security leader, it has gradually come to support a greater security role for Brussels and Tokyo and many of the activities they seek to perform. Although the U.S. never connects its support for these activities with support for greater EU–Japan security cooperation, these documents implicitly show the U.S. supports Brussels and Tokyo cooperating in non-military, non-combat areas.

National Security Strategies

The National Security Strategies (NSS) produced by the George H.W. Bush Administration (1989–1993) maintain the U.S.-Soviet/Russia relationship as its analytical starting point. Still drunk by Cold War victory and the unravelling Communist system in Eastern Europe, a dominant theme is "there is no substitute for American leadership" (Bush, 1991, p. 2). America alone is seen as uniquely placed to tackle the world's challenges because "no other nation has the same combination of moral, cultural, political, economic, and military credibility. No other has won such confidence, respect, and trust. No other has the same potential and indeed responsibility for world leadership" (Bush, 1993, p. 21). Simply put, "the world needs the leadership that only America can provide" (Bush, 1993, p. i).

This does not mean alliances are forgotten. NSS documents indicate the U.S. seeks to "establish a more balanced partnership with [its] allies and a greater sharing of global leadership and responsibilities" (Bush, 1991, p. 3). That said, allies are viewed in terms of their military applicability regarding collective defence. They are a means to help the U.S. deter aggression or, should deterrence fail, assist in repelling or defeating military attack and end conflict on favourable terms (Bush, 1991, p. 3). Rather than allies playing a role in their own right, their role is tied to the U.S. For example, as a means by which the U.S. could "reduce the impact of budget constraints" by greater commitment to national specialization and intra-alliance division of labour based on comparative advantages (Bush, 1990, p. 26).

While there are passing references indicating tacit support for greater European and Japanese efforts, they are not substantial. There is an admission that Germany and Japan assuming a greater political role will assist regional and global stability and the U.S. has a desire to work with the European Community "to adapt NATO's structures to encompass European desires for a distinct security identity within the Alliance" (Bush, 1991, pp. 6–7). The U.S. also has a hope "to see the U.S.-Japan global partnership extend beyond its traditional confines and into fields like refugee relief, non-proliferation and the environment" (Bush, 1991, p. 9).

Bush-era NSS also offer implicit nods to areas that eventually become the main focus of EU–Japan security cooperation. For example, the 1991 NSS states that "If the end of the Cold War lives up to its promise … we should be able to concentrate more on enhancing security … through means that are more political, social and economic than military" (Bush, 1991, p. 8). There is an admission that "the most desirable and efficient security strategy is to address the root causes of instability and to ease tensions before they result in conflict" (Bush, 1993, p. 7). With a desire to contribute to the early attenuation of conflict, rather than allowing it to expand into a more serious threat, the U.S. sees a role for its allies to collectively "develop multinational capabilities necessary for enforcing peace, and enhance our capability to contribute to monitoring, verification and reconnaissance, as well as peace rebuilding after conflict" (Bush, 1993, p. 19).

The William J. Clinton Administration (1993–2001) places a continued priority on U.S. leadership, but is accompanied by an acknowledgement of the constraints on U.S. power. Although there is continued belief that "without [U.S.] active leadership and engagement abroad, threats will fester and our opportunities will narrow" (Clinton, 1994, p. 1), there is also recognition that "it is clear we cannot police the world" (Clinton, 1994, p. 5). Like Bush, therefore, Clinton recognizes the value of allies, seeing that "an important element of [U.S.] security preparedness depends on durable relationships with allies and other friendly nations" (Clinton, 1994, p. 6). But their value is still not what they can do independent of the U.S. Instead, it is allies playing a role in their respective regions in cooperation with the U.S., which remains prima inter pares, "prepared to act alone" (Clinton, 1994, p. 10). Functionally, their value is still seen primarily through the lens of collective defence (Clinton, 1994, p. 6).

More than Bush, Clinton's NSS show more acceptance of areas important to EU–Japan security cooperation. There is recognition of the importance of preventive diplomacy "to help resolve problems, reduce tensions and defuse conflicts before they become crises" (Clinton, 1994, p. 5), of the difficulties of applying military force to conflicts within and among states (Clinton, 1994, p. 21), and of helping support democracy, sustainable economic development and resolution of conflicts through negotiation, diplomacy and peacekeeping by focusing on strengthening civil societies and mechanisms for conflict resolution (Clinton, 1994, p. 26). These are mentioned annually as they are seen as offering the best "prospect of resolving problems with the least human and material cost" (Clinton, 1996, p. 11), but there are very few details to back this up.

Things begin to change in 1996. In speaking about Bosnia, the NSS emphasizes international cooperation and coordination of humanitarian assistance to deal with civilian tasks associated with rebuilding, reconstructing and return of refugees after conflict that are seen as "absolutely essential to making the peace endure" (Clinton, 1996, p. 36). Importantly, in a first that identifies a division of labour between military and non-military cooperation, in view of the large role the U.S. will play in implementing the military aspects of the peace agreement, the NSS recognizes the role of burden sharing the EU and Japan will take in reconstruction (Clinton, 1996, p. 36).

Subsequent Clinton-era NSS include items more familiar to agenda items prioritized by the EU and Japan. This begins in 1997, when the NSS places an emphasis on non-military tools to shape the international environment. Many of these tools, and their targeted objectives, are like EU–Japan cooperation not only in substance, but in the hope that these "U.S. initiatives reduce the need for costly military and humanitarian interventions" (Clinton, 1997, p. 9). These include:

- Efforts "to discourage arms races, halt the proliferation of weapons of mass destruction and reduce tensions in critical regions" (Clinton, 1997, p. 9).
- Sustainable development programs that "promote voluntary family planning, basic education, environmental protection, democratic governance and

rule of law, and the economic empowerment of private citizens" (Clinton, 1997, p. 9).

- Efforts "to promote democracy and human rights ... complemented by [U.S.] humanitarian assistance programs, which are designed to alleviate human suffering, to help establish democratic regimes that respect human rights and to pursue appropriate strategies for economic development. These efforts also ... help prevent humanitarian disasters with far more significant resource implications" (Clinton, 1997, p. 24).

Importantly, there is mention, for the first time, of the need for "closer cooperation with our European partners in dealing with non-military security threats through our New Transatlantic Agenda with the EU" (Clinton, 1997, p. 25).

While the programs detailed in subsequent Clinton-era NSS are similar in nature, they hint at supporting other countries' independent cooperative efforts in security. Examples include:

- Instead of U.S. leading, the U.S. would "foster regional efforts led by the community of democratic nations to promote peace and prosperity in key regions of the world" (Clinton, 1998, p. 2).
- The U.S. would support "promoting an international community that is willing and able to prevent or respond effectively to humanitarian problems, and strengthening international non-governmental movements committed to human rights and democratization (Clinton, 1998, p. 5).
- The U.S. will work "to strengthen the capacity of the international community to prevent and, whenever possible, stop outbreaks of mass killing and displacement ... [W]hen the world community has the power to stop genocide and ethnic cleansing, we will work with our allies and partners, and with the United Nations, to mobilize against such violence" (Clinton, 1999, p. 26).

By 2000, the Clinton Administration offers active support of Europe's independent security initiatives. This includes both the development of the European Security and Defence Policy (ESDP) as well as "European efforts to increase and improve capabilities for collective defence and crisis response operations, including the capability to act militarily under the EU when NATO, as a whole, is not engaged" (Clinton, 2000, p. 52). Reflecting the still evolving relationship with Japan following the 1997 Defence Guidelines, the NSS only recognizes the need to build on the alliance "to define new approaches to post-Cold War threats" (Clinton, 2000, p. i).

The George W. Bush Administration's (2001–2009) two NSS focus heavily on counter-terrorism. This means the breadth of the 2002 NSS agenda is limited. One exception is a section focused on development assistance (Bush, 2002, pp. 21–23). There is shift in emphasis towards supporting other states' efforts, the need to appreciate their interests, and the need for the U.S. to coordinate with them, rather than lead. It calls on "concerned nations ... [to] remain actively engaged in critical regional disputes to avoid explosive escalation and minimize human suffering" (Bush, 2002, p. 9). Similarly, it refers to "coordination"—rather than leading or cooperation—with European allies as an essential means for conflict mediation and peace operations (Bush, 2002, p. 11). Finally, in discussing America's will to organize coalitions, it recognizes the need for "an appreciation of others' interests, and consistent consultations among partners with a spirit of humility" (Bush, 2002, p. 25). Importantly, for the first time, there is strong support for roles played by the EU and Japan. The U.S. "welcome[s] our European allies' efforts to forge a greater foreign policy and defence identity with the EU" and "look[s] to Japan to continue forging a leading role in regional and global affairs based on our common interests, our common values, and our close defence and diplomatic cooperation" (Bush, 2002, p. 26).

While the 2006 NSS still emphasizes counter-terrorism, it also acknowledges non-traditional security issues. This includes, among others, pandemic diseases, human trafficking, and natural disasters (Bush, 2006, preface). The tools identified to fight this broader aperture of challenges harmonize well with the 2001 *Action Plan* but differ from past NSS in their non-military focus to address underlying security challenges. The NSS lays out a strategy for addressing regional conflicts that include three levels of engagement: conflict prevention and resolution; conflict intervention; and post-conflict stabilization and reconstruction (Bush, 2006, p. 15). Among many of the tools cited include:

- Use of "tools of economic assistance, development aid, trade, and good governance to help ensure that new democracies are not burdened with economic stagnation or endemic corruption" (Bush, 2006, p. 4).
- Use "foreign assistance to support the development of free and fair elections, rule of law, civil society, human rights, women's rights, free media, and religious freedom" (Bush, 2006, p. 6).
- Tailor "assistance and training of military forces to support civilian control of the military and military respect for human rights in a democratic society" (Bush, 2006, p. 6).

Importantly, while the EU and Japan are not explicitly mentioned, the NSS recognizes that capable partners are needed, particularly democratic nations, including an acknowledgement of the value of "nongovernmental organizations and other civil society voices" (Bush, 2006, p. 6).

The Barack H. Obama Administration (2009–2017) continues the trend towards implicit embrace of the EU–Japan security agenda. There is a recognition that "a smart national security strategy does not rely solely on military power" (Obama, 2015, p. ii). Toward this end, the U.S. commits itself to "work with partners and through multilateral organizations to address the root causes of conflict before they erupt and to contain and resolve them when they do" (Obama, 2015, p. 2). From this, there is a focus on the need to "address the underlying political and economic deficits that foster instability, enable radicalization and extremism, and ultimately undermine the ability of governments to manage threats within their borders and to be our partners in addressing common challenges" (Obama, 2010, p. 26). The 2010 NSS lays out the need to (1) foster security and reconstruction in the aftermath of conflict; (2) pursue sustainable and responsible security systems in at-risk states; and (3) prevent the emergence of conflict (Obama, 2010, pp. 26–27). This is coupled with a call to accelerate sustainable development to help address states' insecurity and poor governance (Obama, 2010, pp. 33–34).

Like previous NSS, there is continued recognition that current challenges "cannot be solved by one nation or even a group of nations" (Obama, 2010, p. 47). As powerful as the U.S. may be, the Obama Administration recognizes that "our resources and influence are not infinite" (Obama, 2015, p. ii). Recognizing that other states have interests and power to achieve those interests, the Obama Administration's view of the international environment is one "in which different nations are exerting greater influence, and advancing our interests will require expanding spheres of cooperation around the word" (Obama, 2010, p. 43). Following from this, and given the diplomatic space for greater EU–Japan cooperation, the NSS emphasizes the need for collective action with those closest allies and partners that share interests and values with the U.S. Both Europe and Japan are identified as such. With Europe, which is referred to as "the cornerstone for U.S. engagement with the world, and a catalyst for international action" (Obama, 2010, p. 41), the U.S. is "committed to partnering with a stronger European Union to advance our shared goals" (Obama, 2010, p. 42). With Japan (along with South Korea), an "increasingly important leader in addressing regional and global issues", the U.S. is committed to "to develop a positive security agenda for the region" (Obama, 2010, p. 42). There is also an admission that the U.S. will expand its "scope of cooperation to encompass other state partners, non-state and private actors, and international institutions—particularly the United Nations (U.N.), international financial institutions, and key regional organizations" (Obama, 2015, p. 3).

Quadrennial Defense Review

Conducted every four years, the Quadrennial Defense Review (QDR) is a legislatively mandated review of Department of Defense (DOD) strategy and priorities that sets a long-term course as it assesses the threats and challenges the U.S. faces and re-balances DOD's strategies, capabilities, and forces to address today's conflicts and tomorrow's threats (U.S. Department of Defense, n.d.) To date, five have been conducted: 1997, 2001, 2006, 2010, and 2014 but it has since been eliminated by Congress and replaced by the National Defense Strategy. Because these documents set defence priorities and outline military requirements for determining the size and structure of the U.S. military to respond to the changing strategic environment, the focus is on traditional, combat-related military issues. Non-combat items are mentioned, but not as much.

For the first two QDRs, there is little reference to EU–Japan security cooperation. In the 1997 QDR, there are scant references to alliances and non-combat type cooperation. The only relevant references appear in a section about humanitarian crises that admits, "cooperative, multinational approaches that distribute the burden of responsibility among like-minded states" is sometimes needed and the U.S. military may generally not be the best means to address this type of crisis, except if civilian relief agencies are completely overwhelmed by the scope of the crisis (Cohen, 1997). While the 2001 QDR includes references to alliances as "a centerpiece of American security" (Rumsfeld, 2001, p. 5), the references are related to collective security and deterrence against threats. With an eye on strengthening these relationships, it states a primary objective of U.S. cooperation is to help them "create favorable balances of military power in critical areas of the world to deter aggression or coercion" (Rumsfeld, 2001, p. 11).

It is not until the 2006 QDR that more elements in sync with the EU–Japan security relationship are included. First and foremost, the importance of U.S. alliances is explicitly stated. Through allies and partners, the U.S. shares risks and responsibilities (Rumsfeld, 2006, p. 88). NATO and Japan are mentioned often. Although EU–Japan security cooperation is not, there is acknowledgement that U.S. allies will share "military and security burdens around the world" (Rumsfeld, 2006, p. 6). Importantly, there is support of "tailoring national military contributions to best employ the unique capabilities and characteristics of each ally" (Rumsfeld, 2006, p. 88). While the 2014 QDR places Japan as one of its main allies in the U.S. rebalance to the Asia-Pacific (Hagel, 2014, p. 16), the 2010 QDR recognizes the importance of the EU, the security work the EU is performing in Afghanistan, and "the need for NATO to develop its own comprehensive civil-military approach, as well as greater cooperation with the EU" (Gates, 2010, p. 58).

Second, there is recognition of early measures to prevent problems from becoming crises, to help alleviate suffering, and to set the conditions for security; rather than fighting wars. "By alleviating suffering and dealing with crises in their early stages, U.S. forces help prevent disorder from spiralling into wider conflict or crisis" (Rumsfeld, 2006, p. 12). Capacity building is therefore important, as it "can help prevent conflict from beginning or escalating, reducing the possibility that large and enduring deployments of U.S. or allied forces would be required" (Gates, 2010, p. 10). Toward this end, the QDRs express an interest in using U.S. power to address the same civilian, non-combat areas of cooperation outlined by the EU and Japan. In addition to humanitarian assistance and disaster relief, other items include:

- Helping "build up the capacity of local security forces to police their own countries (Rumsfeld, 2006, p. 14).
- Improving "states' governance, administration, internal security and the rule of law in order to build partner governments' legitimacy in the eyes of their own people and thereby inoculate societies against terrorism, insurgency and non-state threats" (Rumsfeld, 2006, p. 90).
- Taking "quick action to relieve civilian suffering, train security forces to maintain civil order and restore critical civilian infrastructure" to deny the

enemy opportunities to capitalize on disorder following military operations (Rumsfeld, 2006, p. 91).

- Utilizing an "integrated use of diplomacy, development, and defence, along with intelligence, law enforcement, and economic tools of statecraft to help build the capacity of partners to maintain and promote stability" (Gates, 2010, p. 13).
- Addressing threats to a state by assisting governments "in the fields of rule of law, economic stability, governance, public health and welfare, infrastructure, and public education and information" (Gates, 2010, p. 24).

Bilateral U.S. statements/agreements

A final way to investigate U.S. views on EU–Japan security cooperation is to look at bilateral statements and agreements it releases with the EU and Japan. Like the pattern witnessed above, these statements and agreements show a growth in U.S. support of the same type of non-combat areas emphasized by the EU and Japan.

EU–U.S.

Understanding the EU–U.S. relationship is primarily economic in focus, economic related issues dominate summit meetings. While items like non-proliferation and cooperation to deal with Southeast Europe are also frequently discussed, cooperation with Japan never makes it on summit agendas in the 1990s.

This changes with the 1995 EU–U.S. Summit where the New Transatlantic Agenda (NTA) is adopted. Although its focus remains almost exclusively on Southeast Europe, one of its four major goals echoes items prioritized by the EU and Japan: promoting peace and stability, democracy and development around the world (European External Action Service, n.d.). The EU and U.S. agree to work on recovery of war-ravaged nations; contribute humanitarian assistance and to the task of reconstruction; to work together more closely in preventive and crisis diplomacy; to promote sustainable development and the building of democratic societies; and to support human rights (European External Action Service, n.d., pp. 2–3). At subsequent summits, the NTA becomes a vehicle by which to discuss these types of issues, although anything security-related almost always focuses on Southeast Europe. It is not until 2005 that their agenda broadens with agreements on democracy promotion and support of rule of law and human rights worldwide (U.S. White House, 2005a) and the promotion of peace, prosperity, and good governance in Africa (U.S. White House, 2005b) as well as peace, prosperity and progress in the Middle East (U.S. White House, 2005c). Renewal of this commitment continues at subsequent summits, culminating in George W. Bush's final summit in 2008 where they lay out a global agenda for promoting international peace, stability, democracy, human rights, international criminal justice, the rule of law and good governance and working together in conflict prevention and post-conflict reconstruction (Office of the Press Secretary, 2008).

Barack Obama initially did little to change this, as his first three summit meetings result in the same reaffirmation of shared commitment to strengthen collaboration in security and development issues and a desire to promote security around the world (Office of the Press Secretary, 2010). This changes at the 2011 summit where, for the first time, they explicitly state a shared strategic interest "in enhancing co-operation on political, economic, security, and human rights issues in the Asia-Pacific region to advance peace, stability and prosperity" (Office of the Press Secretary, 2011). Toward that end, they agree to increase "dialogue on Asia-Pacific issues and coordinate activities to demonstrate an enduring, high-level commitment to the region and encourage regional integration, including through the region's multilateral organizations" (Office of the Press Secretary, 2011).

The following year, the U.S. and EU issue a joint statement on the Asia-Pacific region that lays out their shared interests in closely consulting and cooperating towards the advancement of regional security, development, well-being and prosperity (Office of the Spokesperson, 2012). In this, they include Asia-specific items important for the EU and Japan. This includes:

- a commitment to strengthening cooperation in counter-piracy, including its root causes
- increasing maritime security based on international law
- advancing a Code of Conduct in the South China Sea
- lending assistance to the development of confidence building measures to reduce the risks of crises and conflict
- promoting democracy and human rights
- engaging governance and development challenges.

Much of this agenda is included in 2014 EU–U.S. Summit (Office of the Press Secretary, 2014). In what can arguably be called tacit support for EU–Japan security cooperation, the same Joint Statement welcomes the EU's efforts to strengthen its CSDP, "including by working together with key partners" (Office of the Press Secretary, 2014).

Japan–U.S.

Like NATO, the Japan–U.S. alliance focuses on hard military issues. This means most summit meetings and ministerial meetings focus on military issues regarding the defence of Japan and the roles and missions of alliance. Reflecting the growth seen in NSS and QDR documents, however, these meetings display a similar evolution that culminates with the 2015 revision of their defence guidelines that includes items included in the EU–Japan security agenda.

Throughout the 1990s, most attention at U.S.–Japan summits is on economic issues, the Korean Peninsula, and issues relating to Okinawa. Other issues are discussed, albeit in very small doses. For example, in July 1993 the two coun-tries agree to a Common Agenda for Cooperation in Global Perspective. When expanded in 1996, this means cooperation in addressing emerging non-traditional security issues to include, among others, fighting infectious diseases, trafficking narcotic drugs, strengthen international networks for exchanging data on natural disaster early warning, and coordinate assistance to countries for election moni-toring and strengthening judicial systems (MOFA, 1996a). And in 1996, they agree to strengthen their cooperation in support of the UN and other international organizations through activities such as peacekeeping and humanitarian relief operations (MOFA, 1996b). While these initiatives are never fleshed out, they highlight Japan's non-combat role in global security to complement the non-combat areas of U.S.–EU cooperation highlighted in the Clinton-era NSS. For most of the decade, however, there is not much more.

The 11 September 2001 terrorist attacks change this. The bilateral agenda, still dominated by the issues mentioned above, is increasingly accompanied by an emphasis on the realignment of U.S. forces in the region and the fight against ter-rorism—including Japan's role in the wars against Afghanistan and Iraq. In this context, Japan pursues a civilian power agenda, supported by the U.S., prioritizing assistance to help these countries in their reconstruction and development efforts that included priority areas such as education, infrastructure, and agriculture and rural development (MOFA, 2002). In line with this, the two countries launch the U.S.–Japan Strategic Development Alliance in September 2005 to cooperate towards the "empowerment of individuals and local communities, good govern-ance, strong democratic institutions, and political stability" (MOFA, 2005b). This is reflected in the October 2005 SCC meeting where they emphasize the import-ance of improving bilateral cooperation in humanitarian relief operations, recon-struction assistance operations, peacekeeping operations and capacity building for other nations' peacekeeping efforts (Security Consultative Committee, 2005, p. 4).

This focus fades under Barack Obama. Climate change, Iran's nuclear efforts, and the rise of China dominate the bilateral agenda, although the January 2010 SCC meeting gives fleeting reference to bilateral commitments to combating piracy (Security Consultative Committee, 2010, p. 2). But 2011 marks an important evolution. While issues of nuclear safety, the Transpacific Partnership and the South China Sea dominate their agenda, at the SCC the alliance begins to embrace broader initiatives that include issues highlighted by the EU and Japan.[1] This includes:

- Cooperation in areas of humanitarian assistance, governance and capacity building, peacekeeping operations, and development assistance (Security Consultative Committee, 2011, p. 5).
- Defending the principle of freedom of navigation, including preventing and eradicating piracy … and promoting related customary international law and international agreements (Security Consultative Committee, 2011, p. 5).
- Strengthening international cooperation on disaster prevention and relief (Security Consultative Committee, 2011, p. 6).

This movement towards a broader agenda culminates in the April 2015 release of new Defence Guidelines. While primarily a document outlining military roles and missions, many non-military support roles are detailed, including PKOs, HA/DR operations, maritime security, and partner capacity building (MOFA, 2015a, pp. 18–20). With an increasing number of references to the U.S. supporting Japan (in the context of the alliance) promoting security and defence cooperation with countries that share common values or building networks for security cooperation (Security Consultative Committee, 2011, p. 10; MOFA, 2015b) it is evident the U.S. implicitly supports Japan's outreach to actors like the EU.

Taken together, while the U.S. has never explicitly stated its support for greater EU–Japan security cooperation, a historical look at two-and-a-half decades worth of NSS, QDR, and bilateral agreements/statements show that the U.S. has come to embrace the same agenda as the EU and Japan and supports its allies taking on greater roles in pursuit of that agenda. Implicitly then, the U.S. supports greater EU–Japan security cooperation.

This support continues under the Donald J. Trump Administration (2018–present), although it appears to have changed. At the time of this book's publication, the Trump Administration has been in office just over a year. In December 2017, it released its NSS. Through this, and public statements by officials, it is possible to make a tentative statement on the administration's view on EU–Japan security cooperation. Candidate Trump was dismissive of Europe and Japan as U.S. allies. Since becoming president, his administration has continued to issue critical statements, particularly of Europe, and has not publicly been supportive of efforts like development aid or democracy promotion, for example. Despite this, his administration has publicly stated a commitment to strong alliances, as they help "provide avenues for peace, fostering the conditions for economic growth with countries that share the same vision" (Mattis, 2017). There have also been indications to reinforce the notion of continued U.S. support for issues important to the EU–Japan relationship. This includes:

- Strong commitment to continued cooperation and partnership with the EU and the shared purpose to promote peace and prosperity through freedom, democracy, and the rule of law (Office of the Vice President, 2017).
- Commitment to being an active and fully engaged partner with Japan to promote their shared interests (Office of the Press Secretary, 2017).
- Deep appreciation of the EU's role in promoting peace, security, human rights, and prosperity in Europe and around the world (U.S. Mission to the European Union, 2017).
- A commitment to reinforcing the rules-based international order, including freedom of navigation (Mattis, 2017).

The NSS maintains a focus on these issues important to the EU and Japan. These include:

- "…work[ing] with other countries to detect and mitigate outbreaks early to prevent the spread of disease" (Trump, 2017, p. 9)

- diplomacy "to identify and implement solutions to conflict" (Trump, 2017, p. 33)
- the morality of upholding "the rule of law, empower[ing] women, and respect[ing] individual rights" (Trump, 2017, p. 38)
- "... stand[ing] with those who seek freedom ... [and] committed to supporting and advancing religious freedom" (Trump, 2017, p. 41)
- "... support[ing] efforts to advance women's equality, protect the rights of women and girls, and promote women and youth empowerment programs" (Trump, 2017, p. 42)
- "... advocate[ing] on behalf of religious freedom and threatened minorities" (Trump, 2017, p. 42)
- supporting "food security and health programs that save lives and address the root cause of hunger and disease" (Trump, 2017, p. 42). Africa is mentioned as a place the U.S. will respond to humanitarian needs with other states and organizations "to address the root causes of human suffering" (Trump, 2017, p. 52).

Despite these similarities with previous NSS documents, the emphasis remains on U.S. power and capabilities to directly respond to security challenges, rather than fostering cooperation and addressing underlying causes. And while the importance of allies and partners is recognized, they are viewed through the lens of their ability to magnify U.S. power (Trump, 2017, p. 4) and help the U.S. achieve its interests. There are, however, passing references indicating tacit support for greater European and Japanese initiatives. For example, the NSS "... welcome[s] and support[s] the strong leadership role of our critical ally, Japan" (Trump, 2017, p. 46). Similarly, the NSS states that the U.S. and Europe "... are bound together by our shared commitment to the principles of democracy, individual liberty, and the rule of law" (Trump, 2017, p. 47). But when overlapping issue areas with the EU and Japan are raised, there is often a transactional notion attached. For example, when talking about helping developing states' infrastructure and the need to propel growth, the NSS declares, "Such states can become trading partners that buy more American-made goods and create more predictable business environments that benefit American companies" (Trump, 2017, p. 39). And when discussing the importance of helping states to become stable, the NSS says "Stable, prosperous, and friendly states enhance American security and boost U.S. economic opportunities" (Trump, 2017, p. 38). Finally, when talking about U.S. development assistance, it says the U.S. "... will prioritize collaboration with aspiring partners that are aligned with U.S. interests" (Trump, 2017, p. 39). Likewise, when discussing international organizations, it says the U.S. "will prioritize its efforts in those organizations that serve American interests" (Trump, 2017, p. 40). Together, it appears that the U.S. still implicitly supports the EU and Japan and some of the issues they cooperate on in the security realm, although the nature and strength of the U.S. support appears to have changed.

Impact of greater EU–Japan security cooperation on the U.S. and China

Although the U.S. has never explicitly stated its support of EU–Japan security cooperation, greater cooperation is in its interest. The bilateral relationship represents twenty-nine countries (twenty-eight EU + Japan), which carries the potential for them to have a major influence on international events. Importantly, greater cooperation, if realized, reinforces similar efforts the U.S. is pursuing independently with the EU and Japan, thereby benefiting U.S. interests across a host of domains.

• Combined development assistance and reconstruction support in poor states help lay deeper foundations for sustainable development and prosperity.
• Initiatives aimed at building infrastructure and reforming agricultural sectors in fragile states help address sources of instability.
• Work to promote rule of law, democracy and human rights add legitimacy to U.S.-led efforts against states that do not share these values. Having more partners engaged in these areas means the U.S. alone is not responsible for acting as the world's democracy proselytizer.

Together, it means the EU and Japan's efforts at norm- and rule-making in critical policy areas (Tsuruoka, 2013, p. 2), such as counter-terrorism and non-proliferation, aid U.S. efforts in similar areas.

Operationally, although rooted in non-combat efforts, greater EU–Japan security cooperation act as force multipliers for U.S. efforts. Combined non-proliferation and counter-piracy efforts carry greater impact towards ensuring a more secure world than America's efforts alone. Likewise, cooperation in post-conflict reconstruction and addressing root causes of terrorism and piracy through coordinated development assistance promise more successes to stabilize fragile states. The EU and Japan also can perform peacebuilding missions where the U.S. either does not get involved, or disqualifies itself by naming one party a terrorist organization. Importantly, through capacity building efforts and training of militaries and security forces, the EU and Japan can buttress U.S. efforts to help reduce vulnerabilities in states facing security challenges. This also spreads out costs; rather than the U.S. shouldering these costs alone.

Understandably, closer EU–Japan security cooperation will expand their security involvement into the broader international arena. While this expansion promises to support U.S. efforts, it will have adverse effects on those countries at odds with the EU and Japan. This will be particularly potent if that country opposes U.S. policies. From this perspective, more than any other country, greater EU–Japan security cooperation has the potential to adversely affect China.

It is certainly true that the EU and Japan, acting together, might have the potential to build bridges between the U.S. and other states to mitigate conflict or tensions between them. This is not true with China however given Japan's increasingly hard balance against Beijing in recent years. While the EU and Japan do not agree on all aspects of Washington's China-policy, there are areas in which they do. Arguably, all three support China: (1) playing a constructive, peaceful role in the international arena; (2) avoiding use of its military to threaten or intimidate other countries; and (3) becoming a responsible stakeholder in the international system. Should China appear to move in directions opposite to any of these, greater EU–Japan security cooperation is likely to hurt China across the entire policy spectrum.

- *Military Development:* Greater cooperation can hurt China's military modernization efforts. This has already happened. In 2004–2005, because of increasing economic ties between the EU and China, the EU debated whether to lift its arms embargo on China that had been in place since the June 1989 Tiananmen Square incident (Atanassova-Cornelis, 2010, p. 485; Balme, 2008, pp. 136–138; Tsuruoka, 2011, p. 38). Japan, along with the U.S., strongly opposed this move as it would undermine Japanese strategic interests if a lifting of the embargo helped Chinese military modernization efforts. This resonated with some members in the EU, leading to the embargo remaining in place (although some would argue this continuing embargo is more symbolic than real). What is more, this served as a catalyst to deepen dialogue between Japan and the EU, leading to the 2005 launch of a joint strategic dialogue on the East Asia security environment (MOFA, 2005a).
- *Defence Industrial:* Stronger defence–industrial cooperation between the EU and Japan may give them greater influence and relevance with smaller Asian states, particularly if they can outbid Chinese competitors. This would deny Beijing political influence in third countries, help to more deeply embed Europe in the Asian defence landscape, and possibly aid towards the EU leveraging these relationships to foster closer military-military ties (Smith, Brattberg and Rizzo, 2016, p. 6).
- *Economic:* While it is debatable whether the EU and Japan share a similar understanding of international law, should they view challenges to international law with a unified perspective, it could lead to greater use of sanctions against violators in the Asia-Pacific region. Not only would this reinforce the consensus on international laws, it would impose economic pain on China should they choose to act in response to actions China takes in the South or East China Seas.
- *Operational:* Greater EU–Japan security cooperation means pooling military capabilities for non-combat activities. In Southeast Asia, training military and coast guard officials, pursuing capacity building programs, and establishing new security partnerships with key littoral states all reduce vulnerabilities that China can exploit. Should the EU and Japan conduct increased naval transits and exercises with regional states, it will increase the number of voices by influential states challenging Chinese excessive claims and criticizing Chinese activities.

- *Diplomatic:* Europe and Japan interact across an extensive array of economic and political institutions and mechanisms (Raine and Small, 2015, pp. 13–19). Because many of these institutions are responsible for global rule and norm setting, it gives the EU and Japan an enormous influence should their diplomatic agendas overlap. Should their propensity for diplomacy be translated into advocacy, making the EU and Japan "norm partners" (Hosoya, 2012), China may need to brace itself as the target of joint, rigorous pushes for the rule of law and democracy. This could translate into bolstering of legal mechanisms to deal with Chinese behaviour and more international pressure on China to adhere to UNCLOS and other customary laws.

None of this is without risk. The danger to the U.S. is that greater EU–Japan security cooperation provides a framework for U.S. allies to cooperate without U.S. involvement. If the EU and Japan decide that a problem is best addressed without the U.S., or perhaps aggravated if the U.S. is involved, Brussels and Tokyo may pursue action on their terms. This is not necessarily disagreeable to U.S. interests, but it carries the potential for splits between the U.S. and its allies. Additionally, because many EU member states and Japan are more conservative and sceptical about using force than the U.S., they approach peacekeeping and post-conflict resolution from a non-combat position that may be at odds with the U.S. For example, they may be more reluctant to take sides in conflicts and employ conservative ROEs regarding when to initiate coercive force that will be different from the U.S. (Midford, 2012, p. 292).

Brussels and Tokyo must also brace themselves for a Chinese response. Should Brussels and Tokyo pressure Beijing, it may lead to disproportionate Chinese responses to the initial action. These responses may be more military in nature, to which the EU and Japan may not be equipped to respond. Also, given the EU and Japan are comfortable in non-combat roles, it is questionable how well their efforts can shape Chinese behaviour. Regardless of how much they assist regional states and maintain a maritime presence in East Asia, the Chinese People's Liberation Army Navy is powerful, the maritime militia is overpowering, and Beijing has demonstrated a propensity to ignore international law and reputation.

Conclusion: obstacles preventing turning "potential" into "actual"

Despite twenty-five years since first proclaiming the need for EU–Japan security cooperation and fifteen years since a concrete action plan was agreed upon, little has been accomplished in EU–Japan security cooperation. Lack of greater EU–Japan security is not the fault of the U.S. As strategic documents have shown, the U.S. has come to implicitly support not only the non-combat agenda pursued by the EU and Japan, but greater EU–Japan cooperation. Given the grave security challenges the U.S. faces in an increasingly assertive China—not to mention a provocative North Korea or a revanchist Russia—the more allies with which to share burdens is an opportunity that should not be missed. Yet, the potential of EU–Japan security cooperation continues to remain untapped.

Worse, the window for Brussels and Tokyo to translate their "potential" into "actual" may be closing. In Europe, Brexit promises to keep the EU occupied with internal issues and little bandwidth to expand external security ties. This will be reinforced by continuing differences among member states' China policies and the extent to which they want to get involved in specific issues, like the South China Sea. This was visible when the EU struggled to adopt a common statement on the 2016 Hague ruling (Gotev, 2016). In Japan, because of the deteriorating security environment in Asia, its efforts to build external security ties will likely tend towards harder security issue-areas more appropriate for NATO or the U.S. This will be reinforced by the inability of the EU to speak with a common voice and the Brexit serving as a reminder that EU integration has limits. This will lead Japan to prioritize bilateral hard security ties with individual EU countries when it best suits its interests. Among the possible candidates, ties with France and the United Kingdom are likely to grow, particularly if these countries are more willing to get involved in issues currently important to Japan, like maritime issues.

Even though the U.S. has come to implicitly support greater EU–Japan security cooperation, a final obstacle to turn EU–Japan security ties from "potential" into "actual" may prove to be the U.S. itself. The Trump Administration ushers in uncertainty to otherwise growing implicit U.S. support. His comments about the EU, NATO and Japan have meant the countries of the EU and Japan have focused their energies on firming up their relationships with Washington (Collinson, 2017; Hirano, 2017). Once the relationships between Europe and Japan with Washington are secure, past progress towards greater security cooperation can continue. Whether support from Washington will continue is a still an unknown variable, but assuming it does, it will be the task of policymakers in Brussels and Tokyo to finally turn their "potential" into "actual".

Note

1 The Security Consultative Committee is where the Japanese Ministers of Defense and Foreign Affairs meet with the U.S. Secretaries of Defense and State to consult on security and defence policies in order to examine the direction of the alliance and discuss a range of options to adapt to the changing security environment.

References

Atanassova-Cornelis, E. (2010) The EU-Japan Strategic Partnership in the 21st Century: Motivations, Constraints and Practice. *Journal of Contemporary European Research* 6(4), pp. 478–495.

Balme, R. (2008) A European Strategy towards China? The Limits of Integration in Foreign Policy Making. In Balme, R. and Bridges, B. (eds) *Europe-Asia Relations: Building Multilaterisms*, pp. 125–144. New York: Palgrave Macmillan.

Bush, G. (1990) *National Security Strategy of the United States.* White House. Available from: http://nssarchive.us/NSSR/1990.pdf. [Accessed: 1 December 2016].

Bush, G. (1991) *National Security Strategy of the United States.* White House. Available from: http://nssarchive.us/NSSR/1991.pdf. [Accessed: 1 December 2016].

Bush, G. (1993) *National Security Strategy of the United States.* White House. Available from: http://nssarchive.us/NSSR/1993.pdf. [Accessed: 1 December 2016].

Bush, G. (2002) *The National Security Strategy of the United States of America.* White House. Available from: http://nssarchive.us/NSSR/2002.pdf. [Accessed: 3 December 2016].

Bush, G. (2006) *The National Security Strategy of the United States of America.* White House. Available from: http://nssarchive.us/NSSR/2006.pdf. [Accessed: 3 December 2016].

Clinton, W. (1994) *A National Security Strategy of Engagement and Enlargement.* White House. Available from: http://nssarchive.us/NSSR/1994.pdf. [Accessed: 2 December 2016].

Clinton, W. (1996) *A National Security Strategy of Engagement and Enlargement.* White House. Available from: http://nssarchive.us/NSSR/1996.pdf. [Accessed: 2 December 2016].

Clinton, W. (1997) *A National Security Strategy for a New Century.* White House. Available from: http://nssarchive.us/NSSR/1997.pdf. [Accessed: 2 December 2016].

Clinton, W. (1998) *A National Security Strategy for a New Century.* White House. Available from: http://nssarchive.us/NSSR/1998.pdf. [Accessed: 2 December 2016].

Clinton, W. (1999) *A National Security Strategy for a New Century.* White House. Available from: http://nssarchive.us/NSSR/2000.pdf. [Accessed: 2 December 2016].

Clinton, W. (2000) *A National Security Strategy for a Global Age.* White House. Available from: http://nssarchive.us/NSSR/2001.pdf. [Accessed: 2 December 2016].

Cohen, W. (1997) *Report of the Quadrennial Defense Review.* U.S. Department of Defense. Available from: www.dod.gov/pubs/qdr/sec3.html. [Accessed: 5 December 2016].

Collinson, S. (2017) Trump's Blast Sends Chill across Europe. *CNN.* 17 January 2017. Available from: www.cnn.com/2017/01/17/politics/donald-trump-nato-europe/index.html. [Accessed: 22 January 2017].

Council of the European Union. (2010) *19th EU-Japan Summit Joint Press Statement.* European Council. Available from: www.consilium.europa.eu/uedocs/cms_data/docs/pressdata/en/er/114063.pdf. [Accessed: 5 January 2017].

European Community and Japan. (1991) *Joint Declaration on Relations between the European Community and its Member States and Japan.* Ministry of Foreign Affairs of Japan. Available from: www.mofa.go.jp/region/europe/eu/overview/declar.html. [Accessed: 15 Oct. 2016].

European External Action Service. (n.d.) *The New Transatlantic Agenda.* Available from: http://eeas.europa.eu/archives/docs/us/docs/new_transatlantic_agenda_en.pdf. [Accessed: 13 October 2016].

European Union and Japan (2001). *An Action Plan for EU-Japan Cooperation.* Ministry of Foreign Affairs of Japan. Available from: www.mofa.go.jp/region/europe/eu/summit/action0112.html. [Accessed: 15 October 2016].

Gates, R. (2010) *Quadrennial Defense Review Report.* February 2010. U.S. Department of Defense. Available from: www.defense.gov/Portals/1/features/defenseReviews/QDR/QDR_as_of_29JAN10_1600.pdf. [Accessed: 5 December 2016].

Gotev, G. (2016) EU Unable to Adopt Statement Upholding South China Sea Ruling. *EurActiv*. Available from: www.euractiv.com/section/global-europe/news/eu-unable-to-adopt-statement-upholding-south-china-sea-ruling/. [Accessed: 21 January 2016].

Hagel, C. (2014) *Quadrennial Defense Review 2014*. U.S. Department of Defense. Available from: http://archive.defense.gov/pubs/2014_Quadrennial_Defense_Review.pdf. [Accessed: 23 January 2017].

Hirano, K. (2017) Trump's Stance on Japan-U.S. Alliance Viewed as Key to Asia Stability. *Japan Times*. Available from: www.japantimes.co.jp/news/2017/01/09/national/politics-diplomacy/trumps-stance-japan-u-s-alliance-viewed-key-asia-stability/#.WIZ-SVUrK4Q. [Accessed: 23 January 2017].

Hosoya, Y. (2012) The Evolution of the EU-Japan Relationship: Towards a "Normative Partnership"? *Japan Forum* 24(3), pp. 317–337.

Mattis, J. (2017) *The United States and Asia-Pacific Security*. IISS Shangri-La Dialogue 2017 First Plenary Session. Available from: www.iiss.org/en/events/shangri-la-dialogue/archive/shangri-la-dialogue-2017-a321/plenary-1-6b79/mattis-8315. [Accessed: 26 November 2017].

Midford, P. (2012) By Land and By Sea: The Potential of EU-Japan Security Cooperation. *Japan Forum* 24(3), pp. 289–316.

Midford, P. (2013) Japan-EU Non-Combat Military Cooperation: An Idea Whose Time Has Come. *Japan Spotlight*. Special Article 4, pp. 44–47.

MOFA. (1984) *Major Diplomatic Efforts by Japan in 1983*. Available from: www.mofa.go.jp/policy/other/bluebook/1984/1984-3-1.htm. [Accessed: 17 December 2016].

MOFA. (1996a) *United States-Japan Common Agenda: A Partnership for the 21st Century*. Available from: www.mofa.go.jp/region/n-america/us/agenda.html. [Accessed: 14 January 2017].

MOFA. (1996b) *Japan-U.S. Joint Declaration on Security: Alliance for the 21st Century*. Available from: www.mofa.go.jp/region/n-america/us/security/security.html. [Accessed: 6 October 2016].

MOFA. (2002) *Co-chairs' Summary of Conclusions: The International Conference on Reconstruction Assistance to Afghanistan*. Available from: www.mofa.go.jp/region/middle_e/afghanistan/min0201/summary.html. [Accessed: 16 December 2016].

MOFA. (2005a) *14th EU-Japan Summit Joint Press Statement*. Available from: www.mofa.go.jp/region/europe/eu/summit/joint0505.pdf. [Accessed: 7 December 2016].

MOFA. (2005b) *Joint Statement: Strategic Development Alliance*. Available from: www.mofa.go.jp/region/n-america/us/joint0509.html. [Accessed: 6 October 2016].

MOFA. (2015a) *The Guidelines for Japan-U.S. Defense Cooperation*. Available from: www.mofa.go.jp/files/000078188.pdf. [Accessed: 6 October 2016].

MOFA. (2015b) *Japan-U.S. Summit Meeting*. Available from: www.mofa.go.jp/na/na1/us/page4e_000351.html. [Accessed: 6 October 2016].

Mykal. O. (2011) *The EU-Japan Security Dialogue: Invisible but Comprehensive*. Amsterdam: Amsterdam University Press.

Obama, B. (2010) *National Security Strategy*. White House. Available from: http://nssarchive.us/NSSR/2010.pdf. [Accessed: 21 January 2017].

Obama, B. (2015) *National Security Strategy*. White House. Available from: http://nssarchive.us/wp-content/uploads/2015/02/2015.pdf. [Accessed: 21 January 2017].

Office of the Press Secretary. (2008) *U.S.–EU Summit Declaration*. White House. Available from: https://georgewbush-whitehouse.archives.gov/news/releases/2008/06/20080610-8.html [Accessed: 13 December 2016].

Office of the Press Secretary. (2010) *EU-U.S. Summit Joint Statement*. White House. Available from: https://obamawhitehouse.archives.gov/the-press-office/2010/11/20/eu-us-summit-joint-statement. [Accessed: 21 January 2017].

Office of the Press Secretary. (2011) *Joint Statement: US-EU Summit*. White House. Available from: https://obamawhitehouse.archives.gov/the-press-office/2011/11/28/joint-statement-us-eu-summit. [Accessed: 21 January 2017].

Office of the Press Secretary. (2014) *EU-US Summit: Joint Statement*. White House. Available from: https://obamawhitehouse.archives.gov/the-press-office/2014/03/26/eu-us-summit-joint-statement. [Accessed: 21 January 2017].

Office of the Press Secretary. (2017) *Remarks by President Trump and Prime Minister Abe of Japan in Joint Press Conference*. White House. Available from: www.white house.gov/the-press-office/2017/02/10/remarks-president-trump-and-prime-minister-abe-japan-joint-press. [Accessed: 26 November 2017].

Office of the Spokesperson. (2012) *U.S.-EU Statement on the Asia-Pacific Region*. Department of State. Available from: www.state.gov/r/pa/prs/ps/2012/07/194896.htm. [Accessed: 6 January 2017].

Office of the Vice President. (2017) *Remarks by the Vice President and European Council President Tusk*. White House. Available from: www.whitehouse.gov/the-press-office/2017/02/20/remarks-vice-president-and-european-council-president-tusk. [Accessed: 26 November 2017].

Raine, S. and Small, A. (2015) *Waking up to Geopolitics: A New Trajectory in Japan-Europe Relations*. German Marshall Fund. Available from: www.gmfus.org/publications/waking-geopolitics-new-trajectory-japan-europe-relations. [Accessed: 18 December 2016].

Rumsfeld, D. (2001) *Quadrennial Defense Review Report*. U.S. Department of Defense. Available from: http://archive.defense.gov/pubs/qdr2001.pdf. [Accessed: 5 December 2016].

Rumsfeld, D. (2006) *Quadrennial Defense Review Report*. Department of Defense. Available from: http://archive.defense.gov/pubs/pdfs/QDR20060203.pdf. [Accessed: 5 December 2016].

Security Consultative Committee. (2005) *U.S.-Japan Alliance: Transformation and Realignment for the Future*. Ministry of Foreign Affairs of Japan. Available from: www.mofa.go.jp/region/n-america/us/security/scc/pdfs/doc0510.pdf. [Accessed: 6 October 2016].

Security Consultative Committee. (2010) *Marking the 50th Anniversary of the Signing of The U.S.-Japan Treaty of Mutual Cooperation and Security*. Ministry of Foreign Affairs of Japan. Available from: www.mofa.go.jp/region/n-america/us/security/pdfs/joint1001.pdf. [Accessed: 6 October 2016].

Security Consultative Committee. (2011) *Toward a Deeper and Broader U.S.-Japan Alliance: Building on 50 Years of Partnership*. Ministry of Foreign Affairs of Japan. Available from: www.mofa.go.jp/region/n-america/us/security/pdfs/joint1106_01.pdf. [Accessed: 6 October 2016].

Smith, J., Brattberg, E. and Rizzo, R. (2016) *Transatlantic Security Cooperation in the Asia-Pacific*. Center for a New American Security. Available from: https://s3.amazonaws.com/files.cnas.org/documents/CNAS-Report-TransatlanticSecurityCooperation-Finalc.pdf. [Accessed: 12 January 2017].

Trump, D. (2017) *National Security Strategy of the United States of America*. White House. Available from: www.whitehouse.gov/wp-content/uploads/2017/12/NSS-Final-12-18-2017-0905.pdf. [Accessed: 2 February 2018].

Tsuruoka, M. (2011) Japan-Europe Security Cooperation: How to "Use" NATO and the EU. *NIDS Journal of Defense and Security*. 12, pp. 27–43. Available from: www.nids. mod.go.jp/english/publication/kiyo/pdf/2011/bulletin_e2011_3.pdf. [Accessed: 26 October 2016].

Tsuruoka, M. (2013) *The EU and Japan: Making the Most of Each Other*. European Union Institute for Security Studies. Available from: www.iss.europa.eu/uploads/media/Alert_36_EU_Japan.pdf. [Accessed: 26 November 2016].

U.S. Department of Defense. (n.d.) *Quadrennial Defense Review*.

U.S. Mission to the European Union. (2017) *Press Release by Secretary Tillerson: On the Occasion of Europe Day*. Department of State. Available from: https://useu.usmission. gov/press-release-secretary-tillerson-occasion-europe-day/. [Accessed: 26 November 2017].

U.S. White House. (2005a) *Joint Statement by the European Union and the United States Working Together to Promote Democracy and Support Freedom, the Rule of Law and Human Rights Worldwide*. Available from: https://georgewbush-whitehouse.archives. gov/news/releases/2005/06/20050620-4.html. [Accessed: 10 January 2017].

U.S. White House. (2005b) *EU-US Declaration on Working Together to Promote Peace, Stability, Prosperity, and Good Governance in Africa*. Available from: https:// georgewbush-whitehouse.archives.gov/news/releases/2005/06/20050620-3.html. [Accessed: 10 January 2017].

U.S. White House. (2005c) *Joint Statement by the United States and the European Union Working Together to Promote Peace, Prosperity and Progress in the Middle East*. Available from: https://georgewbush-whitehouse.archives.gov/news/releases/2005/06/ 20050620-7.html. [Accessed: 10 January 2017]. Available from: www.defense.gov/ News/Special-Reports/QDR. [Accessed: 4 January 2017].

Watanabe, H. (2016) *Japan-Europe Relations at the Multilateral Level*. Japan Institute of International Affairs. Available from: www2.jiia.or.jp/en/pdf/digital_library/japan_s_ diplomacy/160330_Hirotaka_Watanabe.pdf. [Accessed: 26 November 2016].

12 From "wider west" to "strategic alliance"

An assessment of China's influence in EU–Japan relations

Lilei Song and Liang Cai

Introduction

During the Cold War, Japanese-European relations can be summed up in two key words: 'dialogue' and 'cooperation.' The institutionalization of EU–Japanese relations took place in 1991, with the adoption of the EU–Japan Hague Declaration, which institutionalized previously irregular bilateral meetings, exchanges and ad-hoc agreements. Later, while Europe and Japan started referring to each other as 'natural,' and/or as 'strategic' partners, bilateral dialogues gradually expanded both in scope and quality. Then, what is referred to as the 'China factor' slowly made it onto the agenda of EU–Japanese exchanges in the twenty-first century. Although China repeatedly stressed that its rise and development will be peaceful, the United States, Europe and Japan, share Nye's (2015) assessment of China belonging to what Nye refers to as 'heterogeneous countries.' Nye argues that there is a normative community in the world, within which countries recognize universal values such as freedom and democracy, reflecting common and shared interests of its members. This group differentiates itself from heterogeneous countries, such as China, which hold skeptical attitudes to universal values.

In this context, Europe and Japan continue to regard each other as the above-mentioned 'natural partners,' and continue to express their joint interest in expanding cooperation on political and security issues based on their shared values. The existing literature typically argues that while the EU pursued a low-profile approach to East Asian politics and security in the two decades since the institutionalization of EU–Japan ties in 1991, recurrent gaps between the rhetoric and the on-the-ground reality of cooperation characterize the EU's strategic partnership with Japan (this is also the case with the EU's strategic partnership with China (Castillo Iglesias, 2012, p. 161). By examining the influence of the China factor on the three dimensions of bilateral cooperation between Europe and Japan, i.e. security, economy and values, this chapter seeks to answer two key questions. First, how does progress in EU–Japan strategic relations impact on the dynamic security environment in Asia? Second, what influence does the EU–China strategic partnership (also referred to as the EU–China 'Comprehensive Strategic Partnership') have on of EU–Japan relations?

Development of Europe–Japan relations and the rise of China's influence after World War II

During the Cold War, EU–Japan relations were dominated by economic and trade issues (as it was the case between the EU and China too). Furthermore, US dominance within the Japan–U.S. asymmetric alliance framework at times set the frame of action for Japanese diplomacy (Morrow, 1991, p. 904). Japan's first 1957 *Diplomacy Bluebook* announced the so-called 'Three Principles' of Japanese foreign policy: (1) Conducting a UN-centric foreign policy, (2) Cooperating with the free world, and (3) Strengthening Japan's position as a 'member of Asia' (MOFA of Japan, 1957). The Japan–U.S. Alliance and the three principles guided Japan's foreign policy during the Cold War. Japan always considered China, the Korean Peninsula, the Soviet Union and Southeast Asia, as well as the United States, political, economic, and security policy priorities. In contrast, although the three principles of Japan's diplomacy included a reference to Western Europe in the context of "the free world," Japan's attention to Europe – due to geographical distance, was not comparable to its attention to the United States and Japan's Asian neighbors (Watanabe, 2013, p. 201).

After the end of the Cold War Japan began looking for a partner in international politics and security who could complement its bilateral security alliance with the U.S. That led to Japan recognizing European countries as 'natural' and 'strategic' partners embedded in the structure of U.S.–European transatlantic relations. Two policy documents outline the EU–Japan partnership: the Hague Declaration of 1991 and the so-called Action Plan (2001 to 2011). As part of this process of institutionalizing bilateral ties between Brussels and Tokyo, Japan sought to ensure that the US–Japan–Europe economic triangle would retain its political centrality after the end of the Cold War through the victory of the Western camp. Japan's Prime Minister at the time, Kaifu Toshiki, declared the desire to strive for a new world order with Japan as co-leader of a tripolar world: Japan, the United States and Europe (MOFA of Japan, 1990). This was the first time a Japanese official laid out a vision to lead the post-Cold War international order. In response, then Japanese Administrative Vice Foreign Minister, Takakazu Kuriyama, proposed the so-called "553 theory" according to which Japan, the United States and Europe agree on the three basic values of freedom, democracy and market economy. They would base their shared concept of governance on their respective economic sizes, political power and common values, which date back to the Cold War (Kuriyama, 1990, p. 16).

Following this principle, in 1991 Kaifu, and the President of the European Communities (EC), Jacques Lucien Jean Delors, held the first Japan–Europe summit in 1991, and signed the Japan–Europe Joint Declaration (The Hague Declaration). Through that declaration both sides recognized each other as countries with similar approaches toward international politics, economy and security, and emphasized the building of a cooperative relationship in economic, political and security affairs. They also pledged to establish a system of continuous and regular exchanges of information, and coordinate with each other on major international issues (EU–Japan Summit, 1991).

Based on The Hague Declaration, a series of communication mechanisms were established. Among them, for example, are the Japan–Europe Strategic Dialogue on Central Asia, and the EU–Japan Dialogue on East Asian Security (Sakamoto, 2012, p. 116). In November 1996, the European–Japanese relationship was upgraded to a global partnership (Watanabe, 2013, p. 206). Japan also cooperated with France, Germany and other European countries on political, economic and cultural affairs. It is worth noting that then Japanese Foreign Minister Yohei Kono gave a speech entitled "A Decade of Japan–Europe Cooperation" in January 2000, which called for the strengthening of political dialogue and cooperation between the two sides (Ueta, 2013 p. 219).

Subsequently, during the 2001 10th EU–Japan Summit, Brussels and Tokyo adopted the follow-up agreement to The Hague Declaration: the Action Plan for EU–Japan Cooperation, entitled "Shaping our Common Future." The Action Plan envisioned a "New Decade of EU-Japan relations" and listed potential new actions and areas of cooperation on more than 100 issues, divided into four areas: (1) promotion of peace and security, (2) strengthening economic partnership, (3) coping with new global and social challenges, and (4) promoting cultural and people-to-people exchanges. The Action Plan confirmed both parties' intention to support cross-regional co-operation through the Asia–Europe Meeting (ASEM) and the Organization for Security and Cooperation in Europe (OSCE) (EU–Japan Summit, 2001). In addition to more generic cooperation fields on the list, such as the promotion of human security and human rights, development, environmental protection, the listed issue areas were primarily emphasized in accordance with their shared identity and common civilian power status. The EU stressed the importance of what Brussels refers to as 'effective multilateralism,' when adopting policies towards East Asia. It identifies its potential role as promoting confidence-building measures in the region, sharing lessons drawn from its own experiences of post-war reconciliation, and promoting effective multilateralism and regional integration (Cameron, 2013, p. 43). The European Commission at the time announced that "the EU should work to contribute to peace and security in the region and globally, through a broadening of our engagement with the region"; statements made in a document it issued entitled: *Europe and Asia: A Strategic Framework for Enhanced Partnerships* in 2001 (European Commission, 2001). Another document, *Guidelines on the EU's Foreign and Security Policy in East Asia*, which the EU Commission adopted in December 2007 and updated in June 2012, touched on the need to develop bilateral strategic dialogues with Asian partner countries. It is worth noting that the EU signed the Treaty on Amity and Cooperation in South East Asia in 2012, when the then EU's High Representative for Foreign Affairs and Security Policy Catherine Ashton attended the ASEAN Regional Forum (ARF). However, the EU's involvement in East Asian politics and security has remained limited and low-profile since the formalization of cooperation, and the strategic partnerships with both China and Japan have, as mentioned above, been characterized by recurrent gaps between the rhetoric of the envisioned cooperation, and the actual cooperation taking place on Asian ground.

Most noteworthy, topics related to China's rise have gradually become one of the main concerns in Japan–Europe strategic dialogue on East Asian security. Both sides believe that in the future, the modernization of China's increasingly potent armed forces will be a challenge to regional and global security. The EU has realized the need for more engagement and involvement in Asian security to achieve stability in the region, and both Tokyo and Brussels have through various announcements and declarations, confirmed their commitment to work together to promote peace and stability in East Asia. In response to Japan's proposal to conclude an Economic Partnership Agreement (EPA) with the EU, both sides agreed to start negotiations in March 2011. Finally, in July 2017, the EU and Japan announced agreement on the final shape of the EPA/FTA 'in principle,' and the agreement was then adopted on December 8, 2017. The above-mentioned SPA on the other hand has yet to be adopted.

China's influence on Europe–Japan cooperation on shared values

Japan and Europe regard each other as strategic partners who adhere to shared values such as democracy, the rule of law and the protection of human rights. This common foundation promotes cooperation and enhances mutual under-standing, which has led in Europe to the formation of a positive image of Japan and likewise to the Japanese perception that Europe is a strategic partner Tokyo can count on. Brussels and Tokyo confirm their shared positions as regards an open market economy and announced to act in accordance with what they char-acterize as the principles of international and universally recognized norms (EU–Japan Summit, 2014). In addition, under the currently negotiated Strategic Partnership Agreement (SPA), both parties seek to jointly share more responsib-ility in regional and global security. At the 23rd Japan–Europe summit meeting in 2015, the two sides announced that they would not only deepen and expand cooperation on issues that directly concerned both parties, but also announced their intention to explore more strategic coordination on global issues. The EU stated its support for Japanese Prime Minister Shinzo Abe's "Proactive Contri-bution to Peace," and voiced opposition to all practices violating international law and damaging the principles of national sovereignty and territorial integrity (EU–Japan Summit, 2015).

Since the beginning of the twenty-first century, the so-called 'China factor' has become one of the most important external factors driving the promotion of common values as part of Europe–Japan relations. This is in part due to the lack of clarity regarding whether China will accept the current international norms and become a status quo power. Many Western scholars have doubts about China becoming a status quo power. As early as 1993, Friedberg (1993) pointed out that Asia would become an arena of great power competition. Similarly, Mearsheimer (2004) went as far as to maintain that China's rise would not be peaceful. Furthermore, scholars like Kang (2008) view the situation through the lens of history and claim that China aims to construct a hierarchical Chinese order in Asia, similar to that of the Chinese Han and Tang Dynasties. Oyane (2016) argued that even if China became a country that endorses universal norms, it would still be accused of being a revisionist country due to its territorial disputes in East and Southeast Asian territorial waters.

Overall, Japanese and European scholars and analysts are relatively consistent in their assessment that China is one of the above-defined 'heterogeneous countries.' Regarding values, both sides have declared that they will adhere to their own values even though they have great economic interests in China. Although Japan and Europe are officially committed to the One China Policy, both parties to some extent regard the status of Hong Kong and Taiwan as disputes over values. For instance, an important motivation for their continuing development of relations with Taiwan is the desire to support the shared value of democracy (MOFA of Japan, 2016).

Sino–Japanese bilateral relations are among the most sensitive and complex bilateral relations in the world today. Abe's cabinet has used the 'China threat theory' to actively lobby for Japan to "get rid of the post-war system" and "turn Japan into a normal state" (Abe, 2013, p. 33). It is accurate to characterize Japan as firmly claiming that the rise of China is a great challenge to the existing international order. Nevertheless, when Abe formed his first cabinet in 2006, he chose China as the first country to visit, and agreed to build a strategic and mutually beneficial relationship with Beijing. Nonetheless, the future direction of bilateral relations is unclear, not least due to the ongoing territorial dispute in the East China Sea (the Diaoyu/Senkaku Islands conflict). Abe declared his intention to contain China, and named China a challenger to the international order, and in this context further emphasized Japan's firm adherence to freedom, democracy and human rights, and willingness to continue cooperating with countries that shared the same values. Hosoya (2016) pointed out that Japan's intention is to establish, under its leadership, values and standards for the Asia-Pacific region with like-minded allies. Based on this school of thought, Japan regards any Chinese action in the South and East China Seas as a challenge to the current international order. It fears that if it were up to China alone, the foundation of the current international order would be in jeopardy. Therefore, Japan, the United States, Australia and India must join to build a so-called 'Values Alliance' in order to, as Beijing fears, contain China (Prime Minister of Japan and His Cabinet, 2015).

The EU primarily adopts a value-based diplomacy, promoting European values as universally applicable and desirable, including effective multilateralism, good governance, recognition and involvement in international organizations, respect for human rights, democracy, promotion of peace and development. To this end the EU applies the principle of conditionality, most notably with countries that strive for EU membership. In relations with third countries, the EU aims to adopt so-called 'Strategic Partnerships,' with the objective of consolidating its bid for effective multilateralism, and an institution- and norm-based international order.

From a Chinese perspective, the EU regards China as the most direct challenge to its norm-based diplomacy, and the EU's claim for the universal validity
of European values. Although the European Commission also mentions the need
to promote universal values in the report 'Elements for a new EU strategy on
China,' it calls on China to accept a greater share of international responsibilities, which would, from a European perspective, require changes to Chinese
domestic policies (European Commission, 2016). The EU for its part is committed to the promotion of human rights globally, and regularly voices concerns
over the human rights situation in China. The EU–China Human Rights dialogue
is held every year. EU Special Representative for Human Rights, Lambrinidis
paid his second official visit to China in 2015 (EEAS, 2016b). Unlike Chinese
policymakers, EU policymakers seem to believe that the protection of human
rights will continue to be one of the core parts of Sino–European relations. EU
member states such as Germany and Sweden have established regular human
rights dialogue mechanisms with China. Japan, for its part, comments on human
rights in China on a regular basis in statements or resolutions (either alone or
jointly with like-minded countries, including the EU). Against the background of
close EU–Chinese relations, it is nonetheless hard to imagine that the EU will
enter into a so-called 'Value Alliance' with Japan directed at China. Japan–
Europe cooperation on values in fact remains largely focused on joint statements
delivered to an international audience. How to deal with China is one of the
greatest challenges facing the EU. Considering China's geopolitical and economic importance, in particular its major global power status and its permanent
seat on the United Nations Security Council (UNSC), the EU's relations with
China are dominated by strategic considerations. From a Chinese perspective,
Beijing can play an important role in consolidating the EU's role as a global
actor and help it realize its foreign policy vision of effective multilateralism.

To sum up, Japan and Europe belong to the above-mentioned 'homogeneous
states,' for which strengthening cooperation is the best way to safeguard their
shared 'universal values' (Oyane, 2016, p. 87). Compared to Japan and Europe,
China belongs to the 'heterogeneous countries' with regards to values. In
response, Japan intends to 'tame' China through a strategy of military and diplomatic encirclement. In addition, and in support of Japanese policies toward
China, the EU urges China to abide by international standards through various
channels of diplomatic dialogue.

China's influence on Europe–Japan security cooperation

Owing to historical grievances, geopolitics and value disputes, Japan is very
concerned about the rise of China, and observes China's regional foreign and
security policies with great interest and indeed suspicion. Therefore, it is not surprising that Japan is a vocal proponent of the so-called 'China threat theory.' In
fact, since the 1990s, Japan's version of a 'China threat theory' has gradually
become more and more extreme. For example, Japan's Ministry of Defence
(2011) began to use the term Chinese 'hegemony' in its Annual White Paper.

The Japanese Ministry of Defence in 2014, like their counterparts in Seoul and Washington, criticized China's establishment of an Air Defense Identification Zone (ADIZ) over the East China Sea. The Japanese Ministry of Defence (2016) condemned China's regional security policies, which had caused great concern in the Asia-Pacific region and the international community. Japanese defence white papers not only regard China as Japan's primary strategic competitor, they also openly blame China for "destroying the peace and stability of the Asia-Pacific region." Consequently, Japan interprets Chinese actions in the South and the East China Seas as challenging the existing international order.

Japan's motivations for warning about China's allegedly aggressive regional policies stem from national interests as well as the desire to portray Japan as the defender of the current international order in the context of Abe's 'Proactive Contribution to Peace.' Furthermore, Japan seeks to gain more support from the international community. To attract support from European countries and encourage them to jointly hedge against China, Japan claimed on several occasions that Chinese acts in the South and the East China Seas constitute attempts to unilaterally change the status quo through military strength, and compared this to the Russian invasion of Crimea (Anami, Ohara and Kamo, 2016, p. 18).

Since the establishment of the Common Foreign and Security Policy (CFSP) under the Maastricht Treaty in 1992, the EU has been consolidating its role as an emerging global political and security actor. Along this road of development, key milestones are the formulation of the European Security Strategy (ESS) in 2003, through which all EU Member States articulated a common vision for the EU as an international actor, and more recently the creation of the European External Action Service (EEAS) under the Lisbon Treaty. Indeed, since the EU's 2004 enlargement, the EU has rather successfully presented itself as a 'civilian' and also 'normative' power, not only in its neighborhood, but even beyond Europe. As a result of its rising concern about stability in East Asia, several reports were published, including a European Parliament briefing that portrays East Asia as a region at considerable risk of military confrontation (Vutz, 2013, p. 1). In particular, the South China Sea, the East China Sea and the Korean Peninsula are identified as areas where tensions are increasing.

The EU intends to cooperate with Japan to strengthen its influence on international security and regional affairs in East Asia. In the context of recent Japan–Europe summits, the EU has repeatedly expressed the hope to become a more effective security provider. Van Rompuy (EU–Japan Summit, 2014b), then the president of the European Council, stated at the 22nd Japan–Europe summit in 2014 that the EU was willing to make more substantial contributions to peace and security in East Asia, and get more involved in the Asian security architecture. Japan and Europe share common interests in the area of security cooperation, and are working together on the construction of a crisis management cooperation mechanism. Japan here plays the 'common ideology' card, reminding the EU to pay attention to the situation in East Asia. At the same time, Japan uses this occasion to promote Abe's 'Proactive Contribution to Peace,' which is linked with the above-mentioned SPA negotiations (EU–Japan Summit,

2015). Thus, for Tokyo, European–Japanese cooperation on Asian security is also aimed at shaping international perceptions of the quality and impact of the Japanese Prime Minister's 'Proactive Contribution to Peace.'

Japan–Europe cooperation regarding the EU arms embargo imposed on China in 1989 went through several stages from oath to action. The EU's arms embargo on China has been a sensitive issue in China–EU relations since 1989, and China has, on numerous occasions, urged the EU to lift the embargo as soon as possible. As EU Member States do not have a common position on the lifting of the weapons embargo, EU institutions in general, and the EEAS in particular, have in the past had difficulties formulating and adopting a common position on the embargo. To prevent the EU from lifting the arms embargo on China, Japan has put pressure on the EU and its member states through formal diplomatic channels. Furthermore, the Japanese Prime Minister, Foreign Minister, Defense Minister, Chief Cabinet Secretary, and even the House of Representatives and House of Counselors members have expressed their opposition to the lifting of the arms embargo during meetings with EU officials and leaders of EU member states. For example, when former French President Jacques Chirac paid a visit to Japan in May 2005, then Japanese Prime Minister Junichiro Koizumi pointed out that Japan strongly opposed the lifting of the EU's arms embargo (MOFA of Japan, 2005). Koizumi knew that Chirac had good relations with China at that time and that he had been in favor of lifting the arms embargo. Current Japanese Prime Minister Abe today spares no effort to persuade the EU to continue to maintain its arms embargo against China whenever he discusses EU–China relations with leaders of the EU and its member states.

Japan seeks to expand its shared values approach with the EU to the security realm. Tokyo has used several international occasions to remind the EU that China's actions in the South and the East China Seas destabilize Asia's security environment. For example, at the 23rd EU–Japan Summit (2015), the two parties reiterated that they will continue monitoring the situation in the East and the South China Seas and oppose unilateral actions that may change the territorial status quo and increase tensions. Japan and Europe encourage all parties to comply with the 2002 *Declaration on the Conduct of Parties in the South China Sea*, and expressed their hope that all parties will conclude a legally binding Code of Conduct for Parties in the South China Sea soon. Another example is the G7 Foreign Ministers Meeting in April 2015. The G7 Foreign Ministers followed the Japanese initiative and published a statement on maritime disputes on April 15, 2015. The statement expressed "concerns over the situation in the East and South China Seas" and opposed "any intimidating, coercive or provocative unilateral actions that could alter the status quo and increase tensions" (MOFA of Japan, 2015). In response, China expressed strong dissatisfaction with the statement (Xin, 2015).

Although the EU is concerned about the situation in the East and South China Seas, the impact of a confrontation between claimant countries on its own security is comparatively small. Consequently, the EU's statements on territorial disputes in the East and South China Seas are less harsh and less dominated by an anti-China bias than the Japanese equivalents. To be sure, the EU too endorsed the July 2017 verdict of the Permanent Court of Arbitration, which ruled that China cannot claim historical territorial rights to waters in the South China Sea as defined by China's so-called 'Nine-Dash Line,' which Beijing uses to demarcate its claims there. The court also ruled that Chinese activities within the Philippines' 200-nautical-mile exclusive economic zone (EEZ) such as fishing and artificial island construction atop geographical features below water at high tide are in violation Manila's sovereign territorial rights.

While the EU also opposes China's unilateral actions that could change the status quo and intensify tensions, it has not named China or called on China and other countries to abide by international law when making sovereignty claims in the South China Sea. In addition, the EU has generally left its position on recent confrontations in East Asia vague. Nonetheless, the EU and its bigger member states issued statements. For example, the EU asked China to accept the Court of Arbitration's adjudications, commit itself to maintain the legal order of the sea according to the principles of the United Nations Convention on the Law of the Sea (UNCLOS), and settle its disputes peacefully (EEAS, 2016a). However, the wording of the EU statement is less harsh than the Japanese statement, and unlike Japan, the EU is geographically very distant from the South China Sea. For the EU, the impact of China's rise on security is not as strong as for Japan due to this geopolitical distance.

The EU is less prepared to promote military encirclement of China than Japan, but seeks to encourage China to make a constructive contribution to regional stability. Specifically it admonishes China to implement confidence-building measures, support the rule-based international order, comply with UNCLOS, and rapidly complete negotiations on the Code of Conduct with ASEAN (EEAS, 2016). China is dissatisfied with EU admonitions to China to comply with the 2016 Court of Permanent Arbitration's findings on the South China Sea dispute with the Philippines. While Brussels had some initial difficulties agreeing on a common position on the verdict, its statement commenting on the verdict is less harsh than the Japanese statement.

The EU is currently preoccupied with its own internal problems, including Brexit and the European refugee crisis, which leaves the EU with less resources to invest into its Asia policies. The EU's position continues to emphasize crisis management and stabilization of the situation to avoid giving the impression that it is siding with Japan against China. The limitations of Japan–Europe security cooperation are only too evident. For example, Japan's largest naval vessel, the Izumo, planned in May 2017 to conduct a three-month-long exercise in the South China Sea with the French navy. While Abe at the time invited France to conduct this exercise in order to increase pressure on China, France instead decided to deploy the training ship Joan of Arc to visit to Japan and to jointly conduct training in the Western Pacific.

China's influence on Europe–Japan economic cooperation

Europe and Japan's relations during the Cold War were largely focused on economic and trade exchanges. Japan became Europe's second largest trade partner in 1988, a rank it maintained until 2000. Today, Japan is the seventh largest trading partner of the EU (EEAS, 2017). The main reason for the decline in volume of trade is the increase of the Sino–Japanese trade volume, which has created a China–Japan–Europe economic triangle, especially in mechanical and electrical products. Japan exports high value-added parts to China and China assembles them to export them to the EU as finished products. At this stage, as Zhang (2013) mentioned, the export similarity index (ESI) of Chinese and European products in the Japanese market is 66. The similarity of Chinese and Japanese products is 58 on the European market index. It is therefore no exaggeration to say that Japan's trade position in the European market is gradually being replaced by China.

According to official Chinese statistics, the total trade volume between China and Europe (EU-27) in 2015 amounted to 574.733 billion dollars, of which the EU's exports to China amounted to 187.077 billion dollars, accounting for 9.4 percent of the EU's total exports. Chinese exports to the EU amounted to 387.656 billion dollars, accounting for 20.2 percent of the EU's total imports. China is the EU's second largest export market and the largest source of imports (MOFA of China, 2017a). In contrast, the total trade volume between Japan and Europe (EU-27) in 2015 was 127.855 billion dollars, of which the EU's exports to Japan amounted to 61.759 billion dollars, accounting for 3.1 percent of the EU's total exports. EU exports to Japan were worth 66.096 billion dollars. Japan was the EU's sixth largest export market and the seventh largest source of imports (EEAS, 2017). Although Sino–Japanese trade has been in decline in recent years, it still amounted to 269.856 billion dollars in 2015, and China is Japan's largest trading partner. Japan's exports to China were worth 109.286 billion dollars, accounting for 17.5 percent of Japan's total exports. China exported goods worth 160.57 billion dollars to Japan, accounting for 24.8 percent of Japan's total imports. China is Japan's second largest export market and the largest source of imports (MOFA of China, 2017b). In terms of trade in goods, China has been the world's largest trading country for several years. From a bilateral trade perspective, Japan's and European member states' largest trade deficit is with China. Japan and Europe are concerned that China, which they view as a 'heterogeneous' country, might exploit its position as the world's largest trading power to increase its influence of shaping the future world trade regime. These concerns have led Japan and the EU to join forces to press China to comply with international trade rules.

This is highlighted in two examples. First, both Japan and Europe refuse to give China full market economy status. The WTO refused to give China full market economy status when it acceded to the WTO on December 11, 2001, on the grounds that China's prices were not determined by demand and supply but by government planning. Since its full market economy status was not recognized, China confronts with very unfavorable conditions in international trade disputes. For instance, other members of the WTO can easily impose penalty taxes against China on the grounds of dumping charges. For example, in order to avoid losses to European companies through Chinese steel product imports, such as seamless steel tubes, the European Commission imposed provisional anti-dumping duties on imports of two steel products from China in October 2016 (European Commission, 2016). In accordance with Article 15 of the WTO Protocol China was supposed to be granted full market economy status within 15 years of its accession to the WTO. However, the United States, Japan and Europe still refuse to recognize China's full market economy status.

Second, Japan and Europe intend to take the lead in establishing rules and regulations for the global trade regime through signing their bilateral free trade agreement. The previous U.S. administration under President Obama promoted the Transpacific Partnership (TPP) negotiations with 11 countries in the Asia-Pacific region (not including China). Through the US–European TTIP negotiations, Europe and the U.S. sought to shape and control a new global trading system, forcing China to become a passive taker of the new rules against its will. Japanese Prime Minister Shinzo Abe announced that Japan would participate in the TPP negotiations in 2013.

In addition, because Japan and Europe are aware that the Japan–Europe FTA could be the key to connecting TTIP and TPP when they started bilateral negotiations in 2013, the two sides at time simultaneously started negotiations on the Japan–EU Strategic Partnership Agreement (SPA). The structure of the two-track negotiations is an important starting point for the EU to exert greater influence in East Asia as a 'normative power' (Xin, 2015, p. 53). For Brussels, concluding the EU–Japan Free Trade Area further develops EU–Japan relations, which helps the EU consolidate its strategic position in the Asia-Pacific region. The EU hopes to work with Japan to resolve pressing security issues in East Asia, including North Korea's missile and nuclear programmes, and the territorial disputes in the South China Sea.

Japan is more interested in concluding an FTA agreement with the EU than vice versa. In Japan's view, China actively supported Europe during the European debt crisis, and once European economies started recovering from the crisis, China would be the first to benefit from that recovery. That in turn, it was feared in Japan, could contribute to the lifting of the arms embargo the EU imposed on China in 1989 (Anami, Ohara and Kamo, 2016). Furthermore, while most EU member states actively cooperate with China on its 'Belt and Road' project, Japan remains skeptical and indeed suspicious about that Chinese-driven initiative. Therefore, the Abe government hopes to contain China's influence on the EU, and maintain its own influence on the EU through the FTA. However, because US President Trump withdrew from the TPP and suspended US–Europe TTIP negotiations, some in China argue that the strategic value of the EU–Japan FTA has almost been eliminated (*Xinhua News*, 2016). Once the Japan–Europe FTA is adopted, it will inevitably force many Chinese enterprises to transfer their production base to the Japan–Europe Free Trade Area. However, China is upgrading its internal industrial structure and actively promotes the RCEP, the China–Japan–Korea FTA, and China–Europe bilateral investment treaty negotiations, as well as the 'The Belt and Road' initiative. Once completed, these trade networks will greatly enhance China's ability to defend itself against the threat of a trade war.

In the meantime, Japan and the EU are hoping gain market share in China. For example, while Tokyo is concerned about China's regional foreign and security policies, in the economic realm, Abe (2013) himself emphasizes that the expansion Sino–Japan trade relations is mutually beneficial. When international media questioned the outlook for China's economy, Abe (2016) pointed out that China's economy was still growing at a steady pace.

The EU also sees itself as China's economic partner, emphasizing that its prosperity is closely linked to China's sustainable development and that European economies benefit from China's 13th Five-Year Plan in areas such as innovation, services, green growth and coordination of urban and rural development. Therefore, it is in the EU's interest to support China's transition to a more sustainable and inclusive socio-economic model. In particular, China–EU technical cooperation has played a positive role in China's economic development, which provided Europe with a stable and reliable market and contributed to its own economic stability through additional employment opportunities. China–EU relations are a model for cooperation and mutual benefit in international relations.

Because Japan and Europe perceive China as a 'heterogeneous' country, both sides hope to cooperate in containing China, based on shared values and ideology. However, the policy of containing China politically co-exists with interest in both Japan and Europe to expand trade ties with China. On the one hand, in the face of huge trade deficits with China, Japan and Europe intend to develop trade rules to balance the deficit, and build a future international trading regime jointly with the U.S. that relegates China to being a passive recipient. On the other hand, due to China's economic development, Japan and Europe both have an eye on China's domestic market's increasing consumption capacity and seek to strengthen economic cooperation. In other words, Japan and Europe are trying to devise new international trade rule to counterbalance China, while simultaneously attempting to obtain more economic dividends from China's development.

Conclusions

Although the EU and Japan are strategic allies of the United States, they are geographically distant. Their shared World War II trauma instilled a sense of commitment to economic recovery, and to a much lesser degree, political cooperation. The weaker commitment to political cooperation was evident by the lack of security cooperation and the focus on economic relations during the Cold War.

After the Cold War, two features gained prominence in EU–Japan relations. First, the EU–Japan strategic dialogue has expanded to encompass values, security and high-level political cooperation. Second, in response to China's perceived 'rise,' China-related issues gradually increased in EU–Japan exchanges and joint statements. Specifically, the 'China factor' in the EU–Japan strategic dialogue mainly focused on three aspects: values, security and economics. However, there is a gap between strategic discourse and action in both EU–China and EU–Japan relations.

The EU and Japan share many similar core values. From a European-Japanese perspective, rising China stands for, and promotes, fundamentally different values. Some European countries and Japan have strong prejudices about China's political ideology and social system. However, European countries' attitudes toward China are contradictory. While the EU officially separates political from economic issues when dealing with China, it nonetheless inserts a portion of ideology into ties with Beijing: while Brussels welcomes and promotes trade and business ties with China, it regards China as an object that has to be 'tamed' by Western norms and values. Through the "China threat theory" the EU and Japan intend to forge cooperation in promoting their values in Asia. In the security realm, Japan and the EU consider all kinds of actions that seek to safeguard what China refers to as its sovereignty in the South and the East China Sea as a challenge to the existing international order. At the same time, when faced with difficult diplomatic situations, the EU seeks to remain neutral – a virtue of the EU's foreign policy. Similarly, the EU's has maintained its neutral position in East Asia and, especially seeks to avoid choosing between Japan and China. Nonetheless, the EU also urged China to accept the above-mentioned verdict of the Permanent Court of Arbitration and commit itself to respecting the maritime legal order according to the principles of UNCLOS. Compared with the EU, Japan is more active in seeking to contain China, which creates difficulties for substantive cooperation on security issues between the EU and Japan.

With regards to economic cooperation, China has become one of the most important economic partners for both Europe and Japan. At the same time since the end of the Cold War, the European–Japanese trade volume declined. Instead, the 'China factor' has become more influential in EU–Japan economic relations. The EU is keeping an equal distance from China and Japan. Largely because of the rapid development of the EU's economic relationship with China, the EU has shown a tendency to prioritize its relationship with China over that with Japan. This is not surprising, considering that China and the EU are not direct strategic rivals, and acknowledge each other's interests in promoting an effective multilateral world order. China's influence on Japan–Europe cooperation can be described by a Chinese proverb: "One body and two wings." The body refers to their shared values, which is the basis of Japan–Europe cooperation. Both sides believe that China's rise economic and military rise poses a challenge to the existing international order, and they must insist on their own values and work together to face this challenge despite their significant commercial ties with China. The two wings represent security and economic cooperation. Japan and Europe intend to join forces to balance China with the normative power of international law and the existing economic and trade rules by building a two-track strategy framework of SPA and FTA.

This sort of Europe–Japan cooperation aimed against China has potentially negative implications for Sino–Japanese relations and Sino–European relations. However, against the backdrop of Chinese overall national strength and its increase in economic proximity with Japan and the EU, both Sino-Japanese relations and Sino–European relations are characterized by competition on the one hand, and cooperation on the other. Neither the EU nor Japan can afford a serious fracture with China. At the same time, the EU and Japan support each other, as it is evident in Japan's endorsement of the EU's engagement in the South China Sea disputes, and the EU's support of Japan in East Asian regional politics. Furthermore, there is a gap between Japan's and Europe's approach to 'China's rise.' Consequently, it may take more time for the EU and Japan to establish a true strategic partner relationship.

References

Abe, S. (2013) *Atarashii Kuni He Utsukushii Kuni He Kanzenban*. Tokyo: Bungeishun-shu.

Abe, S. (2016) Fuanntei suru Sekai, G7 ga Shinro. Nikkei FT Kyodo interview. *Nippon Keizai Shimbun*. January 18, 2016.

Anami, Y., Ohara, B. and Kamo, T. (2016) Handle China's Maritime Assertiveness Through 'Internationalization.' *Diplomacy*. 39(September), pp. 12–22.

Cameron, F. (2013) The Evolution of EU–Asia Relations: 2001–2011. In Christiansen. T., Kirchner, E. and Murray, P. (eds.) *The Palgrave Handbook of EU–Asia Relations*. Basingstoke: Palgrave, pp. 30–43.

Castillo Iglesias, J. (2012) An Assessment of EU-China and EU-Japan Political and Security Relations: Moving the 'Strategic Partnerships' Beyond the Rhetoric Trap. *International Public Policy Studies* 17(1), pp. 159–178.

EEAS. (2016a) *Declaration by the High Representative on Behalf of the EU on the Award Rendered in the Arbitration Between the Philippines and China*. Available from: http://eeas.europa.eu/archives/delegations/vietnam/press_corner/all_news/news/2016/20160715_en.htm. [Accessed: October 19, 2017].

EEAS. (2016b) *EU-China Relations*. 22/06/2016. Available from: http://eeas.europa.eu/archives/delegations/china/press_corner/all_news/news/2016/2016062203_en.htm. [Accessed: October 19, 2017].

EEAS. (2017) *EU and Japan Trade and Investment Relations*. Available from: https://eeas.europa.eu/headquarters/headquarters-homepage/19226/trade-and-investment-relations_en. [Accessed: October 19, 2017].

EU–Japan Summit. (1991) *The Delegation of the European Union to Japan*. Available from: www.euinjapan.jp/relations/political/. [Accessed: October 19, 2017].

EU–Japan Summit. (2001) *Shaping our Common Future: An Action Plan for EU-Japan Cooperation*. Available from: www.mofa.go.jp/region/europe/eu/summit/action0112.html. [Accessed: February 15, 2018].

EU–Japan Summit. (2014a) *EU-Japan Summit Joint Press Statement*. Available from: www.euinjapan.jp/en/resources/news-from-the-eu/news2014/20140507/210016/. [Accessed: October 19, 2017].

EU–Japan Summit. (2014b) *Press Remarks by President of the European Council Herman Van Rompuy following the 22nd EU-Japan Summit*. EUCO 102/14, PRESSE

275, PRPCE 92. Brussels. 7 May. Available from: www.euinjapan.jp/en/resources/news-from-the-eu/news2014/20140507/210016/. [Accessed: October 19, 2017].

EU–Japan Summit. (2015) *23rd Japan-EU Summit Joint Press Statement.* Available from: www.euinjapan.jp/en/resources/news-from-the-eu/news2015/20150529/194003/. [Accessed: October 19, 2017].

European Commission. (2001) *Europe and Asia: A Strategic Framework for Enhanced Partnerships.* COM (2001) 469 final. Brussels.

European Commission. (2016) *Frequently Asked Questions on the Joint Communication: Elements for a New EU Strategy on China.* Brussels. June 22. Available from: http://europa.eu/rapid/press-release_MEMO-16-2258_en.htm. [Accessed: October 19, 2017].

Friedberg, A. (1993/1994) Ripe for Rivalry: Prospects for Peace in a Multipolar Asia. *International Security* 18(3, Winter), pp. 5–33.

Hosoya, Y. (2016) *Anporonso.* Tokyo: Chikuma Shinsho.

Japanese Ministry of Defense. (2011) *The Defense of Japan.* Annual White Paper. Available from: www.clearing.mod.go.jp/hakusho_data/2011/2011/pdf/23010203.pdf. [Accessed: October 19, 2017].

Japanese Ministry of Defense. (2014) *The Defense of Japan.* Annual White Paper. Available from: www.clearing.mod.go.jp/hakusho_data/2014/pdf/26010103.pdf. [Accessed: October 19, 2017].

Japanese Ministry of Defense. (2016) *The Defense of Japan.* Annual White Paper. Available from: www.mod.go.jp/j/publication/wp/wp2016/pdf/28010201.pdf. [Accessed: October 19, 2017].

Kang, D.C. (2008) *China Rising: Peace, Power, and Order in East Asia.* New York: Columbia University Press.

Kuriyama, T. (1990). Gekido no 90 Nendai to Nihon Gaikō no Shintenkai. *Gaiko Forum* (May), pp. 12–21.

Mearsheimer, J. (2004) Why China's Rise Will Not Be Peaceful. September 17. Available from: http://mearsheimer.uchicago.edu/pdfs/A0034b.pdf. [Accessed: October 19, 2017].

MOFA of China. (2017a) *China and EU Relations.* Available from: www.fmprc.gov.cn/web/gjhdq_676201/gj_676203/oz_678770/1206_679930/sbgx_679934/. [Accessed: October 19, 2017].

MOFA of China. (2017b) *China and Japan Relations.* Available from: www.fmprc.gov.cn/web/gjhdq_676201/gj_676203/yz_676205/1206_676836/sbgx_676840/. [Accessed: October 19, 2017].

MOFA of Japan. (1957) Available from: www.mofa.go.jp/mofaj/gaiko/bluebook/1957/s32-1-2.htm. [Accessed: October 19, 2017].

MOFA of Japan. (1990) Available from: www.mofa.go.jp/mofaj/gaiko/bluebook/1990/h02-contents-1.htm. [Accessed: October 19, 2017].

MOFA of Japan. (2005) Available from: www.mofa.go.jp/mofaj/kaidan/s_koi/asia_europe_05/index.html. [Accessed: October 19, 2017].

MOFA of Japan. (2015) Available from: www.mofa.go.jp/mofaj/files/000076374.pdf. [Accessed: October 19, 2017].

MOFA of Japan. (2016) Press Conference by Foreign Minister Fumio Kishida. Press Conference. Available from: www.mofa.go.jp/mofaj/press/kaiken/kaiken4_000353.html. [Accessed: October 19, 2017].

Morrow, J.D. (1991) Alliance and Asymmetry: An Alternative to the Capability Aggression Model of Alliance. *American Journal of Political Science* 35(November), pp. 904–933.

Nye, J.S. (2015) *American Hegemony or American Primacy?* Project Syndicate. 9 March.

Oyane, S. (2016) Shinkokoku no Kunka: 1970 Nendaimatu no Nihon no Summit Gaikō. *International Relations* 183(March), pp. 87–101.

Prime Minister of Japan and His Cabinet. (2015) Available from: www.kantei.go.jp/jp/topics/2015/150814danwa.pdf. [Accessed: October 19, 2017].

Sakamoto, C. (2012). *Europa ni okeru Taminzoku Kyōzon to EU, Gengo Bunka Gender wo megutte, oyobi Nichiō Kankei no Rekishi Bunka Seiji*. Kobe: Kobe Daigaku Daigakuin Kokusai Bunkagaku Kenkyuka Ibunka Kenkyu Koryu Center.

Ueta, T. (2013) Nihon-EU Seiji Anzen Hoshō Kankei. In Ueta, T. (ed.) *EU Studies 1. Taigai Kankei*. Tokyo: Keiso Shobo.

Vutz, C. (2013) *The East China Sea Territorial Dispute: Senkaku, Diaoyu, or Tiayutai Islands?* Library briefing. Brussels: Library of the European Parliament. Available from: www.europarl.europa.eu/RegData/bibliotheque/briefing/2013/130617/LDM_BRI (2013)130617_REV1_EN.pdf. [Accessed: October 19, 2017].

Watanabe, K. (2013) *Takokkanwakugumi no naka no Nichiō Kankei*. In Kokubun, R. (ed.) *Nihon no Gaikō. dai 4 maki. Chiiki Hen*. Tokyo: Iwanami Shoten.

Xin, H. (2015) Analysis on the Mechanism of the EU's Strategic Dual Track Negotiation to Japan. *Contemporary International Relation*. 9, pp. 53–61.

Xinhua News. (2016) US President-elect Trump Vows to Withdraw from TPP on First Day in Office. Available from: www.chinadaily.com.cn/world/2016-11/22/content_274 50101.htm. [Accessed: October 19, 2017].

Zhang, X., Liu, Z., Lu, X. and Zhang, P. (2013) The EU-Japan Free Trade Agreement Negotiations and the Implications to China. *Chinese Journal of European Studies* 4, p. 31.

13 Conclusions

The way forward

Marie Söderberg, Axel Berkofsky,
Christopher W. Hughes and Paul Midford

Are the European Union (EU) and Japan poised to jointly exercise international leadership in finance, free trade, politics, security, and development? Are we about to experience a breakthrough, or even a 'Big Bang', in EU–Japan relations? The timing is right to increase EU–Japan cooperation in regional and global politics and security, albeit for the wrong reasons. The rise of populism, xenophobia and nationalism in Europe and Japan, Brexit, the election of Donald Trump as U.S. President, the rise of China as an illiberal superpower, and the more general allure of illiberal policies and regimes, should prompt Brussels and Tokyo to pool resources to counter this tide of illiberalism.

By concluding an Economic Partnership Agreement (EPA) on 8 December 2017, Brussels and Tokyo took an important joint step in that direction. A Strategic Partnership Agreement (SPA) aimed at intensifying EU–Japan cooperation in global politics and security too is in the pipeline, and with a little bit of luck and Brussels and Tokyo sticking to their promise to do more together, we might even see a new dawn in the joint achievements of Tokyo and Brussels in international trade, politics, and security. However, our volume suggests that EU–Japan cooperation is not yet demonstrating the full potential to lead effectively in these areas. Implementing the EPA and SPA should make a significant contribution to demonstrating effective joint leadership, but gaps are likely to remain. There is also a disturbing lack of urgency in Brussels and Tokyo at the daunting challenges they now face.

This volume has adopted a multidisciplinary approach to analysing Japan–Europe relations, and raised five main questions.

First, how can we assess the significance and impact of EU–Japan cooperation in the areas covered by individual authors?

Starting in the field of economics and trade, the EU–Japan EPA adopted in December 2017 really is significant and potentially path-breaking. Ironically, this is at least as much the case from a political point of view. Both Japan and EU were in the process of negotiating free trade agreements with the US when President Trump came to power and decided, based on his 'America First' approach, to cancel all such negotiations. By instead turning to each other and concluding an EU–Japan agreement, the two sides provided a very strong signal that they will not shift towards protectionism, but instead support and protect the global system of free trade. As Patricia Nelson explains in her chapter, this was a sign of leadership that struck a blow against protectionism. The EPA is a high-level, balanced agreement that could serve as a global model for both fair and free trade once the investment protection rules are finalised.

Commercial interests were also driving forces for the progress and conclusion of the EPA negotiations. For Japan, there was a degree of competition with South Korea which had previously negotiated free trade agreements with the EU and the US. South Korea, for example, did not have to pay the 10 per cent customs duty on car imports to Europe that Japanese carmakers were subject to.[1]

Although it will take well over another year before the EU–Japan EPA has passed through various bureaucratic procedures to be ratified by the relevant political bodies in Japan and all EU member states, it is already likely to prompt both manufacturing and service industries to plan for expanding bilateral trade and investment between Japan and the EU. Once in place the agreement is expected to provide increased economic growth for both parties. All authors in this volume touching on the agreement hail it as a major success.

In the field of monetary policy, the EU and its member states as well as Japan are struggling with the risks of deflation. Central banks learn from each other, as was demonstrated by the implementation of similar monetary policies during the last financial crisis of 2008/2009. Central banks have developed stronger and more cooperative ties on a global level, including coordinating on interest rates, monetary easing, etc. An end to negative interest rates can become parallel future strategies pursued by the Bank of Japan and the European Central Bank that will affect interest-rate setting in national-level central banks in Europe. Enhanced coordination between European central banks and Bank of Japan is important to maintain global financial stability and to prevent future crises.

However, even if the EU and Japan have been influencing each other's respective monetary policies, their central banks' imposition of negative interest rate policies have mostly been parallel responses to global financial instability. There has been minimal EU–Japan cooperation in coordinating the global finan-cial impacts of their radical expansionary monetary policies. Monetary policy-making in both the EU and Japan has fundamentally been inward looking, thus hindering cooperation.

In the fields of politics and security, the SPA (although not yet concluded as of February 2018) is also important, but not necessarily the precondition for Brussels and Tokyo to engage in on-the-ground cooperation in regional and global security. The EU and Japan have over recent years intensified ad-hoc cooperation in various fields of international politics and security as shown, in Axel Berkofsky's chapter. Indeed, the track record of EU–Japan cooperation on both regional and global levels is not unimpressive, and includes various joint missions, conflict mediation and peace-building initiatives in Africa and Asia. The SPA will provide the institutional framework for expanding and regularising such cooperation, but whether this will actually lead to an intensification of cooperation remains to be seen.

Although there is a wide range of untapped potential, Japan–EU security cooperation is more likely to be realised in the field of "soft" or non-traditional security. The fact that the two partners are located in different parts of the world causes their threat perceptions to diverge. The EU is focused on Russia and its illegal annexation of Crimea, whereas Japan is more concerned with Chinese intrusions into its own claimed territorial waters in the East China Sea around the Senkaku/Diaoyu islands, as well as Chinese territorial expansionism in the South China Sea. Tokyo's economic sanctions imposed on Russia following the latter's annexation of Crimea showed a willingness, to some extent, to support European policies aimed at safeguarding international legal norms and standards.

When it comes to the South China Sea, European countries have shown support for the ruling of the Permanent Court of Arbitration in The Hague of July 2016, which states that China has no historical rights to international waters within Beijing's so-called 'Nine Dash Line,' which encompasses approximately 90 per cent of the South China Sea. However, Chinese expansionism in the South China Sea has not led to any EU maritime patrolling there, although a French defence minister has suggested that the EU should undertake such operations. Japan also does not carry out patrolling, but there are efforts led by Japan's Coast Guard, and financed by Tokyo's economic assistance, to train and build up the coast guards of several Southeast Asian countries, and most notably in the Philippines, Vietnam, and Indonesia.

The EU and Japan have cooperated in combating piracy in the Gulf of Aden, and at the same time are providing development assistance to Somalia, and helping to train local maritime security officials and enhance local governance capabilities. A civilian EU Common Security and Defence Policy (CSDP) mission was dispatched in August 2012 to provide training and advice to Niger's security sector. A further CSDP mission was dispatched to help improve Mali's security capabilities. In support of this mission, Japan in March 2015 agreed to provide grant aid for the reconstruction of Mali's national police school, information technology and other equipment.

After years of discussions with Japan about establishing a legal framework to enable regular and long-term contributions to EU CSDP missions, such a framework has yet to be adopted. Even in the absence of such a legal framework, however, Japan has nonetheless been contributing to EU CSDP missions on an occasional basis. As for hard security, Japanese Prime Minister Abe has been more committed to maintaining, and indeed intensifying, security cooperation with the Trump administration, as opposed to intensifying soft security cooperation with Europe. Abe's decisions to meet with Trump before, and then very shortly after, his inauguration have been perceived as very clear messages that security cooperation with the US is of utmost importance for Japan, although a track of increasing security cooperation with the EU could be pursued simultaneously in a complementary manner.

At the same time, we are nonetheless witnessing burgeoning bilateral security cooperation between Japan and individual EU states. In 2015, the UK and Japan held their first joint air force exercises on Japanese territory, followed shortly thereafter by multilateral naval exercises around Japan involving France, the UK, and the US. Japan has concluded, or is in the process of concluding several Acquisition and Cross-Servicing Agreements with European powers (currently negotiations are ongoing with France). The importance that Tokyo accords to France and the UK in its security policy is illustrated by the fact that these countries are among a small number of countries with whom Tokyo holds regular two-plus-two talks: meetings involving Japan's foreign and defence ministers, and their counterparts from London and Paris (AFP-Jiji, 2017; *Asahi Shimbun*, 2016; Kikuchi, 2018).

Since Tokyo started to revise its principles on the export of weapons in 2011, there has been a sudden flurry of high-profile agreements between EU members and Japan (*Asahi Shimbun*, 2017; Aibara, 2017). Arms industry cooperation between the two sides, however, remains nascent and is unlikely to rival trans-Atlantic and trans-Pacific arms industry cooperation anytime soon. Nonetheless, this cooperation is developing, with Japan as an emerging customer, as well as supplier and competitor for European states. Japan's recent decision to buy Norwegian as well as US long-range 'cruise' missiles is an important case in point (*Kyodo*, 2017).

Overall, Japan's growing security ties with the EU, and with EU members, are an integral and important, if still incremental, part of Japan's long-term post-Cold War shift away from centring its security strategy on the US as its only security partner. None of the security cooperation outlined in this chapter and this volume between the EU and its member states on the one hand, and Japan on the other, existed during the Cold War. Although Japan's decentring from its previously exclusive focus on the US as its sole security partner does embrace other partners besides the EU and its member states, the EU and its member states have nonetheless played a crucial role in this process, especially in weapons co-development (Midford, 2018; Hughes, 2018; Vosse, 2017).

In Japan's National Security Strategy (NSS), Europe is identified as a "partner" for Japan "in ensuring the peace and security of the international community", deriving from the fact that, "Japan and European countries ... share universal values of freedom, democracy, respect for fundamental human rights, and the rule of law" (GoJ NSC 2013, pp. 26–27). In line with this view, the NSS calls for enhanced relations with Europe. However, as demonstrated in Paul Midford's chapter on Abe's proactive pacifism and values diplomacy, these new approaches in Japanese foreign policy do not offer many opportunities for greater EU–Japan security cooperation. This is because, as discussed above, European and Japanese strategic threat perceptions and interests are far from identical. Consequently, while Abe's foreign policy may be a sensible realist response to the rising power of China, EU–Japan cooperation cannot be predicated on a realist strategy as the interests of the two sides diverge in significant ways. For EU–Japan cooperation to significantly deepen, it must be founded on shared liberal values. Yet, as Midford's chapter demonstrates, Abe's doctrine of "Pro-active Pacifism" (or a "Pro-active Contribution to Peace") and associated values diplomacy is not matched by a commitment to common liberal values (Hughes, 2015).

Likewise, from André Asplund's chapter it is also obvious that neither Japan, nor Europe, live up to the liberal values espoused in their policy documents. Or at least there is a very mixed picture. Even if Tokyo and Brussels want to raise the issues of the lack of democratic reforms and human rights, their leaders find it difficult to risk forsaking their relationship with a highly-valued partner such as Vietnam. With a large role in the future world economy, as well as in the South China Sea disputes, Vietnam, with a notoriously poor democracy and human rights record, does not provide many opportunities for applying negative sanctions without risking damaging consequences for larger EU and Japanese interests. Although the Lisbon Treaty makes it obligatory to consider democracy and human rights in foreign relations, emerging markets like Vietnam offer economic opportunities that make it hard to impose 'conditionality'. Instead, the EU finds it highly worthwhile to forge ahead with free trade agreements. The example of Vietnam also suggests that EU and Japanese statements of concern about democracy and human rights problems in China – problems comparable in many ways with those found in Vietnam – may in fact be more about power competition and countering China than taking a principled and costly stance in support of these values.

Bacon and Nakamura argue in their chapter that Japan runs the risk of repeating European mistakes, due to its persistent and strident references to democracy and human rights in its diplomatic strategy in the Asia-Pacific. The authors instead suggest that adopting a mix of "ordinary" and "civilian" power identities would be optimal for Japan. Tokyo should not self-identify as either a "post-modern" or "normative" power. These identifications can in themselves be inherently conflict-producing.

The EU and its member states provide more than 50 per cent of all official development assistance (ODA). Japan is a large provider of such aid as well. As Marie Söderberg observes in her chapter, Japanese assistance has always had a strong focus on economic infrastructure (such as roads, railways, power stations and ports), and with the new UN Sustainable Development Goals (SDGs) the EU and its member states are also moving in this direction. At present, there is an EU–Japan discussion on cooperation for infrastructure building in Africa. On the ground, there is significant cooperation between EU and Japanese development cooperation programmes in fields such as education and health. The SDGs are encouraging more cooperation among NGOs, private companies, and ODA agencies. Cooperation between public and private donors is a field where Japan has long experience but which European countries are now also turning to. Hence, many European countries can learn from Japan in this area.

Second, how do China and/or the US, individually or through their bilateral relationship, affect EU–Japan current or potential cooperation in the areas the volume's authors are addressing?

In the field of free trade, it seems obvious that President Trump's withdrawal of US support for the TTP and TTIP provided the EU and Japan with the incentive to forge ahead with their own EPA. For both parties, free trade is important, and, in order to counter Trump's protectionism and China's increasing might in international trade, the necessity is to increase bilateral trade, and thereby boost economic growth.

In the field of security, China's growing military prowess, besides prompting Japan to strengthen its own national defence posture, has also drawn it closer to its ally, the US. Abe is extremely eager to please Trump, whereas European leaders such as German Chancellor Angela Merkel have been lukewarm. Responding to President Trump's request for greater burden sharing and the payment of arrears for alleged past under-spending on defence to compensate for excessive US contributions to NATO, Germany has recommitted to increasing its military spending up to 2 per cent of GDP (a promise it originally made in 2015, long before Trump was elected), whilst also noting that the alliance has other vital missions, including security and development in Africa.

The potential for EU–Japan cooperation in security, however, still remains largely untapped. As shown in Hornung's chapter, the US has implicitly supported not only the non-combat nexus of the security and development agenda but also greater EU–Japan cooperation in general (EJARN and KAS, 2012). Given the grave security challenges the US faces from an increasingly assertive China, not to mention a provocative North Korea and a revanchist Russia, it is beneficial for the US to burden share with as many available allies as possible. Hence, the opportunity of greater burden-sharing via EU–Japan enhanced cooperation is an opportunity Washington should pursue.

In the case of defence production, cooperation between European countries and Japan for the sake of obtaining and developing technology, opening markets for Japanese weapons, and reducing dependence on the US for arms development are important motivations. However, other motivations are narrower, as part of Japan's motivation for nurturing arms industry cooperation with Europe is merely tactical, specifically to prevent the development of an arms industry relationship between the EU and China, and to more generally draw EU countries over to Japan's side in its political competition with China.

In the case of cooperation between the EU and Japan on promoting shared values, such as democracy and human rights, it seems obvious that competition with China for trade and market shares, both within the Chinese market as well as elsewhere in Asia and Africa, has caused the EU and Japan to neglect such values. This does not mean that the EU and Japan are not driven by a genuine wish to see what they regard as universal values become internalised in Asia, Africa, and China itself. But it does mean either that the extent to which they are willing to use their bargaining chips of aid and trade for such purposes is unlimited at least in part by the implications of China's rise economically, and for security in East Asia. Then again, the EU and Japan's reluctance to raise concerns about shortcomings in democracy and human rights in countries such as Vietnam – a reluctance driven by the perceived urgency to counter-balance Chinese influence – suggests that however sincere the EU and Japan may be in wanting to promote these values, eventually strategic concerns and economic gains, take precedence.

Although the EU and Japan remain leading global powers in providing development aid, the rise of China as a major aid power is influencing longstanding EU and Japanese aid policies, pulling them away from the promotion of liberal values in aid policy and more towards the pursuit of narrow national and commercial interests. China's rise as an influential aid power is exerting a gravitational pull on EU and Japanese aid policies, prompting them to turn more towards investments for economic infrastructure and economic development.

In East Asian political economy, China has increasingly been exercising leadership in regional economic multilateralism, and the EU and Japan have been diverging in their responses. Most EU members have joined the Chinese-sponsored Asia Infrastructure Investment Bank (AIIB) and are trying to influence it and Chinese policies through engagement, whereas Japan has sided with the US decision not to join the AIIB and has focused instead on containing China's economic influence. Japan has pursued this by building alternative regional multilateral economic frameworks with the US, most notably the Transpacific Partnership (TPP). After the US withdrew from the TPP in January 2017, Japan continued to push, and eventually succeeded, in realising a paler shadow version of the TPP without the US.

China does not yet know how seriously to treat the EU–Japan "strategic partnership" and SPA. As the authors Song and Cai suggest in their chapter, China sees the EU and Japan teaming up against China under the banner of promoting common values and using intensifying ties and the above-mentioned agreements as tools to contain China economically and politically. On the other hand, they also suggest that China remains fairly relaxed about EU–Japan security relations because these relations remain fairly underdeveloped and the economic ties various EU countries have with China act as a break on the development of an EU–Japan partnership aimed at China. On the other hand, China is very sensitive to any indications that the EU and Japan are adopting positions opposing Chinese policies, especially statements that appear to challenge China's positions on maritime territorial disputes.

Third, how does EU–Japan cooperation in trade, politics and security impact on cooperation between the EU and China and the EU and the US, Japan and the US, and Japan and China respectively?

In the eyes of most Europeans, resisting China's efforts and not joining its new initiatives – the above-mentioned AIIB, but also the China-driven Belt Road

Initiative (BRI) – are not rational options, given that they may result in missed opportunities for both potential funders and entrepreneurs, and eventual beneficiaries in Europe. The European interest in both initiatives is likely to continue and will not be diverted by closer cooperation between EU and Japan through the EPA and SPA agreements. As Beijing's BRI-branding was initiated, most EU member states significantly increased their commercial linkages with China, eagerly trying to become the "foremost gateway" for the implementation of China's New Silk Road in Europe. An EU–China Strategic Partnership was announced in 2003, and since then trade and investment has been growing robustly. Although relatively more enthusiastic than Japan's response, all in all, Europe's response to BRI can, nonetheless, be characterised as relatively cautious, although again attitudes differ from country to country.

Also in Japan's case, trade with China is increasing and recently relations seem to have improved somewhat in the economic field. Although Japan continues to refuse to join the new AIIB, it has through its role as a key player in the Asian Development Bank (ADB) extended cooperation to the AIIB, and in 2017 the Abe administration signalled that it was considering participating in the BRI. As a way of strengthening regional economic cooperation, and in the absence of the Trump administration's interest in undertaking initiatives with Tokyo in this area, Japan has attempted to improve the previously strained political atmosphere with China.

Both the EU and Japan are likely to continue prioritising their economic relations with China. The EU–Japan EPA adopted in December 2017 might still have implications for their trade with China in other ways, namely by promoting rules and standards for fair and free trade that China could eventually feel compelled to follow. Whether these standards could also affect US trade practices with Japan and EU is another issue. Could they convince the Trump Administration of the importance of maintaining, and ideally deepening, the rules-based international system of global economic governance?

In the field of politics and security, the SPA is not likely to have great impact on EU–US or Japan–US relations. Due to diverging geopolitical interests the EU and Japan are likely to continue pursuing their own policies towards the US. Japan, sensing the Chinese threat, and with a moderate defence capability of its own, is going to be much more accommodating of the Trump administration than the EU will be. On the European security scene, the situation is highly complex. The EU in itself is not yet a strong security actor. NATO is the main player, but not all like-minded European countries are members. Then there are a number of EU countries which are strong security actors in their own right. Depending on the issue, some of them will cooperate closely with the US.

Fourth, how does EU–Japan cooperation in trade, politics and security affect Sino–US relations?

For the most part we have little reason to expect that EU–Japan cooperation will have an impact on Sino–US relations. Nonetheless, we can identify a few scenarios where EU–Japan cooperation may have an impact. First, if the EU and Japan hold true to their embrace of liberal values and build effective cooperation in promoting them, there is a greater chance that they will eventually be able to entice the Trump administration or a successor administration to return US foreign policy to its traditional role of championing US-inspired liberal values. This is more likely to happen if effective EU–Japan partnership appears to hold out for Washington the prospect of effective burden-sharing, where the US can be satisfied that it is not bearing a disproportionate burden. Moreover, effective EU–Japan cooperation not only promises reduced burdens for the US, but also enhances the likelihood that such efforts would be successful. In this scenario, EU–Japan cooperation would impact on Sino–US relations by possibly worsening them. Washington's return to championing a liberal order would inevitably lead to more conflict with an illiberal and authoritarian China, one that is attempting to build its own regional order in Asia.

Second, if EU–Japan cooperation does not prove fruitful, the US will be less likely to return to its traditional policy of championing the liberal international order. Lacking a large and effective partner to share the burdens of leadership will not only make Washington think twice about the price of this leadership, but it will also reduce expectations that his leadership can be effective. In this scenario, the failure of EU–Japan cooperation would, ironically, reduce the risk of conflict in Sino–US relations, and perhaps even create greater space for an improvement. Indeed, Trump and Chinese President Xi Jinping share a reluctance to pay for global leadership, thereby reducing the possibility of a competition for global leadership, especially when the EU–Japan partnership is absent as a potential backstop to revived US liberal leadership.

While neither of these scenarios is very likely, they do at least provide an overview of the direction and maximum potential effect the EU–Japan partnership could have on Sino–US relations. There is one more scenario, less likely still, yet worth briefly considering. If Trump's illiberal protectionism becomes truly extreme, it is possible that this might prompt China to become selectively liberal on some issues, most notably trade. This is because China, as the world's largest trading power, has gained the most in recent decades from the liberal international trading system, and would arguably have the most to lose if it were to stop functioning. President's Xi's speech to the Global Economic Summit in Davos in 2017 hinted at this possibility, as did some subsequent Chinese overtures to the EU. Were this scenario, which appears quite unlikely at this point, to become reality, we would likely see worsened Sino–US relations as bilateral trade dries up and the US becomes isolationist, and perhaps even embittered at China, and perhaps even at the EU and Japan, for maintaining at least some aspects of a liberal trading order among themselves in defiance of Trump's protectionism.

Finally, what is the impact of recent instability in the OECD countries on EU–Japan cooperation?

Japan was quicker and more outspoken than any other country in responding to Brexit. The Cabinet Office created a Special Task Force on Brexit in August 2016. MOFA published a fifteen-page message to the UK and the EU on Brexit, reflecting the concerns and interests of the Japanese business community. While the British media described the message as 'unprecedented', a 'dire' warning, a 'stark' threat, or dismissed it as 'doom-mongering', the impact was noteworthy, given the UK was Japan's second largest FDI destination following the US in 2015. More than 1400 Japanese firms have established offices in the UK, some as European headquarters. Japan's ambassador to the UK in talks with Prime Minister Theresa May on 8 February 2018 reiterated Japanese concerns to the UK over Brexit, noting that if frictionless trading arrangements could not be put in place with the EU then Japanese companies could not profit from being located in the UK, and thus a veiled warning that Japan would start to lessen its investment in the UK.

However, so far Brexit does not seem to have a big impact on EU–Japan cooperation. Negotiations for a free trade agreement went on as usual. What really seemed to have speeded up the process was Trump's elections and the decision to end TTP and TTIP negotiations with Japan and Europe. More generally, Trump's election has left Japan and the EU the largest actors still promoting a world order built on past liberal ideas, starting with free trade.

The way forward for EU–Japan relations?

At the conclusion of the twentieth century, the US was talked of as the "lonely superpower", with no parallel in global capability and leadership, and with few partners capable of assisting it to uphold the liberal international order (Huntington, 1999). As the twenty-first century moves towards the end of its second decade, it is perhaps arguable that even if it is still the dominant power in the international system, the US's capabilities are waning relative to those of China as a competitor. Perhaps just as importantly, Washington's willingness to subscribe to and uphold the international order and associated values that were created by itself yet again appears to be waning, and especially under the Trump administration. In this situation the question must be asked whether the EU and Japan can step in and assist the US to maintain the liberal order, or whether perhaps they can even undertake to support much of it in place of the US, as the last two lonely bastions of liberalism.

The answer of this volume has been that the EU and Japan have tremendous potential to move down this path, and are in fact moving with some pace in this direction set against the background of US decline and China's rise that in tandem are producing a growing illiberalism, but are yet to fulfil this role and broaden out their relationship to the greatest extent possible in economic, security and politics. Moreover, in some instances, the EU and Japan have clearly failed to advance their roles, whether individually or in partnership.

The next question that thus arises is how the EU and Japan might yet further their relationship to reach a fuller potential and overcome past and current obstacles. This volume is not a work of policy prescription, but rather one of scholarly analysis. Nevertheless, a few key common policy lessons stand out from the authors' chapters.

First, EU and Japan must address the deficits in their leadership capacity and vision. The EU–Japan relationship is still one largely driven by bureaucratic policy processes in both Brussels and Tokyo, rather than effective leadership and engagement by top political leaders. On the EU side, the EU Commission is unable to convince states to make cooperation with Japan a priority due to conflicting interests among member states. On Japan's side, Prime Minister Abe continues to focus more on ameliorating relations with Trump and counterbalancing China than with exercising leadership to build cooperation with the EU based on shared values. On both sides a lack of vision of what their partnership could produce is hindering the development of bilateral cooperation.

Second, the EU and Japan should have more confidence to actively promote their EPA as a model for other FTAs, for reinforcing existing and setting new global trading rules, whether though the WTO, although progress in that forum is unlikely, or more likely through inter-regional and bilateral FTAs.

Third, the EU and Japan should be more open about promoting a model of security cooperation that does not focus on the use of hard power, but focuses on softer forms of power that are more apt for stabilising post-conflict zones and peace-building, and thus the application of power that will be more effective in preventing future conflicts Although Japan has endorsed this model, under the Abe administration Japan has still cut back on its support for post-conflict reconstruction and peace-building efforts, as symbolised by the fact that as of May 2017 Japan is at "zero PKO" missions (including humanitarian deployments) for the first time in a quarter of a century. Japan needs to recommit itself to these missions, in combination with the EU as its most valuable partner in these endeavours.

Fourth, the EU and Japan should be more full-throated in their defence of multilateralism and negotiations as means for resolving conflicts, starting with nuclear programs in Iran and North Korea.

Fifth, EU and Japan should make greater efforts to harmonise their understanding of maritime laws and norms, given that despite their declarations of shared commitment, they not infrequently diverge regarding specific details.

If the EU and Japan dedicate themselves to forging this kind of agenda and substantive cooperation, then they can make the difference in maintaining stability and liberal values in a highly fluid international environment, and until the US returns to its own previous values and perhaps China shows more comprehensive buy-in to liberal international norms.

Note

1 Trump has recently decided to possibly renegotiate the US FTA with South Korea, so at the time of writing the situation is unclear as to how this relationship will develop.

References

AFP-Jiji. (2017) French Warship Arrives for Joint Drills with Japan as North Korean Tensions Rise. *Japan Times*. 29 April, p. 2.

Aibara, R. (2017) Japan Quietly Inks Deal with Germany on Defense Sharing. *Asahi Shimbun*. 19 July. Available from: www.asahi.com/ajw/articles/AJ201707190028.html. [Accessed: 4 September 2017].

Asahi Shimbun. (2016) *Japan Moves to Solidify Security Relations with British Forces*. 3 November. Available from: www.asahi.com/ajw/articles/AJ201611030061.html. [Accessed: 7 December 2016].

Asahi Shimbun. (2017) *Japan, Britain to Develop Missiles in Move toward 'Semi-alliance'*. 15 December. Available from: www.asahi.com/ajw/articles/AJ201712150 029.html. [Accessed: 29 December 2017].

European Japan Advanced Research Network (EJARN) and Konrad Adenauer Stiftung (KAS). (2012) *A Proposal for a Way Forward on EU-Japan Cooperation at the Nexus of Security and Development*. KAS: Tokyo.

Government of Japan National Security Council (GoJ NSC). (2013) *National Security Strategy*. 17 December.

Hughes, C.W. (2015) *Japan's Foreign and Security Policy Under the 'Abe Doctrine': New Dynamism or New Dead End?* New York: Palgrave.

Hughes, C.W. (2018) Japan's Emerging Arms Transfer Strategy: Diversifying to Re-centre on the US-Japan Alliance. *The Pacific Review*. Forthcoming.

Huntington, S.P. (1999) The Lonely Superpower. *Foreign Affairs* 78(2), pp. 35–49.

Kikuchi, D. (2018) Japan and France Agree to Deepen Maritime Security Ties in 'Two Plus Two' Meeting. *Japan Times*. 26 January. Available from: www.japantimes.co.jp/news/2018/01/26/national/politics-diplomacy/japan-france-agree-deepen-maritime-security-ties-two-plus-two-meeting/#.Wnpqa6hl_IU.

Kyodo. (2017) Defense Ministry Says it Will Seek Funding for Long-range Cruise Missiles. *Japan Times*. 8 December.

Midford, P. (2018) New Directions in Japan's Security: Non-US Centric Evolution, Introduction to a Special Issue. *The Pacific Review*, published online 10 January. Available from: https://doi.org/10.1080/09512748.2017.1417326.

Vosse, W. (2017) Learning Multilateral Military and Political Cooperation in Counter-piracy Cooperation in the Counter-piracy Missions: A Step towards De-centering of Japan's Security Policy? *The Pacific Review*. Published online 6 September. Available from: http://dx.doi.org/10.1080/09512748.2017.1371213.

Index

Page numbers in **bold** denote tables, those in *italic* denote figures.

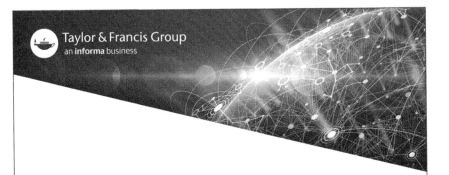

For Product Safety Concerns and Information please contact our EU representative GPSR@taylorandfrancis.com Taylor & Francis Verlag GmbH, Kaufingerstraße 24, 80331 München, Germany

Printed and bound by CPI Group (UK) Ltd, Croydon, CR0 4YY

01/05/2025

01858414-0005